Volume 1 in
Contemporary Perspectives in
Early Childhood Education

Contemporary Perspectives on Early
Childhood Curriculum

Library of Congress Cataloging-in-Publication Data

Contemporary perspectives on early childhood curriculum / [edited by]
Olivia N. Saracho and Bernard Spodek.
    p. cm. – (Contemporary perspectives in early childhood
education)
Includes bibliographical references.
  ISBN 1-930608-27-6 – ISBN 1-930608-26-8 (pbk.)
  1. Early childhood education–Curricula. 2. Early childhood
education–Social aspects. I. Saracho, Olivia N. II. Spodek, Bernard.
III. Series.
  LB1139.4 .C66 2002
  372.19–dc21

                2001007270

Printed in the United States of America

CONTEMPORARY PERSPECTIVES ON EARLY CHILDHOOD CURRICULUM

Edited by

Olivia N. Saracho
University of Maryland

Bernard Spodek
University of Illinois

INFORMATION AGE
PUBLISHING

80 Mason Street
Greenwich, Connecticut 06830

CONTENTS

INTRODUCTION
The Backbone of the Early Childhood Curriculum

Olivia N. Saracho and Bernard Spodek

Over the years, educational scholars have proposed different conceptions of the curriculum. It is as if each scholar, researcher, university educator, and practitioner has developed her or his own personal definition. Unfortunately, there is no one single definition that everybody has agreed upon. Table 1 presents a sample of these definitions.

A universal definition for curriculum may continue to be elusive and may even change through the years to address changes in the social forces and changes in related school goals. Nonetheless, the approach in curriculum development is consistent. Curriculum developers establish goals, develop experiences, designate content, and evaluate experiences and outcomes. Most curriculum developers consistently use such terms as curriculum planning, curriculum development, curriculum implementation, and curriculum evaluation, and many others to describe curriculum related activities. Unfortunately, without a consistent definition of curriculum, it is difficult for the curriculum developers to identify what it is that needs to be planned, developed, implemented, or evaluated. If curriculum developers rely on the curriculum experts' definitions, they will find that their definitions identify a product, a program, determine goals and objectives, and learner experiences. However, its heterogeneity may be inspiring if curriculum developers rely on the components of each definition that depict the richness of the field, which in turn, can provide a foundation for contemporary content, concepts, and creativity.

A curriculum is an anthology of learning experiences, conceived and arranged based on a program's educational goals and the community's social forces. Each curriculum manifests an image of what children "ought to be and become" (Biber, 1984, p. 303) grounded on the awareness of social values and a system that interprets those values into experiences for learners. The concept of curriculum, as a distinctive domain of study within education, arose from the demand to arrange, organize, and translate such awareness into educational programs of study. It integrates the historical study of the goals and content of schooling, analyses of curriculum documents, and analyses of the children's experiences in school. The first formal curriculum text was published in 1918 (Bobbit, 1918), although in the United States contemporary curriculum study goes back to the early 1890's, when lead committees challenged the form and structure of public schooling. Presently curriculum development is fundamental at all educational levels.

EARLY CHILDHOOD EDUCATION CURRICULUM

The curriculum in early childhood education is dramatically different from that at other levels of education. Because children are developing at such a rapid rate during the early years, and because what children are capable of learning and doing is so dependent on their development, curriculum decisions regarding young children's education must take into account each individual's developmental level. While all early childhood educators believe that education should be developmentally appropriate, the meaning of that term may vary in relation to the theory of development each educator espouses. Early childhood education methods and materials also differ from those other educational levels. There is more use of concrete materials and "hands-on" activities in the early years, and curriculum experiences are organized more into activities rather than lessons.

While the early childhood curriculum seems unique as compared with curriculum at other educational levels, there are similarities between early childhood curriculum studies and curriculum at higher levels of education. For example, at all educational levels the curriculum reflects the community's social values and the cultural knowledge available. Education integrates those values and knowledge into the learners' experiences. In addition, at all educational levels, the curriculum focuses on arranging, organizing, and translating those values into educational programs. However, the early childhood education programs' structure, process and content differ at the early childhood level and that difference has been evident throughout the history of early childhood education.

Eisner (1982) offers the idea of a balanced curriculum. He suggests that the content of the curriculum at all levels must include a variety of fields of study, such as the sciences and the arts. It is a common conviction that all these subjects should be integrated into the early childhood curriculum (Bowman, Donovan, & Burns, 2001). A critical goal is to assist children in moving from personal knowledge that comes from activities and experiences to social knowledge, which integrates that knowledge within subjects such as social studies, art, mathematics, language arts, and social science.

This volume seeks to clarify some of the issues related to early childhood curriculum development and its bases in both personal knowledge and knowledge from the different disciplines to achieve a "balanced curriculum." It present the major bases for early childhood curriculum development that can be found in the research literature pertaining to early childhood education. In the first chapter, Bernard Spodek and Olivia N. Saracho discuss the influence on the early childhood curriculum and defines the conflicting concepts of knowledge in human growth and development that were seen as the basis of curriculum models from the 1960s and 1970s up until the present. It also suggests that an understanding of the sociocultural context of school programs is necessary to understand the nature of schooling for young children in various communities and societies. The historical early childhood curriculum models continue to influence early childhood curriculum development today and are related to the sociocultural context of schools for young children. This chapter also suggests that an understanding of young children needs to be established within concepts of human growth and development.

In the following chapter, Kelvin Seifert discusses the various theories of cognitive development that have influenced the field of early childhood education. Seifert categorizes the various cognitive development theories as structural theories, learning theories, information processing theories and socially based theories of learning. He juxtaposes the theoretical understanding of children's learning and development found among scholars with the intuitive understandings that teachers of young children have. He also identifies the dichotomy that exists between individual learning and group learning in a classroom.

Play, and especially sociodramatic play, has been a key element in early childhood programs since their inception. Olivia N. Saracho, in her chapter on children's social pretend play, presents the developmental play theories that influence our understanding of children's imagination and the way we guide their social pretend play. She discusses how pretend play can foster learning in young children and what teachers can do to support this activity in the classroom.

The next two chapters in this volume focus on the differences that can be found among children in an early childhood class. Barbara Wasik and her colleagues focus on the characteristics of effective early childhood curriculum for children at risk. They describe the dichotomy between "developmentally appropriate practices" and "academically oriented programs," characterizing the differences between them as more concerned with method than with content. They then review the characteristics of effective programs for children at risk in terms of both the structural elements of the programs and the content of the programs.

Eugene E. Garcia addresses the issue of the linguistic and cultural diversity among children in early childhood education both from a personal and a social policy point of view. He presents guidelines for dealing with the issue of linguistic and cultural diversity and cites examples of programs that reflect those guidelines. Both of these chapters focus on diversity within the young child community in school today. Presently, researchers and educators have accepted the wide range of individual and group differences that exist among children. The demand for multicultural education and the distinct programs designed for at-risk, gifted, linguistically diverse, and other identifiable groups of children have received much attention in curriculum development.

The next three chapters focus on the different content areas of mathematics, literacy and social studies in the early childhood classroom. Olivia N. Saracho discusses young children's literacy development in the early childhood curriculum. She reports studies that show that (1) children engage in reading and writing activities through play and (2) literacy interactions in a play environment can facilitate and support the development of young children's acquisition of literacy.

Joseph Becker and Daniel Miltner discuss how young children develop reasoning in mathematics. They take a constructivist approach to explore young children's understanding of quantity. They suggest that their understandings develop gradually and that adults should continually monitor their understandings and interacting with them appropriately as required to extent their understanding.

While great emphasis has been placed in recent years on the importance of literacy and numeracy in early childhood education, young children's understanding of social phenomena is equally important. Thomas Weible and Ann J. Dromsky the social studies curriculum ion early childhood education. They see social studies as a vehicle to introduce children to the world of people. They review the various historical approaches to teaching concepts form the social sciences to young children. They also identify principles to guide teachers in offering this element of the early childhood education curriculum to young children.

One major aspect of the early childhood curriculum that can be identified as a new element is the uses of computers in early childhood classrooms. Douglas H. Clements and Julie Sarama present an extensive review of research relating to learning and teaching with computers in early childhood education. They present what we know about integrating computers in programs for young children and the uses of computers in different areas of the curriculum. They look at how the use of computers can help in developing young children's higher order thought processes. They also suggest guidelines for teachers in using computers in the early childhood classroom. They provide guidelines that teachers can use regarding computers and the early childhood classroom.

Douglas Powell and Gary E. Bingham discuss how to strengthen the role of curriculum in child care. Too often, a planned set of experiences to support children's education–a curriculum–is lacking in child care programs. While concern for curriculum has not been part of the traditions of child care, which are rooted more in child welfare concerns than in educational concerns, improving the curriculum of child care settings is seen as a way of improving the quality of programs. The authors identify some of the issues relating to improving curriculum of child care centers, including the preparation and qualifications of personnel. They see curriculum improvement as a significant way of improving the quality of child care services.

Tony Bertram and Christine Pascal explore the issue of what constitutes an effective early childhood education curriculum. They build on the work that has been done in Britain regarding long term achievement of young children. They suggest that such a curriculum should lead to creating in children dispositions to learn, social competence and a positive self-concept and emotional well being. They expand on the meaning of each of these in programs for young children.

The concluding chapter seeks to identify new directions in early childhood curriculum development. Innovative models of early childhood curriculum have emerged through the years reflecting new educational ideologies, new social demands, and new knowledge regarding children's learning and development. The issues addressed in this volume can provide new directions in the development of the early childhood curriculum. Early childhood education will continue to go through transformations. Early childhood researchers and educators need to appreciate the (a) transformations within the cultural context, (b) knowledge relating to young children's development that unfolds in the new programs, and (c) new social and educational systems and institutions that will emerge.

REFERENCES

Bernstein, B. (1971) On the classification and framing of educational knowledge. In M. Young (Ed.) *Educational knowledge.* London: Collier Macmillan.

Biber, B. (1984). *Early education and psychological development.* New Haven, CT: Yale University Press.

Bobbit, F. (1918). *The curriculum.* Boston: Houghton-Mifflin.

Bowman, B., Donovan, M.S. &Burns, M.S. (Eds.). (2001). Washington, DC: National Academy Press.

Caswell, H.L., & Campbell, D.S. (1935). *Curriculum development.* New York: American Book Co.

Doll, R. (1970). *Curriculum improvement.* Boston: Allyn & Bacon.

Eisner, E.W. (1982). *Cognition and curriculum: A basis for deciding what to teach.* New York: Longman.

Harnack, R. (1968). *The teacher: Decision maker and curriculum planner.* Scranton, PA: International Textbook.

Hass, G. (1980). *Curriculum planning: A new approach.* Boston: Allyn & Bacon.

Johnson, M. (1967). Definitions and models in curriculum theory. *Educational Theory, 17.*

Krug, E. (1957). *Curriculum planning.* New York: Harper & Brothers.

Oliva, P. (1982). *Developing the curriculum.* Boston: Little Brown.

Oliver, A. (1977). *Curriculum Improvement.* New York: Harper & Row.

Saylor, J.G., & Alexander, W. (1966). *Curriculum planning for modern schools.* New York: Holt, Rinehart & Winston.

Smith, B.O., Stanley, W.O., & Shores, H.J. (1957). *Fundamentals of curriculum development.* New York: Harcourt Brace Jovanovich.

Taba, H. (1962). *Curriculum development: Theory and practice.* New York: Harcourt Brace Jovanovich.

Tanner, D., &Tanner, L. (1980). *Curriculum development: Decision making and process.* New York: Macmillan.

Tyler, R.W. (1957). The curriculum then and now. In *Proceedings* of the 1956 Conference on Testing Problems. Princeton, NJ: Educational Testing Service.

CHAPTER 1

INFLUENCES ON EARLY CHILDHOOD CURRICULUM DEVELOPMENT

Bernard Spodek and Olivia N. Saracho

INTRODUCTION

Programs of early childhood education have evolved over the years. They have also been modified as they were adapted and adopted by different communities. This chapter will review the various factors that have influenced the development of early childhood curricula over time.

Early childhood education programs are based on both educational theories and child development theories. In the 1890s G. Stanley Hall initiated the child study movement and began the intimate relationship between early childhood education and child development. The merging of the two fields depicted a critical transition in the development of early childhood education curricula since specific developmental theories were used instead of knowledge theories (Spodek & Saracho, 1990).

CHANGES IN CONCEPTIONS OF CHILDHOOD

Until the middle of the nineteenth century, western society viewed the various species of plants and animals as distinct–each created separately. And man was considered a unique species because, according to the Bible, man was created in the image of God. The consequence of this view was that, although other plant and animal species could be studies scientifically, man could only be studied philosophically or spiritually.

All this changes in 1859 when Charles Darwin published *The Origin of the Species*. Darwin suggested that the different species were not created separately, but were the result of natural selection–the process of evolution. One consequence of this new theory was to suggest that humans are related to other animal species and that humans could be studied scientifically just as other species could.

Before this time the development of children was studied either through the diaries of parents who described their children at various ages and stages, or by adults reflecting about what it was like growing up. Neither of these were particularly scientific methods.

Growing out of the emerging field of psychology came the field of child study, later to become child development. One of the first researchers in this field, G. Stanley Hall, used evolution as the basis of his theory of child development. He felt that the development of each human being reflected the development of the entire human race.

Hall, Arnold Gesell, and their followers viewed development as a process of unfolding through maturation. Development was determined by the individual's genetic makeup and was predetermined. While one may thwart development–keeping certain characteristics from unfolding–one could not materially change development. *Maturationist theory* suggested that education should follow development. Teachers were admonished to match their activities to children's developmental levels—to make sure they are developmentally appropriate—and not try to push them or stimulate them beyond that point.

Maturationist theory was one developmental theory that influenced early childhood education. *Behavioral theory*, which was generated in the 1920s, also influenced early childhood practice. As a theory of development, behaviorism suggested that development is primarily influenced by environmental conditions. The major influence in education originally came from the work of Edward Thorndike who posited three laws of learning: The Law of Effect, The Law of Exercise, and the Law of Readiness (Weber, 1984).

The Law of Exercise led teachers to believe in the importance of practice of doing things repeatedly until mastery was achieved. The Law of Effect, stated that a stimulus-response bond is strengthened if it is followed by a pleasurable experience. This was later elaborated into a theory of operant conditioning (a modern version of this behavioral theory) by B.F. Skinner, which then became the basis of applied behavior analysis, a method of instruction that has had more application in the education of children with disabilities or with deviant behavior than in the education of young children who are developing and behaving normally.

Psychodynamic theory, based on the ideas of Sigmund Freud and Eric Erickson, also influenced early childhood education. These psychologists saw in the emotional life of young children the roots of adult behavior. Play–and especially dramatic play–took on importance as a way for children to rid themselves or cope with negative feelings. Mental health became an important goal of early childhood programs since to keep young children mentally healthy would endure that they would mature into mentally healthy adults. Under both Behavioral and Psychodynamic theories, early childhood programs became more proactive in nature rather than just supportive of the natural unfolding of development.

During the last three decades, human development theory and research has focused more on cognitive development than on socioemotional development. The leading paradigms are related to *Constructivism*: the notion that individuals construct their own knowledge. The primary theory originally came from the work of Jean Piaget; later the work of Vygotsky, Bruner and others–sometimes called post-Piagetians—has come increasingly into the limelight (Miller, 1993).

Piaget's theory is a stage theory just as psychodynamic theory is. Piaget posited that children go through a series of transformations in their thinking, moving from sensory-motor thought to hypothetical-deductive, logical thought. The stage element of his theory stimulated the notion of developmentally appropriate practices, which suggest that children's programs should be aimed directly at their level of development since education would not modify the child's level of development.

Piaget's theory inspired a number of new curriculum models in the 1970s. The lone surviving Piagetian model is the High/Scope program, though some educators question whether it actually does reflects Piagetian theory. It has mainly influenced programs in math and science. Constance Kamii's books, *Numbers in Preschool and Kindergarten: Implications of Piaget's Theory* and *Physical Knowledge in Early Childhood Education* are examples of this influence.

Vygotsky and other "Post-Piagetians" differed with Piaget. They suggested that cognitive development consists of cultural development as well as natural development. Vygotsky posited the "zone of proximal development" (ZPD), the area beyond children's current levels of development where children can think logically with help. Adherents to Vygotsky's theories believed that we should teach beyond children's developmental levels, rather than directly to it, while supporting children's learning. As a result, education would influence the child's level of development Post-Piagetian theory also suggests that children need to acquire "cultural tools," which help them make sense of the world and symbolize it. These cultural tools include ways of understanding the world that are developed with each culture.

Vygotsky's work has begun to influence early childhood education and a number of textbooks have been published recently that seek to apply his theory to early childhood education. His greatest influence, though, has been in the area of early reading instruction. The concept of "emergent literacy" has replaced "reading readiness," providing new models for pre-reading and early reading instruction (Mason & Sinha, 1993).

PROGRAMS OF EARLY CHILDHOOD EDUCATION

Innovative programs in early childhood education are often unique because of their particular educational philosophy or the specific goals of the program. Froebel, for example was a philosophical Idealist. His kindergarten was designed to help children understand the relationship between man, God, and nature. The Froebel gifts symbolized the ideas of unity and diversity in that relationship. The gifts and occupations were not presented to help children understand the nature of their shapes or other physical attributes, but rather the abstract ideas they represented.

Montessori, an empiricist, viewed knowledge as gained by gathering information through the senses. Her sensory education helped children sharpen all five of their senses so that they could better use them to gather information through the senses that would allow them to become more knowledgeable. The Montessori materials isolate different aspects of sensory experience to help children sharpen the senses, by comparing and seriating their sensory experiences. While both pioneers of early childhood education were aware of children's developmental levels, neither judged their method simply by its developmental appropriateness. Rather, these two programs represent different concepts of the nature of knowledge and how children can become more knowledgeable.

Progressive kindergartens saw knowledge as embedded in the experience of the community. Studying aspects of the community immediately surrounding the child and having the child reconstruct that knowledge through play, through artistic and linguistic representations, and through activities, was seen as making children more knowledgeable.

Margaret Macmillan's nursery school was as interested in helping children deal with the consequences of poverty as with helping them become more knowledgeable. This early childhood program was originally designed to serve poor children. The key concept underlying the program was Nurturance. Children who came to the nursery school were bathed and fed. Their medical and dental needs were attended to. They were also educated. Play was an important element of the program and Macmillan was interested in educating the imagination.

Each of these programs is still offered, either in its original form or with some modification. Montessori programs and even Froebelian programs still exist. The progressive kindergarten has been manifested in Open Education, the Integrated Day, the Project Approach, the Reggio Emilia

Approach, and in many eclectic programs. And America's Head Start program is very similar in goals and methods to the Macmillan nursery school.

Each program reflects a particular philosophy, a distinct set of goals, and a specific view of the nature of knowledge. One wonders, though, whether parents or educators today, when they select one of these programs, attend to these.

MATERIALS OF EARLY CHILDHOOD EDUCATION

As Harriet Cuffaro (1999) has stated, "Materials are the texts of the early childhood curriculum" (p. 64). The Froebel gifts were unique. For the first time children were given concrete materials to use as the basis for their education. Frank Lloyd Wright, the famous American architect, credits his understanding of shape and space to his use of these gifts (Brosterman, 1997). This idea of using concrete materials continues to be a significant part of early education today. But the physical attributes of the materials are seen as more important than their symbolic meaning.

Building on the ideas of Froebel and Edouard Sequin, a nineteenth century special educator, Montessori developed a set of materials which were specifically designed to enhance the educational value of their physical attributes. Not only were the sensory qualities used to help children become more attuned to these attributes, but concrete materials were used to teach children about the written language and arithmetic.

When the progressive educators reconstructed the kindergarten in America, they removed Froebel's gifts. The gifts were replaced with wooden blocks that children could use to build things with. They also added toys with which children could represent the world around them such as toy kitchens for a housekeeping area. Toys allowed the children to bring their personal experiences down in scale so they could handle them, manipulate them, and use them to make sense of the world around them. The toys are symbolic representations of real things and this play is less fantasy than acted-out representations of reality.

Today, we have added electronic materials to the early childhood classrooms with an increasing number of computers in early childhood classrooms. The computers themselves are not representations that children manipulate. Rather, the programs within them serve as representations, and good computer programs present symbolic representations of many aspects of reality to children. Because they are interactive, they allow children to manipulate them, change them and–in the better programs–create new possibilities that result from their creative imaginations as well as from their understanding of reality.

TARGET POPULATIONS OF EARLY CHILDHOOD PROGRAMS

Some of the earliest programs in early childhood education, including the Montessori program, Macmillan's nursery school, and many kindergartens, were designed to serve poor children. These programs have often been concerned with providing health, nutritional, and social services along with education. Mission kindergartens and free kindergartens, sponsored by religious groups and philanthropic institutions, charged no tuition in order to serve poor children. But most kindergartens, in time, became tuition based and, like Montessori and nursery programs, they came to serve primarily middle class children. The required fees created a barrier to enrolling the poor and early childhood education became an elitist form of education.

This situation changed very slowly in the United States where kindergartens for 5-year-olds. With the War on Poverty, established by former President Lyndon Johnson, the Head Start program was created to serve poor children. The 1970s also saw individual states establishing kindergartens for five-year-olds. Today kindergartens are universal for 5's, and economically challenged 3's and 4's. Although public schools are required to provide such education, parents are not required to enroll their children in these public schools.

In addition, a broader range of children is being served by early childhood education programs. In America, federal law required that schools provide educational programs for children with disabilities from age 3 up and 10% of the enrollment slots in Head Start are reserved for children with disabilities. Schools are required to offer education to children with disabilities in the least restrictive educational settings and increasingly children are being educated in "inclusive" classes serving all children.

BELIEFS ABOUT TEACHING AND CARING

Concern for the care of young children predates a concern for their education. Day nurseries were already being established in the early 1800s in the United States. They were designed to provide basic custodial care for children of poor working mothers. More affluent families used nursery nurses (nannies) or their equivalent and kept their children at home. Even the early infant schools in the United States were valued more for caring for children that for educating them (Strickland, 1982). From the beginning, child care and early childhood education were seen as distinct services. Only in the 1920s, when the idea of the nursery school was transported from England to America, did child care centers begin including educational programs in their service with some regularity.

The changes in the nature of families and in the role of women in our society that began during World War II has continued. Women have increasingly taken professional, technical, and administrative positions, and are concerned with long term careers that continued after marriage and motherhood. Nuclear families with small numbers of children, single parent families, and blended families have become more the norm. Working mothers—whether working class or middle class—need child caring services and such services were created by the private sector. These child care programs are all day programs, often from 8:00 a.m. through 6:00 p.m. In contrast, early educational programs are provided on a half day basis (2 to 3 hours) or a full school day (5 to 6 hours). This has led to a situation where young children may be in more than one early childhood program each day or where school programs are augmented by some type of child care.

To some early childhood educators, the distinction between seems arbitrary. The need to serve all the needs of young children and to deal with the whole child suggests that this distinction may be wrong. They advocate a form of early education they call *educare* which integrates the functions of these two institutions. This idea can actually be traced back to Margaret Macmillan with her idea of education based on *nurturance.*

Teachers of educare must be competent educators, but they also must know about the health, nutritional, and social needs of children. They must work with parents as well as with the children in their classes. This anticipates one of the ways that early childhood education may change in the future.

It may be that the distinction is based on economics, since child caregivers are often payed less than educators. It may be that the distinction also stems from the drive to professionalize the field, with teachers in educational settings having a level of education and credentials seldom found among caregivers. Some suggest that the distinction be eradicated while others suggest creating career ladders that function in a framework of differentiated staffing.

REFORMS IN THE LARGER SOCIAL CONTEXT: INDUSTRIALIZATION, AND URBANIZATION

This education of young children has traditionally taken place in the home. Educational institutions for young children were created beginning in the nineteenth century. This closely paralleled the beginning of the Industrial Revolution in Europe and North America as well as the development of urbanization. These new early childhood institutions included the Infant School in Great Britain, the Kindergarten in Germany, the Children's House of Montessori in Italy, the Nursery School in Britain, and the Progressive kindergarten in America. These institutions were carried to

Asia and to the southern hemisphere in the late eighteenth and early nineteenth century after industrialization took hold there.

Industrialization changed homes and families. It moved the place where people worked from the place where they lived. Earlier, fathers and mothers worked in or around the home, engaging in handicraft industries or farming in fields. Children had been constantly with their parents, learning adult family and work roles by observing them, modeling their behavior, and receiving informal instruction from them. When parents (both fathers and mothers) worked in factories, shops and offices away from home, the bond between parent and child changed. Other adults were needed to undertake up the missing socializing and educating role of parents.

Similarly, as people moved into cities, free, relatively safe, space was no longer available for children to play. Institutions needed to be invented to serve that function in place of the rural landscape. Playgrounds and kindergartens served this purpose. Urbanization also impacted on family structure. Before, children were part of extended families, with grandparents, aunts, uncles and cousins living together or close by. Urbanization led to the creation of nuclear families. While parents and children lived together, members of the extended family lived apart, often at a great distance. This placed greater responsibility for the care and socialization of children on the parents and the support systems for children that had existed for decades, if not centuries, were disbanded. In addition, families became smaller.

FROM PROVINCIAL LIFE TO GLOBALIZATION AND FROM THE INDUSTRIAL AGE TO THE INFORMATION AGE

The industrial revolution not only changed the way goods were produced, it also changed in transportation and communication systems. Steamships and steam locomotives were invented, followed by automobiles, and airplanes. The telegraph was invented, followed by the telephone. The radio extended the range of voice communication. These changes led to increases in the speed in which goods and services could be transported and in which messages and ideas could be disseminated.

There was a great migration of people from Europe to America in the mid-1800s and these immigrants brought their customs and cultures with them. The Germans brought the idea of the kindergarten with them and the first kindergartens in the United States were German language kindergartens. When the ideas of Maria Montessori and Margaret Macmillan traveled to the United States, they came not as the baggage of immigrant, but as ideas gathered from the mass media. These ideas about early childhood education were modified as they arrived in America just as they were when they traveled to Asia. In each country the adoption of ideas in early child-hood education was coupled with the adaptation of these ideas to the local culture (Woollens, 2000).

The new forms of transportation and communication also led to greater interactions among individuals from different countries and cultures. Increasingly there was a need to be aware of and understand people of dif-ferent countries and cultures, both within one's own country as well as within the global community. One result was a need for multicultural edu-cation from the earliest time of a child's education. Thus, even within any particular program model, the content of early childhood education changed. It has been suggested that in America, the kindergarten was the first educational institution to disseminate multicultural education in the schools (Beatty, 2000). Where people earlier felt the need to limit the con-tent of a young child's education to what was directly observable in their immediate environment, there has been increasingly a need to expand the scope of this content both in time and in space.

A major change in technology in recent years has moved us from the industrial age to the information age. Computers and other electronic devices have become increasingly important in our lives. Television has become a pervasive part of children's lives. While we can continue to debate whether the new technologies are a good or bad thing, the process of digitalization continues and impacts on children at younger and younger ages and on their education.

THE FUTURE OF CURRICULUM IN EARLY CHILDHOOD EDUCATION

Although it is difficult to predict any changes in the field of early child-hood education, one can assume that the changes will be gradual rapid since the process of dissemination is a slow one. For example, the changes in technology that have impacted the field in our various countries will continue. Some of the consequences of older technology seems to have reversed, though. While earlier we saw adults moving from their home to separate workplaces, we now see more adults working at home. They are connected to their business establishments by electronic means: cellular or mobile telephones and computers with email and wireless access to the Internet. These have allowed the virtual place of business to replace the office. Women continue to have careers and these careers are increasingly in higher positions, whether working in their homes or away from home. But because the level of technology continues to increase, it is difficult to work and care for young children at the same time even while at home.

Thus, one can assume that technology will not lessen the need for early childhood programs. Family size might, however. In Japan, for example, the number of children being born continues to decline. The preschools there (both kindergartens and child care centers) have shrunk both in numbers and in size. There is also increased competition among kindergartens for clients. As a result, kindergartens are offering an increasing range of services, from transportation and hot lunches, to special classes in foreign languages or computers. This is true for both public and private kindergartens. The trend that we see in Japan may soon be seen in other industrial nations as well.

The call for educare services continues. As parents are away from home for more hours per day, they need child care services, but most do not wish to settle for custodial care. Both care and education needs to be offered. This may be done by requiring child care centers to offer the same curriculum as the kindergarten, as in Japan and in some Scandinavian countries, and by requiring higher educational qualifications for caregivers. We will also see extended child care programs increasing, with young children spending part of the day in kindergarten and part in a child care center in "wraparound" programs. This can work well if the two institutions coordinate their programs.

We will also see increases in public funding for early childhood programs and an increasing range of children in publically supported programs. In the United States most 5-year-olds and some 4- and 3-year-olds are in public school kindergartens although most 3- and 4-year-olds are in private preschools. Increasingly, public schools are offering prekindergarten programs for 4-year-olds, sometimes for all children, and at other times for children with special needs: either those with disabilities or those who are considered at risk of future educational failure. These programs do not require tuition payment for enrolling their children.

In America there are also government subsidies being paid to private child care centers as well as vouchers given to parents to use in child care centers. This is happening particularly as welfare reform has encouraged parents to seek work. In Japan, both public and private kindergartens receive subsidies but tuition is paid by parents in both types of kindergartens

Another trend that can be seen is the increase in the required qualifications for early childhood teachers. Presently in America public school kindergarten teachers must at least have graduated from a four-year program of teacher education. Child care teachers may have as little as six semester hours of child development or education courses beyond high school. Head Start teachers may have a Child Development Associates credential which can be earned by demonstrating certain competencies. Soon, Head Start will require that at least of half their teachers have a minimum of an associate degree in early childhood education or child development. In Japan teachers in kindergarten and child caregivers receive their training separately and kindergarten teachers can have either a 2-year degree or a 4-year degree. Soon they will all be required to have a 4-year degree and kindergarten and child care teachers are beginning to be trained together.

Thus, it seems that early childhood teachers will be better qualified in the future.

The most difficult projection is what will happen to early childhood programs in the future. Some of the oldest historic programs continue to exist. Montessori programs are almost 100 years old. Recently an American manufacturer began producing the entire set of Froebel gifts and advocating the use of these Froebelian gifts in all kindergartens today. The Froebelian program is more than 150 years old. Froebel materials have been manufactured in Japan for some time and there are both Froebelian kindergartens and teacher training programs there. Montessori programs, which had a revival in the United States beginning in 1957, are increasingly being offered in the United States and abroad. Thus, historical early childhood programs will continue to be offered, though in a modified form.

But what about new programs? The Project Approach and the Reggio Emilia Approach have received a great deal of attention and are seen as new and innovative. In the 1960s progressive schools in New York City were doing projects then. Their integrative approach to curriculum was not significantly different from the description of the Reggio Emilia approach. So are these new approaches or just a variation on educational programs that have been around for a long time?

In 1972, Lawrence Kohlberg and Rochelle Mayer published an article in the Harvard Educational Review titled, "Development as the Aim of Education." In this article they identified three streams of educational ideology: *romantic, cultural transmission,* and *progressive.* Each stream was related to a particular set of developmental theories: the *romantic* with the maturationist theory, the *cultural transmission* with the behavioral theory, and the *progressive* with the constructivist theory. Romantics believed that education should follow development as it unfolds. Advocates of cultural transmission believed that the knowledge of the past should be passed on to the new generation in as efficient a manner as possible. And progressives believed that children should be helped to construct their own knowledge by gathering information from their environment and reconstructing that knowledge symbolically.

That same year (1972), The Educational Products Information Exchange published their *Educational Products Report #42* on early childhood education. In their report, they characterized three theories of child development along with their related early childhood program models. These were labeled as a *maturationist-nativist* view, a *behavioral environment* view, and a *comprehensive-interactionist* view. While the two sets of labels are different, the concepts are the same.

Essentially what the two groups of authors were saying is that within the three streams of educational ideologies, there may be many variations, but the underlying principles remain the same. This was evident recently in a research report on Japanese kindergarten (Holloway, 2000). Holloway also sees three streams of educational ideology in today's Japanese kindergartens. Holloway's labels are different from those used in the publications just mentioned. She calls these preschools child-oriented, role-oriented and relationship-oriented. The *child-oriented* programs seem similar to those labeled *romantic*, the *role-oriented* programs seem similar to those labeled *cultural transmission*, and the *relationship-oriented* programs seem similar to those labeled *progressive*. Analyses of programs that were separated by 30 years and by half the globe find programs that are different in name but similar in their ideological characteristics. It may be that early childhood educators will continue to create programs that are different in their labels and their surface characteristics, but are similar in a deeper sense, fitting into ideological frameworks that persist.

During the past century, for example, progressive early childhood education programs were offered periodically with different names attached. Thus, in the 1960s a progressive school in New York was ideologically linked to the Integrated Day of British Infant Schools of the 1960s, the Open Education Movement in America of the 1970s, the Project Approach and the Reggio Emilia Approach. At no one time have any of these progressive approaches to education been put into practice in a majority of schools, but they have continued to be attractive to many early childhood educators.

Similarly, *romantic* programs persist though they may be called "free schools," "child centered" schools, or "developmentally appropriate" programs. And *cultural transmission* programs continue to exist, as "back-to-basics" approaches, or preparation for primary school.

One can assume that in the future we will continue to see early childhood education programs which fit into each of the three steams of educational ideologies. They may carry different names, however. Each will be seen as attractive to some group of educators, of parents, and of community members. While we cannot predict how these ideologies will look in the future, we can assume they will be there. Thus, we can expect that early childhood education programs will remain as diverse as they ever have been.

REFERENCES

Beatty, B. (2000). The letter killed: Americanization and multicultural education in the kindergartens of the United States, 1856-1920. In R. Woolens (Ed.),*Kindergartens and cultures* (pp. 42-58). New Haven, CT: Yale University Press.

Brosterman, N. (1997). Inventing kindergarten. New York: Harry N. Abrams.

Caldwell, B. (1984). Growth and development. *Young Children, 39*(6), 53-56.

Cuffaro, H.K. (1999). A view of materials as the texts of the early childhood curriculum. In B. Spodek & O.N. Saracho (Eds.), *Issues in early childhood curriculum* (pp. 64-85). Troy, NY: Educator's International Press, Inc.

Education Products Information Exchange (1972).*Report #42: Early childhood education.* New York: Author.

Holloway, S. (2000). *Contested Childhood: Diversity and change in Japanese preschools.* New York: Routledge.

Kamii, C. (1982). *Numbers in preschool and kindergarten: Implications of Piaget's theory.* Washington, DC: National Association for the Education of Young Children.

Kamii, C. (1978). *Physical knowledge in early childhood education.* Englewood Cliffs, NJ: Prentice-Hall.

Kohlberg, L., & Mayer, R. (1972). Development as the aim of education.*Harvard Educational Review, 42,* 449-496.

Mason, J.A., & Sinha, S. (1993). Emerging literacy in the early childhood years: Applying a Vygotskian model of learning and development. In B. Spodek (Ed.), *Handbook of research on the education of young children* (pp. 137-150). New York: Macmillan.

Miller, P.H. (1993). *Theories of developmental psychology* (3rd ed.). New York: W. H. Freeman.

Spodek, B. (1973). *Early childhood education.* Englewood Cliffs, NJ: Prentice-Hall.

Spodek, B., & Saracho, O.N. (1990). Early childhood curriculum construction and classroom practice. *Early Child Development and Care, 61,* 1-9.

Strickland, C.E. (1982). Paths not taken: Seminal models of early childhood education in Jacksonian America. In B. Spodek (Ed.). *Handbook of research in early childhood education* (pp. 321-340) New York: Free Press.

Sylva, K. (1986). Developmental psychology and the preschool child. In J. Harris (Ed.), *Child psychology in action* (pp. 127-142). London: Croom Helm.

Weber, E. (1984). *Ideas influencing early childhood education.* New York: Teachers College Press.

Woolens, R. (2000). The missionary kindergarten in Japan. In R. Woolens (Ed.), *Kindergartens and cultures* (pp. 113-136). New Haven, CT: Yale University Press.

CHAPTER 2

SOCIABLE THINKING: COGNITIVE DEVELOPMENT IN EARLY CHILDHOOD EDUCATION

Kelvin Seifert

INTRODUCTION

In a review of cognitive development written in 1993, I wrote that I wanted to promote breadth and flexibility of perspective: there are different theories and informal views of thinking, I said, each with advantages and problems for early childhood educators (Seifert, 1993). Theoretical changes in the intervening years, however, have made me regard this liberal, tolerant view as naive. New models of cognitive development and their embodiments in early childhood education have moved markedly toward socially based theories of learning (SBTLs), theories variously called social constructivism, sociohistorical perspectives, or (less accurately) simply constructivism. In some circles, SBTLs now verge on taken-as-given, universal "truths"—something of an oxymoron given their constructivist premises!

So my challenge as a reviewer has shifted. I still want to avoid "theoretical sectarianism" about cognitive development, but I especially want to avoid evangelizing too hard for the dominant constructivist "churches"— to avoid accepting SBTLs too easily, without critical appraisal. Accomplishing this new task can be challenging, given the support for SBTLs circulating in the current post-modernist *Zeitgeist*. Nonetheless, my hope in this chapter is to encourage an appraisal of SBTLs both directly and indirectly by describing aspects of SBTLs and alternatives theories, and the commenting on what each offer early childhood education and on how much each is partaking of the "new" constructivisms. The appraisals will not aim for full coverage, but emphasize the practical needs of early childhood educators, who I will define as any professionals who work with and support children day-to-day, regardless of institutional affiliation.

I will describe four major theories or models related to cognitive development in early childhood. The first will be learning theory, but learning theory primarily in its recent, relatively cognitive versions. The second will be information processing theory, with special emphasis on the newer ideas about pattern detection and parallel, rather than serial, processing. The third will be structural theory, with emphasis on what might be termed the "organizing inner mind." The fourth will be SBTLs proper, in both individualistic and social forms. This sequence will work, but not perfectly, because versions of SBTL have influenced all schools of developmental thought and early childhood education practice. The problem, it will turn out, is that distinctions between theories and concepts are not fully stable or clear. Blurring conceptual and pedagogical boundaries has mostly been healthy, but the reasons for blurrings need to be understood carefully, in order to make best use of the revisions in daily work with children.

To help fix the conceptual distinctions and shifts, I begin by discussing my understanding of what psychologists and educators tend to mean by the general term *cognitive development,* and its relevance (or lack thereof) for early childhood education. As we will see, the notion of *cognitive development* is problematic for early childhood educators because it implies psychological distinctions not held by them in practice, or even in published reflections on their work. But the mismatch between "classic" cognitive development and the needs of professionals has apparently been noticed by developmental psychologists, some of whom have revised their research projects to bring them more in line with (and also help to create) newer meanings of *cognitive development.* For better or for worse, the new meanings are all more socially based or "social constructivist" than before; hence my cautions in the opening paragraph of this chapter.

THREE PROBLEMS WITH *COGNITIVE DEVELOPMENT*

Although the term *cognitive development* can be understood and analyzed in many ways (Baker, 1999; Burman, 1994), let me highlight three of its assumptions about children and human nature which pose problems for early childhood educators (see also Table 1 for a partial summary). The first is the classic separation of mind and body: in speaking of "cognitive" development, we separate thinking from feeling, and thinking from social interaction. The cognitive becomes attached to the logical, reasoned, rule-governed, and thoughtful; non-cognitive becomes everything else, including the intuitive, the emotional, and the social. By using the term *cognitive development,* we assume that developments on the cognitive side of the fence have a life of their own, one that can be isolated, observed, described and even fostered without directly affecting involvement of non-cognitive processes.

Unfortunately, few teachers, clinicians or others responsible for young children actually find this assumption realistic if stated in such explicit terms; work with children routinely requires attention to the mutual influence of the cognitive and non-cognitive. But neither this reality of professional life, nor generations of philosophical criticism of the mind-body distinction, stop cognitive psychologists from talking as if Descartes were right after all. Textbooks, research programs, and entire academic careers are still organized as if the cognitive can be dissected from the non-cognitive and still yield useful theories and sound professional advice.

The second assumption implied by the term *cognitive development* is that long-term change can in fact be distinguished from short-term change, and that long-term change is especially systematic, predictable, and progressive. In ordinary talk, development refers to changes that take years, although ones spanning only a few months are sometimes called "developmental" if they happen in infancy. The minute we speak of *development,* then, we implicitly split off long, slow changes from faster ones. The latter are often called learning, or named with some category-breaking neologism like "microgenesis" (meaning small-scale or immediate in origin). We generally assume that the longer and slower the change, the more stable and/or systematic it is, and the more it leads to individual betterment or progress (Baker, 1999). These assumptions make truly developmental (i.e., long-term) change more important or worthy than mere daily or hourly change. Yet again, when put so explicitly, many early childhood profession-

TABLE 1
Problematic Assumptions of the Concept of *Cognitive Development*

Assumption	*Problem for Early Childhood Education*
1. Mind-body distinction	ECE requires teaching mind and body simultaneously; cognition not recognizable as such.
2. Long-term change more stable, predictable, and important than short-term change	ECE is intrinsically a matter of blending short-term and long-term goals; ECE does not regard a young child's future as fixed (i.e. as predictable).
3. The child has a stable, unified self capable of making choices and exercising responsibility	ECE regards responsible self-direction as a goal, but not as a current reality in actual classroom practice.

als would deny much of the previous statement. They might share optimism for children's futures (hence their choice of occupation), but they would also point out an important caution: that in the world of young children, *most* changes happen rapidly and *few* have easily predicted outcomes. Learning and development therefore become blended in the actual practice of early childhood education, not separated. By setting up images of "the" normal child, furthermore, developmental psychology implicitly devalues the diversity which early childhood teachers witness among the real, flesh-and-blood children. As a result, research that presents itself as "developmental" in the classic sense becomes a little less useful, because it casts its vision too far into the future and because it implies a universally best way to grow up.

The third assumption lurking in the term *cognitive development* is that a unified self or ego motivates and guides an individual's behavior and activities, including activities that might be called mental or "cognitive." Like Freud's idea of the ego self insures coordination of developmental change; it exercises reason, learns rules and categories' classifications of objects and events. Most important, the single, unified self makes choices about what and how to learn, even if initial choices are awkward, immature, or full of mistakes. As a practical result, what is traditionally called cognitive development implies that children are responsible for their actions and thoughts, or in some sense are their cause. This is not a very post-modernist position, though certainly a commonsense one which many early educators support in principle (Tobin, 1995). The problem is that in practice, early childhood educators also behave as if young children do *not* have a unified, central self and can *not* take responsibility for themselves as individuals! Much early childhood education teaching arranges classroom activities and circumstances so that particular desired behaviors will simply happen to occur anyway—as if this is the best way to insure that desired individual "choices" get made. In preparing the learning environment, teachers seem to believe less in emerging unified identity or self for the child than in the child's *lack* of dependable identity, a lack that requires external, and hopefully benign, influence. Classic notions of cognitive development cannot speak to the decentering of the individual child often implied by classroom practice, except perhaps to criticize teachers for *not* centering their programs enough on individual children, self-choice, and personal responsibility.

Yet in spite of these conceptual criticisms, the idea of *cognitive development* still gives early childhood teachers a way to view children's behavior and the teacher's part in influencing it. As I explain below, this is true even (and especially) for the developmental accounts that are the most classic philosophically, the structural theories. For most other developmental models, the gaps between conceptual assumptions and professional practice have rendered classic versions of the model less directly relevant to early childhood education. But all is not lost: gaps between assumptions

TABLE 2

Theories of *Cognitive Development* Compared (Selectively)

Theory	Key Features	Recent SBTL Influences	Implications for ECE
Structural	Mind organizes experiences; predictable long-term steps and stages	Stages more focused, less global; hence more individuality possible	Teacher's main job is to provide open-ended guidance
Learning Theory	Associations among specific antecedents, behaviors and consequences	Patterns of associations matter more than individual associations; Are inforcement is the entire behavior context, not any specific antecedent	Behavior management should focus on whole context, not on any specific consequence or trigger
Information Processing Theory	Information is organized & processed systematically & logically (like a computer)	Many parts of information are processed in parallel	Repeated, direct exposure to important information and experiences can be helpful
SBTLs	Learning always is a joint (not individual) activity	Knowledge and learning may sometimes be distributed among individuals, not within	Participation is a more important goal than transfer of learning

and practice have also stimulated new directions in the study of children's thinking, and led to more useful, if still implicit, conceptualizations of *cognition* and *development*. The rest of this chapter illustrates these claims, first by exploring new directions in structural theory and then by exploring new directions in other accounts of cognitive development. Because of space limitations, I will confine myself to illustrating trends rather than reviewing research programs comprehensively (see also Table 2 for a partial summary). With one exception, however, the growing hegemony of SBTLs will reveal itself in even a small sample of studies and theories. The exception, interestingly enough, are studies based on traditional structural models of development.

STRUCTURAL MODELS OF COGNITIVE DEVELOPMENT

Structural models of cognitive development are intellectual descendants of rationalist philosophers such as Descartes and Kant, who argued that a person's mind (or "soul") imposes order on knowledge and experience, rather than simply absorbing or detecting it in the environment. When this view has been adopted by developmental psychologists, a top priority has been to discover exactly *how* a child imposes order on experience—the intellectual stages, mechanisms, or order-making processes that are not directly reflected in experience, but are somewhat independent of it and therefore somehow located "in" the child. Whatever the stages, mechanisms, or processes proposed, structural models assume they can be inferred from a child's observable behaviors, but are not identical with them. In recent times the most well-known example of this approach is that of Jean Piaget and his associates at the "Genevan School" (Piaget & Inhelder, 2000). As undergraduates now learn in introductory psychology, Piaget postulated several broad cognitive stages that collectively formed a structural model of development, beginning in infancy with sensorimotor thinking and ending in adolescence with formal operational thinking. In the 1960s and 1970s, immense research energy in both Europe and North America went to working out features of these stages and to testing their breadth, universality, and logical inevitability (Gelman & Baillargeon, 1983).

Structural theory, and Piagetian theory in particular, enjoyed popularity among early childhood educators during this period of research (see Kamii, 1976; Weikart, 1971), but critics identified both theoretical problems and practical limitations for education. For one thing, cognitive stages turned out to be much less general than Piaget had supposed. Slight changes in wording or procedures often affected success at experimental tasks and thereby altered a child's apparent cognitive maturity (Donaldson, 1979). Cross-cultural differences in cognitive performances were common, and related to differences in familiarity with tasks, task materials, and sociolinguistic expectations about conversation during interviews (e.g., teacher-like "test" questions were not construed uniformly). These problems did not invalidate structural theory entirely, but they did lead proponents to define stages more specifically than before (see also Seifert, 1993). Neo-structural studies of cognitive development still looked for broad endogenous ("inner") processes of developmental change, but hypothesized—and seemed to demonstrate—that they unfolded at different rates in different areas of cognition (Case, 1991, 1999). A child might develop numeracy skills and moral thinking, for example, through roughly analogous steps or stages but not necessarily at the same rates.

A more serious theoretical problem was that structural theories often sounded naive or simplistic about how cognitive change actually occurred. According to Piaget, cognitive structures (or "schemata") developed because of an interplay between assimilation (interpreting new experiences or concepts in terms of old ones) and accommodation (modifying existing experiences or concepts to fit with new ones). A child who sees a butterfly may at first name it a "bird" (assimilation to a prior concept), but after additional experience modifies this representation to distinguish two kinds of flying things, "bird" and "butterfly" (accommodation). Although cognitive bootstrapping was all right as an explanation as far as it went, it was also paradoxical and philosophically unsatisfying. Some part of the child—an equilibrating "faculty"—had to make the necessary assimilations and accommodations, and that faculty already had to be cognitively developed enough at birth to do so. It was as if some small piece of the Piagetian child, a mature "homunculus" lurking inside, was cognitively equivalent to the whole child. Yet if this were true, then "whole children" did not develop—only their overt behaviors developed.

The notions of assimilation and accommodation also did not account for the subtle, but common cases of cognitive change involving incommensurability: changes in which a new concept cannot, in principle, be understood either as part of an earlier concept or as a simple combination of earlier concepts. During the preschool years, for example, children differentiate the concepts of *weight* and *density* (Carey, 1991); yet neither concept, if understood accurately, may be either assimilated from or accommodated to the other. Density is not simply a subcategory of weight, nor is it a superordinate category that includes weight plus other elements (e.g., volume); rather it is "weight per volume," usually represented mathematically as a ratio of the two. Developing the concept of density therefore requires accommodating (or modifying) *two* initial concepts, weight and volume, and combining *aspects* of their meanings without also losing track of their original senses. This is a relatively subtle and mysterious intellectual task, and more complex than simple assimilation or accommodation. It is also a task characterizing much of children's cognitive development, and increasingly so as they mature.

The emergence of incommensurable concepts can be explained a number of ways, but most explanations call upon social influences of some form, and therefore compromise the traditional assumptions of structural theory about cognitive development. One explanation, for example, is that new, incommensurable concepts are simply modeled and taught directly. A child witnesses others using the concept of *density*, for example, and (perhaps) is also taught definitions and examples of the concept explicitly. This explanation seems straightforward or even obvious, except that it is not clear whether explicit social transmission actually gives children an intuitive grasp of the new concept, rather than simply a new vocabulary or name for the concept. How is a young child supposed to sense the meaning of a previously incomprehensible idea (e.g., density) if he or she has no prior cognitive furniture with which to interpret it, and cannot be sure which prior experiences might help to build the furniture?

Another explanation for why incommensurable concepts develop is that a child experiences contradictions or (in Piaget's terms) disequilibrium which motivate learning the new concepts. At a water table in an early childhood classroom, for example, a child may note that floating and sinking do not depend on objects' weight; sometimes heavy things float and sometimes light things sink. Theoretically, this anomaly creates cognitive dissonance or instability and motivates development of a new concept, density, to account for the variations. This explanation also seems reasonable as far as it goes, except that it does not account for the uniformities often observed in new concepts that are incommensurable with former ones (Carey, 1999). After working at the water table, why do so many children eventually settle on the identical concept, density? Since density is initially so mysterious, why do not some children finally settle on other possibilities (e.g., wood always floats and rocks always sink, but some things cannot be predicted)?

A similar problem exists with a third explanation: that general reflective (or metacognitive) skills improve with age, and allow children to detect inconsistencies in their thinking and to revise concepts to reduce or eliminate them (Kuhn et al., 1995). This explanation is also based on the disequilibrium idea that contradictions and disequilibrium stimulate cognitive change, but it also asserts that older, more developed children experience disequilibrium *more* fully and *more* effectively than younger, less developed children. Even if this idea were true, however, it is subject to the same criticism as its simpler version: it still does not explain why children tend to develop rather uniform conceptual changes, instead of idiosyncratic ones, even though their prior experiences are highly idiosyncratic and the concepts being learned cannot easily be mapped onto earlier concepts.

Is there a way to account for the uniform development of new concepts without reference either to simple (Piagetian) equilibration or to SBTL? The explanation based most fully on structuralist assumptions assumes that certain broad concepts and beliefs are for all practical purposes innate from birth, and that these "ancestor concepts" develop into a select number of core intuitive theories during infancy and early childhood (Carey, 1999). One ancestor concept, for example, is a belief that objects have underlying essences that are distinct from surface appearances and that determine their true identities. A related belief is that a human being keeps the same identity over time in spite of changes in appearance and setting—basically Piagetian object permanence applied to humans. A third is that living things, whether human or not, have intentions (Johnson, Slaughter, & Carey, 1998). These concepts, among others, allow a young child to develop an intuitive theory of human psychology, based on a central idea that "persons are a sort of living thing that has intentions." This core theory eventually accommodates (in the Piagetian sense) to experiences and to other initial core theories to beget intellectual descendants in the form of more sophisticated intuitive psychologies. The later psychologies include at least some concepts incommensurable with the earlier ones. Later core theories differentiate, for example, between accidental and intentional behavior, and still later ones differentiate unconscious behaviors from conscious ones—two distinctions not comprehensible earlier in development (Bartsch & Wellman, 1995).

Whatever the merits of this structural explanation for conceptual change, it offers only limited help to early childhood teachers because it is still based on traditional assumptions about the nature of cognitive development—that cognitive change is long-term, that it happens "inside" the child even though influenced by "outside" forces, and that cognitive processes can be distinguished from non-cognitive ones. Taken together, these assumptions limit relevance to early childhood education, because they render young children relatively inaccessible to educational influence, and therefore make the early childhood teacher less responsible for the future betterment of her children. As Robbie Case and others have pointed out, the dominant educational strategy in programs guided by structural theories of cognitive development has been guided discovery: providing children with a rich, supportive environment so that development can proceed unimpeded (Baker, 1999; Case, 1998). The chief job of the teacher, according to structural theory, is to understand what children are capable of and where they are headed developmentally; intervention is only a secondary purpose. Emphasizing indirect guidance is certainly consistent with developmentally appropriate practice (Bredekamp & Copple, 1997), but it is not sufficient advice for most programs in early childhood education. In general early childhood educators seek not just understanding, but appropriate intervention strategies as well. So it is necessary to look for additional ideas or theories in order to supplement structural theories of development. This task in turn requires modifying the traditional working assumptions of *cognitive development* embedded in structural theory. One alternative source of ideas that meet these requirements is learning theory.

LEARNING THEORY AS COGNITIVE DEVELOPMENT

Traditionally, learning theory has focused on forms of human change that were, by definition, somewhat peripheral to human development. Learning theory was about relatively rapid associations between stimuli or between responses and reinforcements. When stimuli, responses and consequences were all simple enough and when conditions were properly controlled, the fast-paced (by developmental standards) stimuli and responses displayed lawful properties and allowed for testable predictions about (short-term) behavior change. The resulting changes were called "learning." Connections between stimuli were named associative learning or "classical" conditioning, and those between a response and its consequence were named operant conditioning. Those between a response and consequence that were merely observed by the individual were called modeling, observational learning or "vicarious conditioning."

Assessed in terms of developmental theory and of SBTL, behaviorally oriented learning theory had three blind spots: it did not say enough about long-term change, about the experience of learning, or about how learning and behavior became organized in the minds and lives of learners. Observational learning theory was an early effort to remedy the last two of the three problems (Bandura, 1977), and represented an initial turn toward what SBTL theorists eventually called meaning-making. In observational learning, a person somehow "sees" relationships between a relatively complex behavior and its consequences. A student does not merely see a classmate elevate an arm and vocalize, for example, but sees the classmate "answer a teacher's question." If the teacher then tightens facial muscles, the student sees not merely muscular action, but sees the teacher "smile in response to the student." In observational learning theory, observed concrete behaviors become expressions of meanings perceived as happening in others (Bandura, 1995). This approach is still far from the thorny issues of interpretation discussed by social constructivists, but it is nonetheless a nod toward students' lived experience and personally constructed meanings.

Recent versions of learning theory have moved even more toward meaning-making than did Bandura and his colleagues. In one relatively radical formulation of learning theory, for example, conditioning has been interpreted as not about behavior change per se, but about making meaning (DeGrandpre, 2000). In this view, linkages among overt stimulus cues, responses and consequences are merely cases of this broader process. Operant conditioning is not merely about reinforcing or strengthening specific responses as a result of specific consequences, but about creating perceived *relationships* among responses, the stimuli prior to responses, and the consequences that follow. "Reinforcement" of a behavior is therefore not simply the consequences of a behavior, as in earlier versions of learning theory, but the relationship among all elements of a learning trial—stimuli, responses, and consequences. If a teacher smiles pleasantly at a young child's interesting comment during a circle-time discussion, for example, what is reinforced is not just the child's tendency to make verbal comments in the future. What is reinforced is actually the child's tendency to *associate* or connect the teacher's smile, the child's own verbal contributions, and the setting or conditions when doing so is appropriate. To say that "the teacher reinforces the child with her smile," in fact is misleading because it implies more control on the part of the teacher than the teacher really has. She does contribute to the reinforcement-relationship by smiling, but so do the classroom circumstances and the child's own behavior. All must happen together, and together they constitute reinforcement—and the creation of meaning.

Learning theory has also become more constructivist by developing more complex models of how children learn, and therefore more able to explain concepts and skills that truly matter in the lives of children and caregivers. An example is the "overlapping waves theory" proposed recently by Robert Siegler (1996). This theory makes three assumptions: (1) that children normally use a variety of strategies for solving problems, (2) that strategies can coexist for long periods even when some are suboptimal or incompatible, and (3) that experience changes the relative salience of particular strategies, rather than eliminating any outright. Changes in salience alter the likelihood of particular strategies actually appearing as behavior. When graphed across time, relative salience rises and falls like a series of overlapping waves; hence the name of the model. Learning theory—or at least Siegler's overlapping waves version of learning theory—is about studying these changes in salience and their eventual expression as altered behavior.

The result, compared to older models of learning, are predictions about learning that are more realistic. In actual classroom practice, a child is indeed likely to try a variety of strategies in ways that often seem to be trial-and-error. A child may work two-digit subtraction problems, for example, by using "borrowing" algorithms officially recommended by the teacher, but persist in counting on fingers some of the time, and at other times also try personalized (often bug-ridden) one-digit procedures that work only with particular subsets of problems. Even when a child gains skill with a new strategy—in this case the "borrowing" algorithm—he or she still often regresses to earlier methods now and then, just as adults do. The child sometimes also spends time perfecting existing, suboptimal approaches rather than trying new ones—learning to count on fingers faster or more surreptitiously, for example—since doing so usually has a short-term pay-off. New, more optimal strategies appear both suddenly and intermittently when and if they finally do. The relative importance of a child's alternative subtraction strategies will gradually change with practice, but suboptimal ones will not totally disappear for quite a while, if ever. The results are patterns of behavior that resemble Siegler's "overlapping waves" model of learning (Siegler, 2000).

The educational value of a more meaning-oriented version of learning theory can be seen in the recent professional writing of early educators. Discussions of behavior problems in young children, for example, still draw heavily on concepts of applied behavior analysis (Kaiser & Rasminsky, 1999; Scarlett, 1998). Teachers are often still urged to frame behavior problems in terms of operant conditioning (or as antecedents, behavior, and consequences, which amount to the same idea), in order to influence a child's unwanted behavior. But though this literature is quite behaviorist, it often is also concerned with the *meaning* of antecedents, behavior, and consequences for the child: with the relationships she perceives among these elements, and with how a teacher might influence the perceptions in desirable directions. One result is that teachers are urged to alter not just consequences, but also the connections (or lack thereof) among antecedents, behavior, and consequences. A temper tantrum may be highly disruptive, for example, but the solution may not be simply to avoid paying attention to it (withholding reinforcement in the narrow sense). It may also be necessary to avoid connecting antecedents to the tantrum behaviors—avoid the triggers for tantrums in the first place. Not only is the broader strategy more likely to alter behavior, it is also more likely to help a child "see" his tantrum in new, more acceptable ways—to alter, that is, its personal meaning.

Much of the literature on behavior management also implies a learning theory of "overlapping waves." In discussing how to deal with a tantrum, for example, teachers are reminded that relapses are likely to occur, and that teachers should persevere with altering relationships among antecedents, responses, and consequences in spite of them. Expecting relapses implies that a child is guided by competing responses that are gradually shifting in relative importance or salience. Helping a child respond to frustration in consistently desirable ways is really a matter of developing a high ratio of desirable responses to undesirable ones, and thereby also making the desirable responses highly "meaningful" to the child in the sense of strengthening their connections to antecedents and consequences.

In addition to becoming more compatible with early childhood practice, such revisions to learning theory have had significant influences both on learning theory itself and on traditional meanings of human development, including cognitive development. The ideas about meaningful reinforcement described earlier bring learning theory closer to SBTLs in that it becomes more concerned than before about how learning is experienced by the child and how the child can take responsibility for "constructing" new, learned behaviors. The shifting, overlapping strategies described by Siegler, on the other hand, blur the conventional distinction between short- and long-term change which has been central to the idea of cognitive development. At the heart of the model is a process that is continuous, yet never complete, and in this sense it is neither short- nor long-term, but always both and always lifelong.

Mingling the short- and long-term is consistent with the professional needs of teachers and others with direct responsibilities for children. As professionals, we are fundamentally concerned with connecting the past and the future to a child's present: with helping children to relate previous experience and future intentions to current skills and plans. Classroom practice can be interpreted, in fact, as an active effort to combine the short-term (the current activity) with the long-term (the child's prior skills and knowledge with the child's goals), even though doing so confuses the conventional distinction between immediate learning and long-term growth implied by the term *cognitive development.*

In addition, of course, good teaching of the young integrates children's actions in other ways. Teachers often attend to a child's unstated intuitions and fully conscious reasoning simultaneously; or they deal with a child's individual academic achievements and social relationships at the same time. In order to understand these concerns in parallel, integrated ways, even the revised versions of learning theory are not fully helpful, and early childhood educators must again turn elsewhere, such as to information processing theory or to SBTL itself. The next section considers the first of these alternatives, information processing theory, and its relation to cognitive development and to early childhood education. Following this discussion, we can look directly at what SBTLs have to offer.

INFORMATION PROCESSING THEORY AS COGNITIVE DEVELOPMENT

Information processing theory has intellectual roots in the everyday metaphors of the mind as a container, filing cabinet, bank, and the like. Depending on the metaphor, knowledge (or "information") is an object or substance that either fills the container, gets filed, or is deposited for later use (Olson & Bruner, 1998). Learning consists of sorting and organizing knowledge or information, as well as coordinating already-organized information to determine how and when a person should respond. Knowledge itself is inert or passive, and the mind is neutral with respect to what it stores or organizes. The "energy" to motivate learning is distinct from both knowledge and its storage place, the mind.

The computer and its operations are the most recent version of the container metaphor, and lie at the heart of information processing accounts of learning and cognitive development. Information processing models often use computer-like language to explain thinking (Bereiter & Scarmadalia, 1998). They speak of working memory (like a computer's buffer) for short-term manipulation of information, and they speak of long-term memory (like RAM and/or a hard drive) for permanent organized storage. There are executive processes analogous to computer software, and these direct how information is transformed, categorized, and saved. As with real computers, there are size and speed constraints on each aspect of information processing. The computer-driven language implies that learning and cognitive change are essentially a matter of following already-known rules or instructions, much as a well-programmed computer does. Information processing therefore has been especially successful at explaining learning and thinking with a conscious, linear character, such as solving multi-step problems in arithmetic. To solve a word problem about long division, for example, a child (theoretically) applies a known algorithm, and success depends on correctly mapping the conceptual relations in the word problem to steps of the algorithm. As a child gains experience with word problems involving long division, he or she becomes more skillful at this sort of task.

Modeled in this rather straightforward way, the explanation seems clear enough, although there is little mention of children's common tendency to vacillate among solution strategies, or for them to regress following newly learning strategies, as discussed earlier in the context of behavioral learning theory. Instead, the model portrays children not as becoming more predictable, but as becoming more flexible or strategic in switching from one solution method to another when a first method does not work. Research on mathematical problem solving has found, for example, that five- and six-year-olds often fail to solve arithmetic word problems because they have only a limited repertoire of algorithms with which to interpret the problems (Riley, Greeno, & Heller, 1983). Two or three years later, their repertoire has expanded, and so has their success rate at solving word problems. In this and other ways, information processing is framed as "cognitive development" in the classic sense: long-term gains are distinct from short-term gains, and cognitive behaviors can be described and predicted separately from motivations, social relationships, and emotions. Note, though, that this picture of learning and development most effectively explains problems and cognitions describable as a sequence of steps. When a problem requires several subtasks completed in parallel, classic information processing fares less well, a limitation that is addressed in newer versions of information processing theory, discussed later in this section.

How useful is a linear view of information processing for early childhood education? Its chief educational implication is to highlight the value of direct instruction—activities organized and/or directed by the teacher having clear, focused goals. Such teaching does have a place in early childhood education, but dominant philosophies in the field tend instead to emphasize open-ended, indirect methods such as guided discovery or authentic, apprentice-like practice (Bredekamp & Copple, 1997). Because of this mismatch of philosophical starting points, classic information processing theories, based on linear models of thinking, have had only limited application in early childhood education, for much the same reason that "classic" models of behavioral learning have had only limited impact. They are simply *too* focused and sequential compared to the classroom realities which they are modeling.

To some extent newer versions of information processing theory have remedied this problem by formulating models that account for nonlinear learning and thinking. They have, for example, addressed classroom behaviors like these: (1) carrying a cup of juice without spilling, (2) formulating an intuitive hunch during a class discussion, and (3) sensing when a classmate's behavior is covering up a feeling rather than expressing one (e.g., a smile is hiding anxiety). These are important cognitive skills for children, but they do not have a linear structure and therefore are difficult to explain as a series of linear steps with logical solutions akin to math problems.

The need to describe and predict nonlinear thinking led in the 1980s and 1990s to a form of information processing theory called *connectionism* or *parallel distributed processing* (McClelland, Rumelhart, & Hinton, 1987; Sigel, 1999). These accounts portray the mind as large, multiple networks of associations, each responding to new experience by becoming either stronger or weaker, and each operating independently of and in parallel with the others. After any new experience, the relevant associations in the network individually change so as to optimize a child's performance on future occasions—although perfectly optimal behavior may never be achieved. Balancing a cup of juice, for example, stimulates various sensory associations within a child's hand, arm, and body. Some of these become stronger and others became weaker as experience with cups of juice accumulate, but the eventual result is an optimal (if not perfect) ability to balance a cup. Likewise, immersion in a second language activates numerous associations among phonemes, words, and grammatical forms. As the associations shift in relative strength as a result of language immersion experiences, skillful (if not perfect) ability with the language emerges.

The assumptions supporting connectionism are more compatible with the realities of classroom life than are linear versions of information processing. As early childhood teachers themselves frequently note, learning by children often is less a matter of focused, sequenced steps, than of the broad, simultaneous learning of many associations combined with the optimal integration of separately learned connections. The early childhood teacher's role often consists of assisting this broadly focused process. Developmentally appropriate practice also gives a major role to incidental learning, to serendipitous learning, and active roles for the child in shaping his or her own learning. All of these cognitive processes—breadth of focus, integration of associations, and child initiation—are consistent with imagining learning as a vast network or pattern of associations operating in parallel, rather than in linear sequences.

Connectionism also sits more easily than linear processing with notions of individuality and diversity in learning. Instead of focusing on the learning of relatively preset, step-by-step content like algorithms, logical thinking, and decision rules, connectionism highlights the more open-ended challenges of recognizing patterns, integrating or balancing competing associations, and optimizing responses to diverse stimuli. Since these processes inevitably unfold differently for each child, the model also implies tolerance for the individuality that inevitably accompanies learning. Teachers should expect that no two children will learn to balance a cup of milk in exactly the same way, for example, nor acquire exactly the same version of a second language. Expressed in terms that are less connectionist but more post-modernist, connectionism predicts that each child will be "positioned" by his or her experiences as they unfold; diversity will be the rule, not the exception.

Yet in spite of nods toward diversity, connectionism does not specify *how* diversity among children might develop or how early childhood educators might deal with it under classroom conditions. The connectionist child remains somewhat "disheartened" in the sense of "lacking heart," motivation, or a context for learning. In connectionist theory, the optimizing of associations unfolds automatically, almost machinelike, even though in professional practice, early childhood teachers obviously do not think of children as machines, no matter how complex their mental mechanisms may be. Normally, teachers concern themselves not only with optimizing children's skills and cognitive associations, but also with the social relationships, settings, and scripts that guide children's cognitive activity and allow it to develop. For insight about these social dimensions, teachers must therefore look elsewhere, and most obviously to SBTLs—the socially based theories of learning, described next.

SOCIALLY BASED THEORIES OF LEARNING

Socially based theories of learning (SBTLs) call attention to how learning and development are interactive or socially mediated. Internal cognition is not denied, but treated as derivative to social interactions and cultural processes. In some versions of SBTL, even learning that appears solitary, such as reading a book or writing an essay, is interpreted as interactive: the reader has a (mental) dialogue with the author, for example, and the writer communicates with an (imaginary) audience.

As pointed out earlier, SBTLs have recently gained prominence—even dominance—in educational circles. The philosophical roots of the framework, however, are far from recent. Two hundred years ago, a form of socioculturalism was put forth by George Hegel when he argued that knowledge is synthesized from an intellectual dialogue or "dialectic" among ideas. One hundred years ago, a version of SBTL was also used by Karl Marx in arguing that knowledge and beliefs result from individuals' material positions in society: owners of property, in particular, conceive of human nature and motivations quite differently than do workers, who are positioned only to "sell" their labor. Some form of SBTL is in fact implied by any deliberate teaching, simply because deliberate teaching necessarily entails human interaction, no matter what the local arrangements or practices for doing so (O'Connor, 1998).

Unfortunately the popularity of SBTLs has led to a proliferation of models and theories based on broadly social premises, and therefore fostered ambiguity and misunderstanding about what a "social" perspective on learning means for education (Salomon & Perkins, 1998). For the purposes of understanding cognitive development in early childhood education, it is helpful to distinguish among three main varieties: (1) social mediation of individual cognitive change, (2) the use of cultural tools to learn or develop new concepts or ideas, and (3) participation in a group's efforts to create knowledge jointly. The first variety is the most familiar and compatible with everyday and "traditional" views of education and cognitive change, and the third is the least familiar and most radically challenging. The second variety falls between these extremes, with implications that are at once both more and less familiar.

Social Mediation of Individual Cognitive Change

The most familiar way of framing a SBTL is simply to think of an individual or group helping another individual to learn. A teacher helps a student to write an essay, for example, by offering suggestions or encouraging self-reflection about initial drafts. Three or four children work together to master a common set of mathematics problems, each offering help—but also receiving it—from the others individually. Parents rephrase an incoherent, but well-intentioned comment from their preschool child so that the comment makes more sense. And so on. In all cases help is offered and received, individual learning happens as a result, and over time the learning leads to broader "development" in the sense described at the beginning of this chapter. Note that this sort of social mediation is not confined to classroom instruction. It can happen anywhere, regardless of the setting—at home or school, during class or afterwards, at work or play. In fact, social mediation is virtually universal in human societies (Kruger & Tomasello, 1998). When it happens in a classroom, it takes familiar forms, such as a teacher assisting a child with reading a story, or assisting many children either in groups or one at a time. The constraints of schooling, however, make classroom interaction simply a special case of social mediation, one among many ways to assist individual cognitive change.

Social mediation by and for individuals feels familiar because it relies on the container metaphor for learning, discussed earlier as part of information processing theory. As pointed out before, the container metaphor assumes that learning and development happen "inside" individuals and that resulting knowledge is in some sense portable from one situation to another. A solution strategy for math may have to be learned first with the help of others. Once learned, though, it belongs to the individual and can be used by him or her to solve other similar math problems; assistance will not be needed later. Likewise, new vocabulary or grammar may first have to be acquired by modeling language from others and being reinforced for imitating them; but once learned, the new vocabulary and grammar belong to the individual and can be used without further social assistance. Learning may be social, but the resulting knowledge is individual.

Of course, some social experiences assist learning more than others, and cognitive changes do not happen automatically just because more than one person is involved. In general mediation works best when a learner responds to the mediating person(s) actively, because he or she must take the information or strategies offered by others and transform them into forms that can be truly the learner's own (Rogoff, 1991). Suppose, for example, a preschooler is outdoors gathering autumn leaves. If the teacher wishes to stimulate skills in classification effectively, the child cannot simply be told to group the leaves in particular preset ways. Better (according to SBTLs) is to invite the child to devise categories personally, and to explore the potential of the personally constructed taxonomy that results.

Active construction of knowledge is crucial to the success of social mediation, hence, the oft-used name for this perspective, *constructivism*. Active construction is well-supported by research on individual tutoring—and, of course, by many early childhood teachers' intuitions as well. Adults who tutor children in remedial mathematics, for example, are less successful if they provide only information and corrections, and more successful if they engage in intense interaction, give highly individualized or personal guidance, and ask for frequent, active responses from their tutees (Lepper, Drake, & O'Donnell-Johnson 1997; Rogoff, Matusov, & White, 1998). Interestingly, expert children who tutor less knowledgeable peers can achieve similar success, but are less frequently than adults. Why? Presumably because child tutors, even when comparative experts, are more prone than adults to ignoring a learner's need for active engagement with new knowledge, and more focused on simply completing problems or tasks at hand (Briggs, 1998).

Nonetheless, almost any social mediation of learning may be better than none at all. Whether child or adult, and whether highly skilled or not, live interaction requires a learner to treat emerging ideas with reflective distance, simply to participate in the interaction. The reflective stance thus created implies a lesson that ideas are capable of being manipulated, refined, and elaborated as if they were objects (O'Donnell & King, 1999). The same metacognitive "lesson" may sometimes occur to adults or older children without mediation, particularly if they have had appropriate prior experience with self-reflection. But among the very young, it is hard to imagine metacognition and self-reflection developing far without the expectation and incentive of dialogue, with its attendant requirement of cognitive self-awareness. The importance of mediation for initiating cognitive reflection may account for early childhood teachers' widespread reliance on discussion and on loosely structured group activities as participation structures in the classroom. SBTLs promise to support and enhance these teaching practices by identifying specific conditions where they may be especially successful.

Cultural Tools to Aid Cognitive Development

An extension of the idea of social mediation is to conceive of socially made "tools" which extend individual learning and development. Here the term *tools* refer not just to physical implements (e.g., a desk calculator or a pencil and paper), but also to technical procedures (methods for solving arithmetic problems) or symbol systems (natural languages, musical notations). A cultural tool qualifies as a social mediator in three ways. First, it has conventional structure and use which are agreed on by a social community, though often unconsciously: a pencil is conventionally designed with a certain size and shape and conventionally used for writing, not for stirring soup. Second, a cultural tool extends thinking in particular ways intended and valued by society: a young child can perform more complex multiplication with a desk calculator, for example, than without one. The enhancements are much like what happens during live, in-person mediation, as described previously, though perhaps with effects that are less individualized. Third, a cultural tool stimulates particular new concepts, metaphors or assumptions about thinking and learning that go beyond immediate, practical uses of the tool. A computer not only facilitates children's efforts to solve logic problems, for example, but encourages children (and others) to regard the human mind as a sort of computer. Printed books, for another example, teach content, but they also encourage a modern belief that memory consists not of literal recall of words, but of the essential ideas underlying printed words (Bloch, 1998; Egan, 1997).

By pointing out these effects, SBTLs imply that early childhood teachers have an important responsibility to introduce young children to cultural tools. Computers, for example, should not be delayed to later grades in elementary schools, any more than pencils and pens are. Nor should the acquisition of new vocabulary or new uses for language, whether in a child's first language or in alternate "foreign" languages. Cultural tools can and should be introduced immediately—provided that early childhood teachers understand that the tools are simply being introduced, and that perfection must wait for additional exposure, practice, and maturity (Healy, 1998).

Participation in Joint Creation of Knowledge

The least familiar and most radical version of social mediation sees learning as participation in joint or group creation of knowledge. Sometimes called *social constructivism,* this framework deliberately blurs distinctions between individuals and their social contexts, distinctions that are crucial in other psychological theories. Knowledge, concepts, and meaning emerge through extended interaction and become distributed in complex ways throughout the interacting group. No one person ever "knows it all," but different individuals do learn different parts of "it all" as a result of differences in roles and responsibilities within the group.

The fact that general knowledge is distributed implies that individuals' knowledge is situated or grounded in particular activities and social contexts, and that it is in some sense non-transferable. An early childhood teacher learns much about teaching, for example, through interacting with her actual current students. But her knowledge is grounded in the unique social chemistry of a particular classroom group, a combination that can never be fully duplicated in other classes or in subsequent years. The knowledge of teaching that she acquires from any one class therefore transfers to the next year's class only imperfectly. No matter how experienced a teacher is each new school year quite literally poses new challenges, and inevitably feels both exciting and anxious.

Such a restricted view of transfer is a serious limitation from the point of view of more individualistic models of learning and development. But it is less important within the framework of social constructivism than another problem, that of insuring effective *participation* in joint activities. Portability of knowledge is less important than whether everyone knows at least something relevant to the mission of the group. How can marginal individuals (e.g., children) find a legitimate place in the group's activities, and gradually become able to participate more centrally (Lave & Wenger, 1991; Sfard, 1998)? And if knowledge is indeed situated in particular activities or roles, then the very term *transfer* is a misnomer, since it implies movement of an intact object from one container of knowledge (e.g., my brain) to another (e.g., your brain). When social constructivists engage the problems of transfer, they frame them not in terms of transfer, but of recontextualizing experience: what was learned previously is not transported to new situations, like a suitcase full of tools, but rather combined with new experiences into broader, more enriched knowledge and skills. When classroom learning fails to "transfer," it is because teachers have not helped children to reframe or recontextualize the new with the old: classroom numeracy activities, for example, are not extended clearly enough from numeracy activities engaged in at home or on the playground (Dyson, 1999). The unfortunate result is children who not only fail to develop numeracy skills, but who also risk becoming marginal to the learning community of the class. In this version of SBTL, the latter is the more serious of the two problems, since it interferes with further learning.

The idea of joint construction of knowledge seriously challenges traditional assumptions about cognitive development, the nature of individual differences and the distinctiveness of cognition itself. With knowledge distributed in a social context and not portable in the usual sense, and with it not primarily located in individuals, the outcomes of learning and development become hard to identify in particular children. "What develops" is not the individual so much as the group or activity in which individuals participate. As odd as it may sound, a social constructivist might argue that a group or even an activity can "learn" in some sense, and that such learning does not necessarily imply that the participating individuals also learn.

The joint construction of knowledge, furthermore, is never a strictly "cognitive" affair, since by definition it involves social activity as well as individual thinking. The interactions among participants in a successful activity setting are not only social, but even significantly moral and emotional, and take on the qualities of caring relationships as described by Noddings and others (1992; Goldstein, 1999). In a group constructing knowledge jointly, the central participants focus attention not just on their own contributions, but also on those of marginal participants, and concern for the marginal individuals allows them to frame or scaffold tasks with more sensitivity and effectiveness. More effective distributions of tasks, skills, and problems in turn helps group performance. Under these conditions, some learning usually does accrue to individuals, but only part of it: much learning is better described as happening to the group or community as a whole. When a kindergarten class rehearses a Christmas pageant, for example, individual children do (hopefully) learn their parts, and many also learn bits and pieces of others' parts. But it is the class, not individuals, that "learns" to perform the play.

Because this way of thinking about cognitive development discards the container metaphor of learning, it has proved challenging to use in classroom activities and communities organized around individual learners as the fundamental educational clients. Yet a situated, social perspective on learning has much to recommend it for early childhood education teachers, or indeed for any teacher seeking to offer culturally and developmentally appropriate practice. Why? Because in line with recommendations for developmentally appropriate practice, the perspective highlights participation as a key problem for teaching and emphasizes its importance in early childhood classrooms (Bredekamp & Copple, 1997). The situated, social perspective also steers teachers away from measuring content knowledge in conventional test-like ways, and toward more authentic forms of assessment. Socially situated learning suggests that instead of expecting children to accumulate knowledge or skill along a few key dimensions, teachers should expect numerous qualitative differences—sometimes even radical ones—in what children learn from the "same" project or activity setting.

Given a radical expectation of diversity, the planning and testing of preset, specified goals become less important than in other views of learning or development. Instead, curriculum goals and their assessment grow out of individual children's numerous differences and out of children's dialogues and activities together. These teaching implications are not new to early childhood education (Bredekamp, 1987), but their intellectual alliance with SBTLs, and particularly with social constructivist forms of SBTL, has not been fully recognized.

CONCLUSIONS

In spite of philosophical compatibility between SBTL and developmentally appropriate practice in early childhood teaching—or perhaps because of it—there are dangers if early childhood educators adopt "social revision-ism" too easily. The dangers are both theoretical and pedagogical. Theoretically, SBTLs cannot stand alone. To be truly meaningful, they must say something precise about how individual children learn: what they "get" from mentors, groups, classrooms, and communities. SBTLs must also say something precise about how activity settings are shaped or influenced by the individuals in them, and not just the other way around (Anderson, Greeno, Rider, & Simon, 2000). These conceptual bridges are what early childhood teachers need and seek, given their responsibilities. They can be realized only by taking seriously the more individually oriented theories of cognitive development and learning described earlier in this chapter. As the recent revisions to these theories suggest, rapprochements with SBTLs may indeed be possible, although more philosophical and empirical work still needs to be done.

Pedagogically, the dangers of SBTLs lie with their very popularity among early childhood teachers. As happened with Piagetian constructiv-ism a few decades ago, SBTL may become identified with only parts of itself, and the parts will sanction distorted ideas of what constitutes good teaching practice. Ideas currently vulnerable to becoming stand-ins for entire SBTLs might be Vygotsky's notion of the *zone of proximal development,* for example, or activity theorists' notion of *distributed cognition.* In and of themselves, these two ideas suggest the value of certain socially oriented teaching practices, such as peer tutoring (for the zone of proximal devel-opment) or cooperative group work (for distributed cognition). Yet unless concepts like these become fully situated alongside ideas about individual cognitive development, they are likely to be overused, or else treated as mere philosophical window dressing divorced from actual practices, devel-opmentally appropriate or otherwise (Slavin, 1995).

At bottom maybe Freud was right a century ago, when he argued that an individual and the social community do *not* usually have congruent qualities, needs, or interests, and that the two must constantly negotiate their differences, explicitly or implicitly, in order to realize their respective goals (Freud, 1989/1930). Early childhood teachers may succeed best if they can realize that "civilization and its discontents" can happen in early childhood programs just as much as elsewhere. Translated into the work of teaching, this means that a child's (cognitive) development is one thing, the classroom community is another, and at times their purposes and needs cannot be reduced to each other. Understanding this feature of the human condition, and of early education in particular, may paradoxically help the child and (classroom) community become more congruent: help them both see what they truly hold in common, and where they can mutually thrive.

REFERENCES

Anderson, J., Greeno, J., Reder, L., & Simon, H. (2000). Perspectives on learning, thinking, and activity. *Educational Researcher, 29*(4), 11-13.

Baker, B. (1999). The dangerous and the good? Developmentalism, progress, and public schooling. *American Educational Research Journal, 36,* 797-834.

Bandura, A. (1977). *Social learning theory.* Englewood Cliffs, NJ: Prentice-Hall.

Bandura, A. (1995). *Self-efficacy in changing societies.* New York: Cambridge University Press.

Bartsch, K., & Wellman, H. (1995). *Children talk about the mind.* New York: Oxford University Press.

Bereiter, C., & Scarmadalia, M. (1998). Rethinking learning. In D. Olson & N. Torrance (Eds.), *Handbook of education and human development* (pp. 485-513). Malden, MA: Blackwell.

Bloch, M. (1998). *How we think they think: Anthropological approaches to cognition, memory, and literacy.* Boulder, CO: Westview Press.

Bredekamp, S. (Ed.). (1987). *Developmentally appropriate practice in early childhood education.* Washington, DC: National Association for the Education of Young Children.

Bredekamp, S., & Copple, C. (Eds.). (1997). *Developmentally appropriate practice in early childhood programs* (rev. ed.). Washington, DC: National Association for the Education of Young Children.

Bredekamp, S., & Rosegrant, T. (Eds.). (1995). *Reaching potentials: Transforming early childhood curriculum and assessment* (Vol. 2). Washington, DC: National Association for the Education of Young Children.

Briggs, D. (1998). *A class of their own: When children teach children.* Westport, CT: Bergin & Garvey.

Burman, E. (1994). *Deconstructing developmental psychology.* London: Routledge.

Carey, S. (1998). Sources of conceptual change. In E. Skolnick, K. Nelson, S. Gelman, & P. Miller (Eds.), *Conceptual development: Piaget's legacy* (pp. 293-326). Mahwah, NJ: Erlbaum.

Case, R. (1991). *The mind's staircase: Exploring the conceptual underpinnings of intellectual development.* Mahwah, NJ: Erlbaum.

Case, R. (1998). Changing views of knowledge and their impact on educational research and practice. In D. Olson & N. Torrance (Eds.), *Handbook of education and human development* (pp. 75-99). Malden, MA: Blackwell Publishers.

Case, R. (1999). Conceptual development in the child and in the field. In E. Skolnick, K. Nelson, S. Gelman, & P. Miller (Eds.), *Conceptual development: Piaget's legacy* (pp. 23- 52). Mahwah, NJ: Erlbaum.

DeGrandpre, R. (2000). A science of meaning: Can behaviorism bring meaning to psychological science? *American Psychologist, 55*, 721-739.

Donaldson, M. (1979). *Children's minds.* New York: Norton.

Dyson, A. (1999). Transforming transfer: Unruly children, contrary texts, and the persistence of the pedagogical order. In D. Pearson & A. Iran-Nejad (Eds.), *Review of research in education* (Vol. 24, pp. 141-172). Washington, DC: American Educational Research Association.

Egan, K. (1997). *The educated mind: How cognitive tools shape our understanding.* Chicago: University of Chicago Press.

Freud, S. (1989/1930). *Civilization and its discontents.* (Trans. by J. Strachey.) New York: Norton.

Gelman, R., & Baillargeon, R. (1983). A review of some Piagetian concepts. In J. Flavell & E. Markman (Eds.), *Handbook of child psychology* (Vol. 3, pp. 167-230). New York: Wiley.

Goldstein, L. (1999). The relational zone: The role of caring relationships in the co-construction of mind. *American Educational Research Journal, 36*, 647-673.

Healy, J. (1998). *Failure to connect: How computers affect our children's minds for better and worse.* New York: Simon & Schuster.

Kaiser, B., & Rasminsky, J. (1999). *Meeting the challenge: Effective strategies for challenging behaviors in early childhood environments.* Ottawa, Ontario: Canadian Child Care Federation.

Kamii, C. (1976). *Piaget, children, and number: Applying Piaget's theory to the teaching of elementary number.* Washington, DC: National Association for the Education of Young Children.

Kamii, C. (1994). *Young children continue to reinvent arithmetic: Implications of Piaget's theory.* New York: Teachers College Press.

Kruger, A., & Tomasello, M. (1998). Cultural learning and learning culture. In D. Olson & N. Torrance (Eds.), *Handbook of education and human development* (pp. 369-387). Malden, MA: Blackwell.

Kuhn, D. et al. (1995*). Strategies of knowledge acquisition.* Monographs of the Society for Research in Child Development, Serial #245, Vol. 60(4). Chicago: Society for Research in Child Development.

Johnson, S., Slaughter, V., & Carey, S. (1998). Whose gaze would infants follow? The elicitation of gaze following in 12-month-olds. *Developmental Science, 1*, 233-238.

Lave, J., & Wenger, E. (1991). *Situated learning: Legitimate peripheral participation.* Cambridge: Cambridge University Press.

Lepper, M., Drake, M., & O'Donnell-Johnson, T. (1997). Scaffolding techniques of expert human tutors. In M. Pressley & K. Hogan (Eds.), *Advances in teaching and learning* (pp. 108-144). New York: Brookline Press.

McClelland, J., Rumelhart, D., & Hinton, G. (1987). The appeal of parallel distributed processing. In D. Rumelhart & J. McClelland (Eds.), *Parallel distributed pro-

cessing: Explorations in the micro structure of cognition (pp. 3-44). Cambridge, MA: MIT Press.

Noddings, N. (1992). *The challenge to care in schools: An alternative approach to education.* New York: Teachers College Press.

Piaget, J., & Inhelder, B. (1969/2000). *The psychology of the child.* (Trans. by H. Weaver). New York: Basic Books.

O'Connor, M. C. (1998). Can we trace the efficacy of social constructivism? In D. Pearson & A. Iran-Nejad (Eds.), *Review of research in education* (Vol. 23, pp. 25-72). Washington, DC: American Educational Research Association.

Olson, D., & Bruner, J. (1998). Folk psychology and folk pedagogy. In D. Olson & N. Torrance (Eds.), *Handbook of education and human development* (pp. 9-27). Malden, MA: Blackwell.

Riley, M., Greeno, J., & Heller, J. (1983). The development of children's problem solving ability in arithmetic. In H. Ginsburg (Ed.), *The development of mathematical thinking* (pp. 153-196). New York: Academic Press.

Rogoff, B. (1991). Social interaction as apprenticeship in thinking: Guided participation in spatial planning. In L. Resnick, J. Levine, & S. Teasley (Eds.), *Perspectives on socially shared cognition* (pp. 349-364). Washington, DC: American Psychological Association.

Rogoff, B., Matusov, E., & White, C. (1998). Models of teaching and learning: Participation in a Community of Learners. In D. Olson & N. Torrance (Eds.), *Handbook of education and human development* (pp. 388-414). Malden, MA: Blackwell.

Salomon, G., & Perkins, D. (1998). Individual and social aspects of learning. In D. Pearson & A. Iran-Nejad (Eds.), *Review of research in education* (Vol. 23, pp. 1-24). Washington, DC: American Educational Research Association.

Scarlett, G. (1998). *Trouble in the classroom: Managing the behavior problems of young children.* San Francisco: Jossey-Bass.

Seifert, K. (1993). Cognitive development in early childhood. In B. Spodek (Ed.), *Handbook of research on the education of young children* (pp. 9-23). New York: Macmillan.

Sfard, A. (1998). On two metaphors for learning and the dangers of choosing just one. *Educational Researcher, 27*(2), 4-13.

Sigel, I. (Ed.). (1999). *The development of mental representation.* Mahwah, NJ: Erlbaum.

Siegler, R. (1996). *Emerging minds: The process of change in children's thinking.* New York: Oxford University Press.

Siegler, R. (2000). The rebirth of children's learning. *Child Development, 71*(1), 26-35.

Slavin, R. (1995). *Cooperative learning: Theory, research, and practice* (2nd ed). Boston: Allyn & Bacon.

Tobin, J. (1995). Post-structural research in early childhood education. In J.A. Hatch (Ed.), *Qualitative research in early childhood education* (pp. 223-243). Westport, CT: Praeger.

Wadsworth, B. (1996). *Piaget's theory of cognitive and affective development: Foundations of constructivism* (5th ed.). White Plains, NY: Longman.

Weikart, D. (1971). *The cognitively oriented curriculum.* Washington, DC: National Association for the Education of Young Children.

CHAPTER 3

DEVELOPMENTAL PLAY THEORIES AND CHILDREN'S SOCIAL PRETEND PLAY

Olivia N. Saracho

INTRODUCTION

Even during infancy children develop an understanding of their imagination, drama, and narrative as they become extraordinarily involved in a fantasy world. First, year-old infants normally manipulate and explore objects though not in a symbolic fashion, that is, one object does not represent another. Twelve-and 24-month-old children enjoy exploring the physical features of household devices. They manipulate and bang together objects (e.g., pots, pans, spoons). Two-year-old children frequently use pretend actions with familiar objects. They may position a pot on their head and pretend that it is a hat or propel a spoon across the floor and make movements of a racing car as they shout, "vroom, vroom." Initially these symbolic behaviors surface only as quick and independent actions in young children's play (Kavanaugh & Engel, 1998).

Play facilitates young children's learning about their intellectual and social world as well as their symbolic and language world. When children assume different roles during play, they enrich their social language, using a variety of conversation patterns as they communicate in flexible and expressive tones and come to understand the rules of language. Children apply their language and symbolic systems in conceiving their thoughts and interpreting the ideas of others. Symbolic emergence is a coherent means of relying on the individuals' reflective cognitive development.

A relationship exists between symbolic play and the development of language and cognition. Children's symbolic play enhances children's capacity to exchange language for play actions and objects (Saracho, 1986). When children play, they acquire information about their intellectual and social world. Play is influenced by constructive intentions. Saracho (1986) identifies the cognitive and physical constructs in children's play that are central in young children's learning. These constructs in children's play are related to cognitive, social, emotional and physical development. Studies (e.g., Saracho, in press; 1999, 1998a, 1998b; Saracho & Spodek, 1995, 1998) identify distinctive factors in young children's social play. Saracho's (in press) study demonstrates the importance of (1) imitative experiences, (2) communication of ideas, (3) concrete objects, and (4) parallel/associative levels of socialization. Saracho and Spodek (1998) identify three factors that underlie preschool children's play which includes (1) discussion of ideas in play activities, (2) sociodramatic play behaviors in play activities, and (3) action play in physical play activities. These factors define the importance of discussing ideas, engaging in sociodramatic play, and using actions in their play activities. Saracho (1998a) identifies preschool children's social factors for social and nonsocial children. Social children participate in more social activities and forms of play than do nonsocial children. Social children, more than nonsocial children, manifest more play behaviors, join more in the different play centers, select social play centers, and engage more in associative play. Saracho (1999) also identifies two dimensions of play behaviors for social and nonsocial children. Social children engage in more social play activities, whereas nonsocial children participate more in nonsocial play activities. In understanding the developmental importance of social play in childhood, one must bear in mind the constructive consequence of peer interaction. For young children, the peer group contributes to a crucial and distinctive context in acquiring and implementing social skills.

For more than five decades, theorists have been theorizing the developmental implications of peer interactions and their impact on individual differences in young children's social play. To some degree social play emerges in a clearly definable manner. However, social play is an abstract entity that bears a collection of psychological meanings. In contrast, *non-social* play is even more abstract and multidimensional (Rubin & Coplan, 1998).

Young children's play behaviors vary on an array of important dimensions. In adhering to a Piagetian line of thought, sensorimotor play, pretense, and games-with-rules (Piaget, 1946/1962) occur within a specific social context; while the psychological "meanings" and emphasis of these "cognitive" forms of play differ when they are habitually conceived by a child who is alone or by one who is interacting with playmates. Therefore, the content of children's ludic activity needs to be addressed within the allowed social context. For instance, pretense constructed habitually *on one's own*, in the attendance of a play group must certainly bring with it a very atypical psychological meaning than pretense created habitually while interacting *cooperatively* with social partners. Furthermore, observations of classroom actualized *solitary*-pretense convey more atypical developmental messages than solitary-constructive activities (Rubin & Coplan, 1998). These variations occur within the social contexts during children's social play. Children use their cognitive process in monitoring their social behavior, which has been referred to as social-cognition (Rubin, 1980). Studies in social cognition (e.g., Shantz, 1983) focus on the magnitude of cognitive systems for social behaviors. Play is presumed to be a critical origin for cognitive growth in young children (e.g., Piaget, 1946/1962; Vygotsky, 1962, 1987).

Cognition is basic to children's development of skills in using symbols. Symbolization flourishes in a setting that provides many symbolic representations, where children learn to imagine how one object can represent another. Most theories of cognitive development focus on the importance of understanding the use of symbols. Although symbolic behaviors emerge as temporary and separate actions in young children's play (Kavanaugh & Engel, 1998), these behaviors represent a definite appearance of an innovative way of understanding. Those children who are able to substitute an object from their environment (e.g., a spoon) to portray another one (e.g., a car) have progressed beyond Piaget's sensorimotor (physical) understanding of the world. These children can understand situations that are depicted in their mind. Shortly these "symbolic children" will be able to talk about the past, allude to the future, participate in pretend play, and introduce the construction of narrative segments that relate short "stories" about obvious life events.

Young children's symbolic understanding and pretend play affects their perception of the nonliteral, fantasy world that appears during early childhood such as in the following example:

> A group of children were playing in the dramatic play area. They were playing police officers. They were planning to rob stores and hurt people so that the police officers had something to do.

This play episode encapsulates a most intricate set of thought processes that bear in mind the specific boundaries of the normal preschool child's cognitive ability and creative imagination. According to Sigmund Freud, thought is a form of "trial action." The specifics of Freud's hydraulic energy model can be questioned, but the focus of his theory, which is the importance of trial action through thought, must be recognized. Most great theorists have stressed creative exploration. Kurt Lewin describes the "levels of reality and irreality" in an individual's life; Vygotsky acknowledges the importance of reflective thought in resisting impulsive actions; and Jean Piaget believes that symbolic or creative play is an important period in the appearance of mature thought (Singer & Singer, 1990).

In the social process, children need to communicate and learn from others. Contemporary theoretical perspectives focus on the influence of the social context on cognitive processes, which take into consideration any type of social interaction that modify the development of cognitive processes. Social interactions influence pretend play (El'konin, 1966; Vygotsky, 1935, 1978a, 1978b, 1987). In a make-believe tea party two-year-old children may pretend to feed a doll as well as themselves. Slightly older children may engage in constructing replica objects to express their make believe actions (Fenson, 1984; Wolf, Rygh, & Altshuler, 1984), which is a more complex application of pretense that combines actions, feelings, and thoughts to inanimate objects (e.g., pretending to have a doll go to sleep because "she's tired," or pretending to have a toy animal say, "Ouch, too hot!" as it steps into an imaginary bathtub) (Wolf et al., 1984).

Several researchers demonstrate the importance of the social context in pretend play. Vygotsky suggests a theoretical model that describes how thought is conceived from an external social activity and enriched into an internal mental process. He refers to this process as the development of higher mental functions indicating that the individuals' thought processes are capable of guiding their inner speech. The individuals' inner speech allows them to adapt their own thoughts to their actions. Decades of empirical research support Vygotsky's theory of inner speech (Berk, 1992). His post revolutionary writings integrated the philosophy that *inter*personal experience supports *intra*personal development (Kavanaugh & Engel, 1998). Vygotsky's theory proposes that the children's play with parents or older children has a developmental effect on how young children organize, interpret, and understand their own play.

PLAY THEORIES RELATED TO EARLY CHILDHOOD EDUCATION

Early childhood play theories are identified as classical and modern. Classical theories define the basis for and the purpose of play, whereas modern theories define the practices of play and how they relate to children's development. Typically, the modern theories of play provide an understanding of play through theoretical concepts and empirical research, justifying the play activities in education that have been exclusively characterized as the psychoanalytic and cognitive theories of play.

Psychoanalytic Theory

Psychoanalytic theory, developed by Sigmund Freud and his followers, grew out of clinical practice where individuals described their early experiences. Therapy helped them to deal with their suppressed conflicts that occurred during earlier periods of development but that remained in their subconscious.

Freud hypothesized that play served a special purpose in the children's emotional development. Play enables children to relieve themselves of negative emotions and replace them with more positive ones as play provides a catharsis. By playing out their negative experiences, children rid themselves of negative feelings that might result from traumas in their lives. These negative feelings would otherwise remain with them, though on an unconscious level.

Play activities and explorations help the children to understand distressing events and search for alternative meanings that would help them substitute pleasurable feelings for unpleasant ones.

Freud's theory was modified by other psychoanalysts over time. Some theorists related play to wish fulfillment, anxiety, and ego processes (Takhvar, 1988). Erikson (1963), modified Freud's theory of psychosexual development into a theory of psychosocial development that continues throughout the individual's life (Erikson, 1950). According to Erikson, children play to enact the past, the present, and the future. Play occurs at each developmental stage. Peller (1952), another of Freud's supporters, suggested that children's imitations of life during play reflect their basic emotional feelings, including love, admiration, fear, and aggression. Both Erikson and Peller assumed that the structure of play influenced the individual's psychosocial or psychosexual development.

According to psychoanalysts, children dramatize adult roles in play to give them a sense of competence to be able to handle actual predicaments. As children enact personally distressing experiences, they can overcome the emotional pain of real life as it is reflected in play. Play also helps children manage the affective components of positive life events (Murphy, 1956). For instance, a situation in which a child becomes sick and needs to be rushed to a hospital may leave negative emotional impressions. The child suddenly has to leave his warm and familiar environment to go to unfamiliar surroundings with people that he or she does not know. This distress is added to the child's pain and suffering from the illness and may lead to emotional trauma. Once the child regains good health, he or she may reenact the experiences of the illness through hospital play. While Freud believed that play serves as a catharsis, Murphy believed that the child's hospital play could lead to a better understanding of the experience. Since the child controls the play situation, the child will act out only those fearful situations which he or she is able to cope with them.

A clinical application of the psychoanalytic theory of play is play therapy, a treatment that is employed with children who have emotional problems. Through play therapy children are able to express themselves and enact emotions of tension, fear, and insecurity. The therapist draws out the children's emotions through interactions during play. By observing children during play the therapist can gain insight into the children's problems and create play situations to assist children to deal with their problems. Play therapy helps children to manage their emotions and obtain security (Axline, 1974).

Cognitive Theories of Play

The child development theorists and researchers who have explored the relationship between play and cognitive development include Jean Piaget and Lev. S. Vygotsky. Their ideas are presented here.

Piagetian theory states that children acquire new levels of knowledge through the dual processes of assimilation and accommodation. In assimilation, children gain information from their experiences in the external reality. Then they assimilate or integrate such information into existing mental structures. For accommodation, children modify their mental structures as the new information they acquire does not match the information that they already know. These two processes function to achieve a state of balance. In spontaneous play, children accommodate the world into their mental structures. Children use their present mental schemes and patterns of actions as they imagine that the world is different. Piagetian theory conveys that dramatic play is appropriate for young children, because it is at their developmental level. In dramatic play children access information and acquire meaning from their experiences (Saracho & Spodek, 1995)

Piaget (1946/1962) believes that children go through three sequential stages of play: (1) sensory-motor play, (2) symbolic play, and (3) games with rules. As individuals proceed through the stages, their mental structures gradually blend into later stages.

In the first stage of play, children's repetitive actions concentrate on physical activity, where accommodation is most important. The second of Piaget's stages, from about age 18 months to age seven years, sees make-believe or symbolic play emerge. Because of the symbolic nature of this play, it has a strong influence on literacy development. In symbolic play, any object can be represented and be given the characteristics of the original. For instance, a wooden box can portray a car or truck. Piaget's last stage of play, games with rules, evolves during Piaget's concrete operational stage at the age of 6 or 7 years. Games with rules (such as checkers, chess, and card games) require the participation of at least two children. When children begin to participate in these games, sensorimotor play and symbolic play decrease throughout the individuals' lives.

According to Piaget, modifications in his stages of cognitive development establish the grounds for alterations in the stages of play. Piaget's belief that play develops the individuals' cognitive development is challenged by Vygotsky.

Vygotskian Theory. The Russian psychologist, Lev S. Vygotsky (1896-1934), believes that play affects more than the children's cognitive development. Vygotsky proposed his general theory in 1924. The first description of his research on play was published as *The Prehistory of Written Language* (Vygotsky, 1935, 1928(29)/1978a, 1987) where Vygotsky deliberates the gestural-symbolic nature of the object substitutions made during pretend play:

> . . .The child's own movements, his own gestures are what assign a symbolic function to the corresponding object, that communicate meaning to it. All symbolic representational activity is full of such indicatory gestures; thus, a stick becomes a riding-horse for the child, because it can be placed between the legs and it is possible to apply a gesture to it, which will indicate to the child, that a stick in this case designates a horse.

From this point of view children's symbolic play can be understood as a very complex system of speech with the help of gestures, communicating and indicating the meaning of different playthings. It is only on the basis of these indicatory gestures that playthings gradually acquire their own meaning, just as drawing, at first supported by gesture becomes an independent sign. Only from this point of view is it possible for science to explain two facts, which up to this time still have not had a proper theoretical explanation.

The first fact consists of this—that for the child anything can be anything in play. This can be explained thus, the object itself acquires an unction and a symbolic meaning only thanks to the gesture, which endows it with this. From here follows the idea that meaning consists in the gesture and not in the object. That is why it is unimportant what an object is in any given case. The object is only a point of support for the corresponding gesture.

The second fact consists of this, that it is only early in the play of 4- to 5-year-old children that the verbal conventional symbol appears. Children agree among themselves "this will be a house for us, this is a plate" and so on. At about this age extraordinarily rich verbal connections arise, indicating, explaining, and communicating the meaning of each movement, object, and action. The child not only gesticulates, but also converses, explaining his own play. Gesture and speech mutually intertwine and are united. (1935, pp. 77-78, cited in Smolucha & Smolucha, 1998).

In his research, Vygotsky identified the kind of object substitution children impersonate during their play.

> . . . The object itself performs a substitution function: a pencil substitutes for a nursemaid or a watch for a drugstore, but only the relevant gesture endows

them with meaning. However, under the influence of this gesture, older children begin to make one exceptionally important discovery–that objects can indicate the things they denote as well as substitute for them. For example, when we put down a book with a dark cover and say this will be a forest, a child will spontaneously add, "yes, it's a forest because it's black and dark." She thus isolates one of the features of the object, which, for her, is an indication of the fact that the book is supposed to be a forest. . . . Thus, the object acquires a sign function with a developmental history of its own that is now independent of the child's gesture. This is second-order symbolism, and because it develops in play, we see make-believe play as a major contributor to the development of written language–a system of second-order symbolism. (Vygotsky, 1935, pp. 79-80, cited in Smolucha & Smolucha, 1998; refer to *Mind in Society,* Vygotsky, 1978b, pp. 109-110)

In 1933 Vygotsky published *Play and its Role in the Mental Development of the Child* where he stated that play creates a "zone of proximal development" for the preschool child (Vygotsky, 1966). He defines the zone of proximal development *as "the distance between the actual developmental level as determined by independent problem solving and the level of potential development as determined through problem solving under adult guidance or in collaboration with more capable peers"* (italics in the original text, translated from *Mind in Society,* Vygotsky, 1978a, p. 86).

According to Vygotsky (1962), symbolic or dramatic play fosters the children's abstract thinking. Their make-believe play helps them in their interpretations of the objects. While initially, the representation needs to be similar to the objects, in later stages of development this becomes less relevant. Vygotsky characterizes play as the children's creation of make-believe incidents of real life problems.

Vygotsky's theory added to Piaget's theory manifesting that the children's play experiences stimulated their cognitive development in the social context of culture where the cultural aspects of cognitive development occur. Playing with peers promotes the children's cognitive development.

SOCIAL PRETEND PLAY

Pretend play is a function of three- to seven-year-old children; it creates a micro world of social roles and relationships. Children spontaneously develop and act out different adult roles. Children frequently act out roles in the way they believe and comprehend them and include components of fantasy that are remote from reality. Children also utilize objects to represent something different than its authenticity, such as a doll may represent a baby, a stick a horse, or a piece of hose a gas pump.

Children create their own scenarios in pretend play. They determine the play activity and may use objects to compliment the play episode. They plan the play event, let the plot unfold and develop a spontaneous dialogue. Through pretend play young children express themselves, test out their ideas, give expression to their feelings, and learn to get along with others when they agree in different points of view in social situations. During play children understand the world around them and manage their environment.

Pretense is actually an appealing mental state concerning the children's understanding of the mind. According to Lillard (1996), the fundamental chain of reasoning in understanding anything so erratic in observing a mother talking into a banana is to interpret her mental state to determine she was mentally using the banana to represent the telephone. Scholars (e.g., Lillard, 1996, 1998; Vygotsky, 1978a, 1978b, 1987) acknowledge that strand of reasoning that identifies pretense with the "zone of proximal development" for young children.

Social pretend play, precisely role play, prompts children to explore the world from another person's point of view. When young children enthusiastically carry out a role (e.g., baker, firefighter, police officer, mail carrier, teacher, mother), they briefly become aware about another person's point of view. Understanding someone else's point of view is a prerequisite in preparation for adult life. Therefore, pretend play among 2-and 3-year-olds introduces them to higher levels of thought.

Pretending consists of two levels: (a) *out of frame* and (b) *within frame.* Children at the *out of frame* level mediate their plans for pretending, such as, "You be the mommy, and I'll be the daddy," or "Let's say there was a fire in the house." Children at the *within frame* level of pretense in reality carry it out. Both of these levels relate to pretending and theory of mind (Lillard, 1998).

During the *out of frame* level, pretending assists young children to develop mentalistic understanding when they engage in profound mediating of various players' wishes. When children engage in pretending young children have many opportunities to experience other players with different points of view, such as expressing, "No, I don't want to be the mommy! I want to be the daddy!" According to Garvey and Berndt (1975), "a great deal of speech is devoted to creating, clarifying, maintaining, or negotiating the social pretend experience" (1975, p. 10; see also Giffin, 1984). Compromise among players usually occurs in pretend play, because the success of the pretense interaction centers on adapting all of the players' requests. Players continuously need to negotiate to solve differences among them to create a pretend play scenario (Lillard, 1998) that accommodates everybody's point of view.

Social pretend play offers young children critical knowledge on ways to interact with more mature play partners, which promotes their pretense development. Even very young children can participate in joint pretend scenarios without completely understanding the nonliteral meaning of the play partner. They can behave correctly because of the reasonable model that more mature play partners (such as adults or experienced peers) provide, including props, verbal cues, and pretend demonstrations.

Pretend Play with Adults

Young children's pretend play with adults usually begins with their parents. Early parent-child play develops the children's social skills behavior. The way parents play with their infants contributes to their development of secure attachment (Belsky, Rovine, & Taylor, 1984). Kisler, Bates, Maslin, and Bayles (1986) show that securely attached 13-month-old infants are those whose mothers entertain and engage in their infants' play. These infants also are later rated as securely attached and are more active in maintaining interactions during play episodes.

Children's spontaneous pretend play with their mothers usually involves two situations: (1) the child's mother is nearby and occupied and (2) the child's mother participates as a play partner (Fiese, 1990; O'Connell & Bretherton, 1984; Slade, 1987a, 1987b). The mothers' active involvement enriches their children's pretend play. When the mother of two-year-olds is a play partner, the duration of pretend play, diversity in pretend episodes, and preparation or planning in pretend episodes increases (O'Connell & Bretherton, 1984; Slade, 1987a, 1987b).

Mothers enhance their children's pretend play through direct suggestions for pretense and demonstrations of pretend sequences that the child can partially or completely imitate (O'Connell & Bretherton, 1984; Kavanaugh & Harris, 1991). When mothers respond with nonliteral words and actions to the children's vague prompts, they are skillfully creating and encouraging pretense play to assist children to invent make-believe episodes (Kavanaugh, Whittington, & Cerbone, 1983). In addition, when mothers organize events where play occurs and present appropriate props (e.g., dolls, dishes, bottles), they are actively designing pretend play (Miller & Garvey, 1984).

The capacity to generate pretend actions is important, but pretense comprehension, where children are able to understand their play partner's make-believe goal, justifies their interactive social pretend play. In engaging in pretend play with a partner, children can initiate make-believe scenarios and respond appropriately to the make-believe interest of their play partner. Two and a half year-old children are able to understand their play partner's make-believe structure to fully engage with them in shared pretend play.

The type of parent-child physical play determines the children's social competence. Kindergarten children who engage in "resistant child-highly controlling parent" dyadic play interactions are dependent, feel lonely, and express hostility toward others over the course of the school year. Barth and Parke (1993) conclude that highly dependent children with overly controlling parents may have difficulty initiating and organizing effective interactions in new settings. These children may find hostility or rejection within the peer group. Barth and Parke (1993) also show that parents and children who engage in physical play have low dependency, low hostility, and good relationships with others during kindergarten. If sustaining physical play depends on both the parent's and child's proficiency to monitor and modify their behavior based on the play partner's affective and behavioral cues (e.g., Parke & Waters, 1989), communication becomes essential for children to be able to join peer networks at school. In fact, studies indicate that parent-child synchrony during play interactions predicts later peer acceptance (Lindsey, Smith, & Benedict, 1995). Parke and Waters (1989) claim that the wide range of emotional and social behaviors in parent-child physical play may bond the breach between parent-child and child-peer social contexts.

Pretend Play with Peers

Children's pretend play with peers differs from their pretend play with adults. Mothers tend to use props and toys to motivate their children to convey specific nonliteral actions, which prompt pretend progression. In comparison, peer-play frequently consists of mutually conceiving rich scenarios with pretend roles and psychological states (Dunn & Dale, 1984).

At an early age, children participate in social pretend play with siblings and peers. Dunn and Dale (1984) show how two-year-olds engage in role play, a form of social pretend play. Role play is a refined model of social pretend play where children imitate the other people's attitudes and behaviors.

During preschool, peer groups exhibit their social competence in their play. Successful peer play requires children to use advanced social skills such as verbal recruitment of play partners (e.g., "Come on, let's play Star Trek"); blending into a group in a polite, friendly passive style (e.g., "Can I play, too?"); and adapting to the other children's reactions (Howes, 1985, 1987). Also over the preschool years peers become more competent at mediating play themes, based on the children's proficiency to interpret their peers' verbal and nonverbal cues (Goncu, 1989).

Children's stages of social play have been identified as unoccupied, solitary play, onlooker, parallel play, group activity, associative group play, and organized supplementary group play (Parten, 1932). Some researchers (e.g., Rubin, 1976; Rubin, Maioni, & Hornung, 1976; Rubin, Watson, & Jambor, 1978; Saracho, 1997, 1998a, 1998b, 1999; Saracho & Spodek, 1981,

1986) demonstrate that children engaging in parallel play may prefer for other children to play next to them, whereas those who successfully consider their peers' points of view prefer to join their peers in associative or cooperative play (Rubin et al., 1976; Rubin, 1976; Saracho, 1997, 1998a, 1998b, 1999; Saracho & Spodek, 1981, 1986). These findings suggest that young children's degree of sociability may be related to their personality. Children who are more social, look for facial cues as a source of information from those around them, have an interest in people, and like to be physically close to those with whom they are communicating (Saracho & Spodek, 1981, 1986) engage in parallel, cooperative, and associative play while children who have the reverse attributes may engage in solitary play (Saracho, 1997, 1998a, 1998b, 1999). However, many believe that parallel play, where children play the same way along side their peers, is the best predictor of children's transition to sophisticated group play. Therefore, it is believed that these skills are the exclusive facilitator of more complex, interactive play, where children can shift gracefully from just about any type of play activity to more sophisticated social play. Consequently, participating in particular types of play (e.g., parallel play) provides a worthwhile tie between solitary and joint, cooperative behavior.

Popular and socially skilled children in peer interactions participate in symbolic solitary play rather than functional play, cooperative sociodramatic play (e.g., Connolly & Doyle, 1984; Rubin, 1982; Rubin & Maioni, 1975), and enthusiastically in both peer- and parent-play (MacDonald, 1987; MacDonald & Parke, 1984). They also participate in high levels of fantasy play regardless of their sex and intellectual ability (Connolly & Doyle, 1984). Sociodramatic play as well as rough and tumble play provides evidence of the children's social competence. Both unpopular and popular children equally partake in rough and tumble play (Coie & Kupersmidt, 1983), although the quality of their play centers on their sociometric status. Popular children's rough and tumble play generally becomes a more constructive type of play, while unpopular children's rough and tumble play increases their aggressive behavior (Pellegrini, 1988). Most children can identify the difference between aggression and "playful wrestling." Rejected children tend to misinterpret their peer players' purposes and misconstrue certain harmless play behaviors as threatening or hostile (Costabile, Smith, Matgheson, Aston, Hunter, & Boulton, 1991; Smith & Boulton, 1990).

Children use three strands during social pretend play: (1) negotiation of pretend play plans (e.g., "Hey, the Ninja Turtle just bashed you!"), (2) spontaneous pretend acts by one member of the dyad, or (3) a merger of children's solitary pretend activities (Doyle, Doehring, Tessier, de Lorimer, & Shapiro, 1992). Negotiation of pretend play in the children's plans, is usually perceived as a social skill required to "start up" social play (e.g., Howes, 1985). This is more important in maintaining sociodramatic play instead of initiating it. Nonpretend activities are hardly important in developing complex social pretend play among peers. Solitary pretend play and spontaneous pretend play acts by one member of a peer dyad are other kinds of play, which are important precursors of such social play. Some types of play (especially solitary pretend play) serve as a major connection between solitary and cooperative social play activities.

Social play with peers develops the children's pretend play. Children who participate in more complex play (e.g., complementary play with peers, such as peekaboo and chase) at an early developmental period are more sociable, more cooperative, less aggressive, and less withdrawn during the preschool years than children who repeatedly participate in simpler types of play (e.g., parallel) during toddlerhood. Socially competent toddlers play in more complex ways when they play socially with peers. Thus, early complex play may reflect rather than foster social competent behavior (Howes & Matheson, 1992).

Early social play helps children develop their social skills. When young children are asked to describe the basis of their friendships, "we like to play" is a rationale that young children frequently provide. Gottman (1983) found that the children's play provide some vital purposes. First, children who play together usually share with each other play materials and activities (e.g., "How do you make this work?" They answer, "You gotta push this button first," and ask untangible details that are outside the play theme ("Why is the sky blue?"). Also children talk about meaningful personal concerns (e.g., "My mommy and daddy don't like one another"). Play serves two major functions among peers: (1) pursuing support for both informational and emotional basis as a conforming survival strategy that decreases the insecure influence of anxiety on psychological adjustment (e.g., Carver, Schier, & Weintraub, 1989) and (2) providing an essential context for social support.

When children's play becomes more intricate, it also becomes "riskier" and may create conflict. Children need to search for means to diminish their negative emotions, settle their quarrels, and restructure their play. Complex social play yields a meaningful context for children to generate conflict management skills (Gottman, 1983). Of course, this possibility may fail to occur in play activities where conflict resolution does not emerge, such as building block structures side by side or watching television together.

Children whose play is simultaneous, who are able to deal with conflict, and who take part in knowledge exchange and self-disclosure usually become friends. Inasmuch as a child's ongoing social skills unquestionably develop such behaviors, young children who do not know one another eventually become friends when they play with each other (Creasy, Jarvis, & Berk, 1998).

Play is an important facilitator of social ability. Within the framework of play interactions, parents and infants initiate concurrent dialogues fundamental to the development of healthy joint relationships. At an early age, parent-child play is a fundamental context in developing and refining social skills that are fundamental for establishing peer interactions. Finally, child-peer play is an important context to acquire conflict management skills, intimacy, and role-taking opportunities. Also peer-play contributes to a safe haven, free from adult restraints, where children are able to deal with information and concerns. Saracho (1991a, 1991c) shows that the most popular children select other popular children more often as play-mates. She validates this outcome with the teachers' assessments, where popular children were assessed as more socially competent. In addition, these popular children were the ones who were more often selected as playmates whereas the unpopular children tended to mutually reject each other as playmates. However, children who were rejected as playmates by other children were found to engage in more social play. The problem of the rejected child must be addressed in children's play, because these children continually articulate that they do not like to play with rejected peers (e.g., Coie & Kupersmidt, 1983), these rejected children circumvent atypical developmental opportunities of the play context, which in turn, adds to the rejected child's social incompetence (Creasy et al., 1998).

Children's play is a mirror for universal social competence. The caliber of the children's play applies to their early infant-caregiver attachment patterns, childrearing surroundings, and social competence within the peer group. Later, many use the quality of peer play as a dominant evidence of established social competence (Howes, 1987).

EDUCATIONAL IMPLICATIONS

Some children's play is considered educational. Spodek and Saracho (1997) differentiate between educational and noneducational play. The distinction is not so much in the activity as in the intentions and expected consequences assigned to the activity. In educational play children's learning is planned to achieve a goal. It is used to (1) assist children in exploring and attaining information from their world; (2) develop that information to establish meaning; (3) promote physical, social, and intellectual goals; and (4) aid children in understanding and dealing with their feelings. Teachers need to plan for this form of children's play so that while it is spontaneous, it also has educational value.

Good early childhood programs engage young children in active learning through play which allows children to reconstruct their experiences and generate ideas. They test these ideas in play as they construct knowledge. Teachers need to develop children's play activities in order that they are related to the program's educational goals. Play also allows children to integrate the ideas and experiences in order that many goals might be achieved simultaneously through play.

Teachers should know the different components of play and be flexible in using these components with children. Teachers also need to be careful in guiding children's play. If play loses its spontaneity, or if children lose control of the play situation because the teacher is heavy-handed, the activity will no longer be play. An understanding of how the elements of play relate to different children's characteristics can help in providing careful guidance. Holloway and Reichart-Erickson (1988) found relationships between the quality of interaction with teachers, the arrangement of the physical play space, and the spaciousness of the environment and children's involvement in solitary play and the use of their knowledge to solve social problems. Teachers need to know that there is a vast variability among groups of children. Such variability needs to be considered in the teachers' play curriculum, because the quality of the early childhood environment can have an impact on children's play. The components of play are influenced by the children's age and sex differences, the play environment (including the space inside and outside the classroom), the materials available, and the teacher.

Age and Sex Differences

The play of children, is influenced by their sex and age. Pinkett and Quay (1987), for example, suggest that boys engage more in social interaction. Black (1989) reports that girls discuss issues about taking turns and engage in conversation dialogues. Girls and younger boys prefer play topics related to daily incidents while older boys prefer imaginary topics. Younger children use more props and themes in their play that relate to daily life incidents. Boys like to play by themselves. Howes (1988) shows that older girls like to play with girls, whereas boys either ignore or decline girls' invitations to play games. Teachers need to consider individual differences in children's play, especially any age and sex differences. Knowledge about sex and age differences can help teachers with their curriculum planning.

Environment

High quality play environments support academic learning and young children's development. Teachers must devise both indoor and outdoor play environments that promote children's play. Early childhood classrooms should have an environment that is organized into play centers (Spodek, Saracho, & Davis, 1991). Each play center must have appropriate space, materials, and equipment that promote educational play. Although play centers are appealing, teachers need to be sure that the play centers support the curriculum goals and that the care of the centers does not become an end in itself (Saracho, 1991b).

Outdoor play areas can also be organized into play centers. Frost and Dongju (1998) suggest designing play zones for outdoor play. The playground needs to be zoned to take in consideration the children's natural play behaviors. For instance, three- to five-year-old children require areas or zones for gross motor activity, construction play, and dramatic play. Older preschool children who are approximating five years of age require flat, grassy areas, and hard surfaced areas to play games with rules and chase games. The format of these spaces can be the basis for skill and training but should not be arranged simply on the grounds of tradition. An assortment of portable materials (boarded in a storage facility or storage buckets on the playground) and large-motor equipment (super-structures) can be adeptly culled for an additional enhancement of the playground. Gardens, nature areas, and sand and water areas can complement this ecumenical composition. Frost and Dongju (1998) recommend that outdoor play space have play activities that correspond to indoor play areas. However, both indoor and outdoor play areas must consider safety factors and supervision of all play areas.

Materials

It has been suggested that toys represent the texts of early childhood classes just as books are the texts of classes for older children (Cuffaro, 1999). Children use toys as instruments of learning when they play. The way young children use play materials differs with age (Westby, 1980). Hence, the children's age should be considered in selecting toys. For instance, a classroom of three- to five-year-olds generally has a collection of miniature toys representing objects and symbolizing the children's life (e.g., dolls, doll furniture, wagons, engines). These toys (1) encourage children to act out a number of adult roles; (2) bestow meaningful information to young children; and (3) provide young children with a way to understand the social life of the community, including adult roles and relationships.

The quality and quantity of play materials is a factor in the way children immerse themselves in different kinds of play. Children play by themselves with some play materials such as play-dough, clay, and sand and water. On the other hand, art materials allow young children to engage in constructive, nonsocial play. A careful selection of play materials can assist teachers to foster children's play and to achieve the teachers' educational goals.

Play materials can be selected based on a specific topic or play theme. Play activities that present children with knowledge (e.g., going for a walk around the neighborhood, visiting the post office, reading a book on a specific play topic, or seeing a video) can help them to become motivated in a play topic or theme (Saracho, 1991b).

Roles

Teachers assume several roles in fostering children's play, such as a facilitator and participant. When teachers are facilitators, they choose, arrange and introduce objects, materials, props, and formulate experiences about certain concepts or themes. Teachers intercede to extend any crucial components of play that are sparse. The intercession must reinvigorate, define, and explain the play situation; but the intervention should not control the play activities. Before interceding, teachers should watch the children's play to know the crucial components of the play that children need, evaluate the way children assume roles, use relevant props, and utilize appropriate language.

Introducing Play. Teachers introduce play to children in several ways. Teachers design environments that allow children to immerse themselves in educational play. Teachers can introduce play by offering children aesthetically pleasing play materials, likely play opportunities, and something new to the play setting. A brief planning period before play time can guide children in selecting play activities and help them know what they should do in each play area. In the planning session children become familiar with new equipment or toys and their functions, uses, and restrictions (Saracho, 1991b).

Children can be motivated with diversity and novelty in the play activities. Therefore, new play materials need to be added and existing materials should be presented in new forms. The different play areas can also be rearranged or moved, display new signs in the play areas, or have several new materials added to reproduce an old play activity into a splendid new one. A new play activity needs to motivate the children's attention and creativity.

Prolonging Play. Teachers can use several techniques to prolong children's play. One technique is to carefully enter the children's play making sure that children's independence and the intervention is minimize. Teachers must avoid becoming the center of attention or the primary source of play ideas. This can reduce the children's play motivation. Teachers need to determine how their actions will affect the play situation. They need to become responsive to the children's play (Saracho, 1991b).

Young children's play behavior changes as they develop. Teachers must know the children's play behaviors and the level at which children are playing to be able to initiate play interventions, modify the environment, select new materials, or minimally join the children's play to clarify concepts.

Teachers' interventions should avoid making children become aware of reality or lose control of the play situation. Teachers can sustain young children's play by welcoming children's play patterns. Children who prefer not to play should not be coerced into play but should be provided with alternative activities (Saracho, 1991b).

SUMMARY

Play is an activity that, while it is entertaining and imaginary, it also can be educational. Through play young children come to understand their world and learn to function in it.

Teachers have a crucial role in the play curriculum. They need to provide an effective environment, select appropriate materials, and use appropriate intervention strategies to motivate and develop the children's emersion in educational play that fosters their learning.

REFERENCES

Axline, V.M. (1974). *Play therapy.* New York: Ballentine Books.

Barth, J., & Parke, R. (1993). Parent-child relationship influences on children's transition to school. *Merrill-Palmer Quarterly, 39,* 173-195.

Belsky, J., Rovine, M., & Taylor, D. (1984). The Pennsylvania Infant and Family Development Project, III: The origins of individual differences in infant-mother attachment: Maternal and infant contributions. *Child Development, 55,* 718-728.

Berk, L. (1992). Children's private speech: An overview of theory and the status of research. In R. Diaz & L. Berk (Eds.), *Private speech* (pp.17-54). Hillsdale, NJ: Erlbaum.

Black, B. (1989). Interactive pretense: Social and symbolic skills in preschool play groups. *Merrill-Palmer Quarterly, 35,* 370-397.

Carver, C., Scheier, M., & Weintraub, J. (1989). Assessing coping strategies: A theoretically based approach. *Journal of Personality and Social Psychology, 56,* 267-283.

Coie, J., & Kupersmidt, J. (1983). A behavioral analysis of emerging social status in boys' groups. *Child Development, 54,* 1400-1416.

Connolly, J.A., & Doyle, A. (1984). Relation of social fantasy play to social competence in preschoolers. *Developmental Psychology, 20,* 597-608.

Costabile, A., Smith, P. K., Matgheson, L., Aston, J., Hunter, T., & Boulton, M. (1991). Cross-national comparison of how children distinguish serious and playful fighting. *Developmental Psychology, 27,* 881-887.

Creasey, G.L., Jarvis, P.A., & Berk, L.E . (1998). Play and social competence. In O.N. Saracho & B. Spodek (Eds.), *Multiple perspectives on play in early childhood education* (pp. 116-143). Albany: State University of New York Press.

Cuffaro, H. (1999). A view of materials as the texts of the early childhood curriculum in B. Spodek & O. N. Saracho (Eds). *Yearbook of early childhood education: Issues in early childhood curriculum.* Troy, NY: Educator's International Press, Inc.

Doyle, A., Doehring, P., Tessier, O., de Lorimier, S., & Shapiro, S. (1992). Transitions in children's play: A sequential analysis of states preceding and following social pretense. *Developmental Psychology, 28,* 137-144.

Dunn, J., & Dale, N. (1984). I a Daddy: 2-year-olds' collaboration in joint pretend with sibling and with mother. In I. Bretherton (Ed.), *Symbolic play: The development of social understanding.* New York: Academic Press.

El'konin, D. (1966). Symbolics and its functions in the play of children. *Soviet Education, 8,* 35-41.

Erikson, E.H. (1963). *Childhood and society.* New York: Norton.

Fenson, L. (1984). Developmental trends for action and speech in pretend play. In I. Bretherton (Ed.), *Symbolic play: The development of social understanding.* New York: Academic Press.

Fiese, B.H. (1990). Playful relationships: A contextual analysis of mother-child interaction. *Child Development, 61,* 1648-1656.

Frost, J.L., & Dongju, S. (1998). Physical Environments and Children's Play. In O.N. Saracho & B. Spodek (Eds.), *Multiple Perspectives on Play in Early Childhood Education* (pp. 255-294). Albany: State University of New York Press.

Garvey, C., & Berndt, R. (1975). *Organization in pretend play.* Paper presented at the meeting of the American Psychological Association, Chicago.

Giffin, H. (1984). The coordination of meaning in the creation of shared make-believe play. In I. Bretherton (Ed.), *Symbolic play* (pp. 73-100). Orlando, FL: Academic Press.

Goncu, A. (1989). Models and features of pretense. *Developmental Review, 9,* 341-344.

Gottman, J. (1983). How children make friends. *Monographs of the Society for Research in Child Development, 48,* (3, Serial No. 201).

Holloway, S.D., & Reichart-Erickson, M. (1988). The relationship of day care quality to children's free-play behavior and social problem-solving skills. *Early Childhood Research Quarterly, 3,* 39-53.

Howes, C. (1985). Sharing fantasy: Social pretend play in toddlers. *Child Development, 56,* 1253-1258.

Howes, C. (1987). Social competence with peers in young children: Developmental sequences. *Developmental Review, 7,* 252-272.

Howes, C. (1988). Peer interaction in young children. *Monographs for the Society for Research in Child Development, 53,* (No. 217).

Howes, C., & Matheson, C. (1992). Sequences in the development of competent play with peers: Social and social pretend play. *Developmental Psychology, 28,* 961-974.

Kavanaugh, R.D., & Engel, S. (1998). The development of pretense and narrative in early childhood. In O.N. Saracho & B. Spodek (Eds.), *Multiple perspectives on play in early childhood education* (pp. 80-9). Albany: State University of New York Press.

Kavanaugh, R.D., & Harris, P.L. (September, 1991). *Comprehension and production of pretend language by 2-year-olds.* Paper presented at the annual meeting of the developmental section, British Psychological Society, Cambridge.

Kavanaugh, R.D. , Whittington, S., & Cerbone, M.J. (1983). Mothers' use of fantasy in speech to young children. *Journal of Child Language, 10,* 45-55.

Kisler, L., Bates, J., Maslin, C., & Bayles, K. (1986). Mother-infant play at six months as a predictor of attachment security at thirteen months. *Journal of the American Academy of Child Psychiatry, 25,* 68-75.

Lillard, A.S. (1998). Playing with a theory of mind. In O.N. Saracho & B. Spodek (Eds.), *Multiple perspectives on play in early childhood education* (pp. 11-33). Albany: State University of New York Press.

Lillard, A.S. (1996). Body or mind: Young children's categorizing of pretense. *Child Development, 67,* 1717-1734.

Lindsey, E., Smith, T., & Benedict, K. (1995, March). *Father-child play and children's peer relations.* Paper presented at the Biennial Meeting of the Society for Research in Child Development, Indianapolis, IN.

MacDonald, K. (1987). Parent-child physical play with rejected, neglected, and popular boys. *Developmental Psychology, 23,* 705-711.

MacDonald, K., & Parke, R. (1984). Bridging the gap: Parent-child play interaction and peer interactive competence. *Child Development, 55,* 1265-1277.

Miller, P., & Garvey, C. (1984). Mother-baby role play: Its origins in social support. In I. Bretherton (Ed.), *Symbolic play: The development of social understanding.* New York: Academic Press.

Murphy, L. (1956). *Methods for the study of personality in young children.* New York: Basic Books.

O'Connell, B., & Bretherton, I. (1984). Toddlers' play alone and with mother: The role of maternal guidance. In I. Bretherton (Ed.), *Symbolic play* (pp. 337-368). New York: Academic Press.

Parke, K., & Waters, E. (1989). Security of attachment and preschool friendships. *Child Development, 60,* 1076-1081.

Parten, M.B. (1932). Social participation among preschool children. *Journal of Abnormal Psychology, 27,* 243-269.

Pellegrini, A.D. (1988). Elementary school children's rough-and-tumble play and social competence. *Developmental Psychology, 24,* 802-806.

Peller, L.E. (1952). Models of children's play. *Mental Hygiene, 36,* 66-83.

Piaget, J. (1946/1962). *Play, dreams and imitation in childhood.* New York: Norton (original publication, 1946).

Pinkett, K.E.L., & Quay, L.C. (1987). Race versus social class: Social orientation and cognitive play in black and white middle SES preschool children. *Journal of Applied Developmental Psychology, 8,* 343-350.

Rubin, K.H. (1976). Relation between social participation and role-taking skill in preschool children. *Psychological Reports, 39,* 823-826.

Rubin, K.H. (1980). Fantasy play: Its role in the development of social skills and social cognition. *New Directions for Child Development, 9,* 69-84.

Rubin, K. (1982). Nonsocial play in preschoolers: Necessary evil? *Child Development, 53,* 651-657.

Rubin, K.H., & Coplan, R.J. (1998). Social and non-social play in childhood: An individual differences perspective. In O.N. Saracho & B. Spodek (Eds.), *Multiple perspectives on play in early childhood education* (pp. 144-170). Albany: State University of New York Press.

Rubin, K.H., & Maioni, T.L. (1975). Play preference and its relationship to egocentrism, popularity, and classification skills in preschoolers. *Merrill-Palmer Quarterly, 21,* 171-179.

Rubin, K.H., Maioni, T.L., & Hornung, M. (1976). Free-play behaviors in middle- and low-class preschoolers: Parten and Piaget revisited. *Child Development, 47,* 414-419.

Rubin, K.H., Watson, K.S., & Jambor, T.W. (1978). Free play behaviors in preschool and kindergarten children. *Child Development, 49,* 534-536.

Saracho, O.N. (1986). Play and young children's learning. In B. Spodek (Ed.), *Today's kindergarten: Exploring the knowledge base, expanding the curriculum* (pp. 91-109). New York: Teachers College Press.

Saracho, O.N. (1991a). Cognitive style and social behavior in young Mexican American children. *International Journal of Early Childhood, 23*(2), 21-38.

Saracho, O.N. (1991b). The role of play in the early childhood curriculum. In B. Spodek & O.N. Saracho (Eds.). *Yearbook of early childhood education: Issues in early childhood curriculum* (Vol. 2, pp. 86-105). New York: Teachers College Press.

Saracho, O.N. (1991c). Social correlates of cognitive style in young children.*Early Child Development and Care, 76,* 117-134.

Saracho, O.N. (1997). *Teachers and students' cognitive styles cognitive styles in early childhood education.* Westport, CT: Greenwood Publishing Group, Inc.

Saracho, O.N. (1998a). Socialization factors in the cognitive style and play of young children. *International Journal of Educational Research, 29,* 263-276.

Saracho, O.N. (1998b). What Is Stylish about Play? In O.N. Saracho & B. Spodek (Eds.), *Multiple perspectives on play in early childhood education* (pp. 240-254). Albany: State University of New York Press.

Saracho, O.N. (1999). A factor analysis of preschool children's play strategies and cognitive style. *Educational Psychology, 19,* 165-180.

Saracho, O.N. (in press). Factors in three- to five-year-old children's play.*Play and Culture Studies, 3.*

Saracho, O.N., & Spodek, B. (1981). The teachers' cognitive styles and their educational implications. *Educational Forum, 45,* 153-159.

Saracho, O.N., & Spodek, B. (1986). Cognitive style and children's learning: Individual variation in cognitive processes. In L.G. Katz (Ed.),*Current topics in early childhood education* (Vol. 6, pp. 177-194). Norwood, NJ: Ablex.

Saracho, O.N., & Spodek, B. (1995). Children's play and early childhood education: Insights from history and theory.*Journal of Education, 177*(3), 129-148.

Saracho, O.N., & Spodek, B. (1998). Preschool children's cognitive play: A factor analysis. *International Journal of Early Childhood Education, 3,* 67-76.

Shantz, C. (1983). Social cognition. In P. Mussen (Ed.),*Handbook of child psychology, Vol. 3: Cognitive development.* New York: Wiley.

Singer, D.G., & Singer, J.L. (1990). *The house of make-believe.* Cambridge, MA: Harvard University Press.

Slade, A. (1987a). A longitudinal study of maternal involvement and symbolic play during the toddler period. *Child Development, 58,* 367-375.

Slade, A. (1987b). Quality of attachment and early symbolic play.*Developmental Psychology, 23,* 78-85.

Smith, P.K., & Boulton, M. (1990). Rough-and-tumble play, aggression and dominance: Perception and behavior in children's encounters.*Human Development, 33,* 271-282.

Smolucha, L., & Smolucha, F. (1998). The social origins of mind: Post-Piagetian perspectives on pretend play in children. In O.N. Saracho & B. Spodek (Eds.), *Multiple perspectives on play in early childhood education* (pp. 34-58). Albany: State University of New York Press.

Spodek, B., & Saracho, O. N. (1997). The challenge of educational play. In D. Bergen (Ed.), *Play as a learning medium for learning and development: A handbook of theory and practice* (pp. 11-28). Olney, MD: Association for Childhood Education International.

Spodek, B., Saracho, O.N., & Davis, M.D. (1991).*Foundations of early childhood education* (2nd ed.). Englewood Cliffs, NJ: Prentice Hall.

Takhvar, M. (1988). Play and theories of play: A review of the literature.*Early Child Development and Care, 39*, 221-244.

Vygotsky, L.S. (1935). Predistoria peismennoy rechi [The prehistory of written language]. In *The mental development of children during education* (pp. 73-95). Moscow/Leningrad: Uchpedgiz. (Original work written in 1928 or 1929)

Vygotsky, L.S. (1962). *Thought and language.* Cambridge, MA: M.l.T. Press.

Vygotsky, L.S. (1966). Play and its role in the mental development of the child. *Soviet Psychology, 12*(6), 62-76.

Vygotsky, L.S. (1978a). *Mind in society: The development of higher mental processes* (M. Cole, V. John-Steiner, S. Scribner, & E. Souberman, Eds. & Trans.). Cambridge, MA: Harvard University Press. (Original works published 1930, 1933, 1935)

Vygotsky, L.S. (1978b). The role of play in development. In M. Cole, V. John-Steiner, S. Scribner, & E. Souberman (Eds.),*Mind in society* (pp. 92-104). Cambridge, MA: Harvard University Press.

Vygotsky, L.S. (1987). Thinking and speech. In R. Rieber, A.S. Carton (Eds.), & N. Minick (Trans.), *The collected works of L. S. Vygotsky: Vol. 1: Problems of general psychology* (pp. 37-285). New York: Plenum. (Original Work published 1934)

Wolf, D.P., Rygh, J., & Altshuler, J. (1984). Agency and experience: Actions and states in play narratives. In I. Bretherton,*Symbolic play: The development of social understanding.* New York: Academic Press.

Westby, C.E. (1980). Assessment of cognitive and language abilities through play. *Language, Speech, and Hearing Services in Schools, 11*, 154-168.

CHAPTER 4

EFFECTIVE EARLY CHILDHOOD CURRICULUM FOR CHILDREN AT RISK

**Barbara A. Wasik, Mary Alice Bond, and
Annemarie Hindman**

INTRODUCTION

There is considerable research documenting the positive impact of early education on the development of disadvantaged children (Karweit, 1993, 1994; Ramey & Ramey, 1998a; Wasik & Karweit, 1994). Specifically, studies have shown that interventions that occur early in life can have positive long-term effects on the educational achievement of disadvantaged children (e.g., Ramey & Ramey, 1998a, 1998b). Recent data from Head Start has suggested that the most important factor that determines the effectiveness of a particular Head Start program is the quality of the intervention (Resnick & Zill, 2000; Zill, Resnick, & McKey, 1999). Less is known, however, about the specific curriculum components and practices that contribute to the quality of effective early intervention programs. Some research has shown that the organizational aspects of preschool classrooms such as teacher-child ratios and class size affect the quality of the intervention (Barnett, 1995; Frede, 1995). What is lacking, however, is a discussion of the specific curriculum components that are necessary for an effective preschool program. The core questions concern which curriculum practices an early intervention program should include and how these components should be implemented.

The goal of this chapter is twofold. The first objective is to present central issues in the debate over which methods of classroom organization and instruction are most appropriate for disadvantaged children. This discussion sets the context within which more specific curriculum issues can be interpreted. The second objective is to outline the components identified in research as essential for an effective early intervention program. Knowledge of the program characteristics and the research concerning preschool programs will help educators and policymakers discern practices likely to close the gap between children at risk and their more advantaged peers.

Understanding preschool education is becoming more critical as the nation's policies and perceptions about educating young children evolve. But this agenda can succeed only if the nature of effective practices is well understood. At the beginning of this new millennium, Head Start and other publicly funded preschool programs are expanding at increasingly rapid rates. Two states, New York and Georgia, are setting precedents by mandating funding for universal preschool for all children who are at risk, and many states will follow this plan (Bowman, Donovan, & Burns, 2000). The rationale for this approach is to provide at-risk children with enriched opportunities early in life.

THE EARLY YEARS AND CHILDREN AT-RISK

Experiences that occur in the early years have a profound effect on later development. Recent research on brain development has shown that early cognitive and social experiences affect the neurological foundation of children's later learning (Bruer, 1999; Shore, 1997). Studies have shown that children who experience enriched language interactions show an increase in the number and intricacy of neural connections compared to children with more limited experiences. The National Academy of Sciences report *Preventing Reading Difficulties in Young Children* (Snow, Burns, & Griffin, 1998) documents the importance of early reading and literacy-rich experiences on children's later success in school. Access to good health care, proper nutrition, and quality interactions with adults provide children with the opportunity to get off to a good start in the early years.

Unfortunately, children raised in poverty have very different experiences from their more advantaged peers. In a longitudinal study, Hart and Risley (1995) found that, by the age of three, children from low-income families had significantly lower vocabularies compared to children from middle- and high-income homes. These findings are consistent with the Carnegie Foundation report *Ready to Learn: A Mandate for the Nation* (Boyer, 1991), which found that 35% of the children entering school lacked necessary educational skills. Of these children, a disproportionate number were from low-income homes. Other research indicates that socioeconomic status is one of the strongest predictors of performance differences in children at the beginning of the first grade (Alexander & Entwisle, 1988), and that the gap persists as children progress from elementary to high school (Puma, Karweit, Price, Ricciuti, Thompson, & Vaden-Kiernan, 1997).

In this chapter, the term "disadvantaged" refers to these children who are living in poverty and do not have access to resources, experiences, and learning opportunities that prepare them to succeed in school. The lack of learning opportunities places these children at risk for school failure. Effective preschool interventions can help close the gap between children of access and children of poverty (Freede, 1995).

ISSUES IN EARLY CHILDHOOD CURRICULUM FOR DISADVANTAGED CHILDREN

It is reasonable to assert that curriculum practices should not be different for disadvantaged and advantaged children, and that equal access to quality education should be provided for all children regardless of their economic background. However, differences in the policies and curriculum practices for disadvantaged children do exist, often as a result of the perceptions of educators, researchers, and parents regarding the best methods of instruction for disadvantaged children. Research on the education of disadvantaged children has revealed controversy surrounding three particular issues. One issue involves the debate over which instructional approaches are most appropriate and effective for disadvantaged children. A second issue concerns varied interpretations of school readiness and cultural diversity, as well as the roles that these concepts play in the delivery of curriculum. The third issue pertains to the intensity and quality of the curriculum for the disadvantaged population.

Developmentally appropriate practices vs. academic curriculum. In the early childhood field, there has been a long debate concerning the type of curriculum that is best for young children. It is important to understand this debate because it is central to curriculum issues for disadvantaged children. The tension has been between advocates of what is considered Developmentally Appropriate Practices (DAP) and proponents of a so-called "academic" approach to early instruction that is modeled after elementary school practices. Developmentally Appropriate Practices, described as methods of instruction suited to the developmental level of young children, encourage learning through hands-on, constructive activities and creative play. In an attempt to qualify what developmentally appropriate practices are, the National Association for the Education for Young Children (NAEYC) (Bredekamp & Copple, 1997) established guidelines for instruction addressing children's individual needs and skills. The underlying message of the statement on DAP was that teaching preschoolers was fundamentally different from teaching elementary-aged children, since developmental research has shown that young children learn best when actively engaged in constructing knowledge from their environment (Byrnes, 2001). The DAP statement encouraged preschool teachers to engage children in playful activities that presented important information about the world and helped them learn to process their experiences. Unfortunately, the DAP guidelines were misinterpreted to mean that it was not appropriate to teach young children readiness skills such as the alphabet or any precursors to reading and math. In addition, with the focus on what was developmentally appropriate for young children, issues concerning what was appropriate for the individual child became obscured. This was particularly a concern for special education and disadvantaged children for whom curriculum needs to be both individually appropriate along with being developmentally appropriate (Atwater, Carta, Schwartz, & McConnell, 1994).

In reaction to this interpretation of DAP, educators who believe that young children, especially disadvantaged children, need to acquire school readiness skills at an early age have come to favor an academic focus in early childhood education. Unfortunately, the effectiveness of the academic approach has been limited by its method of instruction that is more closely aligned with teaching older children. In early childhood programs with an academic focus, there is often a "push down" of first and second grade content and instructional practices to the preschool and kindergarten classrooms. Concepts presented in the elementary grades are frequently too difficult for young children to master, and many who consequently struggle are unfairly labeled unready for school.

Recently, there has been increasing consensus that young children need to learn reading (Neuman, Copple, & Bredekamp, 1999) and math readiness skills (National Council of Teachers of Mathematics [NCTM], 2000), an idea which redefines the issues concerning DAP and academic instruction. Research in early literacy and math has shown that very young children acquire precursor skills, which later serve as a solid foundation for language and numeracy (Campbell, 1999; Neuman et al., 1999; NCTM, 1998). But while the general content of an effective early childhood curriculum is becoming more clearly defined, educators continue to debate which methods are most appropriate to teach these readiness skills to young children. These issues are especially relevant for disadvantaged children, as they often acquire school readiness skills through early intervention programs. It is important to understand these issues concerning DAP and academic approaches as background for a discussion of instructional methods, readiness, and diversity in educating disadvantaged preschoolers.

Instructional approaches and disadvantaged children. Instructional approaches in early childhood span a wide continuum, with child-centered approaches on one end and didactic approaches on the other. The child-centered approach refers to a curriculum that is initiated by children and in which the teacher takes cues from the children's interests. The goals of this approach are (a) to allow children opportunities to construct meaning from their environment, and (b) to help them be actively involved in shaping the curriculum. A frequent misconception about the child-centered curriculum is that the focus is entirely on play and does not address the necessary skills that children need to develop in order to be successful in school. Proponents of this approach, however, argue that concepts and skills are taught within the child-directed curriculum.

The didactic approach is more structured, with the curriculum initiated by the teacher. This approach is often associated with commercially prepared materials and a precise program. Typically, didactic programs focus explicitly on academic skills and often incorporate practices such as whole-group instruction, teacher-directed instruction, workbooks, and grading that are generally characteristic of the first grade or later. Although social, emotional, and self-help skills are addressed in the didactic program, the main emphasis is on the child acquiring school-related skills.

The debate about the advantages of child-centered versus didactic approaches has been informed by a limited body of empirical research on the education of disadvantaged children. Supporters of the didactic approach point to successful didactic intervention programs that improved the achievement of low-income, minority children. Specifically, these researchers argue that the direct training in basic skills allows young children to experience success in school, which in turn in enhances learning and self-esteem (Becker & Gersten, 1982; Bereiter, 1986; Carnine, Carnine, Karp, & Weisberg, 1988; Gersten, Darch, & Gleason, 1988).

In addition, research has shown that a significant number of parents and teachers of disadvantaged children favor the didactic approach. In a survey, 551 parents of both disadvantaged and advantaged preschoolers were asked about their perceptions and attitudes toward curriculum practices (Stipek & Byler, 1997; Stipek, Milburn, Clements, & Daniels, 1992). Parents of disadvantaged children were found to believe that a structured curriculum focused on academic skills would best prepare children for formal school (Stipek et al., 1992). Learning the alphabet and the letters in one's name were considered skills necessary for later school success. In other words, activities modeled after more traditional educational practices (in which children were seated at desk working on skills in isolation) were perceived as effective. This survey also revealed that parents of disadvantaged children perceived playing and learning as orthogonal activities and believed that the school should present a balance between the two entities. In contrast, parents of more advantaged children perceived play as a vehicle for learning and were less concerned about the specific skills that their children acquired in preschool.

These perceptions regarding the education of disadvantaged children are, however, inconsistent with the research on effective practices in early childhood. In opposition to the idea that learning and playing are two separate, unrelated activities, studies have shown that curriculum that is appropriate for the developmental age of young children and that provides opportunities for meaningful, playful learning experiences is the most effective (Roskos & Christie, 2000; Stipek, 1991). A curriculum that is appropriate for the developmental needs of young children can teach children academic content using a method of instruction that emphasizes play and exploration. For example, learning the alphabet is considered an academic school readiness skill. Whereas trying to teach young children the alphabet through drill and practice might result in children learning letter names, this approach does not help children to attach meaning and understanding to the letters and letter names. On the other hand, teaching children the alphabet in relationship to the words and experiences in their world will help them learn concepts and skills in a meaningful way.

Research has also shown that curriculum practices that favor the didactic approach may have some negative effects on children's development. In a series of studies, Stipek and her colleagues (Stipek, 1991; Stipek, Feiler, Daniels, & Milburn, 1995; Stipek, Feiler, Byler, Ryan, Milburn, & Salmon, 1998; Stipek & Ryan, 1997) examined the effects of different early childhood curriculum approaches on young children's achievement and motivation. Stipek et al. (1995) conducted a study comparing child-centered and didactic curriculum approaches in low-income and middle-class preschools and kindergartens. The results revealed that children in the didactic programs that stressed basic skills had significantly higher scores on letter identification and pre-reading achievement tests compared to their peers in the child-centered programs. Children in the didactic and child-centered programs scored similarly on their understanding of numbers. However, being enrolled in a didactic program was associated with negative outcomes on most of the motivation measures. Compared to those in the child-centered programs, children in the didactic programs rated their abilities significantly lower and expressed lower expectations for success on academic tasks. Children in the didactic programs also showed more dependency on adults for permission and approval, worried more about school, and evidenced less pride in their accomplishments. Although they scored lower on the academic assessments, children in the child-directed programs appeared to have more positive perceptions about themselves as learners. These findings were consistent for both economically disadvantaged and middle-class children in both preschool and kindergarten. Marcon (1999) also reported similar findings.

In an extension on this work, Stipek et al. (1998) compared the cognitive and motivational competencies of 228 preschoolers and kindergarteners in either child-centered and didactic curriculum. All children's math and reading competencies were assessed with an adapted version of the

Woodcock-Johnson Achievement Test (1989) and supplemented with 66 items of the Peabody Individual Achievement Test (PIAT, Dunn, & Markwardt, 1970). In addition, the short form of the McCarthy was used. To assess motivation, the Young Children's Feelings About School (FAS), a measure developed specifically for the study, was administered. The results showed primarily negative effects on both cognitive and motivational measures in preschool classrooms that emphasized basic skills using structured, teacher directed approaches. This further supports the positive aspects of child-centered curriculum on cognition and motivation of preschoolers.

These studies pose a dilemma to those interested in determining the most effective curriculum for young children. Acquisition of basic early literacy and numeracy skills sets an important foundation for children's later success in school (Snow et al., 1998). However, having the motivation to learn and to trust in one's ability as a learner are important characteristics of engaged learners (Guthrie & Wigfield, 2000). A successful curriculum addresses both the achievement and motivational aspects of young children's development. Programs that present basic skills, while allowing children opportunities to direct their own learning about these subjects, represent the best approach for early childhood programs.

Readiness, cultural diversity, and curriculum. The issue of readiness has played an important role in shaping curriculum for young children. However, our understanding of readiness has evolved over the past 20 years. Historically, the question has been asked, "Is the child ready for school?" Readiness was viewed as a characteristic inherent in the child: a combination of cognitive, psychomotor, and socioemotional development congruent with the child's chronological age. Children were expected to naturally be ready for the school's curriculum; if they were not, this discrepancy was attributed to a problem within the child rather than a problem with the curriculum.

With our increasing understanding of learning in young children, this definition of readiness has been changing. The question that is now asked is, "Are schools and children ready for each other?" Today, readiness is described as a dynamic construct that involves the characteristics of the child, the perceptions and expectations of teachers and schools, and the context of the school and the individual classroom (Graue, 1993). The current definition of readiness concerns not only whether the child is prepared to enter the classroom, but also whether the learning environment—created by the school and the teacher—is ready to support and nurture the child (Graue, 1993). Consequently, curriculum today is more flexible, with the classroom activities adapting more to the needs of the child.

Despite the changing views of readiness, there are still several problems with our perceptions of readiness as this relates to curriculum for disadvantaged children. Current standards upon which readiness is measured remain restrictive. The common definition of readiness is still based on behaviors characteristic of the development and expectations of white, middle-class children (New, 1994). Because of this, the standard curriculum often represents the experiences and values of the majority culture and does not acknowledge the contributions that others make to the learning environment. This cultural bias is reflected in assessments (Meisels, 1994) and teachers' perceptions (Karweit, 1999) of what is expected of three-, four-, and five-year-olds.

Our definition of readiness needs to be expanded to include behaviors of children who are ethnically and linguistically diverse. Curriculum designed to address the values and experiences of children at risk needs to go beyond containing a unit on diversity or city life. Teachers who work with children in poverty need to understand the children's cultures and integrate experiences that the children would be familiar with into the curriculum. If teachers and schools do not understand or acknowledge the experiences of the children whom they teach, how can they provide a learning context in which children will successfully acquire knowledge? This is especially important with regard to language development, in general, and vocabulary development, in particular. Language is the means by which children communicate their ideas, needs, and feelings. When children's language is different from that of the majority culture or if their culture uses vocabulary that is different from that of the majority culture, children will have difficulty communicating (Tabors, 1997). Teachers need to acknowledge the language and vocabulary that children bring to school so that they can scaffold their students' language experiences to take advantage of the broader range of experiences.

Teachers' perceptions of readiness and cultural background play an important role in making curriculum adapt to diversity. Teachers need to learn to value children's home cultures (Edwards, Danridge, & Pleasant, 1999). Often practices that are different from what occurs in the majority culture are viewed negatively rather than celebrated and used as a learning experience. Children come to school with experiences that are particular to their families. Teachers need to learn to respect this diversity and acknowledge that differences can become learning opportunities for children to explore how other people live. Teachers can talk with children and their families about their traditions and routines and then incorporate these diverse experiences into the classroom curriculum with culturally sensitive books, themes, and projects. The goal should not be to have children conform to the values and practices of the majority culture, but to incorporate diversity into the curriculum (Tabors, 1997).

Ready for now and ready for later. Readiness has two meanings and this dual meaning has a complicated effect on the content of curriculum for disadvantaged children. One meaning focuses on the readiness of children to learn in their current educational environment. How ready are the children for the curriculum, and how does the curriculum need to be tailored to meet the needs of the children? Research has consistently shown that children from low-income backgrounds enter preschool less ready to learn than their more advantaged peers (Snow et al., 1998). The curriculum needs to be ready for the children, designed to start where each child is by building new information upon the child's level of knowledge and experience.

The other meaning of readiness focuses on preparing young children for the future. How will the current classroom experiences lay the foundation upon which children can build useful knowledge for the future? This second aspect of readiness creates a challenge for educators of young children. While the curriculum needs to begin where the diverse needs of the children are, the curriculum must also prepare all children for their next steps in learning by laying the foundation for early language, literacy, numeracy skills, and social skills. For disadvantaged children, this often means that the preschool must facilitate learning in order to prepare them for their next educational experience and keep them from falling further behind their more advantaged peers.

Educators of disadvantaged preschoolers are faced with a challenge. Their goal is to provide the most informative early childhood curriculum possible, so that these children might acquire the same skills as their more advantaged peers. However, all of this must be delivered in the context of developmentally appropriate practices. Unfortunately, educators are inclined to increase the rigor and intensity of the curriculum by focusing on skills in isolation. As previously discussed, research has shown that this is not the best method of instruction for children, regardless of their socioeconomic background. Instead, educators need to focus on effective instructional practices that will increase opportunities to learn and ensure that children in preschool are prepared for their next educational experience.

Two approaches are used in providing effective curriculum to young children. One is to vary the delivery of the instruction through extending the length of the day, reducing class size, and providing opportunities to work one-to-one or in small groups. These approaches will be presented in the next section. The second solution is to ensure that the content of the curriculum lays the appropriate foundation for at-risk children and adequately prepares them for their future educational experiences. In combination, these strategies are essential in creating an effective preschool curriculum.

STRUCTURAL ASPECTS
OF EFFECTIVE EARLY CHILDHOOD PROGRAMS

The organization of early childhood programs has an impact on the effectiveness of the program. The amount of time spent in school, either full- or half-day, affects the amount of instruction to which children are exposed. In addition, the number of children in the class and the size of groups play a role in the effectiveness of curriculum.

Full-day versus half-day programs. Although the issue of full- versus half-day instruction has been central in early childhood education, there is limited empirical research on this topic. In general, studies have shown modest, though not always consistently positive, effects for full-day kindergarten programs (Holmes & McConnell, 1990; Johnson, 1974; Oliver, 1980; Winter & Klein, 1970). However, studies that focused specifically on disadvantaged children have shown unequivocal positive results (Karweit, 1993, 1994).

Research has indicated that interventions that increase the quality of the program are more effective than those that simply extend the length of the day. Meyer (1984), for example, found that some half-day kindergartens had more high-quality instructional time than did full-day kindergartens. In addition, Puleo (1988) reports that time on task can be lower in full-day classes (64%) than half-day classes (80%). As Karweit (1994) points out, full-day programs create more opportunities to learn. However, the curriculum implemented during the full-day program needs to take advantage of the increased time and provide quality experiences for young children. More time is not necessarily better; it is what is done with the time that can result in positive educational impacts on children.

Reduced class and group size and one-to-one instruction. Young children can benefit from individualized attention and instruction. Research has consistently shown that reducing the group size in the early grades can have positive effects on students' achievement (Finn & Achilles, 1999). State laws have mandated the maximum teacher-student ratio in early childhood classrooms. For most programs, the ratio is one teacher and an assistant for 10 to 12 children for three-year-olds, one teacher and an assistant per 16 children for four-year-olds, and one teacher for 16 to 18 children for five-year-olds (Kagan & Cohen, 1996; Karweit, 1994). This can vary greatly from state to state and program to program, depending on the availability of funds. However, conducting activities in small groups of three to five children increases each child's opportunity to express him/herself verbally and to receive more direct feedback from the teacher (Morrow & Smith, 1990). Small group activities also provide additional opportunities for the teacher to learn about each child's strengths and weaknesses and to tailor experiences to each student's individual needs. Even though full-day programs theoretically provide more opportunities to learn than do half-day programs, the instruction will not be effective without structuring time for small group activities (Karweit, 1994).

Providing one-to-one instruction for young children is an important component of effective programs (Wasik, 1998). Additional resources in the classroom, for example a teaching assistant or a parent volunteer, can make one-to-one experiences possible. In a one-to-one activity, the adult can expose a child to rich language, offer feedback to a child's statements or requests, and encourage and motivate a child to ask intriguing questions and learn new things. One-to-one experiences, which are most often provided in the home, can be structured into the preschool program. This will strengthen each child's knowledge base and also enhance the collective knowledge of the class.

COMPONENTS OF EFFECTIVE EARLY CHILDHOOD PROGRAMS

In the previous section, meta-curriculum issues concerning delivery of instruction, expectations and perceptions of teachers, and the organization of the classroom were discussed. In this section, specific components that are necessary for an effective curriculum for disadvantaged children are presented.

A curriculum for at-risk children that begins where the children are and prepares them for their elementary school needs to comprehensively address the cognitive, social, and emotional aspects of developing children. According to the joint statement from the International Reading Association and the National Association for the Education of Young Children (Neuman et al., 1999) as well as the research summary from the National Academy of Sciences (Snow et al., 1998), young children need to develop strong language and pre-literacy skills in preparation for reading. The National Council of Teachers of Mathematics (1998) recommends that young children develop knowledge of relationships and numbers as precursor skills. Research also indicates that young children have the ability to learn these concepts at an early age (Hartnett & Gelman, 1998). Providing an environment that allows opportunities to acquire readiness skills is essential to preventing school failure in disadvantaged children.

In the following sections, curriculum components that are essential for effective preschool instruction are outlined. This analysis of components is based on research in the field of effective practices and programs in early childhood, as well as on research on cognitive theory and development. These essential curriculum components are discussed in light of providing the most effective and appropriate curriculum for disadvantaged children.

Theme-Based Instruction

The theme is the central component of the curriculum. Young children learn best when information is presented in an integrated fashion around a topic, theme, or project that is or can be related to the children's experiences (Helm & Katz, 2001; Seefeldt & Galper, 1998). When the activities are related to a single topic or theme, children have repeated exposures to the vocabulary, concepts, and language associated with that theme. Theme-based learning allows children to encounter new information in a meaningful context and not in isolation. Theme or project topics in early childhood classrooms are often based on social science or science information. The topics can be selected by the children, by the teacher, or through negotiations between the teacher and children. An example of a theme is the study of seeds, plants, and how things grow. The teacher can focus the theme lessons upon several specific learning objectives, helping children to understand (a) what materials a seed needs in order to grow, (b) the process through which a seed grows, and (c) how the different parts of the seed change as the plant grows.

Time allotted to themes can range from one week to four weeks of instruction, depending on the depth of the children's interest in the topic. The topic of the theme or project integrates the curriculum. Curricular activities such as book reading, development of mathematical skills, art, and gross and fine motor development are based on the theme. For example, children might listen to, read, and talk about books on planting and seeds; count out seeds and arrange them for an art project; categorize different seeds; and imitate seed sprouts swaying in the wind. Teachers would use these and other activities to first introduce seeds and plants that are particular to the children's own environment and then offer information about less familiar plants.

Developing Language Skills

An effective preschool curriculum must emphasize the development of language skills. Language development is the most important milestone of the preschool years (Halliday, 1975; Snow et al., 1998; Whitehurst & Lonigan, 1998) and is an especially important readiness skill for disadvantaged children (Snow et al., 1998; Whitehurst & Fischel, 2000). Important elements include oral language skills, vocabulary, and knowledge about the syntax and structure of language. Language development can occur only when children have opportunities to engage in a dialogue with adults and to learn new vocabulary words in the context of meaningful activities. When the home does not provide this context for rich language development, schools must take on a more significant role in this process. To this end, it is important that the preschool curriculum provides at-risk children with opportunities to express their ideas in words, to explore the use of language, and to talk and receive feedback from both children and adults.

By the time many at-risk children begin pre-kindergarten, they will already have significantly more limited vocabularies than their more advantaged peers (Hart & Risley, 1995). In addition, children for whom

English is not the primary language typically enter schools with severely limited English vocabularies. Unfortunately, this gap in knowledge persists and widens as children enter kindergarten and elementary school (Karweit, 1999). In order to narrow this gap and provide children with enriched language experiences, the preschool curriculum needs to allow for the explicit development of vocabulary skills and the use of connected language. Vocabulary development is extremely important as children are developing new concepts in math, reading, music, and social science. Many at-risk children arrive at preschool without the fundamental vocabulary that will help them express their wants and needs in a manner that is understood by the teacher and other adults. Opportunities to express ideas and feelings in complete and intelligible language are important experiences for children at risk.

Teachers need to actively think about and plan for vocabulary development. They should identify words to focus on during a theme and design book reading and hands-on activities that ensure that children hear, use, and discuss these vocabulary words (Wasik & Bond, 2001). Explicit instruction of vocabulary words is also important. Often, teachers assume that children know the meaning of commonly used words such as *sandwich* or *backpack*. However, at-risk children may be exposed to words infrequently and, therefore, might not understand the information presented in the classroom.

Research has shown that direct experience with vocabulary words, accompanied by book reading and other related activities, can result in the increase of vocabulary skills of children at risk. For example, Wasik and Bond (2001) found that four-year-olds who were given multiple opportunities to hear vocabulary words through book reading, creative play with concrete representations of the vocabulary words, and other activities were able to learn more of the vocabulary words than were children in a comparison group who only read stories that contained the words.

A theme-based curriculum rich in language development opportunities sets a foundation for a good preschool curriculum. Yet, there is specific curriculum content that disadvantaged children need to be exposed to that will increase their opportunities for learning. These activities and the research that supports this are presented below.

Book Reading

Book reading is intimately tied to language development and is an essential component of an effective preschool curriculum. Research on book reading has consistently shown that reading to young children contributes significantly to language and vocabulary development (Karweit & Wasik, 1996; Neuman et al., 1999; Robbins & Ehri, 1994; Whitehurst & Lonigan, 1998). Through books, many disadvantaged children experience things and learn words that they would not likely encounter in their every-day lives. A book may take them to an ocean that they will never see, an instrument that they may never hold, and a word that they may never hear. Dickinson and Snow (1987) refer to this as learning decontextualized language. Learning decontextualized language through books facilitates vocabulary development, which in turn leads to increased comprehension of spoken and written language.

Unfortunately, recent research on Head Start has shown that book reading is not as common an activity as would be expected. In an observational study of Head Start centers, Dickinson (1999) found that teachers did not read to their classes on a daily basis. In some classrooms, book reading occurred as infrequently as one time per week. Work by Wasik, Bond, and Hindman (2000) also reports that the quality of book reading varies greatly among preschool teachers. Wasik and her colleagues (2000) coached six Head Start teachers in book-reading strategies. Observations of the teachers before the intervention revealed that, after reading a book, none of them discussed the content with children, nor did they relate the vocabulary or the concepts in the book to other classroom activities. The book reading experience was not integrated into other classroom activities. Using a book as a springboard for discussion and related activities allows children multiple opportunities to hear vocabulary words, review unfamiliar concepts, and make connections.

Research on storybook reading also suggests that the methods used to present stories to young children influence their processing of the story. Whitehurst and his colleagues have produced much influential work on book reading and disadvantaged children (Arnold, Lonigan, Whitehurst, & Epstein, 1994; Payne, Whitehurst, & Angell, 1994; Valdez-Menchaca & Whitehurst, 1992; Whitehurst, Arnold et al., 1994; Whitehurst, Epstein et al., 1994; Whitehurst et al., 1988). In a program of shared reading, called *dialogic reading*, Whitehurst demonstrated that when adults asked open-ended questions, created opportunities for children to participate in story-telling, encouraged a discussion of the story, and actively listened to children's comments, significant changes occurred in low-income preschoolers' language skills. Although the findings for dialogic reading were more robust when reading is done one-to-one, children also derived benefit when dialogic reading was implemented with a high degree of fidelity in groups of one teacher and 10 children in preschool classrooms. Children improved significantly on measures of writing and concepts of print, and their scores approached significance on language measures.

Other book reading strategies have been found to be important for disadvantaged children. Rereading and retelling of stories facilitates young children's comprehension of a story (Karweit & Wasik, 1996). In addition, research tells us that limiting the number of questions that children are asked while being read a story is the most effective method of improving comprehension (Dickinson & Smith, 1994). Asking too many questions can be a distraction and may interfere with children's comprehension. Also, reading books to small groups or one-to-one significantly increases children's vocabulary development and comprehension (Morrow & Smith, 1990). Finally, choosing stories that are developmentally appropriate for young children is important in making storybook reading an effective activity in promoting literacy skills. For disadvantaged children, it is important that teachers select stories that reflect the culture and experiences of their students.

Through book reading, children also learn concepts about print. Concepts about print refer to an understanding of the conventions of book reading and the printed word (Clay, 1998; Morrow, 1993). Through repeated exposure to storybooks and big book activities as well as various types of print in the environment, young children learn that print is read from left to right, that reading is done from the front to the back of a book, that individual letters are different from single words, and that there is a one-to-one correspondence between what is read and what is written on a page. Children who have limited exposure to print often do not have an understanding of concepts of print. The curriculum must support activities that allow children to discover these structural aspects of book reading and print.

Mathematics

For disadvantaged children, one of the most important, yet least emphasized, activities in preschool education is mathematics. This neglect often comes from teachers' misconceptions about the role and importance of mathematics in an early childhood curriculum. There are several reasons for the limited attention given to mathematics in at-risk preschools. One reason is that teachers argue that, because disadvantaged children are so behind in language and literacy skills, there is not enough time to devote to math (Pound, 1999). Instead of integrating math concepts into language arts and the creative arts, math is left out. Another reason math is neglected is that preschool teachers are less comfortable with teaching math than language arts and, therefore, assign it lower priority in the daily schedule. Knowledge of math needs to receive as much attention as literacy because of the important role that it will play in children's later learning.

In the preschool years, children need to develop a sense of quantity and number (Campbell, 1999). Attention to patterns, to similarities and differences, and to relative size and amount are important concepts for children of this age. The curriculum needs to provide opportunities for children to experience these mathematical concepts in the context of their environment. Playing with blocks, matching patterns, identifying objects that are bigger and smaller, and measuring ingredients for a recipe allow children to learn the precursors to more complex math concepts such as counting and ordering. Often children from advantaged homes enter preschool with the understanding and the vocabulary of age-appropriate math concepts. However, children from disadvantaged homes often lack these experiences. Frequently, these children can understand mathematical concepts but do not know the associated vocabulary words (Pound, 1999). For example, children can indicate that two objects are different but do not have the vocabulary to describe the nature of the difference. A preschool curriculum for disadvantaged children needs to provide explicit instruction of math-related vocabulary that is reinforced in the context of math and related activities.

Mathematical concepts should be integrated into the theme or project (Helm & Katz, 2001). Whether the children count the number of their classmates present each day, graph the number of children who like chocolate, or make comparisons among each other's shoes, children are thinking about relationships and numbers. Research has shown that children who come from homes where parents make numbers and number concepts a visible part of their daily lives are more likely to be successful in math (Young-Loveridge, 1989). There is also evidence that preschool children do not naturally focus on numbers but will do so if the adults around them encourage them (Munn & Schaffer, 1993). This data suggests that both teachers and curriculum play a significant role in making children aware of mathematical concepts and in preparing them to be interested, motivated learners.

Phonemic Awareness

In the last decade, research has indicated that phonemic awareness is one of the most important predictors of success in reading (Blachman, 2000; Perfetti, Beck, Bell & Hughes, 1987; Stahl & Murray, 1994; Stanovich, 1998; Stanovich & Stanovich, 1995; Wasik, 2001a). Phonemic awareness is the ability to recognize and manipulate sounds in words. Young children need to be aware that words are made up of sounds, which they can learn to hear and manipulate. This paves the way for them to benefit later from more systematic phonics instruction.

An effective preschool curriculum for disadvantaged children needs to incorporate activities that promote the development of phonemic awareness (Wasik, 2001a). Young children learn phonemic awareness through exposure to nursery rhymes, jingles, poetry, and books that contain words with rhymes and alliteration. Playing with language allows children to learn to hear and manipulate the sounds in words. Unlike their more advantaged peers, disadvantaged children do not always have opportunities to develop phonemic awareness skills in the home. Therefore, the school curriculum needs to include opportunities to learn that sounds make up words and to explore these parts of language.

Research has shown that children as young as three years of age can identify words that rhyme (Bradley & Bryant, 1983). Research also suggests that young children can produce words with similar beginning sounds (Blachman, 2000) and that they can identify the number of syllables in words (Treiman & Zukowski, 1992). This suggests that these skills are developmentally appropriate for young children. In the context of playful activities, young children can learn to break words into beginning sounds, ending sounds, and syllables. These activities can help children understand how sounds relate to words. A curriculum rich in poetry, rhymes, and songs, combined with teachers' guidance in attending to the sounds within these texts, will support the development of phonemic awareness. Music and movement activities that emphasize the rhyme and rhythm of language will further support the development of phonemic awareness.

Alphabet Knowledge

Knowledge of the alphabet is also one of the best predictors of success in early reading (Adams, 1990). However, the field of early childhood has debated the role that alphabet instruction should play in the preschool curriculum (Wasik, 2001b). While professional educators were questioning this theoretical construct, middle class parents were teaching their children the alphabet at home. Many middle-class children consequently arrived at school knowing the alphabet, which set an important developmental precedent for later reading. Unfortunately, many preschools serving economically disadvantaged children continued to debate the appropriateness of teaching the alphabet. Currently, there is growing consensus about the importance of learning the alphabet before children enter formal schooling (Wasik, 2001b). However, the most appropriate methods for teaching the alphabet are still being discussed.

Research has shown that teaching young children letters in isolation is ineffective (Ehri, 1983). Pointing to a letter on the chalkboard and asking children to copy it does not provide them with a deep and lasting understanding of the letter. Instead, children need to learn letter names and letter sounds in the context of a rich literacy and oral language experience (Wasik, 2001b). This is especially important for children who come to school with little book reading and alphabet knowledge. A curriculum that integrates letter learning into the theme, for example, by presenting a series of theme-related vocabulary words that begin with a specific target letter, allows young children to attach meaning to—and therefore retain information about—these letters. Children are particularly interested in learning the letters in words that are intimately tied to their personal experiences. Their own names, as well as those of their teachers, friends, and class pets, help translate the abstract concept of a letter into a meaningful symbol. Learning to identify and print letters as well as to understand that letters make up words are important accomplishments of the preschool curriculum.

Recent research has indicated a relationship between letter knowledge and phonemic awareness skills. Stahl and Murray (1994) showed that kindergarteners need alphabet knowledge to separate the beginning sound of a word (the onset) from the remaining part of the word (the rime). Torgesen, Wagner, Rashotte, Burgess, and Hecht (1997) also found that individual differences in letter-name knowledge in kindergartners were related to individual differences in phonological awareness skills. This further supports the importance of learning letter names.

Writing

Reading and writing are connected. Writing allows children the opportunity to make transitions from the spoken word to the printed word (Clay, 1998). Initially, writing can take many forms, such as pictures, scribbling, and letter-like strokes (see Sulzby, 1986, for a complete description of the developmental sequence of writing). As children progress to writing words and using invented spelling, they become increasingly focused on the names and sounds of letters and the structure of words. This can facilitate connections between speaking, reading, and writing activities (Adams, 1990).

Teachers of young children often have the misconception that young children cannot write, and, hesitate to spend curriculum time on this activity. However, research has shown that children who are provided with opportunities to write at an early age develop a more sophisticated understanding of print and phonemic awareness (Blachman, 2000; Morris, 1999). Pre-writing activities, which allow children to express their ideas in some form of picture or scribbling, help children begin to understand the relationship between the spoken word and print.

Art

Creative expression fosters both cognitive and physical development in children. Through drawing or creating an arts and crafts activity, children have the opportunity to express their ideas and feelings, to develop fine motor skills, and to learn about important concepts including color and shapes. Children learn to hold a crayon or pencil, grasp scissors, cut paper, apply paint, and use glue. Art also helps children identify shapes, investigate colors, and experiment with different combinations of media.

With an increasing emphasis on reading and math skills for disadvantaged children, art is receiving a decreasing amount of attention in preschool classes. This is unfortunate, given the important cognitive benefits of art. The ability to represent one's experiences with symbols is a major cognitive achievement for children (Golomb, 1993; Thompson, 1995). In creating art, children need to organize their thoughts and actions into patterns and symbols. Within the context of a drawing, children are presented with opportunities to create, invent, solve problems, and reason. Many children come to school with little experience with art and art projects and with limited opportunities to express themselves creatively. Art allows children to produce something concrete that they can be proud of and provides another way for them to communicate their ideas about the world.

Family Involvement

An effective curriculum for disadvantaged children would be incomplete without a family involvement component. The family is a child's first teacher. Encouraging parents or other significant adults in children's lives to be actively involved in their children's development will ultimately result in positive effects on the children (Edwards et al., 1999). Workshops for pre-kindergarten and kindergarten parents that explain (a) what is going on in school, (b) what can be reinforced at home, and (c) why certain home activities such as reading are important will strengthen the home-school partnership. Parents want to be a part of their children's education, but they often do not know how to do this. A curriculum designed with home-school extensions that provide opportunities for families to participate both in and out of the classroom will empower families to help their children.

Fostering Motivation to Learning

As important as it is to expose young children to oral language, vocabulary, phonemic awareness activities, and the alphabet, it is equally important to consider the affective factors that influence early literacy development. Young children need to feel a sense of efficacy, motivation, and interest in learning (Guthrie & Wigfield, 2000). For children to become lifelong learners, they must learn for the sheer pleasure of learning. Finding pleasure in learning and receiving feedback on their competencies as learners will motivate and encourage children who find many of the experiences in school foreign to what they experience at home. A curriculum that motivates children to learn and respects the individual strengths of each child can provide a positive context for learning.

CONCLUSIONS

The components presented in this chapter are essential to an effective curriculum for disadvantaged children. Children who enter preschool with limited experiences are at a disadvantage for learning language, literacy, math, and art in the context of a central science and/or social studies theme. This learning is essential for the children to catch up to their more advantaged peers. Young children from economically disadvantaged homes need to be provided with the same opportunities to learn as their more advantaged peers (Karweit, 1999). In order to do this, the preschool curriculum needs to provide children with multiple opportunities to build language skills, explore and gain information about the world around them, and think independently. This needs to occur in an environment in which teachers value and respect children, hold high expectations for their accomplishments, and believe that all can learn regardless of their economic status.

ACKNOWLEDGMENT

This research was supported under funding from the Office of Educational Research and Improvement, U.S. Department of Education (Grant No. R-117D-40005). However, the opinions expressed are those of the authors and do not necessarily represent the positions or policies of the U.S. Department of Education.

REFERENCES

Adams, M.J. (1990). *Beginning to read: Thinking and learning about print.* Cambridge, MA: MIT Press.

Alexander, K.L., & Entwisle, D.R. (1988). Achievement in the first two years of school: Patterns and processes. *Monographs of the Society for Research in Child Development, 53* (2, Serial No. 218).

Arnold, D.H., Lonigan, C.J., Whitehurst, G.J., & Epstein, J.N. (1994). Accelerating language development through picture book reading: Replication and extension to videotape training format. *Journal of Educational Psychology, 86,* 235-243.

Atwater, J.B., Carta, J.J., Schwartz, I.S., McConnell, S.R. (1994). In B. Mallory & R. New (Eds.), *Diversity and developmentally appropriate practices: Challenges for early childhood education* (pp. 65-83). New York: Teachers College Press.

Barnett, W.S. (1995). Long-term effects of early childhood programs on cognitive and school outcomes. *Future of Children, 5*(3), 25-50.

Beals, D.E., DeTemple, J.M., & Dickinson, D.K. (1994). Talking and listening that support early literacy development of low-income children. In D.K. Dickinson (Ed.), *Bridges to literacy: Children, families, and schools* (pp. 19-40). Cambridge, MA: Blackwell.

Becker, W.C., & Gersten, R. (1982). A follow-up of follow-through: The later effects of the direct instruction model on children in fifth and sixth grades. *American Educational Research Journal, 19,* 75-92.

Bereiter, C. (1986). Does direct instruction cause delinquency? *Early Childhood Research Quarterly, 1,* 289-292.

Blachman, B.A. (2000). Phonological awareness. In M.L. Kamil, P.B. Mosenthal, P.D. Pearson, & R. Barr (Eds.), *Handbook of reading research* (Vol. III, pp. 483-502). Mahwah, NJ: Lawrence Erlbaum Associates, Inc.

Boyer, E.L. (1991). *Ready to learn: A mandate for the nation* (Carnegie Foundation Special Report). Lawrenceville, NJ: Carnegie Foundation for the Advancement of Teaching/ Princeton University Press.

Bradley, L., & Bryant, P.E. (1983). Categorizing sounds and learning to read: A causal relationship. *Nature, 301,* 419- 421.

Bredekamp, S., & Copple, C. (Eds.). (1997). *Developmentally appropriate practices in early childhood programs* (rev ed.). Washington, DC: NAEYC.

Bruer, J.T. (1999). *The myth of the first three years: A new understanding of early brain development and lifelong learning.* Riverton, NJ: Simon and Schuster.

Bus, A.G., van Ijzendoorn, M.H., & Pelligrini, A.D. (1995). Joint book reading makes for success in learning to read: A meta-analysis on intergenerational transmission of literacy. *Review of Educational Research, 65,* 1-21.

Byrnes, J.P. (2001). *Cognitive development and learning in instructional contexts* (2nd ed.). Needham Heights, MA: Allyn and Bacon.

Campbell, P. (1999). Fostering each child's understanding of mathematics. In C. Seefeldt (Ed.), *The early childhood curriculum: Current findings in theory and practice* (3rd ed., pp. 106-132). New York: Teachers College Press.

Carnine, D., Carnine, L., Karp, J., & Weisberg, P. (1988). Kindergarten for economically disadvantaged children: The direct instruction component. In C. Warger (Ed.), *A resource guide to public school early childhood programs* (pp. 73-98). Alexandria, VA: Association for Supervision and Curriculum Development.

Clay, M.M. (1998). *By different paths to common outcomes.* New York: Stenhouse.

Cornell, E.H., Sénéchal, M., & Broda, L. (1988). Recall of picture books by three-year-old children: Testing and repetition effects in joint activities. *Journal of Educational Psychology, 80,* 537-542.

Crain-Thoreson, C., & Dale, P.S. (1992). Do early talkers become early readers? Linguistic precocity, preschool language, and emergent literacy. *Developmental Psychology, 28,* 421-429.

Debaryshe, B.D. (1993). Joint picture-book reading correlates of early oral language skill. *Child Language, 20*, 455-461.

DeTemple, J.E., & Snow, C.E. (1992, April). *Styles of parent-child book reading as related to mothers' views of literacy and children's literacy outcomes.* Paper presented at the Conference on Human Development, Atlanta, GA.

Dickinson, D.K. (1993). Features of early childhood classroom environments that support development of language and literacy. In J.F. Duchan, L.E. Hewitt, & R.M. Sonnenmeier (Eds.), *Pragmatics: From theory to practice.* Englewood Cliffs, NJ: Prentice-Hall.

Dickinson, D.K. (1999, December). Dimensions of reading style and patterns of book use in preschool. In B. Wasik (Chair), *Multiple perspectives on book reading in early childhood classrooms.* Symposium conducted at the annual meeting of the National Reading Conference, Orlando, FL.

Dickinson, D.K., Cotes, L., & Smith, M.W. (1993). Learning vocabulary in preschool: Social and discourse contexts affecting vocabulary growth. In C. Daiute (Ed.), *The development of literacy through social interactions* (pp. 67-78) [*New directions in child development* Series, no. 61]. San Francisco: Jossey-Bass.

Dickinson, D.K., & Smith, M.W. (1994). Long-term effects of preschool teachers' book readings on low-income children's vocabulary and story comprehension. *Reading Research Quarterly, 29*, 104-122.

Dickinson, D.K., & Snow, C.E. (1987). Interrelationships among pre-reading and oral language skills in kindergartners from two social classes. *Early Childhood Research Quarterly, 2*, 1-25.

Dickinson, D.K., & Tabors, P.O. (1991). Early literacy: Linkages between home, school, and literacy achievement at age five. *Journal of Research in Childhood Education, 6*, 30-46.

Dunn, L., & Markwardt, F. (1970). *Peabody Individual Achievement Test* (Vol. 1). Circle Pines, MN: AGS.

Edwards, P.A., Danridge, J.C., & Pleasant, H.M. (1999). Are we all on the same page? Administrators' and teachers' conceptions of "at-riskness" in an urban elementary school. In T. Shanahan & F.V. Rodriguez-Brown (Eds.), *National reading conference yearbook* (Vol. 48, pp. 329-339). Chicago: National Reading Conference.

Ehri, L.C. (1983). A critique of five studies related to letter-name knowledge and learning to read. In L. Gentile, M. Kamil, & J.S. Blanchards (Eds.), *Reading research revisited* (pp. 143-153). Columbus, OH: Merrill.

Eller, R.G., Pappas, C.C., & Brown, E. (1988). The lexical development of kindergartners: Learning from written context. *Journal of Reading Behavior, 20*, 5-24.

Finn, J.D., & Achilles, C.M. (1999). Tennessee's class size study: Findings, Implications, Misconceptions. *Educational Evaluation and Policy Analysis, 21*(2) 97-110.

Frede, E.C. (1995). The role of program quality in producing early childhood program benefits. *The Future of Children, 5*(3), 115-132.

Gersten, R., Darch, C., & Gleason, M. (1988). Effectiveness of a direct instruction academic kindergarten for low-income students. *Elementary School Journal, 89*, 227-240.

Golomb, C. (1993). Art and the young child: Another look at the developmental question. *Visual Arts Research, 19*, 1-15.

Graue, M.E. (1993). *Ready for what? Constructing meanings of readiness for kindergarten.* Albany: State University of New York Press.

Guthrie, J.T., & Wigfield, A. (2000). Engagement and motivation in reading. In M.L. Kamil, P.B. Mosenthal, P.D. Pearson, & R Barr (Eds.),*Handbook of reading research* (Vol. III, pp. 403-422). Mahwah, NJ: Lawrence Erlbaum Associates, Inc.

Haden, C.A., Reese, E., & Fivush, R. (1996). Mothers' extratextual comments during storybook reading: Stylistic differences over time and across texts.*Discourse Processes, 21*, 135-169.

Halliday, M.A.K. (1975). *Learning how to mean: Explorations in the development of language.* London: Edward Arnold Ltd.

Hart, B., & Risley, T.R. (1995). *Meaningful differences in the everyday experience of young American children.* Baltimore: Brookes Publishing Company.

Hartnett, P., & Gelman, R. (1998). Early understandings of numbers: Paths or barriers to the construction of new understandings? *Learning and Instruction, 8,* 341-374.

Helm, J.H., & Katz, L.G. (2001). *Young investigators: The project approach in the early years.* New York: Teacher's College Press.

Holmes, C.T., & McConnell, B.M. (1990, April).*Full-day versus half-day kindergarten: An experimental study.* Paper presented at the annual meeting of American Educational Research Association, Boston, MA.

Huttenlocker, J., Levine, S., & Vevea, J. (1998). Environmental input and cognitive growth: A study using time-period comparisons. *Child Development, 69,* 1012-1029.

Johnson, E. (1974). *An experimental study of the comparison of pupil achievement in the all-day kindergarten and one half-day control group.* Walden University. (ERIC Document Reproduction No. ED 115 361).

Kagan, S.L., & Cohen, N.E. (1996). *Reinventing early care and education: A vision of a quality system.* San Francisco: Jossey-Bass.

Karweit, N. (1989). The effects of a story reading program on the vocabulary and story comprehension skills of disadvantaged pre-kindergarten and kindergarten students. *Early Educational Research Journal, 21,* 767-787.

Karweit, N. (1993). Effective preschool and kindergarten programs for students at-risk. In B. Spodek (Ed.). *Handbook of research on the education of young children.* New York: Macmillian.

Karweit, N. (1994). Can preschool alone prevent early learning failure? In R. Slavin, N. Karweit, & B.A. Wasik (Eds.), *Preventing early school failure: Research, policy, and practice* (pp. 58-77). Boston: Allyn and Bacon.

Karweit, N. (1999). *Maryland Kindergarten Survey Report.* Baltimore, MD: Johns Hopkins University Center for Research on the Education of Students Placed At Risk.

Karweit, N., & Wasik, B.A. (1996). The effects of story reading programs on the development of disadvantaged preschoolers.*Journal of Students Placed At Risk, 1*(4), 319-348.

Leung, C.B., & Pikulski, J.J. (1990, December). Incidental learning of word meaning by kindergartners and first grade children through repeated readings and read aloud events. In *Yearbook of national reading conference* (Vol. 40). Chicago: National Reading Conference.

Lonigan, C.J. (1994). Reading to preschoolers exposed: Is the emperor really naked? *Developmental Review, 14,* 303-323.

Lonigan, C.J., & Whitehurst, G.J. (1998). Relative efficacy of parent and teacher involvement in a shared-reading intervention for preschool children from low-income backgrounds. *Early Childhood Research Quarterly, 13*, 263-290.

Marcon, R.A. (1999). Differential impact of preschool models on development and early learning of inner-city children: A three-cohort study.*Developmental Psychology, 35*, 358-375.

Mason, J., & Dunning, D. (1986, April). *Toward a model of relating home literacy with beginning reading.* Paper presented at the annual meeting of the American Educational Research Association, San Francisco, CA.

Meisels, S.J. (1994). Designing meaningful measurements for early childhood. In B. Mallory & R. New (Eds.), *Diversity and developmentally appropriate practices: Challenges for early childhood education* (pp. 202-222). New York: Teachers College Press.

Meyer, L.A. (1984, November). *A look at instruction in kindergarten: Observations of interactions in three school districts* (Technical report no. 383). Paper presented at the annual meeting of the National Reading Conference, St. Petersburg, FL.

Morris, D. (1999). Preventing reading failure in the primary grades. In T. Shanahan & F.V. Rodriguez-Brown (Eds.), *National reading conference yearbook* (Vol. 48, pp. 17038). Chicago: National Reading Conference.

Morrow, L.M. (1993). *Literacy development in the early years: Helping children read and write* (2nd ed.). Needham Heights, MA: Allyn and Bacon.

Morrow, L.M., & Smith, J.K. (1990). The effect of group size on interactive storybook reading. *Reading Research Quarterly, 25*, 213-231.

Munn, P., & Schaffer, H.R. (1993). Literacy and numeracy events in social interactive contexts. *International Journal of Early Years Education, 1*, 61-80.

National Council of Teachers of Mathematics. (1998). *Principles and standards for school mathematics.* Washington, DC: National Council of Teachers of Mathematics.

National Council of Teachers of Mathematics. (2000). *Principles and standards for school mathematics.* Washington, DC: National Council of Teachers of Mathematics.

Neuman, S.B., Copple, C., & Bredekamp, S. (1999).*Learning to read and write: Developmentally appropriate practices for young children.* Washington, DC: NAEYC.

New, R.S. (1994). Culture, child development, and developmentally appropriate practices: Teachers as collaborative researchers. In B. Mallory & R. New (Eds.), *Diversity and developmentally appropriate practices: Challenges for early childhood education* (pp. 65-83). New York: Teachers College Press.

Ninio, A., & Bruner, J. (1978). The achievement and antecedents of labeling.*Child Language, 5*, 1-15.

Oliver, L.S. (1980). The effects of extended instructional time on the readiness for reading of kindergarten children. *Dissertation Abstracts International, 41*(5-A), 1943-1944.

Payne, A., Whitehurst, G.J., & Angell, A. (1994). The role of home literacy environment in the development of language ability in preschool children from low-income families. *Early Childhood Research Quarterly, 9*, 427-440.

Perfetti, C.A., Beck, I., Bell, L.C., & Hughes, C. (1987). Phonemic knowledge and learning to read are reciprocal: A longitudinal study of first grade children. *Merrill-Palmer Quarterly, 33*, 283-319.

Pound, L. (1999). *Supporting mathematical development in the early years.* Phildelphia: Open University Press.

Puleo, V.T. (1988). A review and critique of research on full-day kindergarten.*The Elementary School Journal, 8,* 427-439.

Puma, M., Karweit, N., Price, C., Ricciuti, A., Thompson, W., & Vaden-Kiernan, M. (1997). *Prospects: Final report on student outcomes.* Washington, DC: U.S. Department of Education, Planning and Evaluation Services.

Ramey, C.T., & Ramey, S.L. (1998a). Early intervention and early experience.*American Psychologist, 53,* 109-120.

Ramey, C.T., & Ramey, S.L. (1998b). Prevention of intellectual disabilities: Early interventions to improve cognitive development. *Preventive Medicine, 27,* 224-232.

Resnick, G., & Zill, N. (2000). *Is Head Start providing high-quality educational services? Unpacking classroom processes.* Report to the Department of Health and Human Services. Washington, DC: Department of Health and Human Services.

Robbins, C., & Ehri, L. E. (1994). Reading storybooks to kindergartners helps them learn new vocabulary words. *Journal of Educational Psychology, 86,* 54-64.

Rosenthal, R., & Rosnow, R.L. (1991). *Essentials of behavioral research: Methods and data analysis* (2nd ed.). New York: McGraw Hill.

Roskos, K.A., & Christie, J.F. (Eds.). (2000). *Play and literacy in early childhood: Research from multiple perspectives.* Mahwah, NJ: Erlbaum.

Scarborough, H., & Dobrich, W. (1994). On the efficacy of reading to preschoolers. *Developmental Review, 14,* 245-302.

Seefeldt, C., & Galper, A. (Eds.). (1998).*Continuing issues in early childhood education.* Upper Saddle River, NJ: Merrill.

Sénéchal, M. (1997). The differential effect of storybook reading on preschoolers' acquisition of expressive and receptive vocabulary.*Journal of Child Language, 24,* 123-138.

Sénéchal, M., & Cornell, E.H. (1993). Vocabulary acquisition through shared reading experiences. *Reading Research Quarterly, 28,* 360-374.

Sénéchal, M., LeFevre, J., Hudson, E., & Lawson, E.P. (1996). Knowledge of storybooks as a predictor of young children's vocabulary.*Journal of Educational Psychology, 88,* 520-536.

Sénéchal, M., LeFevre, J., Thomas, E.M., & Daley, K.E. (1998). Differential effects of home literacy experiences on the development of oral and written language. *Reading Research Quarterly, 33,* 96-116.

Sénéchal, M., Thomas, E.H., & Monker, J. (1995). Individual differences in 4-year-old children's acquisition of vocabulary during storybook reading.*Journal of Educational Psychology, 87,* 218-229.

Shore, R. (1997). *Rethinking the brain: New insights into early brain development.* New York: Families and Work Institute Press.

Snow, C.E. (1983). Literacy and language: Relationships during the preschool years. *Harvard Educational Review, 53,* 165-189.

Snow, C.E., Burns, S., & Griffin, P. (Eds.). (1998).*Preventing reading difficulties in young children.* Washington, DC: National Academy Press.

Stahl, S.A., & Murray, B.A. (1994). Defining phonological awareness and its relationship to early reading.*Journal of Educational Psychology, 86*(2), 221-234.

Stanovich, K.E. (1998). Refining the phonological core deficit model.*Child Psychology and Psychiatry Review, 3*(1), 17-21.

Stanovich, K.E., & Stanovich, P.J. (1995). How research might inform the debate about early reading acquisition. *Journal of Research in Reading, 18*(2), 87-105.

Stipek, D.J. (1991). Characterizing early childhood education programs. In L. Rescorla, M. C. Hyson, & K. Hirsh-Pasek (Eds.). *Academic instruction in early childhood: Challenge or pressure?* (pp. 47-55). San Francisco: Jossey-Bass.

Stipek, D.J. (1997). Success in school-for a head start in life. In S.S. Luthar, J.A. Burack, & D. Cicchetti (Eds.), *Developmental psychopathology: Perspectives on adjustment, risk, and disorder* (pp. 75-92). New York: Cambridge University Press.

Stipek, D.J., & Byler, P. (1997). Early childhood education teachers: Do they practice what they preach? *Early Childhood Research Quarterly, 12,* 305-325.

Stipek, D.J., Feiler, R., Daniels, D., & Milburn, S. (1995). Effects of different instructional approaches on young children's achievement and motivation. *Child Development, 66,* 209-223.

Stipek, D.J., Milburn, S., Clements, D., & Daniels, D.H. (1992). Parents' beliefs about appropriate education for young children. *Journal of Applied Developmental Psychology, 13,* 293-310.

Stipek, D.J., & Ryan, R.H. (1997). Economically disadvantaged preschoolers: Ready to learn but further to go. *Developmental Psychology, 33,* 711-723.

Sulzby, E. (1986). Writing and reading: Signs of oral and written language organization in the young child. In W. H. Teale & E. Sulzby (Eds.), *Emergent literacy: Writing and reading.* Norwood, NJ: Ablex.

Tabors, P.O. (1997). *One child, two languages: A guide for preschool educators of children learning English as a second language.* Baltimore: Brooks.

Thompson, C.M. (1995). What should I draw today? *Sketchbooks in Early Childhood Art Education, 48*(5) 6-11.

Torgesen, J.K., Wagner, R.K., Rashotte, C.A., Burgess, S., & Hecht, S. (1997). Contributions of phonological awareness and rapid automatic naming ability to the growth of word-reading skills in second- to fifth-grade children. *Scientific Studies of Reading, 1,* 161-185.

Treiman, R., & Zukowski, A. (1992). Levels of phonological awareness. In S.A. Brady & D.P. Shankweiler (Eds.), *Phonological processes in literacy: A tribute to Isabelle Y. Liberman* (pp. 67-83). Hillsdale, NJ: Lawrence Erlbaum Associates.

Valdez-Menchaca, M.C., & Whitehurst, G. (1992). Accelerating language development through picture book reading: A systematic extension to Mexican day care. *Developmental Psychology, 28,* 1106-1114.

Wasik, B.A. (1998). Volunteer tutoring programs in reading: A review. *Reading Research Quarterly, 33,* 266- 291.

Wasik, B.A. (2001a). Phonemic awareness and young children. *Childhood Education, 77,* 128-138.

Wasik, B.A. (2001b). Teaching the alphabet to young children. *Young Children, 56,* 34- 39.

Wasik, B.A., & Bond, M.A. (2001). Beyond the pages of a book: Interactive book reading and language development in preschool classrooms. *Journal of Educational Psychology, 93,* 243- 250.

Wasik, B.A., Bond, M.A., & Hindman, A. (2000, December). Getting the most out of a book: Teacher training and interactive book reading. In L. Klenk (Chair), *Literature-based instruction: Impacts of genre, culture, and teacher training.* Symposium conducted at the annual meeting of the National Reading Conference, Scottsdale, AZ.

Wasik, B.A., & Karweit, N. (1994). Off to a good start: Effects of birth to three interventions on early school success. In R. Slavin, N. Karweit, & B.A. Wasik (Eds.), *Preventing early school failure: Research, policy, and practice* (pp. 13-57). Boston: Allyn and Bacon.

Wells, G. (1985). *Language development in the preschool years.* New York: Cambridge University Press.

Wells, G. (1986). *The meaning makers: Children learning language and using language to learn.* Portsmouth, NH: Heinemann.

Whitehurst, G.J., Arnold, D.S., Epstein, J.N., Angell, A.L., Smith, M., and Fischel, J.E. (1994). A picture book reading intervention in day care and home for children from low-income families. *Developmental Psychology, 30,* 679-689.

Whitehurst, G.J., Epstein, J.N., Angell, A.L., Payne, A.C., Crone, D.A., & Fischel, J.E. (1994). Outcomes of an emergent literacy intervention in Head Start. *Journal of Educational Psychology, 86,* 542-555.

Whitehurst, G.J., Falco, F.L., Lonigan, C.J., Fischel, J.E., Debaryshe, B.D., Valdez-Menchaca, M.C., & Caufield, M.B. (1988). Accelerating language development through picture book reading. *Developmental Psychology, 24,* 552-559.

Whitehurst, G.J., & Fischel, J.E. (2000). Reading and language impairments in conditions of poverty. In D.V.M. Bishop & L.B. Leonard (Eds.), *Speech and language impairments in children: Causes, characteristics, interventions, and outcomes* (pp. 53-71). Philadelphia: Psychology Press/Taylor & Francis.

Whitehurst, G.J., & Lonigan, C.J. (1998). Child development and emergent literacy. *Child Development, 69,* 848-872.

Whitehurst, G.J., Zevenbergen, A., Crone, D.A., Schultz, M., Velting, O., & Fischel, J.E. (1999). Outcomes of an emergent literacy intervention from Head Start through second grade. *Journal of Education Psychology, 91,* 261-272.

Winter, M., & Klein, A.E. (1970). *Extending the kindergarten day: Does it make a difference in the achievement of educationally advantaged and disadvantaged pupils?* (ERIC Document Reproduction No. ED 087 534).

Woodcock, R., & Johnson, M. (1989). *Woodcock-Johnson Psycho-Educational Battery* (rev.). Allen, TX:DLM.

Young- Loveridge, J.M. (1989). The relationship between children's home experiences and their mathematical skills on entry to school. *Early Child Development and Care, 43,* 43-59.

Zill, N., Resnick, G., & McKey, R.H. (1999, April). *What children know and can do at the end of Head Start and what it tells about the program's performance.* Paper presented at the annual meeting of the American Educational Research Association, Montreal, CA.

CHAPTER 5

ADDRESSING LINGUISTIC AND CULTURAL DIVERSITY IN EARLY CHILDHOOD:
From Equity to Excellence, From "Raîces" to "Alas"

Eugene E. Garcia

INTRODUCTION

During my assignment in Washington, DC as the Director of the Office of Bilingual Education and Minority Languages Affairs in the U.S. Department of Education, I attempted to engage my professional experience and expertise as an educational researcher and my personal cultural and linguistic experiences. The task was addressing national educational policy and practice for multilingual, bilingual populations in the United States. The professional in me was, and continues to be, nurtured in some of the best educational institutions of this country. And, the nonprofessional in me was, and continues to be, nurtured in a large, rural, Mexican American family—speaking Spanish as our native language. I found bringing these *personas* (the Spanish term for "persons") together not as difficult as I might have expected and even came to conclude that this intersect was quite helpful to me. The following discussion is my attempt to put into writing these intersecting but distinct voices and to help further our understanding of living in a diverse society, but particularly for linguistically and culturally diverse children in this country during their early childhood years. Moreover, I will emphasize the role of educational institutions that strive to serve this population today and will need to serve them even better in the future. For there is no doubt that the historical pattern of the education of these children in the United States is a continuous story of under achievement. It need not be that way in the future.

The voices in this discussion that address these issues of the past, the present, and the future recognize the multiple selves that not only make up my persona, but the multiple selves that are a reality for all of us. It has been useful to recognize that I am walking in varied and diverse cultures. But we all do this. Diversity within each individual is as great as diversity between individuals and the many cultures they belong to or represent at any one moment. Today, within our borders, English First, an organization committed to English as the United States's official language is passionately concerned that multilingualism will produce "balkanization" and a significant blood bath within our borders. At the same time, indigenous people, mourn just as passionately the loss of their languages and cultures. Additionally, immigrants keep making this historical country of immigrants their home. As this country and the world shrinks communicatively, economically, and socially our diversity becomes more visible and harder to hide. But it has been and will always be there. For children in their early years of schooling, this diversity focuses primarily, but not singly, on their linguistic attributes.

A PERSONAL PROLOGUE

At times, it is quite inappropriate to include in scholarly discussion of a professional area of intellectual interest, any personal commentary related to one's own experiences. In this discussion, I cannot proceed with that scholarly discussion of such a *text* without a personal *context*. In my large and quite Catholic family, to baptize a child was a distinct honor and in recognition of that honor *los padrinos*—the Godparents—were given the authority to name the child. My eldest sister and her husband were selected by my parents to serve as my *padrinos*. My sister was enchanted with the name "Eugene" and that is how I came to have a Greek name in a cohort of brothers and sisters named Antonio, Emelio, Cecelia, Ciprianita, Abel, Federico, Tiburcio, Christina and born of parents named Lorenzo and Juanita. Of course, my mother could not pronounce "Eugene," so to her and my immediate family I became "Gino."

"Gino" carries a distinct sense of cultural "Hispanic-ness," "Chicanismo," "Latino-ness," "Raza-ness." These all reflect a deep regard for the linguistic and cultural roots that foster who he is. These roots are best exemplified by a lesson from my father. As farm workers and sharecroppers, winter was a time to prepare for work—there just was not the quantity of work to do during this period. And, it was during one farm winter in the high plains of Colorado where I was born and raised that my father pointed to an árbol— a cottonwood tree as I recall—near our home. He asked simply, "Por qué puede vivir ese árbol en el frio del invierno y en el calor del verano?" (How can that tree survive the bitter cold of winter and the harsh heat of summer?) My father was not a man of many words—he was often characterized by relatives as quiet and shy—but when he spoke we all listened very carefully. I remember struggling to find an answer. I was also characterized as quiet and shy. But I tried to respond to my father—it was the right thing to do. I rambled on for some time about how big and strong the tree was and how its limbs and trunk were like the strong arms and bodies of my elder brothers, particularly the two who were serving in the U.S. Army during the last phases of the Korean war.

Then he kindly provided a different perspective by referring to a common Spanish dicho/consejo (proverb/advisory): El árbol fuerte tienen raíces maduros. (A strong tree has mature/strong roots). In articulating this significant piece of the analysis that was absent from my youthful ramblings, he made very clear that without strong roots, strong trees are impossible—and we don't even see the roots! In a Spanish class many years later, a teacher extended this lesson further by pointing me to a more elaborate dicho/consejo: Del árbol caido, todos hacen leña. (From a fallen tree, anyone/everyone can make firewood.) What became clear to me at that moment was the more substantive lesson my father was framing—if you have no roots, how can you withstand the tests of the environment that surely will come and prey on your vulnerabilities. That without those roots, any tree can be transformed from a beautiful living organism to a fallen entity that can easily be transformed, or more profoundly, destroyed, never to be recognized as the strong tree it once was. For me as an individual with a set of cultural and linguistic roots, if my roots were to die and I was to be stripped of the integrity that lies in those roots, then I will also disappear along with all that is me.

For many linguistically and culturally diverse children in this country, their roots have either been ignored or stripped away in the name of growing strong. Many have been directed to stop speaking their native language, to perceive their culture as one less-than, and to assimilate as quickly as possible so they can succeed in American society (Chavez, 1991, 1995). And, unfortunately, many have suffered the fate of the rootless tree—they have fallen socially, economically, academically and culturally. Like that fallen tree they have been transformed and forever lost the individual and cultural integrity that once thrived in their ancestors, even in circumstances of greater poverty and social hostility.

But for "Gino," my mother made it very clear, roots/*raíces* and their concomitant integrity and self-respect was not enough. As a mother, she wanted the very best for all her children, certainly not the long and painful fieldwork that she had endured for a lifetime. She wanted us "bien educados"—to have a set of formal and marketable skills. She made very clear that children needed wings, like the wings she insisted we children grew every night upon falling to sleep so as to fly to heaven to be with God. All children, she said, were angels. My mother made it clear that she could not provide the kind of wings that God and a good education could provide. She knew that the teachers and schools would have to take me further than she could so personally. Education would need to provide the strong and elaborate wings for me to succeed where she often felt she had failed: "Go to school—strong wings like those of an eagle are also what you need in this world to raise your family and provide for them all that we have been unable to provide for you."

For linguistically and culturally diverse children in this country, the emphasis on building wings during the early years of schooling has strategically focused on teaching English language skills: "Teach them English well and then they will succeed." Yet all educators realize that in today's information age, education must provide broad and strong intellectual wings related to the fundamental linguistic, mathematical, scientific and technological literacy. English literacy is important but it is not enough. "Gino" feels that these children and their families, like those represented by him and his family, have been educationally short-changed. This country can no longer afford these deplorable educational outcomes. Our growing students should have the educational excellence—the wings—promised all children in the most recent wave of educational reform aimed at equity and excellence (Garcia, 2001).

THE "LANGUAGE/CULTURE" DEBATE

I realize that many Americans do not embrace these sentiments. Most critical of such views of the interactive relationship of *raices y alas* are two well regarded and influential authors, each in their own way refuting the importance of roots and the relationship of those roots to educational development of our diverse populations. Linda Chavez, an advisor in the Reagan White House, journalist commentator and author of *Out of the Barrio: Toward a New Politics of Hispanic Assimilation* (1991) suggests that:

Every previous group—Germans, Irish, Italians, Greeks, Jews, Poles—struggled to be accepted fully into the social, political and economic mainstream, sometimes against the opposition of a hostile majority. They learned the language, acquired education and skills, and adapted their own customs and traditions to fit an American context. (1991, p. 2)

The key for success in America, Chavez argues, is minimizing the public/governmental recognition of non-English, cultural and ethnic roots and the individual and governmental promotion of assimilation. She chides the federal government, particularly federal Bilingual Education programs and "ethnic" leaders, for promoting permanent victim status with these groups vying for the distinction of being the poorest, most segregated and least educated minority, thereby, entitling them to government handouts. These in turn, her conclusion advances, encourages these groups to maintain their language and culture, their specific identity in return for rewards handed out through federal, state and local educational policies which thwart assimilation. This doesn't sound like my father's concern for the importance of roots.

Yet another "minority" author is relevant here: Richard Rodriguez. He is very eloquent in his description of his upbringing in a "Mexican" home and a Catholic school where the English-speaking nuns literally beat the Spanish language and the "Hispanic-ness" out of him. His book, *Hunger of Memory* (1982) describes this forced assimilation, painful as it was, that propelled him to new heights of educational achievement. And although he never really articulates the conclusion himself, he leaves open the suggestion that such treatment of other immigrant stock like him is exactly what they need to get over their "problems." As you have read earlier, reach a very different conclusion in this discussion. But you should know that the debate exists.

BEYOND THE DEBATE

The following discussion will not directly address this debate, but will include an expanded research related discussion of "vulnerability" factors both within and outside the education arena along with related data related to the "optimal" treatment of this growing population of young children and families by addressing the following:

1. An overall demographic assessment of factors related to the schooling of cultural diverse populations including issues of poverty, family stability, and immigrant status.
2. A particular analysis of the challenges associated with the growing number of Latino language minority students—students who come to school in their early years with no or limited proficiency in English.

3.   A presentation of conceptual and empirical perspectives that sets the stage for a more informed approach to the education of Latinos in early childhood, and, more recent assaults of the "roots and wings" metaphor.

THE DEMOGRAPHIC PICTURE

The U.S. Census Bureau in its attempts to provide clarifying demographic information never fails in confusing us. With regard to documenting the racial and ethnic heterogeneity of our country's population, it has arrived at a set of highly confusing terms that place individuals in separate exclusionary categories: White, White non-Hispanic, Black, and Hispanic (with some five subcategories of Hispanics). Unfortunately, outside of the census meaning of these terms, they are, for the most part, highly ambiguous and non-representative of the true heterogeneity that the Bureau diligently seeks to document. Therefore, it is important to note at the outset of this discussion that these categories are useful only as the most superficial reflection of our nation's true diversity. I do not know many census identified "Whites," "Blacks," or "Hispanics" who truly believe they are "White," "Black," etc., but given the forced-choice responses allowed them in census questionnaires they are constrained by these choices. Racially and culturally we are not "pure" stock and any separation by the Census Bureau, the Center for Educational Statistics or other social institutions that attempt to address the complexity of our diverse population representation is likely to impart a highly ambiguous sketch.

Having consented to this significant restriction with regard to efforts aimed at documenting population diversity in this country, I must still conclude that an examination of the available data in this arena does provide a fuzzy but useful portrait of our society and the specific circumstances of various groups within our nation's boundaries. That sketch is one of consummate vulnerability for non-White and Hispanic (usually referred to as "minority") families, children and students. On almost every indicator, non-White and Hispanic families, children and students "at-risk" are likely to fall into the lowest quartile on indicators of "well-being": family stability, family violence, family income, child health and development, and, educational achievement. Yet, this population has grown significantly in the last two decades and will grow substantially in the decades to come.

The demographic transformation that has become more evident in the last decade was easily foreseen at least that long ago. Our future student growth is as predictable: In a mere 40 years, White students will be a minority in every category of public education as we know it today. Unfortunately, these emerging majority ethnic and racial background students continue to be placed "at risk" in today's social institutions. The National

Center for Children in Poverty (1995) provided a clear and alarming demographic window on these "at risk" populations. Of the 21.9 million children less than six years of age in 1990, who will move slowly through society's institutions—family, schools, the work place—five million (25%) were living in poverty. Although less than 30% of all children under six years of age were non-White, more than 50% of these children in poverty were non-White. In addition, these children continue to live in racial/ethnic isolation. Some 56% lived in racially isolated neighborhoods in 1966; 72% resided in such neighborhoods in 1994; 61% of these children in poverty live in concentrations of poverty, where 20% of the population is poor.

Recent national data regarding Head Start (Phillips & Cabrera, 1996) indicates that only one-third of the programs had an enrollment characterized by a single language, with a range of 1-32 languages represented in programs while 72% of programs had enrollments of between 2-3 languages. The predominate languages represented in these programs were Spanish and English.

Combined with the contemporary educational "zeitgeist" which embraces excellence and equity for all students, best reflected in the 1983, *A Nation at Risk,* and the more recent national goals statement, *Goals 2000* (1994), attention to the Hispanic children, families and students has been significant. The major thrust of any such effort aimed at these populations has been centered on identifying why such populations are not thriving, and, how institutions serving these populations can be "reformed" or "restructured" to meet this educational challenge. Following this theme are recent analysis and recommendations by the California State Department of Education in its efforts to better train infant and toddler caregivers in state supported programs (California State Department of Education, 1992) and the U.S. Department of Education regarding reforms for federally funded education programs (Garcia & Gonzalez, 1995), The National Academy of Education in its discussion of standards-based reform (McLauglin & Shepard, 1995), The Roundtable on Head Start Research of the National Research Council in its efforts to provide an issue analysis of research needed to producing a thriving future for Head Start for a highly diverse population of children and families (Phillips & Cabrera, 1996), the National Council of Teachers of English and the International Reading Association in their treatment of language arts standards (NCTE/IRA, 1996), and, the National Association for the Education of Young Children's position statement regarding linguistic and cultural diversity (NAEYC, 1996). All of these articulations have attended to the "vulnerabilities" of linguistic and cultural "minorities" and have addressed issues of language and culture, given this country's past treatment of this population and the present conceptual and empirical understanding of how institutions must be more responsive. Much of this future thinking related to policy and practice is based on the issues and research findings that follow in this discussion.

OUR PAST APPROACH: AMERICANIZATION

Historically, "Americanization" has been a prime institutional education objective for Latino young children and their families (Elam, 1972; Garcia, 2001; Gonzalez, 1990). Schooling practices were adopted whenever the population of these students rose to significant numbers in a community. This adaptation established special programs, and was applied to both children and adults in urban and rural schools and communities. The desired effect of "Americanizing" was to socialize and acculturate the targeted diverse community. In essence, if public efforts could teach these children and families English and "American" values, then social, economic, and educational failure could be averted. Ironically, social economists have argued that this effort was coupled with systematic efforts to maintain disparate conditions between Anglos and "minority" populations. Indeed, more than anything else, past attempts at addressing the "Black, Hispanic, Indian, Asian, etc., educational problem" have actually preserved the political and economic subordination of these communities (Spencer, 1988).

Coming from a sociological theory of assimilation, "Americanization" has traditionally been recognized as a solution to the problem of immigrants and ethnicity in the modern industrialized United States. Linda Chavez (1991, 1995) continues to champion this solution today. In California in 1996 and 1998 and more recently Arizona in 2000, specific state referendums have attempted to restrict the education of immigrants or to provide for their rapid integration into "English only" educational programs (Dueñas González & Ildikó Melis, 2000)

The "Americanization" solution has not worked. Not even in California after restricted educational codes were adopted in 1998 to restrict multilingual education efforts in early childhood (Garcia & Curry, 2001). Moreover, "Americanization" policies depend on the flawed notion of group culture. The "Americanization" solution presumes that culturally different children are, as a group, culturally flawed. To fix them individually, we must act on the individual as a member of a cultural group. By changing the values, language, etc. of the group we will have the solution to the educational under achievement of students who represent these groups.

EARLY CHILDHOOD PRACTICES THAT MEET THE CHALLENGE

The debate regarding early childhood education of Latino students in the United States has centered on the role of cultural and developmental appropriateness of curriculum and pedagogy along with Spanish language use and the development of English in these early childhood settings. With regard to the broader schooling process, the issue has been the effective instruction of a growing population of ethnic minority students who do not speak English and, therefore, are considered candidates for special educational programming that takes into consideration this language and cultural difference. Discussion of this issue has included cross disciplinary dialogues involving psychology, linguistics, sociology, politics, and education.[1] The central theme of these discussions has to do with the specific role of the native language.

Supporters of cultural sensitive and native language instruction are at one end of this debate. Proponents of this specially designed instructional strategy recommend the utilization of the child's native language and mastery of that language prior to the introduction of an English and more "mainstream" curriculum. This approach (Fishman, 1989) suggests that the competencies in the native culture and language, particularly as relate to academic learning, provide important cognitive and social foundations for second language learning and academic learning in general—"you really only learn to read once." At the other end of this debate, introduction to the English curriculum is recommended at the onset of the students' schooling experience with minimal use of the native language. This specially designed approach calls for English language "leveling" by instructional staff (to facilitate the understanding on behalf of the limited English proficient student) combined with an English-as-a-second-language component. In essence, the earlier the student confronts English and the more time it is confronted, the greater the English linguistic advantage (Rossell, 1992; Rossell & Baker, 1996).

Each of these approaches argues that the result of its implementation will be short-term linguistic advantages which will lead to more long-term psychological, linguistic and educational advantages resulting in direct social and economic advancement (Cardenas, 1986; Rossell & Baker, 1996). Simply put, each of these approaches suggests that a simple twist of the educational curriculum particularly in the early years, one that focuses on the language of the curriculum, will fix the problem. Thus, it has been the case that this debate and its related assumptions regarding the importance of the language character of the Hispanic student have driven policy and practice.

The "native language" debate has ignored the contributions of Brice-Heath (1986), Ogbu (1986), Tharp and Gallimore (1989), Rose (1989), Moll (1992), Krashen (1996), and Garcia (1999, 2001) who have suggested that the schooling vulnerability of such students must be understood within the broader contexts of this society's treatment of these students and their families in and out of educational institutions. That is, no quick fix is likely under social and early education conditions which mark the Hispanic language minority student for special treatment of his/her language difference without consideration for the psychological and social/cultural circumstances in which that student resides. This is not to suggest that the linguistic character of this student is insignificant. Instead, it warns

us against the isolation of this single attribute as the only variable of importance. This more comprehensive view of the education, particularly, early
childhood education, includes an understanding of the relationship
between home and school, the sociocultural incongruities between the two
and the resulting effects on learning and achievement (Garcia, 1994, 1997;
Kagan & Garcia, 1991).

Recent findings from research have redefined the nature of the educational vulnerability of our diverse children in early childhood. This
research has destroyed common stereotypes and myths and laid a foundation on which to reconceptualize present educational practices and launch
new initiatives. This foundation recognizes the homogeneity/heterogene-
ity within and between diverse student populations. No one set of descriptions or prescriptions will suffice. However, a set of commonalties deserves
particular attention.

California Tomorrow (1995) in a study of early childhood care in California, concluded that a set of principles guided quality child care across a
variety of care settings which serve a growing community of linguistically
and culturally diverse families:

1. Support development of ethnic identity and anti-racist attitudes
    among children.
2. Build upon the cultures of families and promote cross-cultural
    understanding among children.
3. Foster the preservation of children's home language and encourage
    bilingualism among all children.
4. Engage in ongoing reflection and dialogue. (California Tomorrow,
    1995, p. 8)

Cohen and Pompa (1994) interviewed experts in the early childhood field
and conducted a formative literature review of research on multicultural
early childhood approaches, came to the same conclusion, making a particular note that universal notions of "developmentally appropriate"
approaches must recognize the more specific issues of "culturally appropriate developmental" issues.

Related research focusing on early childhood classrooms, teachers,
administrators and parents revealed an interesting set of perspectives
regarding the treatment of children (Cole, 1995; Garcia, 1991, 1994;
Hakuta & Gould, 1987; Moll, 1992; Ramirez, Yuen, Ramey & Pasta, 1991;
Rose, 1989; Wong Fillmore, 1991). In this research, classroom instructors
were highly committed to the educational success of their students; perceived themselves as instructional innovators utilizing "new" learning theories and instructional philosophies to guide their practice; continued to be
involved in professional development activities including participation in
small-group support networks; had a strong, demonstrated commitment to

student-home communication (several teachers were utilizing a weekly parent interaction format); and felt that they had the autonomy to create or change the instruction and curriculum in their classrooms, even if it did not meet with the exact district guidelines. Significantly, these instructors "adopted" their students. They had high academic expectations for all their student ("everyone will learn to read in my classroom") and also served as an advocate for their students. They rejected any conclusion that their students were intellectually or academically disadvantaged.

Administrators tended to be highly articulate regarding the curriculum and instructional strategies undertaken at their sites. They were also highly supportive of their instructional staff, taking pride in their accomplishments. They reported that their support of teacher autonomy although they were quite aware of the potential problems regarding the pressure to strictly conform to "standard" policies regarding the standardization of curriculum and the need for academic accountability (testing). Parents expressed a high level of satisfaction and appreciation with regard to their children's education experience in these classrooms. All indicated or implied that their students academic success was tied to their child's future economic success. Anglo parents and Hispanic were both quite involved in the formal parent support activities of the schools. However, Anglo parents' attitudes were much more in line with a "child advocacy," somewhat distrustful of the schools specific interest in doing what was right for their child. Conversely, Hispanic parents expressed a high level of trust for the teaching and administrative staff.

The following presents a series of classroom/school snapshots reported by research and demonstration programs funded by the U.S. Department of Education. They come directly form specific research reports submitted to the Department and are available for more thorough review. The intent of these snapshots is to provide a picture of a developing empirical base supporting a new vision of educational programming intended to serve Latino children and families from diverse cultural backgrounds (Garcia, 1999; Garcia & Stein, 1997).

Watsonville. In Erminda Garcia's third grade classroom at Alianza school in Watsonville, California, students were asked at the very outset of the academic year to consider the thematic study of the "Three R's: Resourcefulness, Responsibility, and Respectfulness." In essence, they were asked to study how they could become responsible, respectful, and resourceful in relationship to each other and in what they had to accomplish in their classroom. In this regard, the languages (Spanish and English) were immediately identified as resources and students articulated the ways in which these and other resources (parents, family, books, computers, etc.) could be used to enhance their academic pursuits. This study coupled with the issue of "what do we want to learn?" started this classroom in an analysis of both where they needed to go academically and the resources available to get there. In Erminda's classroom, she has made certain to organize desks in ways which promote sharing of students language resources by seating children in desks facing each other in groups of four. Even in whole-group instruction, children are paired for interactive response discussion. Students select from Spanish and English resources materials often using each other for assistance in selecting those materials. The display of knowledge acquired is available in published works, in brainstorm charts, in related posted student products—examples of learning are always put on display in whatever language that learning was accomplished. And, students keep individual learning logs and participate in daily interactive journal communication with selected peers using their language of choice—sometimes relying on their native English or Spanish and other times using their second language. Similarly, learning logs and dialogue journals are shared with parents and significant family members at home. In such circumstances, they are asked to share each other's language resources and related expertise. *Students and parents are asked to maximize the use of language in getting learning accomplished not in getting language learned.* This approach places a maximum on using language as a learning tool and does not focus on learning language. Although, the latter is achieved through the former, language continues to be operated on as a resource for learning.

Traditional methods of bilingual education and English-as-a-second-language (ESL) instruction have been tied to teaching English and the native languages as languages by themselves and for themselves. The language was dissected and fed to the students in little bits, usually in the form of vocabulary words and verbs to be conjugated. These traditional methods are ESL pullout and early-exit (one to three years) traditional bilingual education. Research and experience has shown these methods to be faulty for both learners of English and of other second language learners. The ESL pullout method pulls students away from content classes and causes them to miss out on the content instruction. At best it leads to a quick-fix verbal English that leaves the student proficient in English speech, but unable to read and write in the native language and unprepared to read and write in English. Research findings imply that ESL pullout can lead to a puzzling situation—one in which that which it sets out to do are confounded by what it actually does.

A newer ESL method is designed to fully embed an enriched second language within a content subject matter as well as in areas such as consumer issues to health issues to survival skills. This method is called sheltered English and is geared toward the one way learning of English. Two-way (also called dual immersion or developmental bilingual) programs involve students from English and a non-English language background learning content and language together. In this two-way program the students from each language background serve as peer coaches and interact with one another to facilitate the learning of both languages through the medium of native speakers. Both languages and cultures are equal and both are developed into full fluency.

Chicago. Sixth graders in Chicago's Inter-American Magnet School cluster in small groups for a Writer's Workshop. The two-way plan works here; all instruction throughout the K-8 school is in both English and Spanish. The teacher asks them to write sentences using these words: Unintelligibly, committee, prop, rambunctious, intention, loyalist, instinctively, elaborated, defiantly, and daintily. Students discuss the assignment among them and write down sentences in their journals in either Spanish or English. Then a first grade class enters and the younger students pair up with the older ones; each pair has an English and a Spanish-speaker. The older ones read stories they have written to the younger ones. The first graders have a million questions and push the sixth graders to explain and elaborate on what they have written. In the last part of the class, the teachers ask the class to focus on what they like and dislike about the stories.

The teacher has created a learning environment distinct from that seen in traditional classrooms. Students assume responsibility for their learning, serve as resources for one another, get feedback on their work from an audience, and engage in teaching experiences for younger children. This level of interaction did not happen by accident; these sixth graders are enrolled at a school where the pedagogical approaches have been designed to support students who play an active role in their learning process.

Teachers often develop their curriculum around themes many, that are drawn from the study of the Americas. For example, teachers plan their curriculum together and use social studies-based themes to create eight thematic units per year. One unit was a study of Mayan civilization; as part of this unit, classes visited the Field Museum to see an exhibit on Mayan culture, architecture, and religion. Teachers used the thematic unit as an opportunity to integrate across curriculum areas. In social studies, students studied the geographic spread of the Mayan civilization as well as its religion and cultural traditions. In science, students studied Mayan agriculture and architecture, while in language arts, students wrote about the Mayans. Thematic instruction lets students see the natural connections between traditional disciplines, while linking themes to student cultures allows students to learn about their culture and the cultures of their fellow students.

Arlington. Entering Arlington, Virginia's Key Elementary School you feel the pulse of the learning process. Clusters of classes are located in the pod matrix that allows students to easily move back and forth from learning centers in the classroom to activity centers in the oval-shaped pods which encircle the classroom clusters. On a Spanish day, you hear only Spanish. Learning is going on. The kids seem perfectly at home; they are adding to their home experience, not deleting it. They are being encouraged to communicate with their parents and grandparents, not to ignore them or put them down for being foreign.

San Diego. The Linda Vista School in San Diego goes out of its way to absorb the needs of its Asian and Latino communities: "To accommodate the constant flow of newcomer students and the widely varying educational backgrounds of students, Linda Vista established developmental ungraded wings (early childhood, primary, middle, and upper). The wings function like four schools within the school, each composed of students within a relatively narrow age range (typically spanning two grade levels), but with mixed levels of English language fluency and various educational backgrounds. In typical elementary schools the classroom is the only entity at the sub-school level. But Linda Vista has added another level of organization—the wing—between school and the classroom. This distinction is important because students receive all their instruction within their wing, as opposed to a self-contained classroom as in most elementary schools. The teachers in that wing design the instructional program within each wing. For example, in the upper wing's daily schedule, students are homogeneously grouped by home language or English language level for language arts, ESL, and social studies instruction and heterogeneously grouped and regrouped during the rest of the day for mathematics, science, art, music, and physical education.

San Francisco. In a more quantitative analysis of schooling success for children in bilingual programs, a district wide analysis of longitudinal results on reading and math scores makes clear the advantage of native language instruction for non-English speaking students, the majority of these students being Latino. The analysis compares students in three language categories: those who spoke English only; those who entered the school district fluent in two languages, and, those who were "re-designated" or became fluent in English after completing their bilingual program. Specifically, the data presented in Figure 1 indicates that those students that entered district bilingual education programs and remained in them over a period of time, outperformed English only students.

Particularly significant were the results for those students that entered the district's bilingual education program as LEP students that were instructed in their native language, and then were subsequently re-designated as Fluent English Proficient (FEP) and placed in English-only instructional settings. These students consistently scored higher in measures of reading and math. It is this type of longitudinal/cohort data that makes more evident the significance of native language instruction and its relationship to eventual English academic success.

Imbedded in the activities of these educational enterprises for Latino students was the understanding that language, culture, and their accompanying values are acquired in the home and community environment, that children come to school with some knowledge about what language is, how it works, and what it is used for, that children learn higher level meta-cognitive and meta-linguistic skills as they engage in socially meaningful activities, and that children's development and learning is best understood as the interaction of linguistic, sociocultural, and cognitive knowledge and experiences. In particular for students who do not speak English, their

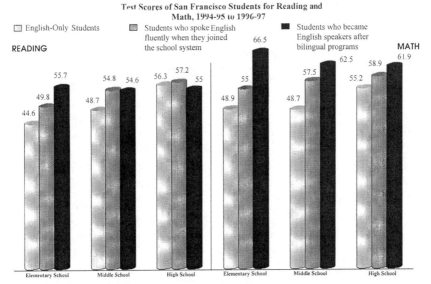

Source: San Francisco Unified School District

FIGURE 1
Bilingual Programs and Student Performance

native language is perceived as a resource instead of a problem. *In general terms, this research suggests moving away from a needs assessment and non-English-proficiency-as-a-problem approach to an asset inventory and native-language-as-a-resource approach. Students are asked to maximize the use of language in getting learning accomplished not in getting language learned.* This approach places a maximum on using language as a learning tool and does not focus on learning language. Although, the latter is achieved through the former, language continues to be operated on as a resource for development and learning.

CONCLUSION

In summary, early education effective curriculum, instructional strategies, and teaching staffs recognize that development and learning has its roots in sharing expertise and experiences through multiple avenues of communication. Further, effective early childhood education for linguistically and culturally diverse children encourages them to take risks, construct meaning, and seek reinterpretation of knowledge within the compatible social contexts. Within this nurturing environment, skills are tools for acquiring knowledge, not ends in themselves, and the language of the child is an incredible resource. The curriculum recognizes that any attempt to address the needs of these students in a deficit or "subtractive" mode is counter productive. Instead, this knowledge base recognizes, conceptually, that educators must be "additive" in an approach to these students, that is, adding to the rich core of cognitive, linguistic, academic, and cultural understanding and skills they bring with them. Early childhood needs to confront these challenges systematically in its program endeavors and each of us can assist in the development of a practice which more fully explores the issues raised here.

Recent articulations regarding these challenges reinforce this charge. The National Council of Teachers of English and the International Reading Association in their enunciation of standards for English language arts recognize that:

- Students develop an understanding of and respect for diversity in language use, patterns, and dialects across cultures, ethnic groups, geographic regions, and social roles.
- Students whose first language is not English make use of their first language to develop competency in the English language arts and to develop understanding of content across the curriculum.
- Celebrating our shared beliefs and traditions are not enough; we also need to honor that which is distinctive in the many groups that make up our nation. (*IRA/NCTE Standards for the Language Arts*, 1996, p. 3)

The National Association for the Education of Young Children echos these same concerns in its position statement related to educational practices regarding linguistic and cultural diversity in early childhood:

> Early childhood educators can best help linguistically and culturally diverse children and their families by acknowledging and responding to the importance of the child's home language and culture. Administrative support for bilingualism as a goal is necessary within the educational setting. Educational practices should focus on educating children toward the "school culture" while preserving and respecting the diversity of the home language and culture that each child brings to the early learning setting. (NAEYC Position Statement: Responding to Linguistic and Cultural Diversity—Recommendations for Effective Early Childhood Education. *Young Children*, 1996, p. 12)

In the present era, this challenge must be met within the context of philosophical, ideological and political debates surrounding our professional efforts to do things right and to do the right things for all children and families, recognizing the significance of their "roots" and need for "wings."

NOTE

1. For a more thorough discussion of these issues allow me to refer you Hakuta and Gould (1987), August and Garcia (1988), Crawford (1989), Baker (1990), Kagan and Garcia (1991), Garcia (1994, 1999), Cole (1995), Garcia and Gonzalez (1995), Rossell and Baker (1996), August and Hakuta (1997), and Dueñas González and Ildikó Melis (2000).

REFERENCES

August, D., & Garcia, E. (1988). *Language minority education in the United States: Research, policy and practice.* Chicago: Charles C. Thomas.

August, D., & Hakuta, K. (1997). *Improving schooling for language-minority children: research agenda.* Washington, DC: National Council Research.

Baker, K.A. (1990). Language minority education: Two decades of research. In A. Barona & E. Garcia (Eds.), *Students-at-risk* (pp. 3-41). Washington, DC: National Association of School Psychologist.

California State Department of Education. (1992). *The program for infant/toddler caregivers: A guide to language development and communication.* Sacramento: California Department of Education.

California Tomorrow. (1995). *The unfinished journey: Restructuring schools in a diverse society.* San Francisco: Author.

Cardenas, J. (1986). The role of native-language instruction in bilingual education. *Phi Delta Kappan, 67,* 359-363.

Chavez, L. (1991). *Out of the barrio: Toward a new politics of Hispanic assimilation.* New York: Basic Books.

Chavez, R.C. (1995). *Multicultural education in the everyday: A renaissance for the recommitted.* Washington DC: The American Association of Colleges for Teacher Education.

Cohen, N.E., & Pompa, D. (1994). *Multicultural perspectives on quality in early care and education: Culturally-specific practices and universal outcomes.* Manuscript submitted for publication.

Cole, R.W. (1995). *Educating everybody's children: What research and practice say about improving achievement.* Alexandra, VA: Association for Supervision and Curriculum Development.

Crawford, J. (1989). *Bilingual education: History, politics, theory, and practice.* Trenton, NJ: Crane Publishing.

Cummins, J. (1986). Empowering minority students: A framework for intervention. *Harvard Educational Review, 56,* (1), 18-35.

Dueñas González, R. & Melis, I. (2000) *Language ideologies: Critical perspectives on the official English movement.* Urbana, IL: National Council of Teachers of English.

Elam, S. (1972). Acculturation and learning problems of Puerto Rican children. In F. Corradasco & E. Bucchini (Eds.), *The Puerto Rican community and its children on the mainland.* Metuchen, NJ: Scarecrow Press.

Fishman, J. (1989). Bias and anti-intellectualism: The frenzied fiction of "English only." In *Language and Ethnicity in Minority Sociolinguistic Perspective.* London: Multilingual matters.

Garcia, E. (1991). *Education of linguistically and culturally diverse students: Effective instructional practices. Education Report #1.* Washington, DC: Center of Applied Linguistics and the National Center for Research on Cultural Diversity and Second Language Learning.

Garcia, E. (1993). Language, culture and education. In L. Darling-Hammond (Ed.) *Review of research in education* (pp. 51-97). Washington, DC: American Education Research Association.

Garcia, E. (1994). The impact of linguistic and cultural diversity in American schools: A need for new policy. In M.C. Wang & M.C. Reynolds (Eds.),*Making a difference for students at risk* (pp. 156-182). Thousand Oaks, CA: Corwin Press.

Garcia, E. (1997, March). The education of Hispanics in early childhood: Of roots and wings. *Young Children, 52* (3), 5-14.

Garcia, E. (1999). *Understanding and meeting the challenge of student diversity.* Boston: Houghton Mifflin.

Garcia, E. (2001). *The education of Hispanics in the United States: Ra es y alas.* Boulder, CO: Rowen and Littlefield Publishers.

Garcia, E., & Curry, J. (2001) The effects of implementing Proposition 227 in California. *Bilingual Research Journal* (in press).

Garcia, E. & Gonzalez, R. (1995). Issues in systemic reform for culturally and linguistically diverse students. *Teachers College Record, 96*(3), 418-31.

Garcia, E., & Stein, C. B. (1996). Multilingualism in U.S. schools: Treating language as a resource for instruction and parent involvement.*Early Childhood Development and care, 127-128,* 141-155.

Goals 2000: Educate America Act. Pub. No. L. (103-227), 108 Stats. 125 (1994).

Gonzalez, G. (1990). *Chicano education in the segregation era: 1915-1945.* Philadelphia: The Balch Institute.

Hakuta, K., & Gould, L.J. (1987) Synthesis of research on bilingual education.*Educational Leadership, 44*(6), 39-45.

Heath, S.B. (1986). Sociocultural contexts of language development. In California Department of Education, *Beyond language: Social and cultural factors in schooling language minority students* (pp.143-186). Los Angeles: Evaluation, Dissemination, and Assessment Center, California State University.

Kagan, S.L., & Garcia, E. (1991). Educating culturally and linguistically diverse preschoolers: Moving the agenda.*Early Childhood Research Quarterly, 6* (3), 427-444.

Krashen, S. (1996). Is English in trouble?*Multicultural Education, 4*(2), 16-19.

McLaughlin, M.W., & Shepard, L.A. (1995). *Improving Education through Standards-Based Reform. A Report by the National Academy of Education Panel on Standards-Based Education Reform.* Stanford, CA: National Academy of Education.

Moll, L. (1992). Bilingual classroom studies and community analysis: Some recent trends. *Educational Researcher, 21*(2), 20-24.

National Academy for the Education of Young Children (NAEYC). (1996). NAEYC Position Statement: Responding to Linguistic and Cultural Diversity—Recommendations for Effective Early Childhood Education.*Young Children,* p. 12.

National Center for Children in Poverty. (1995).*Five million children: A statistical profile of our poorest young citizens.* New York: Columbia University.

National Commission on Excellence in Education. (1983). *A nation at risk: The imperative for education reform.* Washington, DC: United States Department of Education.

National Council of Teachers of English & International Reading Association. (1996). *Standards for the English language arts.* Urbana, IL & Newark, DE: Authors.

Ogbu, J. (1986). The consequences of the American caste system. In Ulric Neisser (Ed.), *The school achievement of minority children: New perspectives.* (pp. 126-132). Hillsdale, NJ: Erlbaum.

Phillips, D.A., & Cabrera, N.J. (Eds.). (1996). *Beyond the blueprint: directions for research on Head Start's families.* Washington, D.C: National Academy of Sciences.

Ramirez, J.D., Yuen, S.D., Ramey, D.R., & Pasta, D.J. (1991).*Final report: Longitudinal study of structured English immersion strategy, early-exit and late-exit transitional bilingual education programs for language-minority children.* San Mateo, CA: Aguirre International.

Rodriguez, R. (1982). *Hunger of memory: An autobiography.* Boston: D.R. Godine.

Rose, M. (1989). *Lives on the boundary.* New York: The Free Press.

Rossell, C.H. (1992). Nothing matters?: A critique of the Ramirez, et al. longitudinal study of instructional programs for language-minority children.*Bilingual Research Journal: The Journal of the National Association for Bilingual Education, 16*(1-2), 159-186.

Rossell, C., & Baker, K. (1996). The educational effectiveness of bilingual education. *Research in the Teaching of English, 30*(1), 7-74.

Spencer, M.B. (1988). Self-concept development. In D.T. Slaughter (Ed.),*Black children and poverty: A developmental perspective* (pp. 103-116). San Francisco: Jossey-Bass.

Tharp, R.G., & Gallimore, R. (1989). *Challenging cultural minds.* London: Cambridge University Press.

Wong-Fillmore, L. (1991). When learning a second language means loosing a first. *Early Childhood Research Quarterly,6*(3), 323-346.

CHAPTER 6

YOUNG CHILDREN'S LITERACY DEVELOPMENT

Olivia N. Saracho

INTRODUCTION

Reading is a complicated experience that integrates (1) multifaceted maturational achievements such as attention, memory, language and motivation (National Research Council, 1998), and (2) writing and other creative or analytical behaviors that require specific knowledge and skills in different disciplines such as history, physics, or mathematics (Anderson & Pearson, 1984). Reading is a cognitive psycholinguistic and social activity where literacy functions may include reading a listing in a telephone book, a Shakespearean play, and a dissertation on electromagnetic force. A good reader accumulates functional knowledge of the culture's writing system (e.g., the English alphabetic writing system) and features of its orthography; its preparation begins at an early age. Before actually reading, young children learn the parts, products, and purposes of the writing system and the way reading and oral language complement each other and differ from each other (National Research Council, 1998). Reading requires individuals to identify words, interpret their meanings, and know the context of the words' grammatical structure, speech phrasing and intonation, literary forms and devices, and print conventions (National Reading Panel, 2000). Individuals who are good readers usually succeed in society, are highly respected, and become an important individual who contributes social and economic prosperity.

CHILDREN'S EMERGENT LITERACY DEVELOPMENT

Prior to the 1960s, there was limited research of pre-first-grade reading and writing. The emphasis in the 1960s was primarily on the reading readiness paradigm and the general belief was that literacy development did not begin until the child encountered formal instruction in school (Sulzby & Teale, 1986). At that time, studies (e.g., Durkin, 1966) concluded that the paradigm was theoretically and pragmatically inappropriate. In 1967 Clay's (1975) ground-breaking research revealed that there is nothing "that suggests that contact with printed language forms should be withheld from a five-year-old child on the ground that he is immature" (p. 24). According to Sulzby and Teale (1986), literacy development in the past decade has resulted in the following notions:

1. Literacy development begins long before children start formal instruction.
2. The view that reading precedes writing, or vice versa, is a misconception.
3. Literacy develops in "real-life" settings for real-life activities in order to "get things done."
4. The functions of literacy are as integral a part of learning about writing and reading during early childhood as are the forms of literacy.
5. Children are doing critical cognitive work in literacy development during the years from birth to six.
6. Children learn written language through active engagement with their world.

Our world is filled with print. The overflow of print that young children encounter daily serves an elusive but important role in motivating children to learn to read for personal and social purposes. Nowadays preschoolers achieve much more and are inherent and cognizant about print and its functions. In 1958 Hymes suggested that reading "sells itself" to young children, because print messages are "in the limelight" constantly. Everyday living "beats the drums" for literacy as the children's world is flooded with print that is nowhere equivalent to any formal instructional program (Vacca & Vacca, 2000).

Learning to read and write begins long before the school years. Children's literacy concepts are acquired from the earliest years when they notice and interact with readers and writers as well as when they strive to read and write (Sulzby & Teale, 1991). In these circumstances their understanding about literacy develops and is impelled by their existing models of written language. Children's knowledge of these models changes as they ponder language, text, and meaning. Beyond incremental learning, particular modifications in concept reconstructions and points of view are imperative. The magnitude, intensity, and disposition of the children's interest with text define their literacy learning.

Children acquire an extensive complicated and decontextualized understanding of the world as their brains develop during their first years of life. This process varies based on the individuals' biological and experiential influences. Their total developmental pattern can influence development and later literacy development. Components that have an impact on preschool reading include counting number concepts, learning letter names and shapes, possessing a phonological awareness, having an interest in literacy, and cooperating with peers (National Research Council, 1998).

The process begins when very young children understand the idea that one object or incident can represent another (Marzolf & DeLoach, 1994). Becoming aware that the alphabet is a symbol system that relates to sounds, melds into this developmental flow. Mastery in understanding and using symbols steadily grows during the first years of life as children first decipher and formulate first iconic and then graphic depictions.

During ages two and three, children advance from babbling to making comprehensible speech and from seeing print in books to making marks in their attempts to write. By the end of age two or at the beginning of age three, most children make reading-like and drawing-like scribbles and recognizable letters or letter-like forms. Sometimes adults introduce two and three-year-olds to examples of letters and related sounds by using television sources such as *Sesame Street*. Many of these children are in child care settings where teachers and caregivers expose them to patterns of reading and writing (National Research Council, 1998). By the time children are three-years-old, they know that the golden arches "stand for" MacDonald's. Although most three-year-old children can utilize symbols in one situation or realm, they might not be able to implement this mastery across all situations and realms without distinctive rehearsal. Young children also begin to understand the way symbols operate including: (1) both hash marks and numerals to depict numerical information, (2) the difference between numerals and letters, (3) difference between the way letters function in their own and their friends' written names, and (4) making the letters correspond with the sounds within words).

Orthographic development supports the complexity and consistency of children's mental models (Ehri, 1991; Gough & Juel, 1991). Children become aware of visual symbols when they understand that written language is composed of letters that represent speech sounds. Even when children know the spellings of words, they need to generate more advanced knowledge to understand the meaning in a text in relation to pictures and secluded words. They need to blend their thinking to the nature of a word, sentence, paragraph, and text structures. This kind of knowledge relies on the individual's experience, exploration, and particular abstract intuition.

Simultaneously children compose many different texts and display miscellaneous types of systems of writing. Read (1971) and Chomsky (1975) show that young children's initial attempts to write indicate that their untutored spellings demonstrate an analysis of phonetic and phonological speech. Clay (1975) provides some insight into the way children develop their writing skills during the early years. She describes young children's early nonconventional writings. Clay (1975) describes the irrational scribbles and nonphonetic letter sequences in children's writing. Saracho (1990) documents the development of the children's writing perception and explores the potential features related to the differentiation process. Levels for each developmental level include (1) aimless scribbling, (2) horizontal movement, (3) separate symbol units, (4) letters written with incorrect form, and (5) correct spelling of first name. Spodek and Saracho (1994) summarized these levels:

> *Level 1—Aimless Scribbling:* Children attempt to write their name by moving the writing tool on the paper. Using their arms and hands, they make longitudinal and circular motions. Many times they draw a picture instead of writing their name.
>
> *Level 2—Horizontal Movement:* The children's marks on paper have a considerable tendency toward the horizontal and some systematic "up and down" squiggling. They make hasty scribbling in an up and down motion progressing across the page. Subjects attempt to imitate the adult's manner in rapid cursive writing.
>
> *Level 3—Separate Symbol Units:* Though horizontal movement (with greater regularity in the vertical strokes) still exists, children have a tendency to make discrete symbol units, some of which are scarcely recognizable as letters.
>
> *Level 4—Incorrect Written Letters:* Letters are written incorrectly. The waviness in imitation of adult cursive writing is almost absent. Most letter units are recognizable. There is more construction in space. Subjects have discovered separate letter units and have developed an interest in writing those letter symbols.
>
> *Level 5—Correct Spelling of First Name:* A mixture of correct and incorrect letters appear in this level. Correct spelling of the first name is seen (p. 324).

These levels should be considered as estimates of competencies rather than a reflection of developmental stages. Variations for each child for the different levels reflects in part their writing developmental patterns.

Children have an interest in the writing process and question its process. During their development they attempt to imitate the adults' writing activities. Such attempts to correct their writing in a literate atmosphere rely on the children's learning capability, interest in the writing process, level of writing maturation, and writing experiences. Young children conform to the characteristics that they communicate about print including linearity and recursive characteristics. Read (1975) demonstrates how chil-

dren at these ages have already developed conceptual categories for conso-
nant and vowel sounds in spoken English that are linguistically sound and
underlie the invented spellings in children's writing.

These writing behaviors indicate that young children are aware of the
relationship between print and language. This procedure suggests that
young children misinterpret the specific nature of this relationship. Young
children's remarks when they read while they write usually indicate they
are solving the written language puzzle. Saracho and Spodek (1996) found
that children have their own concepts about writing.

> *Maria* likes to write because she likes to make words, but she knows that
> some children would rather play than write. She likes to use mark-
> ers and some of the things she likes to do to write when not told to,
> are to draw pictures, make a plane, and write numbers and letters.
>
> *Steve* likes to write in order to learn how to write his name and those of
> other members of his family. He also thinks that some children
> would rather play than write. He prefers pens to pencils because
> they "write pretty." He like to draw a house with boys playing with a
> small dog and its mother. He does not like to be told what to write.
>
> *Flora* likes to write because all children like to write because they like to
> work in school. She likes to use markers because they come in all
> colors. She likes to draw a picture of a clown and prefers to be able
> to write what she wants to, not what a teacher tells her to write. But
> teachers can help because "they know what to do."

When children are three- and four-years-old, they experiment with writing by constructing scribbles, random strings of letters, and letter-like
forms. Several children start to associate noticeable sounds within words,
while several four-year-olds can write using invented spelling with initial
consonants. Such children have played with toys and manipulatives that
have letters, numerals, and playful indications of letter sounds and other
symbol systems. *Sesame Street* on television and CD-ROMS also support useful assistance with letters, sounds, word, and text levels; whereas children at
this age usually manage the duplication of these stimuli using VCRs and
computers (National Research Council, 1998; Saracho & Spodek, 1996,
1998).

When children are regularly read to, they usually "read" their favorite
books by engaging in oral language-like and written language-like acts
(Sulzby & Teale, 1991). Most three- and four-year-old children display
emergent reading practices such as reading pictures and periodically con-
spicuous print like the one found in illustrations or labels. Some young
children start to notice the print in the dominant body of the text, while
others make the transition into traditional reading using their favorite
books (Jackson, 1991). Later most children identify and discuss items in
pictures, relate actions in pictures, enter in occasional question-and-answer

conversation and/or formulate voices for characters in pictures (Kader-avek & Sulzby, 1998a, 1998b; Sulzby & Kaderavek, 1996).

At all ages children need to experience literacy activities that foster reading and writing. These activities must help children to differentiate between print and non-print to advance their understanding of the letters of the alphabet and their sounds. Activities should encourage them to invent symbols and messages and acquire English literacy practices (e.g., left to right and top to bottom progression, apply capitalization and punctuation).

Children need to be provided with activities and materials that relate to relevant instruction. Examples of these activities and materials include books on tape, puppet theaters; computer-based reading, writing, and storybook activities; board games; activity sheets; children's magazines; and all manner of individual and group projects. In addition, literacy strategies that incorporate the children's interests and concentration should be used. The National Research Council (1998, p. 189) suggests the following activities:

- Oral language activities for fostering growth in receptive and expressive language and verbal reasoning.
- Reading aloud with children to foster their appreciation and comprehension of text and literacy language,
- Reading and book exploration by children for developing print and concepts and basic reading knowledge and processes.
- Writing activities for developing children's personal appreciation of the communicative dimensions of print and for exercising printing and spelling abilities,
- Thematic activities (e.g., sociodramatic play) for giving children opportunity to integrate and extend their understanding of stories and new knowledge of spaces,
- Print-directed activities for establishing children's ability to recognize and print the letters of the alphabet,
- Phonemic analysis activities for developing children's phonological and phonemic awareness, and
- Word-directed activities for helping children to acquire a basic sight vocabulary and to understand and appreciate the alphabetic principle.

At first glance, children seem to be playing and exploring in most of these activities. However, they are engaged in intense work in their language and literacy learning.

The National Research Council (1998) identified a set of particular accomplishments that the successful literacy learner typically display during the preschool and kindergarten years (see Table 1). Research suggests

TABLE 1
Developmental Accomplishments of Literacy Acquisition

Birth to Three-Year-Old Accomplishments

- Recognize specific books by cover.
- Pretends to read books.
- Understands that books are handled in particular ways.
- Enters into a book-sharing routine with primary caregivers.
- Vocalization play in crib gives way to enjoyment of rhyming language, nonsense word play, etc.
- Labels objects in books.
- Comments on characters in books.
- Looks at picture in book and realizes it is a symbol for real object.
- Listens to stories.
- Requests/commands adult to read or write.
- May begin attending to specific print such as letters in names.
- Uses increasingly purposive scribbling.
- Occasionally seems to distinguish between drawing and writing.
- Produces some letter-like forms and scribbles with some features of English writing.

Three- and Four-Year-Old Accomplishments

- Knows that alphabet letters are a special category of visual graphics that can be individually names.
- Recognizes local environmental print.
- Knows that it is the print that is read in stories.
- Understands that different text forms are used for different functions of print (e.g., list for groceries).
- Uses new vocabulary and grammatical constructions in own speech.
- Understands and follows oral directions.
- Is sensitive to some sequences of events in stories.
- Shows interest in books and reading.
- When being read a story, connects information and events to life experiences.
- Questions and comments demonstrate understanding of literal meaning of story being told.
- Displays reading and writing attempts, calling attention to self: "Look at my story."
- Can identify 10 alphabet letters, especially those from own name.
- "Writes" (scribbles) message as part of playful activity.
- May begin to attend to beginning or rhyming sound in salient words.

Kindergarten Accomplishments

- Knows the parts of a book and their functions
- "Reads" familiar texts emergently, i.e., not necessarily verbatim from the print alone.
- Recognizes and can name all uppercase and lowercase letters.

(continued)

TABLE 1
Continued

Kindergarten Accomplishments

- Understands that the sequence of letters in a written word represents the sequence of sounds (phonemes) in a spoken word (alphabetic principle).
- Learns many, though not all, one-to-one letter sound correspondences.
- Recognizes some words by sight, including a few very common ones (a, the, I, my, you, is are).
- Uses new vocabulary and grammatical constructions in own speech.
- Makes appropriate switches from oral to written language situations.
- Notices when simple sentences fail to make sense.
- Connects information and events in texts to life and life to text experiences.
- Retells, reenacts, or dramatizes stories or parts of stories.
- Listens attentively to books teacher reads to class.
- Can name some book titles and authors.
- Demonstrates familiarity with a number of types or genres of text (e.g., storybooks, expository texts, poems, newspapers, and everyday print such as signs, notices, labels).
- Correctly answers questions about stories read aloud.
- Makes predictions based on illustrations or portions of stories.
- Demonstrates understanding that spoken words consist of a sequences of phonemes.
- Given spoken sets like "dan, dan, den" can identify the first two as being the same and the third as different.
- Given spoken sets like "dak, pat, zen" can identify the first two as sharing a same sound.
- Given spoken segments can merge them into a meaningful target word.
- Given a spoken word can produce another word that rhymes with it.
- Independently writes many uppercase and lower case letters.
- Uses phonemic awareness and letter knowledge to spell independently (invented or creative spelling).
- Writes (unconventionally) to express own meaning.
- Builds a repertoire of some conventionally spelled words.
- Shows awareness of distinction between "kid writing" and conventional orthography.
- Writes own name (first and last) and the first names of some friends or classmates.
- Can write most letters and some words when they are dictated.

Source: National Research Council (1998). Preventing reading difficulties in young children. Washington, DC: National Academy of Sciences.

that this index is neither complete nor disputable, but it does provide most of the focal points of the children's literacy acquisition.

TRANSITION FROM EMERGENT LITERACY TO FORMAL READING

Young children usually begin as readers well before they are provided with formal reading instruction. When they attend school, they join a group that is expected to follow routines and structures. During the first school year, the children's experience in this environment has an enduring effect on their school performance (Alexander & Entwisle, 1996; Pianta & McCoy, 1997).

Knowledgeable teachers throughout the United States state that children bring to school a unique background, set of experiences, and set of abilities (Vacca & Vacca, 2000). Many kindergarten children have attended group settings for three and four years; few are attending school for the first time. They also vary in ability levels and classes include children with identified disabilities and children with exceptional abilities as well as children who are independent readers or who only now are beginning to acquire some basic literacy knowledge and skills. Kindergarten children could vary in the language they speak and/or their range of language proficiency. Many distinct experiential differences are usually found within a kindergarten classroom in relation to children's literacy-related skills and functioning. According to Riley (1996), "What this means is that some kindergartners may have the skills characteristic of the typical three-year-old, while others might be functioning at the level of the typical eight-year-old" (pp. 4-5). In teaching reading and writing teachers need to use a developmentally appropriate approach to every child even in the primary grades.

In 1998 the International Reading Association (IRA) and the National Association of the Education of Young Children (NAEYC) adopted a position statement on young children's literacy development. This position statement proposed a continuum of children's literacy development, taking into consideration that children at any age could perform at in stage along the continuum. The continuum of children's literacy development embodies the following progression of apparent stages (Vacca & Vacca, 2000).

1. *Awareness and Exploration Stage* is initiated at birth and advances through the children's preschool years. In constructing the groundwork for learning to read and write, young children observe their environment and inquire about print and print-related activities (e.g., listening and discussing stories). In this stage, young children (1) discover that print communicates a message; (2) display logographic knowledge when they specify environmental print such as

labels, signs, cereal boxes, and other kinds of print; (3) pretend to read; (4) make marks (such as assorted shapes of scribbling and writing expressions) in an intent to write; (5) relate some letters to their speech sound; and (6) print letters or estimations of letters to characterize the written language.

2. *Experimental Reading and Writing Stage* usually occurs in kindergarten when young children become aware of and explore spoken and written language. At this time, they (1) understand the basic concepts of print (such as left-to-right progression and top-to-bottom direction); (2) enjoy listening to others read; (3) embark in sustained reading and writing experiences; (4) prevail in letter-recognition and letter-sound relationships; (5) engage in rhyming experiences; and (6) initiate the writing of alphabet letters and high-frequency words.

3. *Early Reading and Writing Stage* generally develops in first grade when teachers initiate formal reading instruction. At this stage, young children initiate (1) reading simple stories; (2) writing about topics that they know and are of interest to them; (3) reading and retelling familiar stories; (4) the acquisition of comprehension strategies; (5) accelerating their knowledge of letter-sound patterns to achieve accurate word identification skills; (6) their ability to read with fluency and recognize an extensive amount of sight words; (6) becoming knowledgeable about grammar (including punctuation, capitalization) when they maintain their writing about topics that are personally meaningful to them.

4. *Transitional Reading and Writing Stage* occurs by second grade when young children initiate their transition from their early stages in reading and writing to engaging in more advanced literacy tasks. At this stage, young children (1) read with extensive fluency; (2) skillfully apply cognitive and metacognitive strategies in reading and writing; (3) display an expanding skill in all reading and writing components (e.g., word identification skills, sight word recognition, reading fluency, sustained silent reading, conventional spelling, proofreading).

5. *Independent and Productive Stage* usually occurs in third grade when young children mature into independent and productive readers and writers. At this stage, young children (1) read and write gracefully based on their purpose and audience, (2) continue to develop as readers and writers, and (3) broaden and enhance their literacy skills and strategies.

Young children usually experience the beginning of formal reading instruction between the ages of five and seven. Many five-year-olds with rich literacy experiences immediately develop their literacy skills. Young children begin to develop reading knowledge and skills long before they are challenged with the difficult task of decoding print. Some of these children may begin be memorizing and identifying some sight words. According to Hiebert (1994), young children need rich literacy experiences prior to attending school. Even in the early literacy stages they can apply their knowledge of language, literature, and the world by finding a number of ways of handling a text. They are able to coordinate their own reading experiences and use their own reading skills and knowledge (National Reading Panel, 2000).

Young children learn the features and forms of written language by exploring print as a cultural object (Ferreiro & Teberosky, 1983). Studies on how children learn the features and forms of written language have contributed substantially to our growing understanding of the early stages of literacy development. The context or situation-of-use of written language serves to make encounters with print meaningful (Goodman, 1986; Harste, Woodward, & Burke, 1984). Gardner (1983) notes that "children acquire skills through observation and participation in the contexts in which these skills are customarily invoked. In contrast, in the standard classroom, teachers talk, often presenting material in abstract symbolic form and relying on inanimate media such as books and diagrams in order to convey information" (p. 357). By failing to fully draw upon what Gardner (1983) refers to as multiple intelligence, schools fail to use the types of experiences that contribute to the emergence of literacy in children in non-school settings.

Emergent literacy places children in the position of active learners, problem-solvers and meaning makers. In contrast to reading readiness theories, emergent literacy recognizes that early literacy behaviors and knowledge are not pre-anything (Sulzby & Teale, 1986). There is much research to suggest that environment affects children's literacy interactions, explorations, expressions and behaviors. According to Chambliss and McKillop (2000), "Having a collection of well-chosen materials within a reading community can have an impact on children's engagement and achievement" (p. 104).

Preschool programs based on an emerging literacy philosophy provide a variety of print-related experiences for their students (Watson, Layton, Pierce, & Abrams, 1994). Purposeful interactions with print and story-related activities are important in developing emergent writing and oral language skills (International Reading Association, 1986).

The National Research Council (1998) concludes from research findings with preschoolers that (a) adult-child shared book reading that stimulates verbal interaction can enhance language (especially vocabulary) development and knowledge bout concepts of print, and (b) activities that direct young children's attention to the sound structure within spoken words (e.g., play with songs and poems that emphasize rhyming, jokes, and games that depend on switching sounds within words), and to the relationship between print and speech can facilitate learning to read. These findings suggest that knowledge of word meanings, an understanding that print conveys meaning, phonological awareness, and some understanding of how printed letters relate to the sounds of language contribute directly to successful reading. Other preschool skills (i.e., identifying letters, numbers, shapes, colors) usually link with future reading achievement, although neither research literacy outcomes nor theories show a relationship to learning to read.

DEVELOPMENTALLY APPROPRIATE LITERACY PRACTICES

The concept of developmentally appropriate practice implies that the curriculum match young children's learning developmental levels (Bredekamp & Copple, 1997; Schickedanz, 1998). Children need to engage in a creative learning process and the construction of knowledge. From a developmental point of view, children, as learners, are considered to have developing abilities. Most children are able to acquire these abilities informally, although some children who enroll in school may lack the necessary abilities to read and write at the same proficiency level. Consequently, individual differences among children must be considered in designing initial literacy experiences (Vacca & Vacca, 2000).

Preprimary children differ physically, emotionally, socially, and intellectually from children in other age groups (Saracho, 1993b). In relation to their literacy development, the initial interface with a language and literacy curriculum in the school should be related to their level of emergent literacy. Young children need to "try out" literacy at their own pace by exploring and experimenting with print (Vacca & Vacca, 2000). They need a reading program that reflects their characteristics and takes into account how they come to know and understand concepts and relationships through active experiences and explorations (Eheart & Leavitt, 1985). Such a reading program can develop literacy-oriented behaviors which facilitate initial reading instruction (Saracho, 1987). Initial reading instruction takes place in literacy environments that promote children's play development (Neuman & Roskos, 1992). In such an environment, young children use objects (e.g., paper, pencil, books) and events (e.g., a bedtime story) to obtain meaning from print. The focus of the natural contexts or enhanced literacy environments is the implicit practice of reading, writing, speaking, listening, and knowing. Process, product, and content are fused and the purposeful use of language is stressed over skill acquisition (Saracho, 1993b) in a play environment.

PLAY: EXPRESSION AND LITERACY

Play has always been an important part of early childhood programs. It supports the social, emotional, physical, and cognitive development of children, since all areas of development are influenced by play. Play gives children an opportunity to express their ideas and feelings as well as to symbolize and test their knowledge of the world. This is needed for all children, especially for those at risk who are not progressing at the rate of their age peers within our educational system. While much of the education of children at risk is concerned with providing direct support for academic and pre-academic learning, play should not be denied its rightful place in their education. In fact, an integrated classroom provides the ideal support for play-learning activities.

Play is intrinsically motivated, is performed for its own sake, and is conducted in a relaxed way to produce positive effects. Play is free from concern with end products. Interference with the spontaneity of play can destroy its essential character. Vygotsky (1967) states that play is invented at the point when unrealizable tendencies appear in development and that children's play must always be interpreted as the imaginary and illusory realization of unrealizable desires.

One form of play is symbolic or sociodramatic play, which children develop between the ages of two and four (Reynolds, 1987). Vygotsky (1967) contends that symbolic play creates the zone of proximal development for preschool-aged children, which in essence is educational pedagogy set appropriately in advance of the children's development. Vygotsky states that children's play is a result of a conflict between their desires and their inability to meet them because of societal constraints. Assuming that sociodramatic play is beneficial to children to "realize their unrealizable desires," what is needed to establish and expand play in the preschool classroom requires a captivating environment, a physical arrangement that facilitates play, and props that are simple, fairly realistic, and durable (Woodward, 1984). Research studies suggest that preschoolers who spend more time at sociodramatic play are advanced in general intellectual development and have an enhanced ability to understand the feelings of others (Berk, 1994).

Play is an essential activity for young children. Through play, young children develop a wide range of verbal and nonverbal communication skills. They also learn about their playmates' feelings and attitudes, and learn to accept their classmates' points of view (Saracho, 1985). The socialization aspects of play helps them learn to get along with others. Play helps young children learn about their social world as they play different roles, express their ideas and feelings and negotiate social relationships with their peers. Play also helps them to gain information, developing and testing ideas to expand their knowledge (Spodek & Saracho, 1998).

Children's play must be planned to offer a supporting environment, making sure that enough materials and equipment are available, extending the children's play, and encouraging positive relations among children.

LITERACY AND PLAY

Play can be used as a curricular tool in emergent literacy. According to Vygotsky (1978) play assumes a major role in literacy development. Play environments stimulate the development of literacy behaviors in young children. Over the last decade, play has been used as a rich contextual setting for observing emerging literacy behaviors (Galda, Pellegrini, & Cox, 1989; Jacob, 1984; Pellegrini, 1985b; Rowe, 1989; Schrader, 1989). Changes in the structural, literature-based features of the play environment may have important consequences for children's emerging conceptions of literacy (Morrow, 1992; Neuman & Roskos, 1992).

In play-based instruction children are helped to consider incidents as they dramatize their own meaning (Galda, 1984; Smilansky, 1968). Environments that offer the opportunity for choice, control, and appropriate levels of challenge can simplify the development of self-regulated, intentional learning (Turner & Paris, 1995). Concurrently, one purpose of sociodramatic play is to develop oral language use. Children interact and utilize new language when they design, mediate, create, and communicate the "script" of their play (Levy, Wolfgang, & Koorland, 1992). In addition, children rehearse verbal and narrative proficiency that are critical to their development of reading comprehension (Gentile & Hoot, 1983).

Play sessions lasting about 20-30 minutes are considered essential for children to develop the detailed scripts that affect the premeditated use of literacy in dramatic play (Christie et al., 1988). Also, children write more recurrently whey they are provided with appropriate materials such as paper, markers, pencils, and stamp pads (Morrow & Rand, 1991; Neuman & Roskos, 1992; Schrader, 1989; Vukelich, 1990). In addition, the teacher needs to take part and assist children to merge literacy materials into their play (Himley, 1986; Morrow & Rand, 1991). Vukelich (1994) show the importance of providing children with opportunities to play in a print-rich center with literacy-related guidance from their teacher. When later tested on their recognition of print these children were able to recognize words, even when presented in a list without the graphics and context of the play environment.

According to the National Research Council (1998, p. 184), kindergarten teachers can facilitate language and literacy development through play-based literacy instruction if they:

- allow enough time and space for play in the classroom,
- provide the needed material resources,
- develop children's background knowledge for the play setting,
- scaffold the rehearsals of dramatic retellings, and
- become involved in play settings as to guide the children's attention and learning through modeling and interaction.

Children need experiences with the written language to understand the functions of written language. Jacob (1984) describes emerging functions of written language in the play of Puerto Rican kindergarten children. In this study, children pretend to construct and use shopping lists, buy goods with food stamps, and get prescriptions from a doctor.

The environment or physical arrangement of the classroom is an important dimension of sociodramatic play (Woodard, 1984). Within the sociodramatic environment, Roskos (1988) reports how children use reading and writing to legitimize their pretend play, to express themselves, and to record information within play events. Children's literacy behaviors can emerge in a play setting where they acquire knowledge of functions and features of print in early literacy development. As children play, they may demonstrate constructive hypotheses about written language as a "sense-making" activity. Furthermore, they can become "meaning makers" in their literacy-enriched environments (Wells, 1986).

Early childhood programs involve young children as active learners by providing them with play experiences that enable them to develop and accumulate their own knowledge. When young children join their peers in dramatic play, they assume and act out a role, usually in relationship to their classmates who are playing other roles. Such informal dramatic play situations usually represent the children's life experiences. This form of play assists children to discover and understand the real world. In cognitive play, children create objects and roles. Although they may use an object as a symbol, they know the original identity and purpose of the object (Saracho, 1993a). Young children ease into writing in much the same manner. They use a writing tool to imitate the writing of adults who are in their environment (Saracho, 1993b).

Studies show that children engage in reading and writing activities through play (Jacob, 1984; Pellegrini, 1985a; Roskos, 1988). Literacy interactions in a play environment can facilitate and support the development of young children's acquisition of literacy (Strickland & Morrow, 1989). Play environments that foster literacy should consider the children's interests. According to Ferreiro and Teberosky (1983), "it is absurd to imagine that four- or five-year-old children growing up in an urban environment that displays print everywhere . . . do not develop any ideas about this cultural object until they find themselves in front of a teacher" (p. 12). Saracho and Spodek (1998) show how family members can interact with their children to support and extend the child's literacy development through play. Family members can use literacy-play materials to encourage family-child interactions during reading and through playfully using concrete literacy objects from the home environment. Their study shows how family members can use strategies and activities that integrate play and literacy, including reading stories, telling stories, listening to children's stories, engaging children in predicting sequence in stories, expanding the children's vocabulary based on the stories, using puppets to retell stories, reading poetry, dramatizing stories, discussing stories, writing stories, and interacting about stories. Neuman and Roskos' (1989) classroom study supports these results. In examining the common functions of reading and writing in two preschools, they show that children exhibit a broad range of uses of literacy on their own and with others in five functional domains: they used literacy (1) to explore their environment, (2) to interact with others, (3) to express themselves, (4) to authenticate events, and (5) to transact with text.

Changes in the structural features of the play environment that are literacy based may have important consequences for children's emerging concepts of literacy (Neuman & Roskos, 1992). This relates to the general aim of this review: the premise that play can be used as a curricular tool to support and influence literacy development. When children engage in literacy-related play experiences, they select and use abilities that are essential for literacy learning in a social context. In fact, play may be an important resource for children to explore their developing conceptions of the functions and features of print in the preschool years.

REFERENCES

Alexander, J., & Entwisle, D. (1996). Schools and children at risk. In A. Booth & J. Dunn (Eds.) *Family-school links: How do they affect educational outcomes?* (pp. 67-88). Hillsdale, NJ: Erlbaum.

Anderson, R.C., & Pearson, P.D. (1984). A schema-thematic view of basic processes in reading comprehension. In P.D. Pearson, R. Barr, M.L. Kamil, & P. Mosenthal (Eds.), *Handbook of reading research* (pp. 255-291). New York: Longman.

Berk, L. (1994). Vygotsky's theory: The importance of make-believe play. *Young Children, 50*(1), 30-39.

Bredekamp, S., & Copple, C. (Eds.) (1997). *Developmentally appropriate practice in early childhood programs* (rev. ed.). Washington, DC: National Association for the Education of Young Children.

Chambliss, M.J., & McKillop, A.M. (2000). Creating a print- and technology-rich classroom library to entice children to read. In L. Baker, M.J. Dreher, & J.T. Guthrie (Eds.) *Engaging young readers: Promoting achievement and motivation* (pp. 94-118). New York: The Guildford Press.

Christie, J.F. et al. (1988). The effects of play period duration on children's play patterns. *Journal of Research in Childhood Education, 3*(2), 123-131.

Chomsky, C. (1972). Stages in language development and reading exposure. *Harvard Educational Review, 42*, 1-33.

Clay, M.M. (1975). *What did I write?* Aukland, NZ: Heinemann.

Durkin, D. (1966). *Children who read early: Two longitudinal studies.* New York: Teachers College Press.

Eheart, B.K., & Leavitt, R.L. (1985). Supporting toddler play. *Young Children, 40*(3), 18-22.

Ehri, L.C. (1991). Learning to read and spell words. In L. Rieben & C.A. Perfectti (Eds.), *Learning to read: Basic research and its implications* (pp. 57-73). Hillsdale, NJ: Erlbaum.

Ferreiro, E., & Teberosky, A. (1983). *Literacy before schooling.* Portsmouth, NH: Heinemann.

Galda, L. (1984). Narrative competence: Play, storytelling, and story comprehension. In A. D. Pellegrini & T.D. Yawkey (Eds.) *The development of oral and written language in social contexts.* Norwood, NJ: Ablex.

Galda, L., Pellegrini, A.D., & Cox, S. (1989, March).*A short-term longitudinal study of preschoolers' emergent literacy.* Paper presented at the American Educational Research Association Conference, San Francisco, CA.

Gardner, H. (1983). *Frames of mind: The theory of multiple intelligence.* New York: Basic Books.

Gentile, L.M., & Hoot, J.L. (1983). Kindergarten play: The foundation of reading. *The Reading Teacher, 36,* 46-49.

Goodman, Y. (1986). Children coming to know literacy. In W. Teale & E. Sulzby (Eds.), *Emergent literacy* (pp. 1-14). Norwood, NJ: Ablex.

Gough, P.B., & Juel, C. (1991). The first stages of word recognition. In L. Rieben & C.A. Perfectti (Eds.), *Learning to read: Basic research and its implications* (pp. 47-56). Hillsdale, NJ: Lawrence Erlbaum & Associates.

Harste, J., Woodward, V., & Burke, C. (1984). *Language stories & literacy lessons.* Portsmouth, NH: Heinemann.

Hiebert, E. (1994). Becoming literate through authentic tasks: Evidence and adaptations. In R.B. Ruddell, M.R. Ruddell, & H. Singer (Eds).*Theoretical models and processes of reading* (4th ed., pp. 391-413). Newark, DE: International Reading Association.

Himley, M. (1986). Genre as generative: One perspective on ones child's early writing growth. In M. Nystrand (Ed.) *The structure of written communication: Studies in reciprocity between writers and readers.* Orlando, FL: Academic Press.

International Reading Association. (1986). *Literacy development and pre-first grade.* Newark, DE: Author.

International Reading Association [IRA] & National Association of the Education of Young Children [NAEYC]. (1998).Learning to read and write: Developmentally appropriate practices for young children. *The Reading Teacher, 52,* 193-216.

Jacob, E. (1984). Learning literacy through play: Puerto Rican kindergarten children. In H. Goelman, A. Oberg, & F. Smith (Eds.),*Awakening to literacy.* Exeter, NH: Heinemann.

Jackson, N.E. (1991). Precocious reading in English: Origin, structure and predictive significance. In A.J. Tannenbaum & P. Klein (Eds), *To be young and gifted.* Norwood, NJ: Ablex.

Kaderavek, J., & Sulzby, E. (1998a). Emergent literacy issues for children with language impairment. In L.R. Watson, T.L. Layton, & E.R. Crais (Eds.).*Handbook of early language impairments in children, Vol. II: Assessment and treatment.* New York: Delmar.

Kaderavek, J., & Sulzby, E. (1998b). Parent-child joint book reading. An observation protocol for young children. *American Journal of Speech-language Pathology.*

Levy, A.K., Wolfgang, C.H., & Koorland, M.A. (1992). sociodramatic play as a method for enhancing the language performance of kindergarten-age students. *Early Childhood Research Quarterly (Special Issue: Research on Kindergarten, 7,* 245-262.

Marzolf, D.P., & DeLoach, J.S. (1994). Transfers in young children's understanding of spatial representation. *Child Development, 65,* 1-15.

Morrow, L.M. (1992). The impact of literature-based program on literacy achievement, use of literature, and attitudes of children from minority backgrounds. *Reading Research Quarterly, 27,* 250-275.

Morrow, L.M., & Rand, M.K. (1991). Promoting literacy during play by designing early childhood classroom environments. *Reading Teacher, 44,* 396-402.

National Research Council. (1998). *Preventing reading difficulties in young children.* Washington, DC: National Academy of Sciences.

National Reading Panel. (2000). *Teaching children to read: An evidence-based assessment of the scientific research literature on reading and its implications for reading instructions.* Bethesda, MD: The National Reading Panel.

Neuman, S.B., & Roskos, K. (1989). Preschoolers' conceptions of literacy as reflected in their spontaneous play. In S. McCormick & J. Zutell (Eds.), *Cognitive and social perspectives for literacy research and instruction* (pp. 87-94). Chicago: National Reading Conference.

Neuman, S.B., & Roskos, K. (1992). Literacy objects as cultural tools: Effects on children's literacy behaviors in play. *Reading Research Quarterly, 27,* 203-225.

Pellegrini, A.D. (1985a). Relations between preschool children's symbolic play and literate behavior. In L. Galda & A. Pellegrini (Eds.), *Play, language and stories* (pp. 79-97). Norwood, NJ: Ablex.

Pellegrini, A. (1985b). The relationship between symbolic play and literate behavior: A review and critique of the empirical literature. *Review of Educational Research, 55*(1), 107-121.

Pianta, R.C., & McCoy, S.J. (1997).The first day of school: The predictive validity of early school screening. *Journal of Applied Developmental Psychology, 18,* 1-22.

Read, C. (1971). Preschool children's knowledge of English phonology. *Harvard Educational Review, 41,* 1-34.

Read, C. (1975) . *Children's categorization of speech sounds in English: Research Report No. 17.* Urbana, IL: National Council of Teachers of English.

Reynolds, G. (1987). When I was little I used to play a lot. In *51st yearbook of the Claremont Reading Conference* (pp 151-164), Claremont, CA: Claremont Graduate School.

Riley, J.L. (1996). The ability to label the Letters of the alphabet at school entry: A discussion on its value. *Journal of Research in Reading, 19*(2), 87-10.

Roskos, K. (1988). Literacy at work in play. *The Reading Teacher, 55,* 107-121.

Rowe, D.W. (1989). Preschoolers' use of metacognitive knowledge and strategies in self-selected literacy events. In S. McCormick & J. Zutell (Eds.), *Cognitive and social perspectives for literacy research and instruction* (pp. 65-76). Chicago: National Reading Conference.

Saracho, O.N. (1985). Young children's play behaviors and cognitive styles. *Early Child Development and Care, 21*(4), 1-18.

Saracho, O.N. (1987). Evaluating reading attitudes. *Day Care and Early Education, 14,* 23-25.

Saracho, O.N. (1990). Developmental sequences in three-year-old children's writing. *Early Child Development and Care, 56,* 1-10.

Saracho, O.N. (1990). Teaching young children: The teachers' function in the early childhood curriculum. *Early Child Development and Care, 61,* 57-63.

Saracho, O.N. (1993a). A factor analysis of young children's play.*Early Child Development and Care, 84,* 91-102.

Saracho, O.N. (1993b). Literacy Development: The Whole Language Approach. In B. Spodek & O. N. Saracho (Eds.) *Yearbook of early childhood education: Early childhood language and literacy* (Vol. 4, pp. 42-59). New York: Teachers College Press.

Saracho, O.N., & Spodek, B. (1996). Literacy activities in a play environment.*International Journal of Early Childhood Education, 1,* 7-19.

Saracho, O.N., & Spodek, B. (1998). A play foundation for family literacy.*International Journal of Educational Research, 29,* 41-50.

Schickedanz, J. (1998). What is developmentally appropriate practice in early literacy? Considering the alphabet. In S. Neumann & K.A. Roskos (Eds.),*Children achieving: Best practices in early literacy.* Newark, DE: International Reading Association.

Schrader, C. (1989). Written language use within the context of young children's symbolic play. *Early Childhood Research Quarterly, 4,* 225-244.

Schrader, C. (1990). Symbolic play as a curricular tool for early literacy development. *Early Childhood Research Quarterly, 5,* 79-103.

Smilansky, S. (1968). *The effects of sociodramatic play on disadvantaged school children.* New York: Wiley.

Spodek, B., & Saracho, O.N. (1994). *Right from the start: Teaching children ages three to eight.* Boston: Allyn & Bacon.

Spodek, B., & Saracho, O.N. (1998). The challenge of educational play. In D. Bergen (Ed.), *Play as a medium for learning and development* (pp. 11-28). Olney, MD: Association for Childhood Education International.

Strickland, D., & Morrow, L. (1989). Environments rich in print promote literacy behavior during play. *The Reading Teacher, 43,* 178-179.

Sulzby, E., & Kaderavek, J. (1996). Parent-child language during storybook reading and toy play contexts: Case studies of normally developing and specific language impaired (SLI) children. *National Reading Conference Yearbook, 37,* 95-106.

Sulzby, E., & Teale, W.H. (Eds.). (1986).*Emergent literacy: Writing and reading.* Norwood, NJ: Ablex.

Sulzby, W., & Teale, W.H. (1991). Emergent literacy. In P.D. Pearson, R. Barr, M.L. Kamil, & P. Mosenthal (Eds.) *Handbook of reading research* (pp. 727-757). New York: Longman.

Turner, J., & Paris, S.G. (1995). How literacy tasks influence children's motivation for literacy. *Reading Teacher, 48,* 662-673.

Vacca, R.T., & Vacca, J.L. (2000).*Reading and learning to read.* New York: Longman.

Vukelich, C. (1990). Where's the paper? Literacy during dramatic lay. *Childhood Education, 66(4),* 205-209.

Vukelich, C. (1994). Effects of play interventions on young children's reading of environmental print. *Early Childhood Research Quarterly, 9,* 153-170.

Vygotsky, L.S. (1967). Play and its role in the mental development of the child. *Soviet Psychology, 5*(3), 6-18.

Vygotsky, L. (1978). *Mind in society: The development of higher psychological processes.* [M. Call, V. John-Steiner, S. Scribner, & E. Souberman, Eds.] Cambridge, MA: Harvard University Press.

Watson, L.R., Layton, T.L., Pierce, P.L., & Abraham, L.M. (1994). Enhancing emerging literacy in a language preschool. *Language, speech and hearing services in schools, 25,* 136-145.

Wells, G. (1986). *The meaning makers.* Portsmouth, NH: Heinemann.

Woodard, C.Y. (1984). Guidelines for facilitating sociodramatic play.*Childhood Education, 60*(3), 172-177.

CHAPTER 7

DEVELOPMENTS IN YOUNG CHILDREN'S MATHEMATICAL REASONING

Joe Becker and Daniel Miltner

ABSTRACT

Both the National Council of Teachers of Mathematics (NCTM, 2000) and the National Association for the Education of Young Children (NAEYC, 1997) link educational practice to constructivist theory. In this chapter we focus on a constructivist account of young children's understanding of quantities of discrete items. We pursue this approach with an emphasis on children's use of symbolic means, such as number words and counting. The basic concept of the number of items in a set is complex. It requires a coordination of the level of individual items with the level of the whole set conceived as a single object. For example, understanding that there are five fingers on a hand, involves coordinating the levels of the individual fingers with the level of all the fingers on a hand taken together as a single object. Furthermore, this coordination is represented by a single symbol, a number word that indicates how many items there are in the set, or, put more formally, the cardinal value of the set. We emphasize the gradual development of young children's understanding of cardinality, and their partial understandings. As their item-whole coordinations become more stable, young children use number words meaningfully without attending directly to the individual items in the set.

INTRODUCTION

The National Council of Teachers of Mathematics' Principles and Standards (NCTM, 2000) states, for grades Pre-K-2, "All students need adequate time and opportunity to develop, construct, test, and reflect on their increasing understanding of mathematics" (p. 76). Furthermore, in their position statement Developmentally Appropriate Practice for Early Childhood Programs Serving Children from Birth through Age Eight, the National Association for the Education of Young Children (NAEYC, 1997) noted that the concept of "developmentally appropriate" educational practice is linked to constructivist theory. While taking care to point out that children's understandings are "mediated by and clearly linked to the sociocultural context," NAEYC states, "From birth, children are actively engaged in constructing their own understandings" (p. 7). This connection between a constructivist approach to understanding and a concern for developmentally appropriate practice is a crucial one. Its significance lies in the idea that the construction of understanding is gradual, and it asks us to confront the idea of partial understanding.

In this chapter we focus on a constructivist account of young children's understanding of quantities of discrete items. However, we pursue this approach with an emphasis on children's use of symbolic means, such as number words and counting. The basic concept of the number of items in a set is complex. It requires a coordination of the level of individual items with the level of the whole set conceived as a single object. For example, understanding that there are five fingers on a hand, involves coordinating the level of the individual fingers with the level of all the fingers on a hand taken together as a single object. Furthermore, this coordination is represented by a single symbol, a number word that indicates how many items there are in the set, or, put more formally, the cardinal value of the set. Young children gradually develop these understandings. Further, as their item-whole coordinations become more stable, young children use number words meaningfully without attending directly to the individual items in the set—as in addition and subtraction. [1]

INTRODUCING PARTIAL UNDERSTANDING, PIAGET'S WORK

According to Ginsburg, Klein, and Starkey (1988), "Today, the notion of constructivism is among the most popular concepts in mathematics education." However, these authors are referring to a very general idea of constructivism, and not to Piaget's theory of the cognitive operations underlying children's concept of number. They write, "[Piaget's] general constructivist approach ultimately proved more enduring and influential.

Piaget proposed that number, like other major cognitive acquisitions, is constructed—it is not innate and it is not "picked up" from stimulation or . . . otherwise imposed by experience" (p. 408). We agree that this general constructivist approach is valuable, and also that it is not necessary to accept the whole edifice of Piagetian theory in order to make progress in understanding young children's mathematical reasoning. However, we consider that there is more worth mining from the Piagetian field. In particular, its approach to partial understanding offers valuable insight.

Over half a century ago, Piaget (1941/1952) brought researchers' attention to children's performance in his number conservation task. In Piaget's task, children were presented with one array and asked to construct a numerically equivalent second array by putting one item of the second array opposite each item of the given array. Then the experimenter lengthened or shortened one of the two arrays, thus removing the perceptual evidence of one-to-one correspondence, and asked the children whether the two sets were numerically equivalent. In general, young children's responses indicated that the one-to-one correspondence no longer existed for them. Mostly, they considered that the longer array had more items.

Piaget's number conservation task has been criticized on several grounds. For example, the task asks children to consider the numerical equivalence of two arrays *twice*, before and after the transformation. This, it is argued, implicitly suggests to children that the second comparison should yield a different answer than the first. As a result, children change from their first conclusion, that the arrays are numerically equivalent, to the opposite conclusion, that they are not (McGarrigle & Donaldson, 1975). The controversy over the interpretation of performance in the number conservation task is contexted in an extensive critical literature on Piagetian constructivism (Donaldson, 1978; Gelman & Baillargeon, 1983; Gelman & Gallistel, 1978), and it is not our purpose here to pursue the controversy in detail. We do, however, borrow from his conceptualization of partial understanding. From a Piagetian perspective, children's susceptibility to implicit suggestions, such as that noted above, is related to the partial character of their understanding of cardinality. For example, four year olds generally have enough understanding of quantity to succeed on the preliminary task of constructing a second array equal to the first through a matching process, using one-to-one correspondence, but not sufficient to succeed on the conservation part of the task.

The partial understanding attributed to young children by the Piagetian work has a strange character. What does it mean, for example, to have some understanding of a quantity of items, and yet think that the quantity is changed when the items are rearranged in space? The very coherence of our own ideas of quantity makes it difficult to imagine such a partial understanding. The fact that changing the spatial arrangement of the items does not alter the quantity of a set of items is for us an inherent part of our concept of quantity. It is difficult for us to make sense of the idea that we could abandon that part of our concept of quantity and retain the rest. How are we to conceptualize such partial understandings? This type of question extends beyond Piaget's work.

PARTIAL UNDERSTANDINGS IN MORE RECENT WORK ON COUNTING A SINGLE SET

Piaget's number conservation task was designed to render counting irrelevant. The idea was that a sufficient understanding of quantity would lead a person to deduce that since there is numerical equivalence before the spatial transformation, there must be numerical equivalence afterwards. The understanding of quantity would obviate the need for any counting. Piaget favored this task in part because he was concerned that children's use of number words and counting might not express an understanding of cardinality. Children may pick up symbols and symbolic procedures without having constructed the conceptual relations that make them meaningful. They might then succeed on tasks that involve counting without really understanding their correct answers. In part, Piaget sought tasks that did not rely heavily on number words and counting because he did not think that these symbolic means play a central role in the development of elementary understanding of quantity.

However, in developing their mathematical reasoning, children must come to use their understandings of quantity in conjunction with number words and counting. In keeping with this, more recent research has examined children's understanding of quantity in the context of their use of these symbols and symbolic procedures. Here too, the question of partial understanding arises. Consider the following from the Principles and Standards (NCTM, 2000), "Young children should learn that the last number named represents the last object as well as the total number of objects in the collection" (p. 79). Is this just a matter of learning conventions that have evolved over time for how to use count words? Or do young children also need to develop the very idea of a quantity of objects, of the "total number of objects in the collection?" After all, as we have noted, this idea is quite complex.

Or consider the following statement from the same source, "[Young children] should learn that counting objects in a different order does not alter the result," (p. 79). This statement raises the question: Could a child have any understanding of quantity and counting and also think that counting in a different order might yield a different result? How can we reconcile such partial understanding with our sense that the irrelevance of the order in which the items are counted is a necessary (integral) part of our own understanding of quantity and counting? Part of the fascination of the research on young children's understanding of quantity and counting is that it continually confronts us with such questions. We will illustrate this with an abbreviated account of two central disputes in the research.

Cardinality

In regard to children's use of number words and counting, the work of Gelman (Gelman & Gallistel, 1978) was seminal. Gelman brought evidence to support the claim that well before the age at which children pass Piaget's conservation task, children have a substantial knowledge of counting linked to a basic understanding of quantity. Gelman attributed a principle of cardinality to young children. She claimed that they understood that the last word of a count lets us know the number of items in the set. Put more formally, the last word of a count gives the set's cardinal value. Gelman (Gelman & Gallistel, 1978; Gelman & Meck, 1983; Gelman, Meck & Merkin, 1986) used liberal criteria to make this determination. When children emphasized the last word of their counts, she took this as indicating knowledge of cardinality. Similarly, when children were asked how many items were in a set they had previously counted and responded with the last word of that count, she took this as evidence that children have a principle of cardinality.

The validity of using such data to support the claim that young children have a principle of cardinality has been questioned. For example, Fuson (1988; Fuson, Pergamont, & Lyons, 1985; Fuson, Pergamont, Lyons, & Hall, 1985) provided evidence that some children learn rote last-word rules such as "emphasize the last word of a count" or "the correct answer to a how many question is the last number word of a count." They do not have an understanding of quantity, and do not use symbols that represent cardinal values in a numerically meaningful way. More recently, Wynn (1992) compared children's performance on two tasks: In the how-many task, she asked 2- and 3-year-old children how many items were in a set they had previously counted. She considered children successful if they replied with the last word of the count they had made previous to the question, and did not need to count again after being asked the question. In the generate-a-set task, Wynn asked the children to give a puppet a specific quantity of items, from one to five. She found that some of the children who succeeded in the how-many task failed the generate-a-set task. Wynn interpreted this as evidence that children who succeed in passing the how-many task do not necessarily have an understanding of cardinal value. However, Wynn's work raises again the issue of partial understanding. Perhaps, children have some understanding of cardinality, enough so that they respond in a mathematically meaningful way to the how-many task but not to the generate-a-set task. This returns us to the question of how to conceptualize partial understanding.

Young children's success in some tasks and failure in others may be explained in terms of information processing demands and procedural knowledge. For example, in the generate-a-set task, children must remember the target cardinal value while counting out the items, compare successive count words to the target cardinal value, and cease when the count word is equal to the target. These information processing and procedural aspects are quite different from what is required in the how-many task. Thus, children may succeed in the how-many task but fail in the generate-a-set task because of these memory and performance aspects. In this view, it is children's information processing abilities and their procedural knowledge that is considered to develop, and the questions we raised about partial understandings receive less attention. [2]

However, we should not take this route too hastily. Researchers (Baroody, 1987; Fuson, 1988, 1992) have pointed out that the how-many task and the generate-a-set task ask children to think in different directions. In responding to the how-many task, children need to produce a cardinal value from counting. In contrast, the generate-a-set task challenges children to think in the opposite direction: to succeed they must use a given cardinal value to direct their counting. These researchers have suggested that children first develop a cardinality rule that involves knowing that counting yields the cardinal value of a set, and still do not reason successfully in the opposite direction. Only later do children develop a cardinal-count rule that involves knowing that given a cardinal value, one can count out a set with that value. Here we confront again the issue of partial understanding that is counter to our sense of the integration of our own knowledge of quantity. In our own understanding of cardinality, the cardinality rule and the cardinal-count rule imply each other. Thus, the question arises as to how we might conceptualize the idea that children can hold one of these rules without having a sense that the other rule must also be true.

Order-Irrelevance

Gelman also claimed that young children's understanding of quantity includes an order-irrelevance principle. That is, she claimed that young children understand that counting a set of items yields the same cardinal value regardless of the order in which the items are counted (e.g., from left to right or from right to left). In one experiment Gelman and Gallistel (1978) presented preschoolers (3-, 4-, and 5-year-olds) with a set of 4 or 5 toy objects (i.e., a doll, a chair, a dog, etc.). They first asked the children to count the objects, making a particular item (e.g., the doll) either number one, or number two, or number three, and so forth. The children were then given a similar task with a different object in the set. The results showed 94% of 5-year-olds, 69% of 4-year-olds and 31% of 3-year-olds both tagged the designated object with the specified number word and counted all objects without error in 60% or more of their trials.

Gelman and Gallistel also explicitly asked the children whether it was acceptable to tag two different objects with the same number word, and whether it was acceptable to exchange the name of two different objects (to call the chair a dog). They found that even many of the 3-year-old children recognized some difference between reassigning number words to the items of a set and reassigning names of objects. For example, the following is from a 3-year-old: "This [the baby] could be number one, right? *Okay.* And this [the dog] could be number one? *Yeah.* Is it silly to call this [the baby] a doggie? *Yeah, cause it's not a dog*," (p. 156). Gelman and Gallistel claimed that such results show that even 3-year-olds demonstrate significant competence. However, as was the case for the cardinality principle, these are liberal criteria, and other research yields results that support a contrary view.

Briars and Siegler (1984) asked children to judge a puppet's counts as acceptable or unacceptable. In some of the counts, the puppet violated an essential feature of counting, one-to-one correspondence of count words and objects. In other counts, the puppet violated one or more common but inessential features of counting: counting adjacent objects consecutively, pointing once to each object, starting at the end of a row, and proceeding in a left to right direction. Briars and Siegler inferred that children considered a feature to be essential if they consistently rejected counts violating that feature. They found that the majority of 4- and 5-year-olds (out of the ten at each age they tested) thought that assigning one number word to each subject was essential and that counting from left to right was not essential, but also thought that counting adjacent objects consecutively and starting at an end were essential—in contradiction to Gelman and Gallistel's claims that children's knowledge includes the order-irrelevance principle.

Furthermore, Baroody (1984) also provided evidence contrary to Gelman and Gallistel's claim. Baroody distinguished between two competencies: (1) knowing that the items in a set do not need to be counted in any particular order (tag reassignment skill) and (2) knowing that the order in which elements of a set are enumerated does not affect the cardinal value of the set (order-irrelevance principle). He claimed that Gelman and Gallistel's evidence spoke to the first competency and not the second. He therefore introduced a reverse-count *prediction* task to examine whether children's knowledge includes the order-irrelevance principle. He asked children to count an array in one direction and then asked, "We got N (where N was the result of the count) by counting this way. What do you think we would get counting the other way?" Baroody found that 55% of 5-year-olds (and 13% of 6-year-olds) were unsuccessful, and regarded this as inconsistent with Gelman and Gallistel's claims.

Gelman et al. (1986) responded to Baroody. They argued that young children's lack of success did not necessarily mean that the children's knowledge did not include the order-irrelevance principle. They theorized that the wording might cause children to respond in an inappropriate way. In his question to the children, Baroody repeated the cardinal value, N, the children had obtained in their count. Gelman and her colleagues argued that children may take this as a clue that they should not give N in response to the reverse-count prediction question. To test their hypothesis, Gelman et al. (1986) dropped the mention of the cardinal value from the question asked of the children. They found that 4-year-olds performed poorly on the original prediction task but did well on the revised prediction task.

Baroody (1993) reexamined Gelman's (Gelman & Gallistel, 1978) position. In attributing the cardinality and order irrelevance principles to young children, Gelman claimed that these principles guided children's perfection of their counting skills. Baroody (1993) argued that if this was so, no child who failed the revised reverse-count question should succeed in tag reassigning (a counting skill). From a reanalysis of Gelman et al.'s (1986) data, Baroody found that the performance of some children ran counter to the above constraint. He explored this further in an empirical study in which he introduced two changes. First, to make the question more reasonable to children, he asked them whether it would be acceptable for someone else (the cookie monster) to count in the reverse direction, and what the result would be. Second, he focused on children who did not predict that the cookie monster would get the same count in the reverse direction, and checked whether these children remembered the result of the first count. He found that 21% the children who were successful in the tag-reassigning task remembered the result of their first count but were not successful in predicting the result of the reverse task. Baroody presented this as further evidence that young children may have a tag reassigning skill and still not have an order-irrelevance principle.

The examination of these issues has continued in subsequent work (e.g., Cowan, 1996). In this debate too, we confront the questions raised by children's partial understandings: children may have some understanding of number but not consider that the order in which the items of a set are counted is irrelevant to its cardinal value.

A CONSTRUCTIVIST CONCEPT OF PARTIAL UNDERSTANDING: THE ITEM-WHOLE COORDINATION AND ITS DEVELOPMENT

How might we conceptualize the possibility that a person to some extent has an understanding of cardinality and yet does not consider that the cardinal value of an array is conserved when the items of the set are rearranged in space? How might we conceptualize the possibility that a person to some extent has an understanding of cardinality and also of counting, and yet does not realize that the order in which the items of a set are counted does not matter?

In asking these questions, we are distinguishing "understanding" from the concepts of knowledge and information. We are connecting understanding to the deep relations whereby various ideas are felt to imply each other. In this sense we are talking about partial understanding, and not only about partial knowledge. Partial knowledge can be made more complete by information. Partial understanding is changed by further construction.

To answer the above questions, we turn to the coordination introduced earlier: the coordination of the level of individual items with the level of the whole set conceived as a single object. For ease of reference, we call this an item-whole coordination.[3] This coordination is central in constructivist approaches to mathematical understanding (e.g., Kamii, 1986; Steffe, 1992; Steffe & Cobb, 1988). It is considered to underlie our sense that we cannot split off certain parts of our understanding of quantity and maintain the rest. To a person with a relatively stable item-whole coordination, it feels necessarily true that the number of items in a set does not change when the items are rearranged in space (conservation). Such a person can meaningfully use the final word of a count to represent the number of items in the set taken as a whole (count-cardinal direction). To a person who has a relatively stable item-whole coordination linked to knowledge of counting, it feels necessarily true that counting out items is a valid way to produce a set with a given cardinal value (cardinal-count direction). Further, it feels necessarily true that counting the items of a set in any order will yield the same cardinal value (order-irrelevance).

In constructivist approaches to understanding, we do not consider children's reasoning primarily in terms of memory or other information processing capabilities, nor in terms of a list of individual rules. In these approaches, we focus on the conceptual power of the item-whole coordination that children construct, exploring to what extent it supports mathematical meaning (including the sense of necessity indicated above) and to what extent it succumbs to challenges. We consider that developmental processes gradually strengthen and improve the item-whole coordinations that children construct. This means that—as judged by an adult with a relatively stable item-whole coordination—there is a period in which children's item-whole coordinations serve them well under some conditions and not others.

In the constructivist perspective elaborated by Piaget, a major characteristic of relatively weak item-whole coordinations is that they do not provide a sufficient basis for the flexibility to think in different directions as part of the same reasoning. Most significantly, they do not provide a sufficient basis for integrating reasoning from the level of the individual items to the level of the set as a whole with reasoning in the reverse direction. In the work cited in the foregoing discussion of young children's numerical reasoning, there are two particular examples of this. First, young children may construct item-whole coordinations that allow them to make sense of the idea that the final number word in a count yields the cardinal value of the set (count-cardinal direction). However, this item-whole coordination may still be too weak to imply also that given a cardinal value, they can use counting to produce a set with that cardinal value (cardinal-count direction). Second, the understanding of order-irrelevance involves the ability to move easily between the level of the individual items and the level of the set taken as a single entity in both directions.

It may be relatively easy and straightforward to focus on such factors as memory and retrieval of information, or the gradual expansion of a list of individual rules. They are part of a very familiar paradigm. So much so that it may require an effort for us to see these concepts as interpretive, or in any way problematic. In contrast, the gap between what we can actually observe, on one hand, and the concept of differences in the strength of item-whole coordinations, on the other, may be much more salient. The focus on item-whole coordination, however, emphasizes our sense of how integrated our own knowledge is. It may help us keep in mind that children may differ from us in precisely this aspect. Their very conception of quantity and their understanding of number words and counting may be in this way different from our own—the result of a significantly weaker and more fragile item-whole coordination. This is the more radical sense in which constructivist approaches to mathematical knowledge relate to the idea of developmentally appropriate practice. In what follows we illustrate how this constructivist perspective applies to further basic issues in young children's mathematical understanding.

NUMERICAL EQUIVALENCE

In their Principles and Standards, NCTM (2000) notes the importance of children's understanding of one-to-one correspondence. In the single-set [4] counting tasks discussed above, children are tested in their understanding of the use of number words to represent the quantity of items in a set. The focus is whether young children construct item-whole coordinations adequate enough for them to make sense of the idea that the last number word of a count labels the set taken as a whole—even as it relates to the level of the individual items. However, these tasks do not provide much insight into children's understanding of the one-to-one correspondence of the items in sets with the same cardinal value. This is, of course, central to an understanding of cardinality, and was the focus of Piaget's number conservation task. We will now examine some of the more recent research on children's understanding of cardinality with respect to the numerical equivalence of two sets.

Gelman (Gelman & Gallistel, 1978) found that even 3-year-olds determined which of two sets is a "winner" by determining which set yields "three" when counted and which yields "two." Gelman's position was that young children have item-whole coordinations linked to counting stable enough for them to understand the comparison of two sets. Gelman considers that even before they are verbal, children have this level of understanding of cardinality and the principles of counting, and that this understanding is independent of symbolic means, perhaps even innate. In her perspective, any difficulty children experience in performing adequately with symbolic means lies in linking this preverbal understanding to actual symbolic means such as number words. However, there is evidence that supports a contrary position.

Mix (1999) found that young children's judgments of the equivalence of two sets were affected by the similarity of items in the sets, and that children's understanding became more abstract over the period in which they learned to use number words. Mix presented children with a target set of items (with cardinal value varying from 2 to 4) and asked them to choose which of two response sets was numerically equivalent to the target set. One of the two response sets had the same cardinal value as the target set and the other differed by plus or minus one. The target sets were linear arrays of black dots, red pasta shells, or different items drawn randomly from a pool of objects. The response sets were always composed of black dots having the same size as the black dots used in one of the target sets.

The results showed a gradual progression in children's success in bringing an understanding of cardinality to bear on comparisons involving sets with dissimilar items. At about 3 years old, children successfully matched sets when the target and response sets were each homogeneous and both sets were composed of the same items; at 3½ they successfully matched two homogenous but different sets; and at 4½ they successfully matched a heterogeneous set with a homogeneous set. Furthermore, Mix measured children's responses to two counting tasks: the how-many task and the generate-a-set task. She found that performance on matching tasks was correlated with performance on these counting tasks. According to Mix, labeling the sets with their cardinal values helped children abstract away from the different appearances of the items. Mix argued that this increased abstraction is a further development of children's understanding and not simply an application of previous understandings.

Saxe (1977) presented 3-, 4-, and 7-year-old children with three tasks in which they were given a set of 9 items and were asked to produce a second set having the same number of items. Very few 3-year-olds initiated counting in these tasks. After direct suggestion (e.g., "Would counting help?") 3-year-olds counted but did not use the counting as a basis to produce the second set. The majority of 4-year-olds initiated counting and used it to produce a second set having the correct number of items. Many of the 4-year-olds used counting in a trial-and-error strategy. They produced a second set that was an approximate copy of the given set, and counted to determine whether or not the two sets were numerically equivalent, and if necessary they modified the second set. All the seven-year-olds counted the given set and then directly produced a second set on the basis of that count. This work suggests that the item-whole coordination linked to counting undergoes important development over this age range. Initially, young children do not have stable item-whole coordinations that they use in reasoning with number words about the equivalence of two sets, and later they do. However, it should be noted that Saxe's task raises the issues we have discussed regarding the generate-a-set task used by Wynn.

Young Children's Use of Number Words in Relation to One-to-One Correspondence

Although the above research uses two-set tasks and explores young children's understanding of numerical equivalence, the relation between children's counting and their understanding of one-to-one correspondence was not directly explored. Children may adopt the criterion that two sets are equivalent only if counting yields the same cardinal value for the two sets, and still not understand that if two sets yield the same final number word there is a one-to-one correspondence between the items. This central question concerning children's use of item-whole coordinations in reasoning about the numerical relation between two arrays was examined more directly in the research described below.

Sophian (1987) examined specifically whether children initiate counting to solve two-set tasks. She presented 3- and 3½-year-olds with two tasks. The first task tested their understanding of a question about the correspondence relation between items in two sets. In this task, the objects from the two sets (e.g., jars and lids) were matched so that children had visual evidence as to whether there was, or was not, one-to-one correspondence between the items of the sets. The children were asked a correspondence question: Are there enough lids so that every jar has a lid? Their performance on this task indicated that these young children understood the question. In the main task, the two sets were spatially separated and arranged in a different geometrical shape (one in a circle, the other in an array), and children were asked the same question about the correspondence between the two sets. Sophian found that about half of the children at each age failed to count at all in this task, even though they successfully counted the sets in a separate counting task. Consistent with the work of Saxe just described, Sophian also found that when children did count, they were not very likely to arrive at a correct answer: They counted only one set, or counted both sets and gave an answer that did not correspond to the results of their counting. In sum, the children did not relate counting to one-to-one correspondence sufficiently to use counting to answer the correspondence question.

Sophian, Wood, and Vong (1995) studied 3-, 4-, and 5-year-olds initiation of counting in another task. They presented children with a story involving two sets (frogs and boats), with the items from the sets initially paired (each frog came to a party in its own boat). They left all the items of one set (the boats) in view but hid the items of the other set (the frogs). There were two conditions, in one condition children were asked to count the visible set (boats) and were then asked how many items were in the hidden set (frogs). In the other condition, children were not asked to count the items of the visible set, instead they were simply asked to move the items to a different place where they remained visible, and then asked how many items were in the hidden set. In both conditions, a majority of 4- and 5-year-olds, but not 3-year-olds, reliably solved the problem. However, children did better in the count condition than in the move condition. The older children, and not the younger ones, used the evidence of one-to-one correspondence to reason that the number word expressing the cardinal value of one set also expressed the cardinal value of the second set.

Sophian (1988) and Becker (1989) used versions of the two tasks introduced by Sophian (1987) to investigate in both directions the relation between children's use of number words and their knowledge of one-to-one correspondence. In one task, the objects from two sets (e.g., dolls and cups) were matched so that children had visual evidence as to whether there was, or was not, one-to-one correspondence between the items of the sets. The children also knew the cardinal value of one of the sets (either because they were told, Sophian, 1988, or because they had counted, Becker, 1989). They were asked whether the cardinal value of the other set was the same (There are six dolls. Is there the same number of cups?). In the other task, the two sets were grouped separately, and children knew the cardinal value of both sets. They were asked whether there was enough of one set to match one item of that set with each item of the other set (there are six dolls and five cups. Is there a cup for every doll?). Taking the two studies together, at a set size of 6, from 40% to over 75% of the 4½-year-olds participating in the studies successfully reasoned about the equality of cardinal values of two sets given information on one-to-one correspondence. They also successfully reasoned about one-to-one correspondence given information about the cardinal values of the sets.

These studies provide clear evidence that, at this age, many children have a firm enough understanding of cardinality linked to number words to reason in both directions about the equivalence of two sets: from cardinal values to one-to-one correspondence, and vice versa. Making judgments of whether the items in one set can be compared with those in the other involves reasoning about each set as a whole, as well as about the individual items. This is even more apparent when, as in the above tasks, the sets are designated by a single symbol representing their cardinal value. Thus, the above results indicate that over these early childhood years, children judge one-to-one correspondence on the basis of cardinal values without actually matching the items in the sets. They develop item-whole coordinations sufficiently stable for them to understand that when two sets have the same cardinal value, and only then, the items in the sets can be put in one-to-one correspondence. That being so, we discuss in the next section whether young children's item-whole coordinations are stable enough to allow them to reason about quantities without attending directly to the individual items.

Before pursuing this question, it is appropriate to note that young children's item-whole coordinations do not serve equally well in all situations calling for a judgment of numerical equivalence. Children first solve the tasks used by Sophian and by Becker, and only considerably later succeed in the conservation task. We have already made reference to critiques of the conservation task, and indicated the response from the Piagetian perspective. From a constructivist perspective, one way to understand the greater difficulty of the conservation task as compared to the tasks used by Sophian and Becker is to consider that the former presents more of a challenge to children's item-whole coordinations. After the spatial transformation in the conservation task, children see two rows spread out over different lengths. Deducing that these two rows must be numerically equivalent, despite how different they look, requires item-whole coordinations that can resist the appearance of inequality. The tasks used by Sophian and Becker did not test children's item-whole coordination in this way, and thus children succeed in these tasks first. At that point their use of number words involves a level of item-whole coordination that is adequate for judging the numerical equivalence of sets in some conditions, but not sufficient to withstand the appearance of inequality in the conservation task (Becker, 1989).

Using Item-Whole Coordinations Without Attending Directly to the Individual Items

As noted by NCTM (2000), "[young children's] strategies for computing play an important role in linking less formal knowledge with more sophisticated mathematical thinking" (pp. 85-86). Young children develop various strategies for combining two sets to produce a total set, and for separating a smaller one from a larger one to quantify the difference. In developing these strategies, young children increasingly use item-whole coordinations without attending directly to each item in the sets.

In the count-all strategy, children produce a total set by counting all the items in two given sets. In this strategy, the children attend to all the items in the sets being combined. Young children use this strategy to combine several smaller sets into a single total. For example, Becker (1993) presented children with an array of 6 dolls and asked them to give two cookies to each of the first two dolls. After the children had done this, they were asked how many more cookies they needed in order to give each of the remaining dolls two cookies. At age 4½, about 50% the children succeeded in this task by pointing twice in front of the first remaining doll and saying "1, 2" then moving onto the next doll and saying "3, 4" etc. to produce an answer of 8.[5] At age 5, about 75% of the children succeeded. Additionally, when the task stipulated a relation of three-to-one instead of two-to-one, about 33% of the 4½-year-olds and 75% of the 5-year-olds succeeded.

The children who succeeded on this task used item-whole coordinations for the small sets (2 or 3) while considering them as part of the item-whole coordination for the total set (8 or 12). Moreover, they succeeded in doing this for a *needed* set, a set that did not yet exist as a set of material items. However, the way the children found the total was by counting each individual item in all the sets. In contrast, in the way we generally perform addition, we do not pay attention to each individual item in the set. Instead, saying, for example, that 5 plus 3 equals 8, we use the cardinal values in a more abstract way—we combine the cardinal values without attending directly to the individual items in the sets they represent.

First graders often invent, without specific instruction, another strategy known as counting-on. In counting-on, children start from the given cardinal value of one of the sets and count from there to get the total of the quantities. Thus given sets 5 and 3, children say, 5 (for the first set) and continue counting 6, 7, 8 allotting one number word for each item in the second set. In this strategy, children use the item-whole coordination of one of the given sets (in the example given here, the set of 5) without attending directly to each item.[6] Using cardinal values to represent the item-whole coordinations, children reason about quantity without attending directly to the individual items in the set. This is, of course, a crucial step of abstraction that children need to take in order to develop their mathematical thinking further. Children take this step gradually.[7]

Young children's use of item-whole coordinations without attending directly to the individual items is further shown when children compute a sum or difference on the basis of arithmetic facts that they know. Various researchers have documented second graders strategies of decomposing and recomposing numbers in order to obtain sums and differences (e.g., Carraher, Carraher, & Schlieman, 1987; Ginsburg, 1989; Resnick, 1992; Saxe, Guberman, & Gearhart, 1987). For example, Ginsburg (1989) describes a 7-year-old boy adding 12 and 6. The boy gets 18 and explains that 12 is 10 plus 2, adding 6 to 10 gives 16, and adding the remaining 2 to this sum gives a total of 18. In such computations children are using item-whole coordinations linked to symbolic means without attending directly to each individual item.

Children use this type of reasoning in various ways depending on the nature of the problem (e.g., Carpenter & Moser, 1982; Carpenter, Fennema, & Franke, 1996). Consider the following two problems: "Robin has 5 toy cars. How many more cars does she need to get for her birthday to have 12 cars altogether?" "Colleen had 12 guppies. She gave 5 guppies to Roger. How many guppies does Colleen have left?" [8] In some strategies children used counting. In others they used addition or subtraction, deriving facts they did not know from those they did. In using derived fact strategies, children responded to the toy car problem as follows, "5 plus 5 is 10, and 2 more is 12, so it's 7." They responded to the guppy problem as follows, "12 take away 2 is 10, and take away 3 more is 7." Thus, children used symbolic means to reproduce the actions and relations in the problems without needing to attend to the individual items. This work shows that young children develop effective item-whole coordinations linked to symbolic means, enabling them to produce a new set from two given sets without attending directly to the individual items.

We have emphasized that number words facilitate reasoning about quantities without attending directly to the individual items. This brings with it a further crucial development. With children's increased use of strategies in which the item-whole coordinations are maintained without attending directly to the individual items, the system of number words and counting begins to attain a standing of its own. We may see the beginning of this process in the distinction between concrete and abstract counting. For example, Fuson noted a progression from the concrete form to the abstract form in children's counting-on (Fuson, 1982; Fuson & Secada, 1986). Consider the example 5 plus 3, already introduced. In the earlier form, children first say "5" to represent the first set, then say "6" pointing to one of the items in the set of 3, then say "7" pointing to another item in that set, and finally say "8" pointing to the last item. They are directly counting the concrete items. In the later form (the abstract form), children say "5" and count from there using the items in the second set, or surrogates for them, as a way of keeping track of how far they should continue counting. That is, rather than count the additional items, or others that represent them, they use the concrete items as tallies to make sure that they count-on by the correct number of extra words. Children's counting may reflect this distinction in the following way. In the concrete form, children may put out three fingers for the second set and then count them. In the abstract form, they may put out the three fingers sequentially, allotting a count word for each finger before putting out another one. [9]

In the concrete form of counting-on, children do not need a means of ascertaining when to stop the counting-on, and in the abstract form they do. In the concrete form, the children directly count the items, and the counting stops when all of them have been included. When children are using the abstract form of counting-on, they do not count the items. Therefore they need some other means of ascertaining when they have counted-on the correct number of additional number words (Baroody, 1987). For example, they may count the fingers that they use for the second set, counting the 6 as 1, the 7 as 2 and the 8 as 3, and thus know that they should stop at 8 because they have added 3 more to the 5. Or, they may visually recognize that they have put out 3 fingers. In either case, there is a new relation between concrete items on one hand, and the symbol system and the symbolic procedure of counting, on the other.

In concrete counting, priority is given to a concrete set of objects that is to be counted. The number words are secondary: a means of determining the cardinal value of the set of concrete items. In abstract counting, the relation between the number words and the concrete items (e.g., the three fingers put out sequentially in the above example) is more complex, and even reversed. To some extent, the number words themselves and the system of counting assume a priority, and concrete items (the original ones or surrogates for them) are secondary—they are used to keep track of the counting. This is a very early step in a crucial aspect of mathematical reasoning: the system of number words and counting begins to attain a standing of its own.

The development in which the symbol system attains a standing of its own is critical to children's progress in mathematical reasoning. As Resnick (1992) noted, "Throughout mathematics, the terms and expressions in the formal notation have both referential and formal functions. As referential symbols, they refer to objects (e.g., a set of three apples) or cognitive entities (e.g., the number *three*) external to the formalism. As formal symbols, they are elements in a system that obeys its own rules, and they can function without continuous reference to the physical or mathematical objects they name" (p. 396).

This issue occurs repeatedly in the development of mathematical reasoning. For example, Hiebert (1988) has made a similar point in discussing how children develop an understanding of place value. He proposed that in this development, "cognitive processes shift from a heavy reliance on referents to a consideration of the symbols and rules themselves" (p. 340). As another example, Pirie and Kieren (1994) noted that at first children consider fractions to refer to empirical referents such as particular kinds of pieces in a set of fraction manipulatives. Later, they use reasoning that "does not reference concrete images of each fraction separately . . . [but deals with] addition of fractions as a method based on the forms of the number. In this understanding [children use] numbers in their own right. They [the numbers] are not *like* anything" (p. 41).

In young children's development of mathematical reasoning, the symbol system begins to attain a standing in its own right. In this development, the relations of the symbols with each other attain a new prominence. The relations between individual symbols and their concrete referents become less direct; they are mediated by the relations among the symbols, particularly as these occur in symbolic procedures. The symbol system continues to function mathematically because the integration within the symbol system is linked to a strong and flexible conceptual understanding of quantity based on relatively stable item-whole coordinations (Becker & Varelas, 1993; Varelas & Becker, 1997).

We saw at the beginning of this chapter that initially young children's item-whole coordinations are not strong enough for them to appreciate, for example, that the validity of the count-cardinal direction implies the validity of the cardinal-count direction. We have now also seen that over the early childhood years, young children develop item-whole coordinations stable enough to reason about quantities without attending directly to the individual items. Also, already in the mathematics of young children, the relation of symbols to more empirical referents is changed. This change is part of the development in which the symbol system and symbolic procedures attain a standing in their own right. On one hand, the more direct links between individual symbols and concrete referents are weakened, and on the other hand, new links are formed in which the relations between any one symbol and its referent are more strongly mediated by relations among the symbols themselves. During these developments, children maintain the links between the symbols and their conceptual understandings of quantity (in particular well-developed item-whole coordinations), so that the formal relations they construct for the symbols and the symbolic procedures are consistent with these understandings. We have seen that children begin this formal use of symbols and symbolic procedures very early in their mathematical reasoning.

EDUCATIONAL IMPLICATIONS

NCTM (2000) states, "teachers must maintain a balance, helping students develop both conceptual understanding and procedural facility (skill)" (p. 77). NAEYC (1996) refers to a polarization between a view that "development of certain cognitive structures was a necessary prerequisite to learning (i.e., development precedes learning)" and an opposing view that instruction "can facilitate development of more mature cognitive structures (learning precedes development)" (p. 8). NAEYC emphasizes its rejection of this polarization, and specifically challenges the field of early childhood education "to move from *either/or* to *both/and* thinking" (p. 1). We are in full agreement with this position. In early childhood, do item-whole coordinations help children understand counting or does counting help children attain item-whole coordinations? Formulated in this way the question is unhelpfully polarizing. We may do well to consider a middle ground. During the early childhood years, there is a continual development of item-whole coordinations. These developments both contribute to children's meaningful use of number words and counting, and are nurtured by children's use of these symbolic means. We believe that this middle ground position is facilitated when we appreciate more fully the insights into partial understanding that we have discussed.

Without these insights, we might tend to think that we need simply to wait for children to have better memory capacity, or give them aids for memorizing. We might think we need simply to focus on the perfection of skills, and symbolic procedures, or to note which rules children have and inform them of the other rules. We may be tempted to overestimate children's understanding. When children demonstrate to us that they have some understanding of a particular mathematical relation, we may implicitly assume that their understanding is more complete than it is. In particular, we may assume that their understanding has the same implications—with the same force of necessity—as does ours.

When we give weight to the idea of partial understanding, distinct from partial knowledge, we may realize more fully what an intriguing balancing act teaching is. This balancing act lies in the interplay of two directions: giving enough room for children's internal mental processes to do their work (and let us admit that it is work that largely remains mysterious), and also giving enough support and direction (Becker & Varelas, 1995; Oyler & Becker, 1997). On one hand, we seek to encourage children to make sense of things using their own mental instruments, their own level of item-whole coordinations. We might well draw patience from the knowledge that their understandings will transform to become more like ours. On the other hand, we seek to offer children whatever help our cultural tools, and the cultural practices that use them (such as number words and counting), can provide to the internal processes that stabilize and strengthen item-whole coordinations.

We work toward classrooms in which young children are encouraged to use their own ways of making sense. Moreover, we seek to create an environment where children feel comfortable presenting their reasoning to each other, and working together publicly to understand the different reasoning presented. At the same time, we need to consider developmental perspectives that focus on how to bring society's cultural achievements to new members of the society. Increasingly, researchers are turning their attention to exploring how these two aspects may best be combined in the classroom (e.g., Ball, 1993; Cobb & Yackel, 1998). A feature of this literature is its concern with the establishment of social norms in the classroom that facilitate children's construction of new mathematical understanding.

It is appropriate at this point to note that there is good reason to consider that interacting with people who already use symbolic means linked to more conceptual understanding actually helps a person achieve that conceptual understanding. People today relatively easily develop understandings that at one time were at the cutting edge of the intellectual achievements of humankind, for example, the idea of negative numbers. This concept is constructed only after the period of early childhood considered here. However, the difficulty of understanding negative numbers when this was first achieved in history, compared to its relative ease now, supports the idea that it is easier for people to develop this concept if they are participants in a culture in which this concept has currency and are interacting with those members of the culture who have already constructed the concept (Becker & Varelas, 1995).

Anderson's (1997) study of parent-child interactions provides evidence of parents interacting with young children in ways that may foster the children's development of mathematical meaning. The question of adults promoting the move to more developed mathematical reasoning may be seen in terms of striking a balance between giving too little encouragement and imposing too much. Saxe et al. (1987; Saxe, Gearhart, & Guberman, 1984) drew on Vygotskian theory to conceptualize the way interaction with a person who has already achieved a higher level of mathematical understanding may help children in their development. These researchers showed how mothers interact in a sensitive way with their children as they engage with them in number activities such as producing a set equal to a given set. They found that mothers tended to offer more explicit help when children did not succeed, and pull back when they were doing well. This presents a picture of an adult closely monitoring where an individual child is, and interacting as required by that particular child. Children differ in terms of how much direction they need in the development of any particular aspect of item-whole coordination, such as abstraction and the changing relation of the symbol system to concrete referents. Therefore, the individualized attention they get out of class, for example, at home, may be a significant boon to some children.

In interacting with children, we seek the joy of sharing with them, and we prefer to impose as little as possible. It is not always easy. Based on a video study of teaching Stigler and Hiebert (1998) noted, "Teachers act as though confusion and frustration are signs that they have not done their job. When they notice confusion, they quickly assist students by providing whatever information it takes to get the student back on track" (p. 92). This is a natural temptation; after all we want children to benefit from our experience and knowledge. A constructivist conception of partial understanding may help us with this. The way many parts of our own understandings are linked together and mutually imply each other may make it difficult for us to enter young children's mental world. The insight into this situation afforded by a constructivist conception of partial understanding may help us orient ourselves better to children's construction of mathematical knowledge, and their meaning making activities.

ACKNOWLEDGMENTS

The authors express their thanks to Ivan K. Ash, Andrew Corrigan-Halpern, and Timothy J. Nokes, members with us of the Math Cognition Reading Group, Fall 2000, for many stimulating and helpful discussions, and to a reviewer for provocative comments that helped us improve on a previous version of this chapter.

NOTES

1. Resnick (1992) distinguishes between the mathematics of protoquantities and of quantities. In the former, no numerical quantification is involved, and its language is descriptive and comparative. Resnick gives as examples, a big doll, many eggs, more milk. In contrast, "In the mathematics of quantities, reasoning is about numerically quantified amounts of material" (p. 404). Using these terms, we are concerned in this chapter with the mathematics of quantities and not with the mathematics of protoquantities. Nor are we concerned with preverbal understandings in infancy (see Ginsburg, Klein, & Starkey, 1998, and Haith & Benson, 1998, for brief reviews from opposing perspectives).

2. For different perspectives on procedural and information processing aspects of young children's developing mathematical reasoning see Ashcraft (1992); Baroody (1985); Rittle-Johnson and Siegler (1998).

3. The term "part-whole" coordination is sometimes used. We prefer "item-whole" coordination as we wish to emphasize that each individual item is cognized as an entity in its own right.

4. In what we have called single-set tasks there is really a second set, the set of number words. A count involves producing a second set in one-to-one correspondence with the items of the counted set. However, it is not at all clear that children consider the number words as a set and are aware that there are now two sets in one-to-one correspondence. For example, they may see the correspondence only at the level of the items and not consider the equivalence at the level of the sets. For this reason, as well as for simplicity of description, we use the terms "single-set" and "two-set" to denote the number of sets ignoring the number words themselves.

5. Prior to responding in this way, children often count the sets individually, saying 1,2, for the first set and again 1,2 for each of the remaining sets. This is an aspect of the gradual development of the combination of two sets even when attending directly to each item individually.

6. There are two versions of both the count-all and the count-on strategies, concrete and abstract. We discuss this distinction later.

7. In some of the tasks discussed above, children may have begun to use number words linked to strong item-whole coordinations without attending directly to the individual items. Specifically, it is possible that in the task used by Sophian (1988) and Becker (1989), children made judgments about one-to-one correspondence on the basis of cardinal values without attending directly to the individual items in the sets. However, we see more clearly children's developing use of item-whole coordinations without attending directly to the individual items in their strategies for combining and separating quantities.

8. We have changed the numbers for the guppy problem cited in Carpenter et al. (1996) so that both problems are illustrated with the same numbers.

9. In some of the strategies that Carpenter et al. (1996) reported, children displayed strategies similar to the later form of counting-on. In describing the preva-

lent strategy for the guppy problem, Carpenter et al. commented that the children used "fingers to keep track of the number of steps in the counting sequence" (p. 17).

REFERENCES

Anderson, A. (1997). Families and mathematics: A study of parent-child interactions. *Journal for Research in Mathematics Education, 28,* 484-511.

Ashcraft, M. (1992). Cognitive arithmetic: A review of data and theory. *Cognition, 44,* 75-106.

Ball, D.L. (1993). With an eye on the mathematical horizon: Dilemmas of teaching elementary school mathematics. *The Elementary School Journal, 93,* 373-397.

Baroody, A. (1984). More precisely defining and measuring the order-irrelevance principle. *Journal of Experimental Child Psychology, 38,* 33-41.

Baroody, A. (1985). Mastery of the basic number combinations: Internalization of relationships or facts? *Journal for Research in Mathematics Education, 16*(2), 83-89.

Baroody, A. (1987). *Children's mathematical thinking.* New York: Teachers College Press.

Baroody, A. (1993). The relationship between the order-irrelevance principle and counting skill. *Journal for Research in Mathematics Education, 24,* 415-427.

Becker, J. (1989). Preschoolers' use of number words to denote one-to-one correspondence. *Child Development, 60,* 1147-1157.

Becker, J. (1993). Young children's numerical use of number words: Counting in many-to-one situations. *Developmental Psychology, 29,* 458-465.

Becker, J., & Varelas, M. (1993). Semiotic aspects of cognitive development: Illustrations from early mathematical cognition. *Psychological Review, 100,* 420-431.

Becker, J., & Varelas, M. (1995). Assisting construction: The role of the teacher in assisting the learner's construction of pre-existing cultural knowledge. In L. P. Steffe & J. Gale (Eds.), *Constructivism in education* (pp. 433-446). Hillsdale, NJ: Erlbaum.

Briars, D., & Siegler, R.S. (1984). A feature analysis of preschoolers' counting knowledge. *Developmental Psychology, 20,* 607-618.

Carpenter, T.P., & Moser, J.M. (1982). The development of addition and subtraction problem-solving skills. In T.P. Carpenter, J.M. Moser, & T.A. Romberg (Eds.), *Addition and subtraction: A cognitive perspective* (pp. 9-24). Hillsdale, NJ: Erlbaum.

Carpenter, T.P., Fennema, E., & Franke, M.L. (1996). Cognitively guided instruction: A knowledge base for reform in primary mathematics instruction. *The Elementary School Journal, 97,* 3-20.

Carraher, T.N., Carraher, D.W., & Schlieman, A.D. (1987). Written and oral mathematics. *Journal for Research in Mathematics Education, 18,* 83-97.

Cobb, P., & Yackel, E. (1998). A constructivist perspective on the culture of the mathematics classroom. In F. Seeger, J. Voigt, & U. Waschescio (Eds.), *The culture of the mathematics classroom* (pp. 159-190). Cambridge: Cambridge University Press.

Cowan, R. (1996). Even more precisely assessing children's understanding of the order-irrelevance principle. *Journal of Experimental Child Psychology, 62,* 84-101.

Donaldson, M. (1978). *Children's minds.* New York: Norton.

Fuson, K.C. (1982). An analysis of the counting-on solution procedure in addition. In T.M. Carpenter, J.M. Moser, & T.A. Romberg (Eds.), *Addition and subtraction: A cognitive perspective* (pp. 67-81). Hillsdale, NJ: Erlbaum.

Fuson, K.C. (1988). *Children's counting and concepts of number.* New York: Springer-Verlag.

Fuson, K.C. (1992). Research on whole number addition and subtraction. In D.A. Grouws (Ed.), *Handbook of research on mathematics teaching and learning* (pp. 243-275). New York: Macmillan.

Fuson, K.C., & Secada, W.G. (1986). Teaching children to add by counting-on with one-handed finger patterns. *Cognition and Instruction, 3,* 229-260.

Fuson, K.C., Pergament, G.G., & Lyons, B.G. (1985). Collection terms and children's use of the cardinality rule. *Cognitive Psychology, 17,* 315-323.

Fuson, K.C., Pergament, G.G., Lyons, B.G., & Hall, J.W. (1985). Children's conformity to the cardinality rule as a function of set size and counting accuracy. *Child Development, 56,* 1429-1436.

Gelman R., & Baillargeon, R. (1983). A review of some Piagetian concepts. In J.H. Flavel & E.M. Markman (Eds.), *Handbook of child psychology; Vol. 3. Cognitive development* (pp. 167-230). New York: Wiley.

Gelman, R., & Gallistel, C.R. (1978). *The child's understanding of number.* Cambridge, MA: Harvard University Press.

Gelman, R., & Meck, E. (1983). Preschooler's counting: Principles before skill. *Cognition, 13,* 343-359.

Gelman, R., Meck, E., & Merkin, S. (1986). Young children's numerical competence. *Cognitive Development, 1,* 1-29.

Ginsburg, H.P. (1989). *Children's arithmetic: How they learn it and how you teach it.* Austin, TX: Pro. Ed.

Ginsburg, H.P., Klein, A., & Starkey P. (1988). The development of children's mathematical thinking: Connecting research with practice. In I.E. Sigel & K.A. Renninger (Eds.), *Handbook of child psychology; Vol. 4. Child psychology in practice* (pp. 401-476). New York: Wiley.

Haith, M.M., & Benson, J.H. (1998). Infant cognition. In D. Kuhn & R.S. Siegler (Eds.), *Handbook of child psychology; Vol. 2. Child psychology in practice* (pp. 199-254). New York: Wiley.

Hiebert, J. (1988). A theory of developing competence with written mathematical symbols. *Educational Studies in Mathematics, 19,* 333-355.

Kamii, C. (1986). Place value: An explanation of its difficulty and educational implications for the primary grades. *Journal of Research in Childhood Education, 1,* 75-85.

McGarrigle, J., & Donaldson, M. (1975). Conservation accidents. *Cognition, 3,* 341-350.

Mix, K.S. (1999). Similarity and numerical equivalence: Appearances count. *Cognitive Development, 14,* 269-297.

National Association for the Education of Young Children. (1997). *Developmentally appropriate practice for early childhood programs serving children from birth through age eight.* Washington, DC: National Association for the Education of Young Children.

National Council of Teachers of Mathematics. (2000). *Principles and standards for school mathematics.* Reston, VA: National Council of Teachers of Mathematics.

Oyler, C., & Becker, J. (1997). Teaching beyond the traditional-progressive dichotomy: Sharing authority and sharing vulnerability. *Curriculum Inquiry, 27,* 453-467.

Piaget, J. (1952) *The child's conception of number.* New York: Norton. (Original work published 1941)

Pirie, S.B., & Kieren, T.E. (1994). Beyond metaphor: Formalizing in mathematical understanding within constructivist environments. *For the Learning of Mathematics, 14*(1), 39-43.

Resnick, L.B. (1992). From protoquantities to operators: Building mathematical competence on a foundation of everyday knowledge. In G. Leinhardt, R. Putnam, & R.A. Hattrup (Eds.), *Analysis of arithmetic for mathematics teaching* (pp. 373-429). Hillsdale, NJ: Erlbaum.

Rittle-Johnson, B., & Siegler, R.S. (1998). The relations between conceptual and procedural knowledge in learning mathematics: A review. In C. Donlan (Ed.), *The development of mathematical skills* (pp. 75-110). Hove, UK: Psychology Press.

Saxe, G.B. (1977). A developmental analysis of notational counting. *Child Development, 48,* 1512-1520.

Saxe, G.B., Gearhart, M., & Guberman, S.R. (1984). The social organization of early number development. In B. Rogoff & J.V. Wertsch (Eds.), *Children's learning in the zone of proximal development.* New Directions for Child Development, No. 23 (pp. 19-30). San Francisco: Jossey-Bass.

Saxe, G.B., Guberman, S.R., & Gearhart, M., (1987). Social processes in early number development. *Monographs of the Society for Research in Child Development, 52* (2, Serial No. 216).

Sophian, C. (1987). Early developments in children's use of counting to solve quantitative problems. *Cognition and Instruction, 4,* 61-90.

Sophian, C. (1988). Early developments in children's understanding of number: Inferences about numerosity and one-to-one correspondence. *Child Development, 59,* 1397-1414.

Sophian, C., Wood, A.M., & Vong, K.I. (1995). Making numbers count: The early development of numerical inferences. *Developmental Psychology, 31,* 263-273.

Steffe, L.P. (1992) Learning stages in the construction of the number sequence. In J. Bideaud, C. Meljac, & J. Fischer, (Eds.), *Pathways to number: Children's developing numerical abilities* (pp. 83-98). Hillsdale, NJ: Erlbaum.

Steffe, L.P., & Cobb P. (1988). *Construction of arithmetical meanings and strategies.* New York: Springer-Verlag.

Stigler, J.W., & Hiebert, J. (1998). *The teaching gap.* New York: The Free Press.

Varelas, M., & Becker, J. (1997). Internalization of cultural forms of behavior: Semiotic aspects of intellectual development. In B.D. Cox & C. Lightfoot (Eds.), *Sociogenetic perspectives on internalization.* Mahwah, NJ: Erlbaum.

Wynn, K. (1992). Children's acquisition of the number words and the counting system. *Cognitive Psychology, 24,* 220-251.

CHAPTER 8

EARLY CHILDHOOD SOCIAL STUDIES

Thomas D. Weible and Ann J. Dromsky

INTRODUCTION

Research in the vast curricular area known as the social studies documents how young children develop concepts across multiple disciplinary structures including economics, anthropology, geography, history, political science, sociology, and other humanistic studies. While an understanding of developmental patterns is critical to effective early childhood instruction, some links to concepts and pedagogy are necessary. The present research base provides much needed knowledge for improving early childhood education while opening the door for new theoretical inquiries and curricular recommendations. This chapter will discuss research across a few disciplines in an effort to draw implications and make appropriate connections to social studies in early childhood education programs.

THREE TRADITIONS OF SOCIAL STUDIES

Social Studies "has emerged as the major part of the K-12 curriculum concerned with the maturation of young citizens in our nation and the world" (Pahl, 1996, p. 345). In examining the role of social studies as a school subject, Barth and Shermis (1970) have identified three traditions. Social studies, historically, has been viewed as citizenship transmission. In this first tradition, patriotism, cultural heritage, core political values and societal perspectives are passed on to our students. A second tradition is to promote civic competence and social development by teaching the social studies as a social science, emphasizing concept attainment and promoting an understanding of the process of inquiry that an historian or a social scientist employs. The third tradition, social studies as reflective inquiry, stresses in-depth study of social issues and developing habits of the mind "to free themselves and public policy from unexamined conventions" and "habits of the heart to have democratic regard for others and for the institutions that promote the common good" (Allen, 1996, p. 6).

These traditions provide an overview of the purposes for the teaching of history, geography, sociology, anthropology, economics and political science—those disciplines typically found in the social studies curriculum. As well, the broad goals of social competence and citizenship afford a central purpose for the disciplines within the social studies. Typically reserved for the later elementary years, these disciplines are now an integral part of early childhood curriculums. The challenge for educators is to identify and integrate developmentally appropriate experiences that introduce young children to the social studies. Central to this task is an understanding of the role of social studies and influential theories in early childhood curriculum.

THE ROLE OF SOCIAL STUDIES IN EARLY CHILDHOOD EDUCATION

To a large extent, the beliefs we hold as individuals and share as a society determine the school curriculum and, in turn, the value and trust we place on children influences what and how we teach. Over the years evolving theoretical models grounded in different beliefs have influenced the early childhood social studies curriculum (Stott & Bowman, 1996). Three influential theories, Maturationist, Behaviorist, and Cognitive/Constructivist range along a continuum of beliefs regarding the nature of children and have influenced approaches to social studies instruction (for a more exhaustive treatment of theories, see Ch. 2 of this volume). How children are perceived by each theory influenced curriculum design and the cumulative knowledge about how children learn and how best to prepare future citizens.

Seefeldt (1984) stated that "social studies for young children are more than a collection of separate, though related disciplines from the social sciences." She further elaborated, "For a society to perpetuate itself, its young must clearly understand its values and attitudes and must develop the skills and knowledge required to live in it. Thus, a social studies curriculum for young children includes value clarification and social living as well as knowledge of the social sciences." In its 1993 definition the National Council for the Social Studies (NCSS), the learned society for social studies education, in part, stated, "The primary purpose of the social studies is to help young people develop the ability to make informed and reasoned decisions for the public good as citizens of a culturally diverse, democratic society in an interdependent world" (NCSS, 1993).

While we could ponder the merits of these and other definitions, in a broad sense, the role of social studies for the early childhood teacher is to "introduce children to the world of people" (Ellis, 1998, p.1). What better way to foster personal competence and responsibility than by studying people? Understanding where and how people live, how they are impacted by and interact with their surroundings, and how we live together by appreciating and exploring the uniqueness, similarity and contributions of all cultures. To effectively introduce children to this "world of people" the teacher must take care in selecting appropriate goals for the social studies program and orchestrate learning activities that are engaging and rich in content, as opposed to a curriculum with a scope and sequence of unconnected, meaningless facts (NCHS, 1994; Seefeldt, 1995). The design, implementation and assessment of such a curriculum requires that the early childhood teacher have a sound knowledge and understanding of the role and content of the social studies, theory, and practice in early childhood education.

Upon reviewing standards across content areas the National Association for the Education of the Young Child (NAEYC) recommends "transforming" curriculum to integrate disciplines and create meaningful experiences grounded in the teacher's knowledge of how children learn (Bredekamp & Rosengrant, 1995). Similarly, NCSS states that at the primary level, ". . . children often learn social studies through learning experiences that are highly integrated across several disciplines" (NCSS, 2000). From the current perspective of constructivism, as well as sociocognitive and interactive theories, learning is viewed as the interaction between the child, the context, materials, and other individuals. The dynamic process of this interaction builds children's background knowledge, concepts about the world and language facility through scaffolded and diverse experiences across disciplines. Thus, active participation combined with a social studies program should enable children to better understand and more effectively participate as citizens.

APPROACHES TO EARLY CHILDHOOD SOCIAL STUDIES

The evolution of approaches to early childhood social studies, in many respects, reflects the influence of child development theory, the thinking of prominent educators, and educational issues. Traditionally, social studies instruction placed the young child in a passive role in the learning experience. Viewing the child as a miniature adult, social studies content was determined by authorities in the field, oftentimes having little meaning to the students or relevance to their lives. Lessons were oriented to a direct instructional approach often requiring students to read, memorize, and recite facts. History and geography dominated social studies content. Inculcation of attitudes and values attributed to famous Americans was a primary vehicle for civic education. The tales of the truthfulness of George Washington and the cherry tree, and the patriotism of Nathan Hale regretting having but one life to give for his country, represent classic examples.

The Progressive Education Era ushered in new thinking about curriculum that would have profound implications for the teaching of children and the social studies. Jarolimek (1981) stated, "The social studies more than any other area of the school curriculum, felt the impact of the progressive education movement," and, "was intended to be socially useful to ordinary citizens." According to Jarolimek the progressive education movement was, "not merely preparation for life, it *was* life!" (p. 6). John Dewey's writings, translated into practice in his laboratory school, brought about new ways of looking at how children learn, the nature of the school curriculum, and instructional methodologies. Dewey's belief that the classroom should be a model for democracy and the curriculum involve students in real world problems, prompted educators to think of the child as a more active participant in the learning process. In Dewey's view, school was a social institution that should be structured as a democratic society (Phillips, 1998). This thinking placed the teacher in a more active role in curriculum decisions and in motivating the child's interest in learning.

The progressive education movement contributed to the development of the "expanding environments" curriculum model that still influences social studies in the primary grades (PreK-3). This model is based on the notion that "students will be introduced during each year of school to an increasingly expanding social environment. Moving from examining the self and family in grades K-1 to the world at large in grade 6" (Martorella, 2001). Lucy Sprague Mitchell later refined this model and determined that the social studies curriculum should actively involve students as learners and be "cased entirely on children's experiences and on their discovery of the world around them." Mitchell's goal was to enhance young children's relationship thinking and the ability to generalize from one experience to another. In her book *Young Geographers* (1934) emphasis was placed on students developing positive relationships with others; cultivating self-concept, self-respect, and self-management behaviors; and appreciating and respecting others in the group. Equally important, however, was the growing need to compete academically with other countries and to accelerate the nation's technological progress. Thus, shortly thereafter, geography disappeared from systematic instruction and was replaced by more trivial units that limited students' exposure to complex concepts (Jantz & Seefeldt, 1999).

The launching of Sputnik in 1957 caused our nation to ponder the effectiveness of our public schools as the "Cold War" intensified. Many Americans questioned whether or not schools were preparing our children to ensure our nation could remain competitive with other global powers. During the late 50s and through the decade of the 60s, the emphasis shifted to the child's "capacity" to learn and process information. Psychologists would challenge us to think about the cognitive development of the child in relation to the appropriateness when and how to teach selected content. The work of both Jean Piaget and Jerome Bruner had a significant impact upon social studies education for young children. Piaget viewed children as "active, exploratory and curious information processors" (Ellis, 1998, p. 31). He concluded that children progress through stages of cognitive development: sensorimotor, preoperational, concrete operations, and formal operations. Early childhood teachers, knowledgeable about Piaget's stages, could now make more informed decisions regarding content selection and sequence as well as determining appropriate strategies for social studies instruction. For example, teachers realized that certain geographic concepts involving direction and distance might be difficult for children at the preoperational stage of development.

Jerome Bruner's influence on social studies was the contribution of the instructional model he utilized in his innovative program, *Man: A Course of Study*. Bruner's model emphasized the importance of students learning the structure of the discipline and the concept of discovery learning (Bruner, 1960). He proposed that social studies instruction should emphasize significant ideas and concepts. The teaching of history, for example, would promote an understanding of chronology and change, rather than the knowledge of a specific date or event. Important in learning the structure of the discipline was Bruner's belief that students should also learn and experience the methods of inquiry an historian or social scientist utilizes. In his instructional model Bruner also stressed the importance of discovery learning, a "hands-on" approach to learning "using the senses as a means of direct encounter with knowledge" (Ellis, 1998, p. 55).

In addition to Bruner, Lawrence Senesh developed *Our Working World*, a program to actively involve students in learning economics. He tested ideas with elementary students that helped link content scholars to teachers, bridging the gap between academia and practice. His program placed economics at the center of the curriculum, believing "students can demonstrate their economic understanding operationally, even if they can't give neat definitions of such concepts as supply and demand curves, GNP, and opportunity cost" (Gross, Messick, Chapin, & Sutherland, 1978).

More recent approaches to social studies instruction have been influenced by the growing body of research on child development and teaching, learning motivation, the changing demographics of the students we teach, and the politics and policies of education. Howard Gardner's (1983) theory of multiple intelligences (linguistic, musical, logical-mathematical, spatial, kinesthetic, intrapersonal, interpersonal) provided early childhood educators with seemingly limitless opportunity for teaching and learning particularly in the social studies. Likewise, the constructivist perspective that supports in the social studies "what is presented by the teacher or in the textbook as public and agreed-upon knowledge or beliefs, is received by the student and given meaning in terms of his or her past experience and cognitive capabilities or structures" is now influencing pedagogical approaches (Torney-Purta 1991, p. 190). As such, the early childhood educator has to consider that constructing knowledge in social studies involves the child in both cognitive and affective processes of learning and that the total life experiences of the child play a significant role in the interpretation and meaning of information.

Geography

One of the earliest concepts children develop is spatial reasoning, and this awareness is the foundation of basic geography (Sunal, 1993). Piaget and Infelder (1967) documented that infants and toddlers demonstrate emerging awareness of their proximity to items in their environment. As young children develop they can communicate their location in reference to how near or far they find themselves from an object. Following this line of research, Blaut, McCleary, and Blaut (1970) found that kindergartners are capable of reading simple maps and understanding concepts such as cardinal directions. These studies clearly indicate that very young children understand their environment and therefore achieve with instruction in geographic concepts.

The benefits of geography instruction with young children are absent in recent research; however, studies in the 1950s and 1970s noted that children in the primary grades demonstrated increased achievement after systematic map skills and higher-level questioning with different materials (Bloom, 1956; Buggey, 1971; & Tyler, 1971). This level of instruction can be integrated throughout the day from whole-group to individual centers that promote young students' thinking about geographical concepts. Investigation and problem solving are prominent in the pre-kindergarten curriculum. Children have access to various centers to construct, observe, classify, categorize and experiment about topics related to social studies.

Considering the many components of the curriculum, one can readily see that the pre-kindergarten program affords ample opportunity for children to be "introduced to the world of people" (Ellis, 1998, p. 2). Children are engaged in learning activities that focus upon holidays such as Martin Luther King Day, neighborhoods and local communities, and physical systems. The few studies related to early geography skills indicate that such celebrations and opportunities provide a dynamic context for well-designed instruction that promotes questioning and inquiry about locations beyond the immediate physical environment.

Economics

Commenting on the Voluntary National Content Standards in Economics, Duval notes that students should "learn about basic economics and the economy as they go through school, so that they will be better informed workers, consumers and producers, savers and investors, and most important, citizens" (NCEE, 1997, p. v). Researchers who focused on young children's development of economic concepts produced numerous "stages" of economic understanding (see Furth, 1980; Fox, 1978). These investigations and subsequent studies highlight the importance of real-life experiences as critical components of instruction, While further research is necessary as to the limitations of children's economic understanding (Sunal, 1993), real-life experiences emerge as a critical feature in exemplary classrooms (Pressley, Rankin, & Yokoi, 1996).

There is little doubt that children experience, on a regular basis, economic concepts such as producer, consumer, goods and services, money, scarcity, and choice. Seefeldt (1985) notes, "Young children are already acquainted with economic concepts. They shop with their parents, receive the services of a physician, nurse, librarian and school teacher; they have wants, perhaps receive an allowance and come into contact with jobs, production of goods and the economic systems of banking and government" (p. 203). Since economics is an integral part of the child's world, the teacher has seemingly unlimited opportunity to develop relevant and meaningful learning experiences.

History

"History is concerned with the totality of human experience, past and present . . . It is past politics, past economics, past society, past religion, past civilization—in short, past everything" (Krug, 1967, p. 4). For the young child history should focus on change and chronology with an understanding of the past, while developing a vision of the future. Building upon a child's prior knowledge and experiences may facilitate historical understanding (Jantz & Seefeldt, 1999). Barton (1997) states, "Teachers who are willing and able to engage students in active investigations to build on what children already know and to address misconceptions will stand a good chance of helping them to develop meaningful historical understanding" (p. 16).

For the very young, developing a sense of the continuity of change must be accomplished through daily personal experiences. Real-life experiences, read-alouds of story and picture books that detail life in the past, or pictures of the local community a hundred years ago, illuminate how people and artifacts change over time, as well as other individuals' points of view. Young children are capable of engaging in discussions that can foster critical thinking about experiences with artifacts or stories of the past (Mazzoni & Gambrell, 1996). Instruction designed to capitalize on these language and creative concepts allow children to represent the "big idea" of change. Developing a basic understanding of time and how people change is critical to more complex treatment of these topics in primary grade textbooks and curriculum. As students enter kindergarten, the ideas and constructs introduced in the early years expand to include more global and multicultural topics.

IMPLICATIONS FOR EARLY CHILDHOOD SOCIAL STUDIES CURRICULUM

In many respects, the social studies in the early childhood curriculum continue to evolve and seek definition. While there are published standards from NCSS and a number of professional organizations specific to the social studies, few address the early childhood curriculum nor consider the research discussed above. Regarding this dilemma, Seefeldt (1992) states:

> When the complexities of the field of social studies meet the confounding factors of early childhood education, the problems involved in specifying appropriate content expand, and the question of how either field can effectively fulfill its overarching purpose—that of preparing children to become members of a democracy—remain unanswered. (p. 216)

While recommendations from NCSS and NAEYC stress the importance of a rich curricular experience for young children, translating the vast knowledge base for social studies into developmentally appropriate practices is a difficult task. Perhaps the most sensible approach for the early childhood educator is offered by Jantz and Seefeldt (1999). They suggest that teachers be the decision makers advocating that they "be aware of the nature of the students, the nature of learning, the nature of society and the nature of knowledge as they make choices about the social studies curriculum" (p. 61). For the teacher to assume this responsibility they ". . . must have a command of the knowledge and the ability to intentionally and selectively draw from the various disciplines: history, geography, sociology, anthropology, global studies, ecology, economics, and moral education" (Spodek & Saracho, 1990, p. 90). The teachers, therefore, needs not only a sound understanding of the subject matter in each of these disciplines, but because of our rapidly changing world, be a lifelong learner of the social studies.

Planning appropriate learning experiences to teach the social studies poses yet another challenge. For children to acquire and understand content the teacher must "provide opportunities for learners to construct knowledge by interacting directly with the content, most typically through the solution of an authentic problem" (Harris & Graham, 1994). In designing instruction for such a program the teacher might be guided by the following principles identified by Brooks and Brooks (1993):

- Pose problems that are relevant and meaningful to students. Constructing problems that challenge children to learn is a trademark of effective early childhood teachers.
- Structure learning around "big ideas" or primary concepts. Broad experiences provide a schema for children to discuss. Teachers can provide access to various centers to construct, observe, classify, categorize and experiment about topics related to social studies.
- Seek and value students' points of view. What children understand prior to instruction will help guide further instruction.
- Modify curriculum to address students' suppositions.
- Assess student learning in the context of teaching. The learner *and* context help the teacher design social studies instruction. The teacher, therefore, must know how to interpret students' developing sense of concepts to make daily and long-term instructional decisions. As important as it is to modify the curriculum, in the pre-kindergarten years a teacher must modify instructional approaches based on students' needs. Observations of how students participate and engage in the above experiences will dictate how to approach more complex tasks.

These principles lend credence to the importance of an integrated curriculum. Children spend a great deal of time reading, writing, speaking, and listening to topics related to their world (Tovey & Weible, 1981). Therefore integrating language activities to enhance social studies understanding is a natural combination (Farris, 2001). Language activities can integrate a wide variety of literature and provide opportunities for children to experience learning through the humanistic studies of art, music, drama, and dance. Tables 1 and 2 provide a framework of how the principles outlined above might look in the early childhood classroom for the concepts of economics and history discussed in this chapter.

TABLE 1
Integrated Experience Framework for Economics

- Pose problems that are relevant and meaningful to students. Primary grade students can easily grasp the concept of needs/wants and supply/demand. Every child can relate to a familiar topic such as housing, food, or popular toys. Engaging children in an exploration of how individuals acquire needs and wants demonstrates a primary economic concept.

- Structure learning around "big ideas" or primary concepts. To activate prior knowledge, the list-group-label technique activates children's background knowledge and helps students organize concepts logically. The teacher introduces a topic such as "wants" or "needs" and students list any words or ideas they believe are related to the topic. In this way children learn to use key vocabulary for writing and reading extensions through scaffolded experiences. Children can document their learning through descriptive writing or planning classroom events or field trips.

- Seek and value students' points of view. What children understand prior to instruction will help guide further instruction. Creating a Venn diagram provides listening and speaking opportunities and permits the teacher to assess how students conceptualize the topic. Students can visualize similarities and differences between producers and consumers and how wants and needs create a demand for production or the diagram might contrast two producers or compare local businesses. At first only one circle may be appropriate to represent a concept. The same would be done with a second circle. Then the circles can be crossed to discuss similarities (what belongs in both circles) and differences (what belongs in separate circles). Students are introduced to the vocabulary of the everyday world of producers, consumers, and decision-making occupations. The teacher guides students in placing the words in categories, discussion the overall logic and negotiating disagreements. Finally, labels are generated for the categories. To scaffold this experience, the teacher may need to provide the categories first and gradually lead children to generate the labels.

- Modify curriculum to address students' suppositions. From the above experiences, the teacher will gain insight into children's developing knowledge of economics. Based on this knowledge, it may be necessary to create a mini-economy within the classroom or plan visits with local businesses. Students might require greater exposure to the concept of producers versus consumers. Activities such as the Venn Diagram can be completed independently or in small groups. This variation in social context affords students multiple opportunities to engage in discussions, language experiences, and artistic activities that foster an appreciation for the social studies. The curriculum should be flexible enough to match students' needs as well as interests.

- Assess student learning in the context of teaching. As noted in the previous section, effective social studies teachers operate within a framework that is not constrained by rote adherence to a manual or guide. Although the content of a curriculum might be guided by the school system, instructional delivery should follow from students' participation in carefully planned lessons. This type of informal assessment occurs on a daily basis.

TABLE 2
Integrated Experience Framework for History

- Pose problems that are relevant and meaningful to students. Chronology and change are difficult concepts for young children, yet the basic understanding is critical to study of the past and the ability to contextualize the present in relation to the past. To pose this problem with three and four olds, the experience must be grounded in a concrete example. Taking a walking field trip of the school community may reveal differences in housing, local businesses opening or closing, construction, and seasonal changes in physical systems like trees and animal life. These experiences provide a schema for children to discuss and observe as examples of change and how the chronological history of the community affects people.

- Structure learning around "big ideas" or primary concepts. For the very young, developing a sense of the continuity of change must be accomplished through daily personal experiences. Discussion of the changes witnessed on a field trip should be discussed modeling the vocabulary and language. Young children are capable of engaging in discussions that can foster critical thinking (Mazzoni & Gambrell, 1996). Discussions about the importance of sharing, listening, cooperating and negotiating directly address that key role of the social studies, citizenship. If students engage with artifacts from the past, the teacher can ask students to participate in the activity and compare the process to the present. For example, pre-kindergartners may take turns churning butter or washing clothes on a washboard. Such opportunities demonstrate change is continuous and affects people. To supplement these experiences, read-alouds of story and picture books that detail life in the past, or pictures of the local community a hundred years ago, illuminate how people and artifacts change over time, as well as other individuals' points of view. These language and artistic activities allow children to represent the "big idea" of change.

- Seek and value students' points of view. In addition to verbal discussion, recording students' statements about their experiences provides an early introduction to reading and writing. Through the Language Experience Approach (see Walker, 1996), teachers can chart students' own statements and provide copies to students. These class charts can be read chorally or with peers. Having experiences recorded will build children's social studies vocabulary and aid in the transfer of oral language into reading and writing tasks. Students should be encouraged to write their thoughts and have speaking opportunities to share writing. Encouraging participation in whole class or small group settings teaches children that individuals have different ideas and perceptions of the same concept.

- Modify curriculum to address students' suppositions. As per the previous principle, reading a variety of texts presents multiple points of view. To help children evaluate their suppositions, an anticipation guide is one pre-reading or pre-listening activity that requires students to activate prior knowledge and modify their ideas. The teacher creates and reads aloud a small number of statements about the content of an historical reading selection. The students are encouraged to discuss the statements and mark whether they agree or disagree with the content. After listening to the selection, the group revisits the statements to evaluate if new information changed individual beliefs. Such discussion promotes speaking and modification and/or revision of ideas. With young children these statements can be written on chart paper and students can check if they agree or disagree with the opportunity to modify their statements throughout the social studies unit.

(continued)

TABLE 2
Continued

- Assess student learning in the context of teaching. The learner and context help the teacher design social studies instruction. The teacher, therefore, must know how to interpret students' developing sense of concepts to make daily and long-term instructional decisions. As important as it is to modify the curriculum, in the pre-kindergarten years a teacher must modify instructional approaches based on students' needs. Observations of how students participate and engage in the above experiences will dictate how to approach more complex tasks. A teacher may discover that a great deal of modeling is necessary for one concept, while students readily engage in drawings or dramatic recreations of other experiences. Some students may eagerly attempt to write, while others will dictate their ideas to an adult. Informal assessment during lessons reveals that children learn similar concepts in different ways. Multiple trips and discussions may need to preface more complex activities, and the teacher must gauge instruction by the students and not a scope and sequence of activities.

CONCLUSION

Early childhood Social Studies instruction is dramatically different today from past decades. Documented in the literature across curricular disciplines are numerous shifts in pedagogy for teaching the young child (Gambrell & Mazzoni, 1996) coupled with more global perspectives of social studies content. In response to new research, major organizations such as the National Association for the Education of the Young Child (NAEYC), National Council for the Social Studies (NCSS, 1994), are publishing curriculum standards and joint position statements regarding developmentally appropriate practices for the young child. Given these perspectives, early Social Studies instruction is no longer characterized by study of the immediate physical environment of the student. Rather young children are exploring a global community across such disciplines as history, geography, economics, and anthropology; and political science aided by technology and instruction that recognizes the young learner's capacity for critical thinking.

There is a paucity of research regarding the social studies in the primary grades and growing concern among many educators that social studies may be neglected in an effort to spend more time on reading and mathematics. Farris (2001) contends that 25% of the curriculum should be devoted to social studies. This is a considerable amount of time, however, not unreasonable given the importance of the social studies disciplines in our everyday lives and the critical role that social studies plays as the primary school subject for citizenship education. Likewise, suggested integrated models for curriculum (Bredekamp & Rosengrant, 1995) would provide the time and context to meet this guideline. Given the significant changes occurring in classroom contexts and early childhood education, it is important to examine curriculum patterns and reconceptualize effective social studies instruction for the young child.

The changing demographics of our society and the children in our charge demand that we continue to explore new ways to meet the needs of a diverse student population. As we implement innovative instructional approaches we will need to continuously assess the social studies curriculum to assure that the knowledge, attitudes and skills we teach are relevant to the children and contribute to preparing them to be effective and participating citizens. Seefeldt (1995) noted that the social studies are well suited to helping young children not only participate in a democratic society, but improve and perfect that society.

During the past decade education has become a central societal issue in local, statewide and national elections. Politicians and policymakers share an interest in and seem to agree that our future as a dominant world player is dependent upon providing all children access to a high-quality education. Much of this attention is focused upon early childhood education and intervention. At this same time we find professional associations, states and accrediting agencies developing a myriad of standards to be met by teachers and students. This demand for accountability has increased along with the public interest and investment in education. While there has been little research as to how the aforementioned will impact the early childhood curriculum and social studies in particular, it seems inevitable that change will occur.

REFERENCES

Barth, J.L., & Shermis, S.S. (1970). Defining the social studies: An exploration of three traditions. *Social Education, 34*, 743-751.

Barton, K. (1997). History—it can be elementary: An overview of elementary students' understanding of history. *Social Education, 61*, 13-16.

Blaut, J., McCleary, G., & Blaut, A. (1970). Environmental mapping in young children. *Environment and Behavior, 2*, 335-349.

Bloom, B. (1956). *Taxonomy of educational objectives: Handbook I: Cognitive domain.* New York: David McKay.

Borchert, J.R. (1983). Questions students ask. *Journal of Geography, 82*, 43.

Bredekamp, S., & Rosegrant, T. (1995a). Reaching potentials through transforming curriculum: Introduction. In S. Bredekamp & T. Rosegrant (Eds.), *Reaching potentials: Transforming early childhood curriculum and assessment* (Vol. 2, pp. 1-4). Washington, DC: National Association for the Education of Young Children.

Bredekamp, S., & Rosegrant, T. (1995b). Reaching potentials through national standards: Panacea or pipe dream? In S. Bredekamp & T. Rosegrant (Eds.), *Reaching potentials: Transforming early childhood curriculum and assessment* (Vol. 2, pp. 5-14). Washington, DC: National Association for the Education of Young Children.

Brooks, J.G., & Brooks, M.G. (1993). *In search of understanding: The case for constructivist classrooms.* Alexandria, VA: Association for Supervision and Curriculum Development.

Bruner, J. (1966). *Toward a theory of instruction.* Cambridge, MA: Belknap.

Bruner, J. (1960). *The process of education.* Cambridge, MA: Harvard University Press.

Dewey, J. (1938). *Experience and education.* New York: Macmillan.

Ellis, A.K. (1998). *Teaching and learning elementary social studies* (6th ed.). Boston: Allyn Bacon

Farris, P.J. (2001). *Elementary and middle school social studies: An interdisciplinary instructional approach* (3rd ed.), New York: McGraw-Hill.

Fox, K. (1978). What children bring to school: The beginnings of economic education. *Social Education, 42*(6), 478-481.

Gardner, H. (1983). *Frames of mind: The theory of multiple intelligences.* New York: Basic Books.

Gross, R.E., Messick, R., Chapin, J.R., & Sutherland, J. (1978). *Social studies for our times.* New York: Wiley.

Harris, K., & Graham, S. (Eds.) (1994). Implications of constructivism for students with disabilities and students at risk: Issues and directions. *Journal of Special Education, 38* (Special Edition).

Jantz, R.K., & Seefeldt, C. (1999). Early childhood social studies. In C. Seefeldt (Ed.), *The early childhood curriculum: Current findings in theory and practice* (3rd ed.). New York: Teachers College Press.

Jarolimek, J. (1981). The social studies: An overview. *The social studies.* Eightieth Yearbook of the National Society for the Study of Education. Chicago: The University of Chicago Press.

Krug, M. (1967). *History and the social sciences.* Waltham, MA: Blaisdell.

Martorella, P.H. (2001). *Teaching social studies in middle and secondary schools* (3rd ed.). Upper Saddle River, NJ: Prentice-Hall.

Mayer, R.H. (1995). Inquiry into place as an introduction to world geography—Starting with ourselves. *Social Education, 86,* 74-77.

Mazzoni, S.A., & Gambrell, L.B. (1996). Text talk: Using discussion to promote comprehension of informational texts. In L.B. Gambrell & J.F. Almasi (Eds.), *Lively discussions! Fostering engaged reading.* Newark, DE: International Reading Association.

McCarthy, J. (1990). The content of early childhood teacher education programs: Pedagogy. In B. Spodek & O. Saracho (Eds.), *Yearbook in early childhood education* (Vol. I). New York: Teachers College Press.

National Center for History in the Schools. (1994). *National standards: History for grades K-4.* Los Angeles: Author.

National Council for the Social Studies. (1993, January-February). Definition approved. *The Social Studies Professional,* p. 1.

National Council on Economic Education. (NCEE). (1997). *Voluntary national content standards in economics.* New York: Author.

Pahl, R.H. (1996). Digital technology and social studies. In B.G. Massiallas & R.F. Allen (Eds.), *Critical issues in teaching social studies K-12.* Belmont, CA: Wadsworth.

Phillips, D.C. (1998). John Dewey's the child and the curriculum: A century later. *The Elementary School Journal, 98,* 403-424.

Piaget, J., & Inhelder, B. (1967). *The child's conception of space.* New York: Norton.

Pressley, M., Rankin, J., & Yokoi, L. (1996). A survey of instructional practices of primary teachers nominated as effective in promoting literacy. *Elementary School Journal 96,* 363-384.

Seefeldt, C. (1995). Transforming curriculum in social studies. In S. Bredekamp & T. Rosegrant (Eds.), *Reaching potentials: Transforming early childhood curriculum and assessment* (Vol. 2, pp. 109-124). Washington, DC: National Association for the Education of the Young Child.

Seefeldt, C. (1992, 1999). *The early childhood curriculum: A review of research* (2nd & 3rd eds.). New York: Teachers College Press.

Stott, F., & Bowman, B. (1996). Child development knowledge: A slippery base for practice. *Early Childhood Quarterly, 11,* 169-183.

Thomas, R.M. (1992). *Comparing theories of development* (3rd ed.). Belmont, CA: Wadsworth.

Vygotsky, L. (1962). *Thought and language.* Cambridge, MA: MIT Press.

CHAPTER 9

LEARNING AND TEACHING WITH COMPUTERS IN EARLY CHILDHOOD EDUCATION

Julie Sarama and Douglas H. Clements

INTRODUCTION

Computers are increasingly a part of preschoolers' lives. Toward the end of the 1980s, only a fourth of licensed preschools had computers. At the beginning of the 21st century, the majority of sites have computers. Estimates vary; some research shows that about half of the sites surveyed in the United States and Japan had computers (Ishigaki, Chiba, & Matsuda, 1996; Wood, Willoughby, & Specht, 1998). In contrast, 80% to 90% of early childhood educators attending the annual National Association for the Education of Young Children national conference report using computers (Haugland, 1997).

During the same time period, we concluded that research on young children and technology had moved beyond simple questions. Instead, research could and should consider the varied uses of technology in early childhood education. For example, researchers no longer needed to ask whether the use of technology is "developmentally appropriate." Young children have shown comfort and confidence in using software. They can understand, think about, and learn from their computer activity (Clements & Nastasi, 1993).

Therefore, we were surprised to find that strong statements against computer use by young children are still being written and promulgated

(Cordes & Miller, 2000). Although we do believe that the general issues have been addressed, we take this as a sign that discussion regarding the appropriateness of computer use with young children needs to be continued. Although we have much empirical evidence as to the benefits of using computers with young children, it is important to achieve consensus regarding how children develop and learn, so that we can both maximize the benefits of using computers and avoid doing any harm. We do this by addressing a series of questions. What do we know about children using computers? How old should children be before computers can have a positive influence in their lives? How do children interact with computers? What is the empirical evidence about possible negative influences of such interaction? How do computers influence children's social-emotional development? How might computers affect their learning and thinking? What are the implications for teachers?

Before we address these questions, it is useful to consider the two major philosophies and theories on which researchers have based their investigations of computers in early childhood education. Most of those studying the effects of drill have used a behaviorist paradigm. Most of those who study children's use of word processing, Logo programming, fine arts and manipulative and other "tool" programs, and so forth often hail from a constructivist perspective. As contributors to the latter research, to the National Association for the Education of Young Children's position statement "Technology and Young Children—Ages 3 through 8," and to the National Council of Teachers of Mathematics' new *Principles and Standards for School Mathematics* (2000), our own constructivist orientation is clear. We believe that the child is a capable active learner, that social relationships form the basis for development, that the environment also serves to support development and learning, that learning and development occur over sustained periods of time, and that the best curriculum is child-centered. However, we do not believe that constructivism dictates or limits approaches to teaching (Clements, 1997). Further, we review research from each perspective, to prevent a biased interpretation.

CHILDREN USING COMPUTERS: APPROPRIATENESS, INTERACTIONS, AND AGE

As mentioned, most schools have some computer technology, with the ratio of computers to students changing from 1:125 in 1984 and 1:22 in 1990 to 1:10 in 1997 according to some sources (Clements & Nastasi, 1993; Coley, Cradler, & Engel, 1997). This matches the minimum ratio favorable to social interaction. That is, higher ratios may lead to arguments between children about who gets to use the computer (Clements & Nastasi, 1993). However, these are averages, and many children do not have equal access.

For example, children attending poor and high-minority schools have less access to most types of technology (Coley et al., 1997).

Furthermore, schools having computers does not mean children use computers. In one study, just 9% of 4th graders (they did not collect data on younger children) said they used a computer for school work almost every day, 60% said they never used one. A survey in Silicon Valley, where computer use might be expected to be as high as any location in the United States, found that although 70% of teachers in kindergarten through third grade had their students work on computers, the students' computer time averaged less than 10 minutes per day (Shields & Behrmann, 2000). Nevertheless, there seems to be an increasing *potential* for children to use computers in early childhood settings. Is such use appropriate?

What is "Appropriate"?

An early concern is that children must reach the stage of concrete operations before they are ready to work with computers. Research, however, has found that preschoolers are more competent than has been thought and can, under certain conditions, exhibit thinking traditionally considered "concrete" (Gelman & Baillargeon, 1983). Furthermore, research shows that even young preoperational children can use *appropriate* computer programs with understanding (Clements & Nastasi, 1992).

A related concern is that computer use demands symbolic competence; that is, *computers* are not concrete. This ignores, however, that much of the activity in which young children engage *is* symbolic. They communicate with gestures and language, and they employ symbols in their play, song, and art (Sheingold, 1986). They use two-dimensional symbols in painting as well as in their storybooks. Therefore, symbolism alone does not militate against computer use in early childhood. Further, there are studies that indicate that appropriate computer work, especially in a social setting, can help children acquire symbol vocabularies and action schemes, for example, getting and using a computer stamp pad for transfigurative symbolism (Labbo & Kuhn, 1998). In another study, children learned to make decisions about the appropriateness of varying symbol systems for different communication purposes, often creating nonconventional forms of symbols and moving from exploration to symbolic play (Escobedo, 1992).

Moreover, what is "concrete" to the child may have more to do with what is meaningful and manipulable than with physical characteristics. One study compared a computer graphic felt board environment, in which children could freely construct "bean stick pictures" by selecting and arranging beans, sticks, and number symbols, to a real bean stick environment (Char, 1989). The computer environment actually offered equal, and sometimes greater control and flexibility to young children. Both environments were worthwhile, but one did not need to precede the other. Other studies show that computers enrich experience with regular manipulatives. Third-grade students who used both manipulatives and computer programs, or software, demonstrated a greater sophistication in classification and logical thinking, and showed more foresight and deliberation in classification, than did students who used only manipulatives (Olson, 1988). The computer provided an alternative medium, but also uniquely aided reflection. Another study similarly compared three groups of third graders, receiving science instruction that was hands-on, hands-on with computer-assisted instruction, and limited to the textbook. Both groups with hands-on activities outscored the textbook group. However, the group that included both hands-on and computer activities also outscored the group that only used hands-on activities (Gardner, Simmons, & Simmons, 1992). Again, the computer provides a medium that aids reflection and analysis, as well as providing feedback, enhancing a child's overall experience.

Even if they do learn from the experience, people ask: Should young children use computers at all? Are they "developmentally appropriate?" We follow NAEYC in creating our definition: "Developmentally appropriate means challenging but attainable for most children of a given age range, flexible enough to respond to inevitable individual variation, and, most important, consistent with children's ways of thinking and learning" (Clements, Sarama, & DiBiase, in press). Therefore, the key question is not, "*Are computers 'concrete'?*," but rather, "*Do computers provide experiences that facilitate children's learning in many spheres in ways consistent with children's development?*"

As we shall see repeatedly, philosophizing without empirical support may lead us astray. As just one initial example, critics have said, about children drawing shapes by giving Logo programming commands to a screen "turtle" (e.g., fd 50 rt 90 fd 100 rt 90 fd 50 rt 90 fd 100 rt 90 draws a rectangle): "What does it mean to children to command a perfect square but still not be able to draw it by themselves?" (Cuffaro, 1984, p. 561). Empirical research indicates, however, that Logo drawing experience allows some children to create pictures more elaborate, or detailed, than those that they can create by hand. Children modify their ideas and use these new ideas in all their art work (Vaidya & McKeeby, 1984). Thus, what it means is that children can extend their experiences, their creative activities, and their joy in learning to draw. This is not to say that all uses of computers are beneficial; most studies that show benefits use carefully designed, open-ended activities (we shall return to the issue of the appropriateness and benefit of specific activities, as well as to the issue of creativity writ large). We can help ensure appropriateness by allowing children to select activities and to work with activities at their own level (Watson, Nida, & Shade, 1986) and, of course, by monitoring the way they work at the computer and the total time they spend. How do children *choose* to use computers?

How Do Children Interact with Computers?

Very young children have shown comfort and confidence in using software that requires single-key presses. They can turn on the computer, follow pictorial directions, and use situational and visual cues to understand and reason about their activity (Anderson, 2000a; Clements & Nastasi, 1993; Watson, Chadwick, & Brinkley, 1986).

Typing on the keyboard does not seem to cause them any trouble; in fact, using this adult device seems to be a source of pride for many (Muller & Perlmutter, 1985; Shade, Nida, Lipinski, & Watson, 1986). Moreover, it is often superior to other devices, such as a joystick. Thus, for simple input, the keyboard often may be the best option (Jones & Liu, 1997). Initial experiences can be eased with simple adaptations such as color-coding important keys, such as a green dot for "go" on the "return" key or similar coding for the space bar and shift key for word processing (Jones & Liu, 1997; Kajs, Alaniz, Willman, & Sifuentes, 1998).

For many software programs, you have to position a cursor (i.e., "point"). Keyboards are less useful for this purpose (King & Alloway, 1992). Both mice and trackballs are better than keyboards or joysticks for moving a cursor, with the trackball being particularly good for initial use (Strommen, 1993). Older children can use the mouse more efficiently, but even 3-year-olds and some 2-year-olds can master its use. Children improve significantly following a couple of experiences (Ishigaki et al., 1996; Lane & Ziviani, 1997; Liu, 1996).

Thanks to the recent modifications in hardware, even children with physical and emotional disabilities can use the computer with ease. Besides enhancing their mobility and sense of control, computers can help improve their self-esteem. One totally mute 4-year-old diagnosed with retardation and autism began to echo words for the first time while working at a computer (Schery & O'Connor, 1992). For children with severe learning disabilities, either a touch screen or a simplified, "concept" keyboard is effective, with no significant difference between the two (Wright, Read, & Anderson, 1992).

Differences in learning styles are more readily visible at the computer when children have the freedom to follow diverse paths toward the goal (Wright, 1994). This is particularly valuable with special children, as the computer seems to reveal their hidden strengths. Throughout the early childhood years, children can "work" computers, have positive attitudes toward them, and can describe and discuss their computer work (Yelland, 1995).

How much do children enjoy using computers compared to other well-liked activities? A computer center may vary from being among the most popular free–time activity to being chosen about the same as many other areas (Jones & Liu, 1997; Picard & Giuli, 1985). Physical setup, teacher interventions, and especially the computer programs (software) used, may cause such variations. Noteworthy is that the computer is used extensively during free play, reflecting focused attention and concentration spans of an impressive order (King & Alloway, 1992). In most cases, it appears that three to five-year-old children spend approximately the same amount of time playing in the computer center as drawing, talking, or playing in the block or art centers (Hoover & Austin, 1986; Picard & Giuli, 1985). This attraction outlives the novelty effect (Bergin, Ford, & Hess, 1993). However, play in other important centers, such as blocks, is not decreased by the presence of a computer. Thus, the computer is an interesting, but not overly engrossing, activity for young children (Anderson, 2000a; Lipinski, Nida, Shade, & Watson, 1986).

What software do children like using? Children prefer programs with a lot of interaction, and those that use animation, sound, and voice (Escobedo & Evans, 1997; Lahm, 1996). Parent-child pairs replayed segments more, showed a stronger cognitive focus, and wrote pertinent stories more when they used software programs that have animated graphics or full motion video (Wright, Seppy, & Yenkin, 1992). Thus, certain features attract children, but these should not be the main reason to choose software. Children prefer some features that are educationally and developmentally appropriate, including open-endedness, process orientation, and child-centeredness. However, they also like some software that is neither oriented toward learning nor appropriate, if it has such features as familiarity, animation, music, surprise elements, and high interest topics (Escobedo & Evans, 1997; Shade, 1994). Therefore, good software should strive to include these elements in an instructionally sound manner, but teachers should be careful of using children's interests as a main criterion for selecting or using software. This is especially important, as some research indicates that many students reported enjoying the method from which they learned the least (Saracho, 1982).

In summary, teachers should seek to fully integrate developmentally appropriate, bias-free software matched to educational goals. Multimedia capabilities should be used when they serve educational purposes. Features such as animation, surprise elements, and especially consistent interaction get and hold children's interest. They can also aid learning, *if* designed to be consistent with, and supporting, the pedagogical goals.

What Types of Educational Software Exist?

Software also can be classified into categories based on their pedagogical approach. Not all of these categories are equally appropriate for young children.

Drill software provides practice on skills and knowledge to help students remember and use what they have been taught. If drill programs are used, they should follow principles based on research on learning. They should be designed to increase automaticity in essential skills. They should emphasize accuracy and speed, present only a few items at once, keep sessions short and spaced, and dynamically adapt instruction to the child. As we shall see, research on drill software does show that it leads to measurable gains in learning. However, drill should not be used inappropriately. For example, preschool children may not learn best from this approach. Children using drill have shown significant losses in creativity (with scores decreasing by 50%). Those using more responsive, open-ended software did not show any such loss but instead made cognitive gains (Haugland, 1992).

Tutorial software teaches new subject-matter content. It attempts to interact with a student in much the same way as a human teacher would in a one-to-one situation. Few presently available tutorials adequately interact with young children and most suffer from the same weaknesses as drill software. The following types tend to move from the behaviorist to the constructivist philosophy.

Simulations are models of some part of the world. Games such as "Life" and "Monopoly" are simulations. Computer simulations are mathematical models based on real-world information which attempt to respond in realistic ways. Simulations should not replace a valuable hands-on activity with an unnecessarily vicarious and abstract one. Some simulations, however, may appropriately extend physical experiences (e.g., simulations of microorganisms in the human body; see Mikropoulos, Kossivaki, Katsikis, & Savranides, 1994). In such a case, careful comparison of a simulation and a real-world event may benefit elementary school children (Clements, 1989). Similarly, simulations of events such as running a store or making ethical decisions when faced with a simulated classroom social problem may lead to excellent conjectures and discussions. So, used carefully and critically, simulations can help children explore and develop intuition about events and situations which are too dangerous, expensive, complex, or time consuming to experience directly.

Instructional games as considered here are not merely drill placed in out-of-context settings (e.g., math drill in an arcade game). In true instructional games, the concepts to be learned are intrinsic to the structure and content of the game. For example, in one program, children learn about coordinates by selecting points on a grid so as to create a picture. Such computer games can be intrinsically motivating.

Computer manipulatives are software versions of physical manipulatives. For example, *Shapes* is a computer manipulative, a software version of pattern blocks, that extends what children can do with these shapes. Children create as many copies of each shape as they want and use computer tools to move, combine, and duplicate these shapes to make pictures and designs and to solve problems (Sarama, Clements, & Vukelic, 1996).

Exploratory and tool programs cover a wide range of software that allows children to paint, move animated pictures, type text or record their voices to tell a story, have text read to them, scan or import photographs, create "slide shows," and much more. Such activities encourage problem solving and planning.

Resources such as online encyclopedias can provide multimedia information for young children. The Internet is a vast array of connected computers and information that includes sources of software and subject matter information that can be useful for both teachers and children.

How Young?

Five-year-olds may be more interested in using computers than younger children (Anselmo & Zinck, 1987). However, no major differences were found between the *way* computers were used by younger and older preschoolers (Beeson & Williams, 1985; Lewis, 1981), although 3-year-olds take longer to acclimate to the keyboard than 5-year-olds (Sivin, Lee, & Vollmer, 1985). Newer programs with well-designed multimedia features are interesting to and easily used by 3- to 5-year-olds, even those who were exposed to it for the first time (Liu, 1996). Some research suggests that three years of age (or over) be selected as an appropriate time for introducing a child to discovery-oriented software. However, even children as young as 2 1/2 might be introduced to simple, single-keystroke software (Jones & Liu, 1997; Shade & Watson, 1987). However, one must note that children younger than 4 years should spend most of their time being physically active and the benefits of using computers may be limited; certainly, expenditures and choices for this age should be carefully considered. For all ages, the appropriateness of the design of the software and, of course, the early childhood pedagogy of offering a range of choices from which children can freely choose are of critical importance.

Further, under special circumstances, even very young children can benefit from certain computer applications. Noting that handicapped infants are at high risk for learned helplessness, Brinker (1984) sought ways to use computers to help them exert control over their environment. Infants wore ribbons attached to switches. Their arm or leg movements sent different signals to a computer, which was programmed to turn on a tape recording of the mother's voice or music, show a picture, activate a toy, or the like. These activities built motivation to control such events and increased the infants' smiling and vocalizing. These results have been replicated, with the added result that prompting strategies to teach switch activation should be included (Kinsley & Langone, 1995).

What is the Empirical Evidence about Possible Negative Influences of Such Interaction?

Of course, not always is the use of technology appropriate, and not always does it lead to a good learning experience. Like anything else, it can be used well or badly, and it can be used too much or too little. It all depends on how we design the curriculum and the learning experiences that we provide our children. And, as in most human affairs, it often seems far easier to do things badly than well. Therefore, whether it is manipulatives or computers or text, it is not difficult to find situations in which their use does not benefit children.

In the computer arena, some research indicates that computers are often used in less than ideal ways. For example, most elementary students use computers only occasionally, and then usually only to add "variety" or rewards to the instructional program (Becker, 1990; Hickey, 1993). Often, only those who have finished their seatwork get to use the computer (Hickey, 1993). They use mostly drill software; their teachers state that their goal for using computers is to increase basic skills rather than solve problems or write compositions (Becker, 1990; Hickey, 1993). Simple drill programs similarly predominate in preschool classrooms. Use of only drill software, however, is not consistent with the guidelines of national organizations (e.g., National Association for the Education of Young Children and the International Reading Association, 1998; National Council of Teachers of Mathematics, 2000). Further, many schools are investing heavily in "integrated learning systems" (ILS) that focus on drill. Such ILS programs automatically load one of an extensive sequence of exercises into each student's computer. Evaluations of these systems show a moderate effect on basic skills (Becker, 1992; Kelman, 1990); however, one must consider other aspects of ILS, especially diminished teacher and student control. Also, there are possibilities that children will be less motivated to perform academic work following drill (Clements & Nastasi, 1985) and that their creativity may be harmed (Haugland, 1992).

As we noted in the introduction, some argue that computers have inherent problems. Unfortunately, some critics of computers have spread the misconception that such problems are unavoidable; for "young children, computers have to be converted into teaching machines presenting programmed learning" (Elkind, 1987, p. 8). However, the most promising uses of computers have nothing to do with programmed learning. As mentioned, in one study, only children using drill programs had significant *losses* in creativity. Children using open-ended software made significant gains in intelligence, nonverbal skills, structural knowledge, long-term memory, complex manual dexterity, and self-esteem (Haugland, 1992). Put simply, what we as early childhood educators do the *most* with computers is what research and the national guidelines say we should do the *least*.

Other critics in the United States and Japan (Ishigaki et al., 1996) contend that use of the computer is less "natural." Certainly, overuse of computers might lead to a lack of other experiences, such as outdoor play; however, no advocate of computers in early childhood to our knowledge would condone such overuse. As stated, present-day school use is minimal. Children appear to use computers at home for longer periods, although not excessively, on the average. In one national survey, preschoolers averaged 27 minutes per day, while children 6 to 11 years of age averaged 49 minutes per day (Woodward & Gridina, 2000). Certainly, total screen time should be limited; commercial TV and video games are the largest contributors to such time and should be the first to be curtailed (Clements & Nastasi, 1993; Shields & Behrmann, 2000).

Some complain of possible physical harm, but the issues are complex. For example, declining eyesight due to computer use is a popular myth in Japan, based on data that does show declining eyesight in children (Ishigaki et al., 1996). However, analysis reveals no causal connection, even if more popular video games (often confused with educational software by parents) are considered. The distribution of video games began in 1985, the decline in eyesight began in 1974 and thus the former does not appear to play a decisive role in the latter. Repetitive stress injuries are currently being researched, although if a child is using a keyboard so many hours as to make such an injury conceivable, they have already exceeded the amount of use considered appropriate. Even positive uses should be limited to no more than one to two hours a day, including school and home use (American Academy of Pediatrics, 1999). Further, such time should not be continuous; all people should take breaks for the eyes and the entire body. Given the existence of alternative positive uses of media, and the recommended limit on total screen time, it is not difficult to recommend that children experience no negative media such as violent or adult-oriented video games or TV programming.

SOCIAL AND EMOTIONAL DEVELOPMENT

Contrary to critics' fears, computers do not isolate children. Just the opposite—computers in schools can serve as catalysts for positive social interaction. As one example, children at the computer spent nine times as much time talking to peers while on the computer than while doing puzzles (Muller & Perlmutter, 1985). Other research supports this position as well.

Working Together at the Computer

Children overwhelmingly display positive emotions when using computers (Ishigaki et al., 1996; Shade, 1994). Most of the time, they prefer to work on the computer with a friend rather than alone (Lipinski et al., 1986; Rosengren, Gross, Abrams, & Perlmutter, 1985; Swigger & Swigger, 1984). Further, working on the computer can instigate collaborative work (Clements, 1994). In one third-grade classroom, the teacher gave the students the choice of working at the computer either alone or with a partner. Half the class chose to work alone. Midway through their game, the children who were playing by themselves started to join others. Some even abandoned their own game to offer and take help from their peers. Similar positive results have also been seen regarding children with special needs. The highest proportion of socially contingent discourse was noticed on a computer (Villarruel, 1990). Children show higher positive affect and interest when they use the computer together (Shade, 1994).

The addition of a computer center does not disrupt ongoing play, but does facilitate extensive positive social interaction, cooperation, and helping behaviors (Binder & Ledger, 1985; King & Alloway, 1992; Rhee & Chavnagri, 1991; Rosengren et al., 1985). As an illustration, a teacher-researcher (Anderson, 2000a) stated that her team had a group of very independent, egocentric children, many of whom were accustomed to being the center of their family's attention. They learned cooperation and problem solving with their peers at the computer. Their cooperative play at the computer parallels closely the proportion of cooperative play in the block center (Anderson, 2000b). Further, cooperation in a computer center sometimes provided a context for initiating and sustaining interaction that can be transferred to play in other areas as well, especially for boys. For example, one four-year-old boy with high cognitive skills and low interactional skills relinquished his turn at the mouse to a boy more adept at social skills and less adept at cognitive tasks. Remaining to watch the progress of play in the game he had been playing, he intermittently gave directions to his peer first by merely pointing to the screen and gradually adding verbal suggestions. After working together for a few minutes the boys left the center and continued their interaction on the playground.

Other studies have similar findings. New friendships have been fostered in the computer's presence. There is greater and more spontaneous peer teaching and helping (Clements & Nastasi, 1992; King & Alloway, 1992). Especially encouraging is the finding that preschoolers' participation in computer activities facilitates social interaction between children with disabilities and their normally developing peers (Spiegel-McGill, Zippiroli, & Mistrett, 1989).

The nature of children's interactions appears to follow a developmental trend. Initially, their social exchange consists of an egocentric focus on turn taking. Gradually, they become more peer-oriented, offering to help and to teach and finally, they are able to work collaboratively even without adult intervention (Bergin, Ford, & Meyer-Gaub, 1986; Clements, 1993; Clements & Nastasi, 1992; Emihovich & Miller, 1988; Shade et al., 1986).

Interestingly, this trend emerges both across age levels (e.g., comparing 4-to 6-year-olds) and with greater experience in computer environments.

Given this trend, it is not surprising that preschoolers may find it difficult to take the perspective of their partner and they may also have trouble balancing the cognitive demands of problem-solving tasks simultaneously with managing the social relations (Perlmutter, Behrend, Kuo, & Muller, 1986). Such developmental limitations do not necessarily have to preclude some types of cooperative work for the very young. Children as young as 4 years of age can provide help through verbal instruction and demonstration. They often emulate their teacher's behavior when teaching their peers; therefore, teachers should take extra care to think about their instructional strategies. As an interesting note, preschool children were effective tutors of anxious adults, so much so that their strategies were effective even when used by other adults (Doran & Kalinowski, 1991)! Nevertheless, it may be that most children must be 5 years or more to benefit in both cognitive and social domains by solving substantive problems on the computer.

The Effects of Different Types of Software

The software children use affects their social interactions at the computer. For example, open-ended programs, such as exploratory and tool programs or computer manipulatives, foster collaborative work characterized by goal setting, planning, negotiation, and resolution of conflicts. Logo has been shown to increase preschoolers' self-efficacy and internal locus of control (Bernhard & Siegel, 1994). Drill software, on the other hand, can encourage turn-taking but also engender a competitive spirit. Similarly, video-games with aggressive content can engender aggressiveness in children (Clements & Nastasi, 1992).

Computer-based instructional games specifically designed to involve cooperative interaction and symbolic play can stimulate significant improvement in social behavior (Garaigordobil & Echebarria, 1995). Similarly, a mixture of software has been used successfully as a play therapy tool for preschoolers (Kokish, 1994). So, choosing the right type of software to meet the right goal is an important task for adults. Of course, off-computer activities can also serve these purposes, and a combination can be especially useful.

The Synergy of Social and Cognitive Interactions

We have seen that computers appear to facilitate certain prosocial behaviors. In addition, they facilitate both social and cognitive interactions. Researchers have observed that 95% of children's talking during

Logo is related to their work (Genishi, McCollum, & Strand, 1985). Further, computers produce a more advanced cognitive type of play than other centers (Hoover & Austin, 1986). In one study, the computer was the only activity that resulted in high levels of both language development and cooperative play (Muhlstein & Croft, 1986). Finally, Logo programming has been found to increase both prosocial and higher-order thinking behaviors (Clements, 1986; Clements & Nastasi, 1985). Thus, *computers may represent an environment in which both cognitive and social interactions simultaneously are encouraged, each to the benefit of the other.* As we shall see, research on the cognitive influences of computer use support this claim.

COGNITIVE DEVELOPMENT AND LEARNING

Research has substantiated that computers can help young children learn. For example, one computer-based project showed positive and statistically significant improvement across grades and schools for three areas: reading, mathematics, and total battery scores (Kromhout & Butzin, 1993). Effects were largest for students in the program for more than one year, as well as those from minorities and free-lunch programs. Other general achievement results are similar (Stone, 1996).

Even mundane applications of computers, such as providing practice and feedback, have been shown to be effective. More promising are applications that maximize the unique value of technology as a learning device. They open new and unforeseen avenues for learning. They allow children to interact with vast amounts of information from within their classrooms and homes. They bring children from across the world together (Riel, 1994). This section reviews research on learning in various subject areas and on creativity and higher-order thinking skills.

Language and Literacy—Talking, Practicing, and Writing

Language Development. The previous section reviewed research indicating that computers often facilitate increases in social interaction and positive attitudes. Unsurprisingly, this often helps children increase their use of language. Preschoolers' language activity, measured as words spoken per minute, is almost twice as high at the computer as at any of the other activities, including play dough, blocks, art, or games (Muhlstein & Croft, 1986). In general, the classroom computer is a valuable resource in facilitating language use, particularly interactional language functions (Kent & Rakestraw, 1994).

When children create or manipulate computer graphics, they are especially likely to generate language (Escobedo, 1992). For example, children in a nursery setting tell longer and more structured stories following a computer graphics presentation than following a static presentation or no stimulus (Riding & Tite, 1985). Working within a language experience context, 3- and 4-year-old children verbalized (i.e., dictated) significantly more about their Logo computer pictures than about their hand–drawn works (Warash, 1984). Research with Logo also indicates that it engenders interaction and language rich with emotion, humor, and imagination (Genishi et al., 1985). Children were clearly and directly responsive to other children's requests for information. Experience with Logo embedded in a narrative context similarly enhances language-impaired preschool children's perceptual-language skills (Lehrer & deBernard, 1987) and increases first graders' scores on assessments of visual-motor development, vocabulary, and listening comprehension (Robinson, Gilley, & Uhlig, 1988; Robinson & Uhlig, 1988). Such facilitative effects may significantly help children at risk, who perform poorly when asked to understand and retell orally presented stories (Cognition and Technology Group at Vanderbilt, 1998). When provided with dynamic visual information that supported the text they were learning, these children significantly improved (Cognition and Technology Group at Vanderbilt, 1998).

Computers can also help special populations. Some children are at risk in literacy; for example, children of parents who have a low educational level receive only half the language stimulation than those of average middle-class parents (Cognition and Technology Group at Vanderbilt, 1998). In school, these children perform poorly when asked to understand and retell stories. When provided stories on computer that included dynamic visual information, these students improve significantly, perhaps because the images help decrease working memory requirements. These children enjoyed seeing and then retelling stories into the computer, which recorded and played back their versions. Children made medium to large achievement gains using the software. At-risk kindergartners can similarly use multimedia software to aid the development of listening comprehension, story production, and decoding skills (Mayfield-Stewart et al., 1994).

Computer activity is slightly more effective than toy play in stimulating vocalizations in disabled preschoolers (McCormick, 1987). Computers are also reshaping speech language pathology and special education. Their unique advantages include: being patient and nonjudgmental, providing undivided attention, proceeding at the child's pace, and providing immediate reinforcement (Schery & O'Connor, 1997). These advantages lead to significant improvements for children with special needs.

Reports such as these help allay the fear that computers will de-emphasize play, fantasy, and the corresponding rich use of language. When children are in control, they create fantasy in computer programs beyond the producers' imaginations (Escobedo, 1992; Wright & Samaras, 1986). Some at-risk students have also shown they benefit from direct instruction on computer use and strategies, combined with student-directed exploration (Walker, Elliott, & Lacey, 1994). In summary, computer environments can facilitate language development.

Prereading and reading skills. Unique advantages of computers allow computer-assisted instruction (CAI) drills and tutorials to help students develop prereading and reading skills. For example, computers can be successful in increasing a variety of verbal and language skills, especially when the software provides scaffolding, or assistance to the learning that is gradually withdrawn (Shute & Miksad, 1997). This is especially true for language-delayed preschoolers.

Unique capabilities of CAI include those previously mentioned, as well as visual displays, animated graphics and speech, the ability to provide feedback and keep a variety of records, and individualization (Clements, 1994). When these capabilities are used, drill software increases preschool and primary grade children's prereading or reading skills. As one specific example, computer graphics representation of words enhances word recognition and recall in beginning reading (Shapira, 1995).

The amount of practice is important. A small number of sessions with simple readiness software may have little or no effect (Clements, 1987b; Clements & Nastasi, 1992). In contrast, placing computers in kindergartners' classrooms for several months significantly increases reading readiness skills; placing them in the home as well yields greater gains (Hess & McGarvey, 1987). About 10 minutes work with CAI per day significantly benefits primary grade childrens' reading skill development (Childers, 1989; Lavin & Sanders, 1983; Murphy & Appel, 1984; Ragosta, Holland, & Jamison, 1981; Silfen & Howes, 1984; Teague, Wilson, & Teague, 1984). Similarly, preschoolers can develop such reading readiness abilities as visual discrimination and letter naming (Lin, Vallone, & Lepper, 1985; Smithy-Willis, Riley, & Smith, 1982; Swigger & Campbell, 1981). A large effect has been shown on kindergartners' phonological awareness (Foster, Erickson, Foster, Brinkman, & Torgesen, 1994).

Computers can make a special contribution to special needs children. After six weeks of reading instruction using a microcomputer, 3- to 6-year-old deaf children demonstrated a significant improvement in word recognition and identification (Prinz, Nelson, & Stedt, 1982). Taking advantage of young children's cognitive readiness regardless of their primary mode of communication, the program allowed them to press a word (say, "flower") and see a picture of a flower, the word, and a graphic representation of a manual sign.

This approach, while effective, is not consistent with a constructivist, whole-language approach, especially if it is the only instructional strategy. It might be used in moderation, but the cautions (e.g., possible negative effects on creativity) should be carefully considered. Are there alternatives? At the preschool level, teachers might emphasize language enhancement, as previously described. *Talking books* is another promising application (Hutinger & Johanson, 2000; Lewin, 1997; McKenna, 1998). For example, use of such electronic books supported preschool children's emergent literacy (Talley, Lancy, & Lee, 1997). Preschoolers who were not read to frequently at home and scored low on literacy assessments improved their scores significantly more than a control group after working with talking books; on several measures, their scores sufficiently increased so that they were not significantly different from those children who were read to at home and scored high on the initial assessments. Talking books can pronounce words and read larger language units at the child's request. Therefore, they can make independent reading a reality long before decoding reaches the point of automaticity (McKenna, 1998).

Writing in light: Word processing. Another approach to early literacy is having children write and publish on the computer, one of the most prevalent applications teachers of young children use (not including the most prevalent use, CAI drill, Becker, 1994; Cosden, 1988; Kromhout & Butzin, 1993). The hypothesis is that word processors can help children write more as well as improve their basic language skills in the process of writing. Unique capabilities of computers which may support these benefits include the following: easy text entry, easy and more powerful editing, spell checkers and other tools, and built-in prompting (Clements, 1994). Research indicates that these capabilities encourage a fluid idea of the written word and free young children from mechanical concerns (Bangert-Drowns, 1993; Jones & Pellegrini, 1996). Kindergartners write and edit more like older students (Yost, 1998). In general, children using word processors write more, have fewer fine motor control problems, worry less about making mistakes, and make fewer mechanical errors (Clements, 1987a; Daiute, 1988; Hawisher, 1989; Kurth, 1988; Phenix & Hannan, 1984; Roblyer, Castine, & King, 1988).

Does this make a substantive difference in children's ability to write? Young children can learn to competently revise their text when shown how to use the computer to edit their words. They improve their style using more descriptive phrases and also create better plots with climaxes and character descriptions (Wright, 1994). They improve their attitude toward writing (Green, 1991; Holmes & Godlewski, 1995). Findings regarding holistic ratings of quality are mixed (Shaw, Nauman, & Burson, 1994), but generally positive (Bangert-Drowns, 1989; Clements & Nastasi, 1992; Owston & Wideman, 1997). Quality increases if children are encouraged to use the word processor to edit their text in substantive ways (Wild & Ing, 1994).

Word processors also affect the social context of writing. When writing with a computer, compared to writing with paper, young children cooperatively plan, revise, and discuss spelling, punctuation, spacing, and text meaning and style. For example, Bernardo and Dan discussed the meaning of their text:

Bernardo: That doesn't make sense: "The Pilgrims were scared of the Indians. The found the food."

Dan: Oh yeah, I forgot!

Bernardo: "The found?" The Indians found.

Dan: Oh yeah.

Bernardo: You forgot the Indians. Now are you gonna try and go back and fit "Indians" in there? (Dickinson, 1986, pp. 372-374).

They are, therefore, more "metacognitive" in their writing at the computer than with paper-and-pencil (Jones & Pellegrini, 1996).

Thus, word processing encourages peer collaboration, as well as self- and other-monitoring behaviors (Hine, Goldman, & Cosden, 1990). Learning disabled children working with a partner had fewer errors than those working alone. The partners monitored and helped each other. The shared availability of the text on the screen enabled participation by both partners in creating and editing text.

While the instructional approach may need to be modified, even young preschoolers may benefit from computer environments. For example, three-year-olds began using the computer in a self-selected language experience activity that lasted two years. These children showed steady improvement in spelling and story writing, including invented spellings (Moxley, Warash, Coffman, Brinton, & Concannon, 1997). When they were 4 years of age, they performed better than another group of children who engaged in similar activities but had not received such experiences as 3-year-olds. Kindergartners increased writing and reading competencies working with a picture-word processor system that allowed them to write messages by simply pressing squares of picture-words on an electronic tablet without having to spell words or use extensive eye-hand coordination (Chang & Osguthorpe, 1990). Such findings are supported by the conclusions of another study: Children ages 4 through 7 can use word processors in a creative writing program to promote their developing writing abilities in many ways and in different ways at different stages of their development (Schrader, 1990).

Talking word processors are especially popular with young children. Indeed, one of the longest-term studies of this type of technology involves the "talking typewriter," an early multimedia environment first implemented in the 1960s (Steg, Lazar, & Boyce, 1994). Children using the talking typewriter exceeded controls on many short-term measures, with competencies that often doubled those of control children (Israel, 1968). In addition, delayed effects were assessed; for example, significant positive effects were shown in fourth grade, when independent reading is expected (Steg et al., 1994).

Similarly, using talking word processors, preschool to first-grade children were more able to express ideas, write simple sentences, and take risks in experimenting with their writing (Rosegrant, 1988). In a study comparing writing with and without speech, only voice-aided word process-ing acted as a scaffold for young children's writing by promoting the acqui-sition of several components of preschool literacy including symbol-sound and sound-symbol associations, the importance of vowels and the need to have distinctive boundaries (e.g., spaces) between words, reading of com-positions, and metacognitive awareness of the purposes and processes of writing (Lehrer, Levin, DeHart, & Comeaux, 1987). Of what does such metacognitive awareness consist? For young writers, an important aspect is the need to develop an "inner voice" for constructing and editing text sub-vocally. Computerized speech can provide an external voice to read and reread text during the composing and revising process. Research has dem-onstrated that children eventually read along with the speech synthesizer, adding intonations that complete the meaning, and ultimately become increasingly subvocal—an inner voice is developed. Children then simulta-neously develop the ability to "hear" whether or not the text "sounds right" (Rosegrant, 1988).

This positively affects their writing. The more children in kindergarten and first grade used such spoken feedback, the higher their compositions were rated in length, grammatical cohesion, and lexical density (Jones, 1998; Jones & Pellegrini, 1996). It helps children represent words with gra-phophonic relationships. However, teachers need to use computer speech wisely. Children may have to be ready; if they are in the earliest stages of invented spelling, computerized speech may not be helpful (Shilling, 1997). Another caution is that some young writers have the computer read their compositions a lot—so much so that in one study children using talk-ing word processors wrote shorter compositions than those using word processors without speech; both wrote more than paper-and-pencil groups (Kurth & Kurth, 1987). Later in the year, better readers listened to the computer less. Poor readers continued to use the synthesizer to read their stories. Thus, speech synthesis may be most important for beginning writ-ers or less able readers (Kurth, 1988).

Does such computer-based reading affect children's invented spellings and editing? Although children using speech synthesis do invent spellings (Rosegrant, 1985, 1988), their final drafts include fewer invented spellings than do those of children not using synthesizers. Possibly the synthesizer could not pronounce the word correctly if spellings were not close to the phonetic pronunciation or to the preprogramed spelling (Kurth, 1988; Kurth & Kurth, 1987).

In contrast, talking word processors increase the amount of editing chil-dren performed on their compositions, even compared to non-talking word processing (Borgh & Dickson, 1986). Differences in the length or holistic quality, however, were not found (Borgh & Dickson, 1986; Kurth, 1988; Kurth & Kurth, 1987; Lehrer et al., 1987). It may be that the spoken feedback specifically fostered an awareness of the need to edit.

Computer writing also has tied classrooms from across the world together in cooperative groups (Riel, 1994). In one project, children wrote and illustrated their own stories on the computer and sent them by e-mail to children in other preschools in Nordic countries (Gustafsson, Mellgren, Klerfelt, & Samuelsson, 1999).

Language interventions with special populations have shown similar results. Severely handicapped children who were trained on communication skills using a computer increased their receptive and expressive language more than those with regular classroom training (Schery & O'Connor, 1992). Most were incapable of using the computer intervention without supervision and support from a trainer, but they were able to sustain interest and respond to the format over 10 weeks.

Word processing can have disadvantages. For example, first graders may benefit more from spelling practice involving handwriting than typing (Cunningham & Stanovich, 1990). Beginning writers tend to leave out spaces between words and fail to use the wrap feature of word processors. None of the problems is long-lasting or insurmountable (Neufeld, 1989). Perhaps most important, effective teaching and writing strategies may be more influential than technology. Although more teachers are using word processing, they are often making the computer software the object of instruction—teaching word processing rather than composing (Becker, 1990).

Realizing benefits also requires sufficient computer access and time (Reed, 1996). One group of researchers stated that if they had stopped their evaluation after a couple of months, they would have mistakenly concluded there were no effects. Only after one full year did the rich benefits emerge (Cochran-Smith, Kahn, & Paris, 1988).

Teachers play an important role in building a creative environment and scaffolding the children's efforts. For example, word processors can enhance a creative writing environment but do not by themselves establish it (Clements & Nastasi, 1993). Used within the context of a sound learning theory, the computer can be a valuable language arts tool. Further, integration of an interactive literacy program appears to increase young students' use of computers, enhance computer skills, computer self-efficacy, and enjoyment of computers (Ross, Hogaboam-Gray, & Hannay, 2001).

Thus, it would seem that word processing can be successfully integrated into a process-oriented writing program as early as first grade, and that even younger students can use computers to explore written language. If used within the context of a theoretically-based educational environment, computers can facilitate the development of a new view of writing, and a new social organization (cooperative learning) that supports young children's writing. Software and teaching strategies that support the composing process, especially guiding prewriting, might be most beneficial for young writers. Children plan, write, discuss, and revise more frequently in such environments. They use the computer as a language arts learning tool. They improve their writing and their reading (Green, 1991).

Mathematics and Reasoning

As with literacy skills, children can use CAI to practice arithmetic processes and to foster deeper conceptual thinking. Drill software can help young children develop competence in such skills as counting and sorting (Clements & Nastasi, 1993). Indeed, the largest gains in the use of CAI have been in mathematics for *preschool* (Fletcher-Flinn & Gravatt, 1995) or *primary* grade children, especially in compensatory education (Lavin & Sanders, 1983; Niemiec & Walberg, 1984; Ragosta et al., 1981). Again, 10 minutes per day proved sufficient for significant gains; 20 minutes was even better. This CAI approach may be as or more cost effective as other instructional interventions, such as peer tutoring and reducing class size (Niemiec & Walberg, 1987). Properly chosen, computer games may also be effective. Kraus (1981) reported that second graders with an average of one hour of interaction with a computer game over a two-week period responded correctly to twice as many items on an addition facts speed test as did students in a control group.

Preschoolers and math. How young can children be and still obtain such benefits? Three-year-olds learned sorting from a computer task as easily as from a concrete doll task (Brinkley & Watson, 1987-88a). Reports of gains in such skills as counting have also been reported for kindergartners (Hungate, 1982). Similarly, kindergartners in a computer group scored higher on numeral recognition tasks than those taught by a teacher (McCollister, Burts, Wright, & Hildreth, 1986). There was some indication, however, that instruction by a teacher was more effective for children just beginning to recognize numerals, but the opposite was true for more able children. Children might best work with such programs once they understand the concepts; then, practice may be of real benefit. In addition, students with learning difficulties might be distracted by drill in a game format, which impairs their learning (Christensen & Gerber, 1990).

Again, possible negative effects on creativity and motivation (Clements & Nastasi, 1985) should be carefully considered. Further, exclusive use of such drill software would do little to achieve the vision of the National Council of Teachers of Mathematics (2000) that children should be mathematically literate in a world where mathematics is rapidly growing and is extensively being applied in diverse fields. What other approaches help achieve that vision?

Computer manipulatives. Researchers have observed that children who use computer manipulatives learn to understand and apply concepts such as symmetry, patterns and spatial order. For example, Tammy overlaid two overlapping triangles on one square and colored select parts of this figure to create a third triangle which was not provided by the program. Not only did Tammy exhibit an awareness of how she had made this, but she also showed a higher-order awareness of the challenge it would be to others

(Wright, 1994). As another example, young children used a graphics program to combine the three primary colors to create three secondary colors (Wright, 1994). Such complex combinatorial abilities are often thought out of reach of young children. In both these examples, the computer experience led the children to explorations that increased the boundaries of what they could do.

Computer manipulative programs extend general-purpose graphics programs in allowing children to perform specific mathematical transformations on objects on the screen. For example, whereas physical base-ten blocks must be "traded" (e.g., in subtracting, students may need to trade 1 ten for 10 ones), students can break a computer base-ten block into 10 ones. Such actions are more in line with the *mental actions* that we want students to learn. The computer also links the blocks to the symbols. For example, the number represented by the base-ten blocks is dynamically linked to the students' actions on the blocks, so that when the student changes the blocks the number displayed is automatically changed as well. This can help students make sense of their activity and the numbers.

So, computer manipulatives can provide unique advantages (Clements & Sarama, 1998; Sarama et al., 1996), including: saving and retrieving work, so children can work on projects over a long period (Ishigaki et al., 1996); offering a flexible and manageable manipulative, one that, for example, might "snap" into position; providing an extensible manipulative, which you can resize or cut; linking the concrete and the symbolic with feedback, such as showing base-ten blocks dynamically linked to numerals; recording and replaying students' actions; and bringing mathematics to explicit awareness, for example, by asking children to consciously choose what mathematical operations (e.g., turn, flip, scale) to apply.

Additional illustrations of these advantages might be useful. When a group of kindergartners were working on a pattern with physical manipulatives, they wanted to move it slightly on the rug. Two girls (four hands) tried to keep the design together, but they were unsuccessful. Marisssa told Leah to fix the design. Leah tried, but in re-creating the design, she inserted two extra shapes and the pattern wasn't the same. The girls experienced considerable frustration at their inability to get their "old" design back. Had the children been able to save their design, or had they been able to move their design and keep the pieces together, their group project would have continued. Indeed, moving a design to another area of the screen was the most common reason for using the "glue" tool with these kindergartners (Sarama et al., 1996).

Turtle geometry. Directing the movement of Logo's "turtle" can also provide challenging learning experiences. In Logo, children give commands to direct an on-screen turtle to move through "roads" or mazes or to draw shapes. Primary-grade children have shown greater explicit awareness of the properties of shapes and the meaning of measurements after working with Logo (Clements & Nastasi, 1993). For example, while drawing a face in Turtle Math™ (Clements & Meredith, 1994), Nina decided to draw her "mouth with a smile" with exactly 200 turtle steps. Off-computer she wrote a procedure where the sides of the rectangle were 40 and 20 and the sides of the equilateral triangle were 10. She realized that the total perimeter of these figures was 20 short of 200 and changed just one side of each triangle to 20. Running these procedures on the computer, she remarked that changing the length of one side "messed up" an equilateral triangle and consequently her smile. She had to decide whether to compromise on the geometric shape or the total perimeter. Her final "mouth" was a rectangle of 200 steps and her "smile" was an equilateral triangle of 60 steps.

Logo programming is also a rich environment that elicits reflection on mathematics and one's own problem-solving. Students use certain mathematical notions in Logo programming, such as notions of inverse operation. First grader Ryan wanted to turn the turtle to point into his rectangle. He asked the teacher, "What's half of 90?" After she responded, he typed RT 45. "Oh, I went the wrong way." He said and did nothing, eyes on the screen. "Try LEFT 90," he said at last. This inverse operation produced exactly the desired effect.

Other children may need teacher assistance to link their knowledge of mathematics to their computer work as well as Nina did. Teachers can ask children to reflect on their work; especially "surprises," when the computer does something other than what they want it to do. Such reflection can promote greater self-monitoring and may encourage them to find computer "bugs" themselves (Clements, Nastasi, & Swaminathan, 1993).

Logo sometimes can be difficult for young children to comprehend. However, when the environment is gradually and systematically introduced to the children and when the microworlds are age-appropriate, they do not show any signs of problems (Allen, Watson, & Howard, 1993; Brinkley & Watson, 1987-88b; Clements, 1983-84 #402; Cohen & Geva, 1989; Howard, Watson, & Allen, 1993; Watson, Lange, & Brinkley, 1992). Thus, there is substantial evidence that young children can learn Logo and can transfer their knowledge to other areas, such as map-reading tasks and interpreting right and left rotation of objects.

Benefits are not automatic, of course. Thoughtful use, including carefully selected activities, is the key (Clements & Nastasi, 1992). There must be a reason to use the technology. We know from Piaget that young children learn about geometric shapes not from taking mental pictures of objects, but from actions they perform on objects. For example, children can walk a rectangular path and then program the Logo turtle to draw it on the screen. The programming helps children link their intuitive knowledge about moving and drawing to more explicit mathematical ideas (Clements & Battista, 1989, 1992). One class of first graders was constructing rectangles (Clements & Battista, in press). "I wonder if I can tilt one," mused a boy. He turned the turtle, drew the first side . . . then was unsure about how much to turn at this strange new heading. He finally figured that it must be the same turn command as before. He hesitated again. "How far now? Oh, it *must* be the same as its partner!" He easily completed his rectangle. The instructions he should give the turtle *at this new orientation* were initially not obvious. He analyzed the situation and reflected on the properties of a rectangle. Perhaps most important, he posed the problem for himself.

These studies indicate that Logo, used thoughtfully, can provide an additional evocative context for young children's explorations of mathematical ideas. Such "thoughtful use" includes structuring and guiding Logo work to help children form strong, valid mathematical ideas. Children do not appreciate the mathematics in Logo work unless teachers help them see the work mathematically. These teachers raise questions about "surprises" or conflicts between children's intuitions and computer feedback to promote reflection. They pose challenges and tasks designed to make the mathematical ideas explicit for children. They help children build bridges between the Logo experience and their regular mathematics work (Clements, 1987c; Watson & Brinkley, 1990/91). These suggestions are valid for most types of open-ended software and will be discussed in a latter section.

Logo has some unique advantages (Clements & Battista, 1989, 1992) in that it: links children's intuitive knowledge about moving and drawing to more explicit mathematical ideas, encourages the manipulation of specific shapes in ways that helps students in viewing them as mathematical representatives of a *class* of shapes, facilitates students' development of autonomy in learning (rather than seeking authority) and positive beliefs about the creation of mathematical ideas, encourages wondering about and posing problems by providing an environment in which to test ideas and receive feedback about these ideas, helps *connect* visual shapes with abstract numbers, and fosters mathematical thinking (Clements, 1994).

In summary, computers can help develop young children's knowledge and skills in mathematics and reasoning. Technology helped actuate the mathematical world we find in this young century. Technology—used thoughtfully and creatively rather than as a teaching machine—can engender and support educational environments that will empower children to flourish in this intensively mathematical world.

Creativity and Higher-Order Thinking Skills

Creativity. Besides developing knowledge in the domains of language and mathematics, appropriate computer environments can positively affect children's creativity, at least in some domains. Children have opportunities similar to those provided by concrete art materials, but with interesting and important differences (Escobedo & Bhargava, 1991; Ishigaki et al., 1996). Logo too can have benefits. One early study documented an increase in figural creativity following Logo experience (Clements & Gullo, 1984). Later studies showed similar effects, although gains in some were moderate (Clements & Nastasi, 1992; Reimer, 1985; Roblyer et al., 1988; Wiburg, 1987) and occasionally nonsignificant (Mitterer & Rose-Drasnor, 1986; Plourde, 1987). Another study reported significant gains in creativity, noting that Logo students more fully developed their graphic compositions in completeness, originality, and drawing style (Horton & Ryba, 1986). At least one critical component of creativity, originality, has been consistently and positively affected in every study (Clements, 1986, 1991b, 1995; Clements & Gullo, 1984; Hlawati, 1985; Horton & Ryba, 1986; Plourde, 1987; Reimer, 1985; Wiburg, 1987). These results, in which creativity was measured with various instruments across graphic and verbal domains, provide further evidence that Logo work enhances higher-order creative processes.

Higher-order thinking. Computers can also help develop other higher-order thinking skills. Preschoolers who used computers scored higher on measures of metacognition (Fletcher-Flinn & Suddendorf, 1996). They were more able to keep in mind a number of different mental states simultaneously and had more sophisticated theories of mind than those who did not use computers. Several studies have reported that Logo experience significantly increases both preschool and primary grade children's ability to monitor their comprehension and problem solving processes; that is, to "realize when you don't understand" (Clements, 1986, 1990; Clements & Gullo, 1984; Lehrer & Randle, 1986; Miller & Emihovich, 1986). This may reflect the prevalence of "debugging" in Logo programming. Other abilities that may be positively affected include understanding the nature of a problem, representing that problem, and even "learning to learn" (Clements, 1990; Lehrer & Randle, 1986). Along with the increase in metacognitive talk in writing and mathematics activities, there is a substantial argument that computers can foster young children's metacognition.

Problem-solving computer activities motivate children as young as kindergartners to make choices and decisions, alter their strategies, persist, and score higher on tests of critical thinking (Gélinas, 1986; Riding & Powell, 1987). Specially-designed computer programs can improve analogical thinking of kindergartners (Klein & Gal, 1992); a variety of problem-solving CAI programs significantly increased first and second graders ability to generalize and solve mathematics problems (Orabuchi, 1993). In this study, children in the experimental group worked with a variety of problem-solving programs. For example, one asked children to find the "odd one out" in a group program. After four months, the experimental group scored statistically significantly higher than a control group in generalization, math problem solving, and such affective domains as attitude toward school and toward computers (overall academic achievement and general self-concept were not significantly different).

Several studies reveal that drawing shapes, pictures and designs with the Logo turtle is a particularly engaging activity to young children, fostering higher-order thinking in children from preschool through the primary grades, including special needs students (Clements & Nastasi, 1988; Degelman, Free, Scarlato, Blackburn, & Golden, 1986; Lehrer, Harckham, Archer, & Pruzek, 1986; Nastasi, Clements, & Battista, 1990). Preschool and primary grade children develop the ability to understand the nature of problems and use representations such as drawings to solve them. When given opportunities to debug, or find and fix errors in Logo programs (Poulin-Dubois, McGilly, & Shultz, 1989), they also increase their ability to monitor their thinking; that is, to realize when they are confused or need to change directions in solving a problem (Clements & Nastasi, 1992).

Unique advantages of computers for fostering creativity and higher-order thinking include: allowing children to create, change, save, and retrieve ideas, promoting reflection and engagement; connecting ideas from different areas, such as the mathematical and the artistic; providing situations with clear-cut variable means-end structure, some constraints, and feedback that students can interpret on their own; and so allowing children to interact, think, and play with ideas in significant ways, in some cases even with limited adult supervision (Clements, 1994).

The teachers in most of these studies were consistently mediating children's interactions with the computer (cf. Samaras, 1991). The importance of the teacher's role is the subject to which we now turn.

TEACHING WITH COMPUTERS

Even in preschool, children can work cooperatively with minimal instruction and supervision, if they have adult support initially (Rosengren et al., 1985; Shade et al., 1986). However, adults play a significant role in successful computer use. Children are more attentive, more interested, and less frustrated when an adult is present (Binder & Ledger, 1985). Thus, teachers may wish to make the computer one of many choices, placed where they can supervise and assist children. Next we examine specific strategies for effective classroom use of computers.

Arranging the Classroom Setting

The physical arrangement of the computers in the classroom can enhance their social use (Davidson & Wright, 1994; Shade, 1994). The parts of the computer with which the children interact, the keyboard, mouse, monitor, and microphone, should be at the children's eye level, on a low table or even on the floor. If children are changing CD-ROMs, they can be placed so that children can see and change them easily. Software might be changed, along with other centers, to match educational themes. The other parts should be out of children's reach. All parts can be stabilized and locked down as necessary. If computers are to be shared, rolling carts might be used.

Placing two seats in front of the computer and one at the side for the teacher encourages positive social interaction. If more than two children work with a computer, they assert the right to control the keyboard frequently (Shrock, Matthias, Anastasoff, Vensel, & Shaw, 1985). Placing computers close to each other can facilitate the sharing of ideas among children. Computers that are centrally located in the classroom invite other children to pause and participate in the computer activity. Such an arrangement also helps keep teacher participation at an optimum level. They are nearby to provide supervision and assistance as needed (Clements, 1991a). Other factors, such as the ratio of computers to children, may also influence social behaviors. Less than a 10:1 ratio of children to computers might ideally encourage computer use, cooperation, and equal access to girls and boys (Lipinski et al., 1986; Yost, 1998). Cooperative use of computers raises achievement (Xin, 1999); a mixture of use in pairs and individual work may be ideal (Shade, 1994). It is critical to make sure special education children are accepted and supported. Only in these situations did they like to be included in regular classroom computer work (Xin, 1999).

To encourage children to connect off- and on-computer experiences, place print materials, manipulatives, and real objects next to the computer (Hutinger & Johanson, 2000). This also provides good activities for children who are observing or waiting for their turn.

Managing the Computer Environment

As you might with any center, teach children proper computer use and care, and post signs to remind them of the rules (e.g., no liquids, sand, food, or magnets near computers). Using a child-oriented utility that helps children find and use the programs they want, and prevents them from inadvertently harming other programs or files, makes everyone's life easier.

Monitoring the time children spend on computers and giving everyone fair access is, of course, important. However, at least one study has found that rigid time limits generated hostility and isolation instead of social communication (Hutinger & Johanson, 2000). A better idea is flexible time with sign-up lists that encourage children to manage themselves. The sign-up list itself can have a positive effect on preschoolers' emergent literacy (Hutinger & Johanson, 2000).

Introduce computer work gradually. Initially, use only one or two programs at a time. Expect independent work from children gradually. Prepare them for independence, even having individual or small groups of children work closely with an adult at first, and increase the degree of such work slowly. Provide substantial support and guidance initially, even sitting with children at the computer to encourage turn-taking. Then gradually foster self-directed and cooperative learning.

When necessary, teach children effective collaboration, for example, communication and negotiation skills. For young children, this might include such matters as what constitutes a "turn" in a particular game. However, do not mandate sharing the computer all the time. Especially with construction-oriented programs such as Logo, children sometimes need to work alone. If possible, make at least two computers available so that peer teaching and other kinds of interaction can take place, even if children are working on one computer.

Once children are working independently, provide enough guidance, but not too much. Intervening too much or at the wrong times can decrease peer tutoring and collaboration (Bergin et al., 1986; Emihovich & Miller, 1988; Riel, 1985). On the other hand, without any teacher guidance, children tend to "jockey" for position at the computer and use the computer in the turn-taking, competitive manner of video games (Lipinski et al., 1986; Silvern, Countermine, & Williamson, 1988).

Research shows that the introduction of a microcomputer often places many additional demands on the teacher (Shrock et al., 1985). Plan carefully the use only of computer programs that will substantially benefit your children.

Choosing Software

Using computers positively in these ways assumes that the teacher has chosen high-quality software. Previous sections already described the nature of such software; here we emphasize only that software always should be selected according to sound educational principles. Preschool children respond correctly more often using software that incorporates such principles (Grover, 1986). (Other resources provide additional detail, such as Haugland & Shade, 1990; Haugland & Wright, 1997).

- Actions and graphics should provide a meaningful context for children.
- Reading level, assumed attention span, and way of responding should be appropriate for the age level. Instructions should be clear, such as simple choices in the form of a picture menu.

- After initial adult support, children should be able to use the software independently. There should be multiple opportunities for success.
- Feedback should be informative.
- Children should be in control. Software should provide as much manipulative power as possible.
- Software should allow children to create, program, or invent new activities. It should have the potential for independent use but should also challenge. It should be flexible and allow more than one correct response.
- If you have one, use a digital camera or scanner to incorporate photos of kids and events into computer activities and artwork.
- Remember that more is not always better; inexpensive software that claims to address every developmental area and level may be suspect.
- Perhaps most important, software should enhance the classroom environment, helping and empowering children to learn and meet specific educational and developmental goals more effectively and powerfully than they could without the technology.

This final point serves as an important summary: The computer should not be simply an end unto itself. Computers can help children learn and should be used reflectively by both children and their teachers. Children should learn to understand how and why the programs they use work the way to do (Turkle, 1997).

The Internet

The Internet includes some sources of software and information both for teachers and children. At its best, the Internet, or World Wide Web, can provide lesson plans and resources to promote higher-level thinking processes for teachers. It can allow children to communicate with others of similar interests. Recall that some of the literacy work that we have discussed involves writing for other audiences using such technologies. The Internet can involve students in information gathering, research, and virtual field trips. These opportunities may enrich children's multicultural experiences, support emergent literacy, enhance concept development, and build problem-solving capabilities (Gerzog & Haugland, 1999).

These promises, however, may not be realized. Most questions regarding the Internet are still to be answered. How prevalent are such uses in school and home environments, when children universally prefer to find games? Does using the Internet in the home aid or hinder socialization (Woodward & Gridina, 2000)? We need studies addressing both the advantages and disadvantages of *specific uses of the Internet*. That is, just because the

Internet is the source of a computer activity may have little or no effect on the learning potential of that activity. Similarly, video may be a frivolous addition, an equivalent replacement of animation or video on a CD-based computer program, or a real contribution. As we stated previously, such multimedia capabilities should be used when they serve educational purposes.

One caveat that should be considered carefully is that sites sponsored by media conglomerates and toy companies are increasingly present; content and hidden messages should be carefully considered (Downes, Arthur, Beecher, & Kemp, 1999; Wartella & Jennings, 2000). Also important is parent education. Surveys indicate that about half of all children with home access to the Internet have no parental restrictions on the amount of time or the type of content viewed (Shields & Behrmann, 2000). Given the wide variety of inappropriate content available on the Internet and in video games, professional attention is needed. Parents and teachers need media literacy training, for example, to understand the motives underlying various content on the Internet or to understand how computers in children's bedrooms might be socially isolating. Media literacy training for parents and children can result in young children becoming less vulnerable to the negative aspects of all media and able to make wise choices (American Academy of Pediatrics, 1999).

Effective Strategies for Teaching with Computers

Critical to effective use of computers is teacher planning, participation, and support. Optimally, the teacher's role should be that of a facilitator of children's learning. Such facilitation includes not only physical structuring of the environment, but also establishing standards for and supporting specific types of learning environments. When using open-ended programs, for example, considerable support may need to precede independent use. Other important aspects of support include structuring and discussing computer work to help children form viable concepts and strategies, posing questions to help children reflect on these concepts and strategies, and "building bridges" to help children connect their computer and noncomputer experiences.

Across the educational goals, we find that teachers whose children benefit significantly from using computers are always active. They closely guide children's learning of basic tasks, then encourage experimentation with open-ended problems. They are frequently encouraging, questioning, prompting, and demonstrating, *without* offering unnecessary help or limiting children's opportunity to explore (Hutinger & Johanson, 2000). They redirect inappropriate behaviors, model strategies, and give children choices (Hutinger et al., 1998). Such scaffolding leads children to reflect

on their own thinking behaviors and brings higher-order thinking processes to the fore. Such metacognitively-oriented instruction includes strategies of identifying goals, active monitoring, modeling, questioning,
reflecting, peer tutoring, discussion, and reasoning (Elliott & Hall, 1997).

Effective teachers make the subject matter to be learned clear and
extend the ideas children encounter. They focus attention on critical
aspects and ideas of the activities. When appropriate, they facilitate disequilibrium by using the computer feedback to help children reflect on and
question their ideas and eventually strengthen their concepts. They also
help children build links between computer and noncomputer work.

Whole group discussions that help children communicate about their
solution strategies and reflect on what they've learned are also essential
components of good teaching with computers (Galen & Buter, 2000).
Effective teachers avoid overly directive teaching behaviors (except as necessary for some populations and on topics such as using the computer
equipment), strict time limits (which generate hostility and isolation
instead of social communication), and offering unnecessary help without
allowing children the opportunity to explore (Hutinger et al., 1998).
Instead, effective teachers prompt children to teach each other by physically placing one child in a teaching role or verbally reminding a child to
explain his or her actions and respond to specific requests for help (Paris
& Morris, 1985).

Two studies show clearly that such scaffolding is critical. In the first (Yelland, 1998), children were only given instructions for specific tasks and
then mostly left alone. These children rarely planned, were often off task,
rarely cooperated, displayed frustration and lack of confidence, and did
not finish tasks. In the second study using similar software and tasks (Yelland, 1994), the teacher scaffolded instruction by providing open-ended
but structured tasks, holding group brainstorming sessions about problem-
solving strategies, encouraging children to work collaboratively, asking
them to think and discuss their plans before working at the computer,
questioning them about their plans and strategies, and provided models of
strategies as necessary. These children planned, worked on tasks collaboratively, were able to explain their strategies, were rarely frustrated, and completed tasks efficiently. They showed a high level of mathematical
reasoning about geometric figures and motions, as well as number and
measurement.

Such teaching is difficult. A balance of teacher guidance and children
self-directed exploration is necessary for children to learn to appropriate
this new technology (Escobedo & Bhargava, 1991). In designing curriculum around open-ended software, research has shown that children work
best when assigned open-ended projects rather than when asked merely to
"free explore" (Lemerise, 1993). They spend longer time and actively
search for diverse ways to solve the task. The group allowed to free explore

grew disinterested quite soon. Models and sharing projects may also be helpful (Hall & Hooper, 1993).

Remember that preparation and follow–up are as necessary for computer activities as they are for any other. Do not omit critical whole group discussion sessions following computer work. Consider using a single computer with a large screen or with overhead projector equipment.

Professional Development

We have seen that children can create complex simulations in second grade (Howland, Laffey, & Espinosa, 1997), direct the Logo turtle in preschool, program in the primary grades, and create pictures and text at all age levels. Will teachers take the time to learn to support such challenging experiences? If teachers are to take up that challenge, they need substantial professional development. Research has established that less than ten hours of training can have a negative impact (Ryan, 1993). Further, only 15% reported receiving at least 9 hours of training (Coley et al., 1997). Others have emphasized the importance of hands-on experience and warned against brief exposure to a variety of programs, rather than an in-depth knowledge of one (Wright, 1994). In one study (Sexton, King, Aldridge, & Goodstat-Killoran, 1999), positive computer attitudes were most highly associated with access to a home computer and prior computer training. Students need someone knowledgeable to help them develop strategies to use the computers effectively. Although faculty reported being comfortable with computers, they were not satisfied with their ability to integrate this technology into their courses (Sexton et al., 1999); this needs to be changed.

Student teaching may have an adverse effect. Some preservice teachers' cooperating teachers do not use technology and may actively impede the preservice teachers' attempts at using technology in the practice of teaching (Bosch, 1993). Teachers at all levels need to be assisted in learning how to integrate computers into instruction (Coley et al., 1997), using models that have proven effective (Ainsa, 1992). Learning through networking and collaborating with other teachers is one promising approach (Becker, 2000). Teachers need concrete suggestions. For example, one group of teachers and children used technology in different ways to extend learning of a recent trip to a farm. Children fell into four interest groups. The children fascinated by the machinery created a large floor map of the farm and used battery operated robots to play out the roles of the tractor and trucks, transporting animals and produce to appropriate locations. Children interested in farm animals created families of animals using a program that produced a variety of animal types and sizes. Children who wanted to study the jobs of people on the farm read books and applied what they had seen and read to a program that allowed them to create a farm scene and write a story about the people who lived there. The children who were interested in how we get foods we eat wrote a book of recipes and songs on the computer that was sent home to parents.

Equity

We end this section with a consideration of equity. There are many issues; we consider three here: socioeconomic status, gender, and special needs children.

Socioeconomic status. Given that the research indicates that computers can facilitate young children's development, we must worry about inequitable access. The "digital divide separating children in socioeconomically advantaged homes from children in socioeconomically disadvantaged homes is mammoth" (Becker, 2000, p. 56). About 22% of children living in families with annual incomes under $20,000 had a home computer in 1998, compared with 91% of children living in families with incomes more than $75,000 (Becker, 2000). Even those with computers used them in different ways. For example, 50% of the children from high-SES families with home computers used word processing, compared with only 24% of children from low-SES families with home computers. If all children are considered, not just those with computers, 44% of children from high-SES homes used computers for word processing compared to only 4% of low-SES children. Schools must play a critical role in ensuring equal opportunity for less-advantaged children. They could do so; schools serving families with different levels of income do not have different ratios of computers to children. Unfortunately, higher-income schools, compared to lower-income schools, use computers in more intellectually powerful ways. If teachers in lower-income schools are to meet these challenges, they need time and practice to develop methods for using such challenging software successfully with their students (Becker, 2000).

Gender. In addition, as early as the later elementary school years, boys have more access to computers, own more computers, and use computers more frequently and with more control (Lieberman, 1985; Parker, 1984; Picard & Giuli, 1985). Some studies show that boys use computers more than girls in the early years (Beeson & Williams, 1985; Klinzing & Hall, 1985) and that boys are more interested in creative problem-solving programs, whereas girls tend to stay within the dictates of established drill programs (Shrock et al., 1985; Swigger, Campbell, & Swigger, 1983). Other studies, however, have not revealed such differences (Sherman, Divine, & Johnson, 1985), and the vast majority report that girls and boys do not differ in the amount or type of computer use (Essa, 1987; Hess & McGarvey, 1987; Hoover & Austin, 1986; Johnson, 1985; King & Perrin, n.d.; Lipinski et al., 1986; Muller & Perlmutter, 1985; Shade et al., 1986; Sprigle & Schaefer, 1984; Swigger & Campbell, 1981; Swigger et al., 1983). Furthermore, recent research reveals that girls are often just as interested and just as or more effective at computer tasks (Yelland, 1998) Considering the traditional heavy dominance of computer use by males, these researchers have recommended that the early years are the ideal time to introduce students to computers.

Special needs children. Finally, schools should plan for using computers to help students with special needs. Computers can serve in different ways. Technology can facilitate a broader range of educational activities to meet a variety of needs for students with mild learning disorders. Mildly handicapped children, even of preschooler age, can use existing materials, using lower levels and slower pacing as needed (Hutinger, 1987; Watson, Chadwick et al., 1986). Such uses have proven to be an effective method of giving these students experience with practice, communication, and exploratory activities matched to their individual abilities and needs (Hasselbring & Glaser, 2000). (Recall that many studies and suggestions were described in previous sections.)

In addition, adaptive technology exists than can enable even those students with severe disabilities to become active learners in the classroom alongside their peers who do not have disabilities. Hardware and software alterations are often necessary, such as switches used for input devices for the physically impaired.

For many special populations, the need for teacher support is high initially but declines over time; low-functioning students, however, may require teacher assistance during all their work. With such teacher support, CAI may even be more effective in providing basic skills instruction to special education students than to students in regular education (Swan & Black, 1989), possibly due to its systematic presentation of information in small increments, immediate feedback and positive reinforcement, high frequency of student response, and the opportunity for extended remediation through branching (Watson, Chadwick et al., 1986). Research documents that CAI can provide basic skills instruction to educationally-disadvantaged school-aged children (Swan & Black, 1989) and teach reading and writing skills to preschool and elementary-aged hearing-impaired children (Prinz et al., 1982).

Concern exists, however, that special education teachers use computers predominantly for drill and for rewarding desired behaviors (Christensen & Cosden, 1986). Alternatives are viable; handicapped students benefit from work with Logo or other discovery-oriented software (Lehrer & deBernard, 1987; Watson, Chadwick et al., 1986); even preschoolers can use exploratory programs in which they manipulate characters. Even severely handicapped young children can use voice synthesizers as communication tools, control robots, and some can create computer drawings and program in Logo (Biklen, 1990; Hutinger, 1987). Such use positively affects attention span, retention, social interaction, and aspects of problem solving. In one comprehensive project, special needs preschool children made progress in all developmental areas, including social-emotional, fine motor, gross motor, communication, cognition, and self-help. A measure of development showed that upon joining the program, children were making an average gain of .52 months per month. While participating in the computer-based program, children were making an average rate of progress of 1.81 months per month. After participation, 14 of the 15 children who participated for two years doubled their per month gain; 6 had developmental scores that exceeded their chronological scores for the first time in their lives (Hutinger & Johanson, 2000). For these children, 100% of both parents and teachers indicated that they saw improvements across the same wide variety of areas of development. Results indicated that the computer made a unique contribution. Across 11 common classroom activities, including play, books, computer, art, and snack time, results showed that computer use was most often followed by desirable behaviors such as sharing, communicating, and taking turns and least likely to be followed by aggression (Hutinger & Johanson, 2000).

In summary, both as educational tools and as adaptive devices, computers can provide sensory input; enhance mobility; develop cognitive, language, perceptual and motor skills; and facilitate communication (Clements, 1985). They can enhance sense of control, promote the understanding of cause-and-effect relationships, and provide a means of environmental control for both young children and older, severely-handicapped children. So, computers can enhance the quality of life for many special populations.

Schools should choose options in hardware and software that incorporate universal design features to facilitate access to computers for all children, including those with special needs (Shields & Behrmann, 2000). In addition, effective programs employ a comprehensive approach, making strong home-school connections, and sustain the intervention, helping children and families make the transition to later school settings (Cognition and Technology Group at Vanderbilt, 1998; Hutinger & Johanson, 2000).

FINAL WORDS

The computer can offer unique opportunities for learning through exploration, creative problem solving, and self-guided instruction. Realizing this potential demands a simultaneous focus on curriculum and technology innovations (Hohmann, 1994). Effectively integrating technology into the curriculum demands effort, time, commitment, and sometimes even a change in one's beliefs. One teacher reflected, "As you work into using the computer in the classroom, you start questioning everything you have done in the past and wonder how you can adapt it to the computer. Then, you start questioning the whole concept of what you originally did" (Dwyer, Ringstaff, & Sandholtz, 1991). These are positive results, but just as important is consideration of the potential disadvantages, from the drain on resources to the use of inappropriate software.

Some criticize computer use because computers—by their nature mechanistic and algorithmic—support only uncreative thinking and production. However, adults increasingly view computers as valuable tools of creative production. Educational research indicates that there is no single "effect" of the computer on achievement, higher-order thinking and creativity—technology can support either drill or the highest-order thinking. Research also provides strong evidence that certain computer environments, such as word processing, art and design tools, computer manipulatives, and turtle graphics hold the potential for the computer's facilitation of these educational goals. There is equally strong evidence that the curriculum in which computer programs are embedded, and the teacher who chooses, uses, and infuses these programs, are essential elements in realizing the full potential of technology.

ACKNOWLEDGMENTS

This chapter was supported in part by the National Science Foundation under Grant No. ESI-9730804, "Building Blocks—Foundations for Mathematical Thinking, Pre-Kindergarten to Grade 2: Research-based Materials Development" and Grant No. ESI-9814218, "Planning for Professional Development in Pre-School Mathematics: Meeting the Challenge of Standards 2000." Any opinions, findings, and conclusions or recommendations expressed in this material are those of the author and do not necessarily reflect the views of the National Science Foundation.

REFERENCES

Ainsa, P.A. (1992). Empowering classroom teachers via early childhood computer education. *Journal of Educational Computing Research, 3*(1), 3-14.

Allen, J., Watson, J.A., & Howard, J.R. (1993). The impact of cognitive styles on the problem solving strategies used by preschool minority children in Logo microworlds. *Journal of Computing in Childhood Education, 4,* 203-217.

American Academy of Pediatrics. (1999). Media education.*Pediatrics, 104,* 341-343.

Anderson, G.T. (2000a). Computers in a DAP curriculum.*Young Children, 55,* 90-93.

Anderson, G.T. (2000b, November). *An empirical comparison of the proportion of cooperative play of 4-year-old preschool children observed as they interact in four centers: Block, computer, housekeeping, and manipulative.* Paper presented at the meeting of the National Association for the Education of Young Children, Atlanta, GA.

Anselmo, S., & Zinck, R.A. (1987). Computers for young children? Perhaps. *Young Children, 42,* 22-27.

Bangert-Drowns, R.L. (1989, March). *Research on word processing and writing instruction.* Paper presented at the meeting of the American Educational Research Association, San Francisco.

Bangert-Drowns, R.L. (1993). The word processor as an instructional tool: A meta-analysis of word processing in and writing instruction. *Review of Educational Research, 63*(1), 69-93.

Becker, H.J. (1990). How computers are used in United States schools: Basic data from the 1989 I.E.A. Computers in Education Survey. *Journal of Educational Computing Research, 7,* 385-406.

Becker, H.J. (1992). Computer-based integrated learning systems in the elementary and middle grades: A critical review and synthesis of evaluation reports. *Journal of Educational Computing Research, 8,* 1-41.

Becker, H.J. (1994). *Analysis and trends of school use of new information technologies.* Unpublished manuscript, Department of Education, University of California, Irvine.

Becker, H.J. (2000). Who's wired and who's not: Children's access to and use of computer technology. *The Future of Children, 10*(2), 44-75.

Beeson, B.S., & Williams, R.A. (1985). The effects of gender and age on preschool children's choice of the computer as a child–selected activity. *Journal of the American Society for Information Science, 36,* 339-341.

Bergin, D., Ford, M.E., & Meyer-Gaub, B. (1986, April). *Social and motivational consequences of microcomputer use in kindergarten.* Paper presented at the meeting of the American Educational Research Association, San Francisco.

Bergin, D.A., Ford, M.E., & Hess, R.D. (1993). Patterns of motivation and social behavior associated with microcomputer use of young children. *Journal of Educational Psychology, 85,* 437-445.

Bernhard, J.K., & Siegel, L.S. (1994). Increasing internal locus of control for a disadvantaged group: A computer intervention. *Computers in the Schools, 11*(1), 59-77.

Biklen, D. (1990). Communication unbound: Autism and praxis. *Harvard Educational Review, 60,* 291-314.

Binder, S.L., & Ledger, B. (1985). *Preschool computer project report.* Oakville, Ontario: Sheridan College.

Borgh, K., & Dickson, W.P. (1986). Two preschoolers sharing one microcomputer: Creating prosocial behavior with hardware and software. In P.F. Campbell & G.G. Fein (Eds.), *Young children and microcomputers* (pp. 37-44). Reston, VA: Prentice-Hall.

Bosch, K.A. (1993). Can preservice teachers implement technology during field experiences? In N. Estes & M. Thomas (Eds.), *Rethinking the roles of technology in education* (Vol. 2, pp. 972-974). Cambridge, MA: Massachuseets Institute of Technology.

Brinker, R.P. (1984). The microcomputer as perceptual tool: Searching for systematic learning strategies with handicapped infants. In R.E. Bennett & C.A.

Maher (Eds.), *Microcomputers and exceptional children* (pp. 21-36). New York: Haworth Press.

Brinkley, V.M., & Watson, J.A. (1987-88a). Effects of microworld training experience on sorting tasks by young children. *Journal of Educational Technology Systems, 16*, 349-364.

Brinkley, V.M., & Watson, J.A. (1987-88b). Logo and young children: Are quadrant effects part of initial Logo mastery? *Journal of Educational Technology Systems, 19,* 75-86.

Chang, L.L., & Osguthorpe, R.T. (1990). The effects of computerized picture-word processing on kindergartners' language development. *Journal of Research in Childhood Education, 5,* 73-84.

Char, C.A. (1989, March). *Computer graphic feltboards: New software approaches for young children's mathematical exploration.* Paper presented at the meeting of the American Educational Research Association, San Francisco.

Childers, R.D. (1989). *Implementation of the Writing to Read instructional system in 13 rural elementary schools in southern West Virginia. 1988-89 annual report.* Charleston, WV: Appalacia Educational Lab. (ERIC Document Reproduction Service No. ED ED320744 RC017601)

Christensen, C.A., & Cosden, M.A. (1986). The relationship between special education placement and instruction in computer literacy skills. *Journal of Educational Computing Research, 2,* 299-306.

Christensen, C.A., & Gerber, M.M. (1990). Effectiveness of computerized drill and practice games in teaching basic math facts. *Exceptionality, 1,* 149-165.

Clements, D.H. (1985). *Computers in early and primary education.* Englewood Cliffs, NJ: Prentice-Hall.

Clements, D.H. (1986). Effects of Logo and CAI environments on cognition and creativity. *Journal of Educational Psychology, 78,* 309-318.

Clements, D.H. (1987a). Computers and literacy. In J.L. Vacca, R.T. Vacca, & M. Gove (Eds.), *Reading and learning to read* (pp. 338-372). Boston: Little, Brown.

Clements, D.H. (1987b). Computers and young children: A review of the research. *Young Children, 43*(1), 34-44.

Clements, D.H. (1987c). Longitudinal study of the effects of Logo programming on cognitive abilities and achievement. *Journal of Educational Computing Research, 3,* 73-94.

Clements, D.H. (1989). *Computers in elementary mathematics education.* Englewood Cliffs, NJ: Prentice-Hall.

Clements, D.H. (1990). Metacomponential development in a Logo programming environment. *Journal of Educational Psychology, 82,* 141-149.

Clements, D.H. (1991a). Current technology and the early childhood curriculum. In B. Spodek & O.N. Saracho (Eds.), *Yearbook in early childhood education, Volume 2: Issues in early childhood curriculum* (pp. 106-131). New York: Teachers College Press.

Clements, D.H. (1991b). Enhancement of creativity in computer environments. *American Educational Research Journal, 28,* 173-187.

Clements, D.H. (1993). Computer technology and early childhood education. In J.L. Roopnarine & J.E. Johnson (Eds.), *Approaches to early childhood education (2nd ed.)* (2nd ed., pp. 295-316). New York: Merrill.

Clements, D.H. (1994). The uniqueness of the computer as a learning tool: Insights from research and practice. In J.L. Wright & D.D. Shade (Eds.), *Young children: Active learners in a technological age* (pp. 31-50). Washington, DC: National Association for the Education of Young Children.

Clements, D.H. (1995). Teaching creativity with computers.*Educational Psychology Review, 7*(2), 141-161.

Clements, D.H. (1997). (Mis?)Constructing constructivism.*Teaching Children Mathematics, 4*(4), 198-200.

Clements, D.H., & Battista, M.T. (1989). Learning of geometric concepts in a Logo environment. *Journal for Research in Mathematics Education, 20,* 450-467.

Clements, D.H., & Battista, M.T. (1992). Geometry and spatial reasoning. In D.A. Grouws (Ed.), *Handbook of research on mathematics teaching and learning* (pp. 420-464). New York: Macmillan.

Clements, D.H., & Battista, M.T. (in press). Logo and geometry.*Journal for Research in Mathematics Education Monograph Series.*

Clements, D.H., & Gullo, D.F. (1984). Effects of computer programming on young children's cognition. *Journal of Educational Psychology, 76,* 1051-1058.

Clements, D.H., & Meredith, J.S. (1994). *Turtle math.* Montreal, Quebec: Logo Computer Systems, Inc. (LCSI).

Clements, D.H., & Nastasi, B.K. (1985). Effects of computer environments on social-emotional development: Logo and computer-assisted instruction.*Computers in the Schools, 2*(2-3), 11-31.

Clements, D.H., & Nastasi, B.K. (1988). Social and cognitive interactions in educational computer environments. *American Educational Research Journal, 25,* 87-106.

Clements, D.H., & Nastasi, B.K. (1992). Computers and early childhood education. In M. Gettinger, S.N. Elliott, & T.R. Kratochwill (Eds.),*Advances in school psychology: Preschool and early childhood treatment directions* (pp. 187-246). Hillsdale, NJ: Lawrence Erlbaum Associates.

Clements, D.H., & Nastasi, B.K. (1993). Electronic media and early childhood education. In B. Spodek (Ed.), *Handbook of research on the education of young children* (pp. 251-275). New York: Macmillan.

Clements, D.H., Nastasi, B.K., & Swaminathan, S. (1993). Young children and computers: Crossroads and directions from research.*Young Children, 48*(2), 56-64.

Clements, D.H., & Sarama, J. (1998). *Building Blocks—Foundations for Mathematical Thinking, Pre-Kindergarten to Grade 2: Research-based Materials Development [National Science Foundation, grant number ESI-9730804; see www.gse.buffalo.edu/ org/buildingblocks/].* Buffalo: State University of New York at Buffalo.

Clements, D.H., Sarama, J., & DiBiase, A.-M. (Eds.). (in press).*Engaging young children in mathematics: Findings of the 2000 national conference on standards for preschool and kindergarten mathematics education.* Hillsdale, NJ: Lawrence Erlbaum Associates.

Cochran-Smith, M., Kahn, J., & Paris, C.L. (1988). When word processors come into the classroom. In J.L. Hoot & S.B. Silvern (Eds.),*Writing with computers in the early grades* (pp. 43-74). New York: Teachers College Press.

Cognition and Technology Group at Vanderbilt. (1998). Designing environments to reveal, support, and expand our children's potentials. In S. Soraci & W.J. McIlvane (Eds.), *Perspectives on fundamental processes in intellectual functioning: Volume 1—A survey of research approaches* (pp. 313-350). Stamford, CT: Ablex.

Cohen, R., & Geva, E. (1989). Designing Logo-like environments for young children: The interaction between theory and practice. *Journal of Educational Computing Research, 5,* 349-377.

Coley, R.J., Cradler, J., & Engel, P.K. (1997). *Computers and classrooms: The status of technology in U.S. schools.* Princeton, NJ: Educational Testing Service.

Cordes, C., & Miller, E. (2000). *Fool's gold: A critical look at computers in childhood.* Alliance for Childhood. Available: http://www.allianceforchildhood.net/projects/computers/computers_reports.htm [2000, November 7].

Cosden, M.A. (1988). Microcomputer instruction and perceptions of effectiveness by special and regular education elementary teachers. *The Journal of Special Education, 22,* 242-253.

Cuffaro, H.K. (1984). Microcomputers in education: Why is earlier better? *Teachers College Record, 85,* 559-568.

Cunningham, A.E., & Stanovich, K.E. (1990). Early spelling acquisition: Writing beats the computer. *Journal of Educational Psychology, 82,* 159-162.

Daiute, C. (1988). The early development of writing abilities: Two theoretical perspectives. In J.L. Hoot & S.B. Silvern (Eds.), *Writing with computers in the early grades* (pp. 10-22). New York: Teachers College Press.

Davidson, J., & Wright, J.L. (1994). The potential of the microcomputer in the early childhood classroom. In J.L. Wright & D.D. Shade (Eds.), *Young children: Active learners in a technological age* (pp. 77-91). Washington, DC: National Association for the Education of Young Children.

Degelman, D., Free, J.U., Scarlato, M., Blackburn, J.M., & Golden, T. (1986). Concept learning in preschool children: Effects of a short–term Logo experience. *Journal of Educational Computing Research, 2*(2), 199-205.

Dickinson, D.K. (1986). Cooperation, collaboration, and a computer: Integrating a computer into a first-second grade writing program. *Research in the Teaching of English, 20,* 357-378.

Doran, L.A., & Kalinowski, M.F. (1991). Reducing adult computer anxiety: Lessons from preschool child tutors. *Journal of Computing in Childhood Education, 2*(3), 41-50.

Downes, T., Arthur, L., Beecher, B., & Kemp, L. (1999). *Appropriate EdNA services for children eight years and younger.* University of Western Sydney, Macarthur.

Dwyer, D.C., Ringstaff, C., & Sandholtz, J.H. (1991). Changes in teachers' beliefs and practices in technology-rich classrooms. *Educational Leadership, 48,* 45-52.

Elkind, D. (1987, May). The child yesterday, today, and tomorrow. *Young Children,* 6-11.

Elliott, A., & Hall, N. (1997). The impact of self-regulatory teaching strategies on "at-risk" preschoolers' mathematical learning in a computer-mediated environment. *Journal of Computing in Childhood Education, 8*(2/3), 187-198.

Emihovich, C., & Miller, G.E. (1988). Talking to the turtle: A discourse analysis of Logo instruction. *Discourse Processes, 11,* 183-201.

Escobedo, T.H. (1992). Play in a new medium: Children's talk and graphics at computers. *Play and Culture, 5,* 120-140.

Escobedo, T.H., & Bhargava, A. (1991). A study of children's computer-generated graphics. *Journal of Computing in Childhood Education, 2,* 3-25.

Escobedo, T.H., & Evans, S. (1997, March). *A comparison of child-tested early childhood education software with professional ratings.* Paper presented at the meeting of the American Educational Research Association, Chicago.

Essa, E.L. (1987). The effect of a computer on preschool children's activities.*Early Childhood Research Quarterly, 2,* 377-382.

Fletcher-Flinn, C.M., & Gravatt, B. (1995). The efficacy of computer assisted introduction (CAI): A meta-analysis. *Journal of Educational Computing Research, 12,* 219-242.

Fletcher-Flinn, C.M., & Suddendorf, T. (1996). Do computers affect "the mind"? *Journal of Educational Computing Research, 15*(2), 97-112.

Foster, K.C., Erickson, G.C., Foster, D.F., Brinkman, D., & Torgesen, J.K. (1994). Computer administered instruction in phonological awareness: Evaluation of the DaisyQuest program. *Journal of Research and Development in Education, 27,* 126-137.

Galen, F.H.J. v., & Buter, A. (2000). *Computer tasks and classroom discussions in mathematics.* Paper presented at the International Congress on Mathematics Education (ICME-9), Tokyo/Makuhari, Japan.

Garaigordobil, M., & Echebarria, A. (1995). Assessment of a peer-helping game program on children's development.*Journal of Research in Childhood Education, 10,* 63-69.

Gardner, C.M., Simmons, P.E., & Simmons, R.D. (1992). The effects of CAI and hands-on activities on elementary students' attitudes and weather knowledge. *School Science and Mathematics, 92,* 334-336.

Gélinas, C. (1986). *Educational computer activities and problem solving at the kindergarten level.* Quebec City, Quebec: Quebec Ministry of Education.

Gelman, R., & Baillargeon, R. (1983). A review of some Piagetian concepts. In P.H. Mussen (Ed.), *Handbook of child psychology* (4th ed., Vol. 3, pp. 167-230). New York: John Wiley & Sons.

Genishi, C., McCollum, P., & Strand, E.B. (1985). Research currents: The interactional richness of children's computer use.*Language Arts, 62*(5), 526-532.

Gerzog, E.H., & Haugland, S.W. (1999, Winter). Web sites provide unique learning opporunties for young children. *Early Childhood Education Journal, 27*(2), 109-114.

Green, L.C. (1991). The effects of word processing and a process approach to writing on the reading and writing achievement, revision and editing strategies, and attitudes towards writing of third-grade Mexican-American students.*Dissertation Abstracts International, 52-12,* 4245. (University Microfilms No. DA8426831)

Grover, S.C. (1986). A field study of the use of cognitive-developmental principles in microcomputer design for young children. *Journal of Educational Research, 79,* 325-332.

Gustafsson, K., Mellgren, E., Klerfelt, A., & Samuelsson, I.P. (1999, August).*Preschool teachers—Children, computers, and IT: An exploratory study.* Paper presented at the meeting of the EARLI 99: The 8th European Conference for Research and Learning, Gothenburg, Sweden.

Hall, I., & Hooper, P. (1993). Creating a successful learning environment with second and third graders, their parents, and LEGO/Logo. In D.L. Watt & M.L. Watt (Eds.), *New paradigms in classroom research on Logo learning* (pp. 53-63). Eugene, OR: International Society for Technolopy in Education.

Hasselbring, T.S., & Glaser, C.H.W. (2000). Use of computer technology to help students with special needs. *The Future of Children, 10*(2), 102-122.

Haugland, S.W. (1992). Effects of computer software on preschool children's developmental gains. *Journal of Computing in Childhood Education, 3*(1), 15-30.

Haugland, S.W. (1997). How teachers use computers in early childhood classrooms. *Journal of Computing in Childhood Education, 8*, 3-14.

Haugland, S.W., & Shade, D.D. (1990). *Developmental evaluations of software for young children*. Albany, NY: Delmar.

Haugland, S.W., & Wright, J.L. (1997). *Young children and technology: A world of discovery*. Boston: Allyn and Bacon.

Hawisher, G.E. (1989). Research and recommendations for computers and composition. In G.E. Hawisher & C.L. Selfe (Eds.), *Critical perspectives on computers and composition instruction* (pp. 44-69). New York: Teachers College Press.

Hess, R.D., & McGarvey, L. (1987). School-relevant effects of educational uses of microcomputers in kindergarten classrooms and homes. *Journal of Educational Computing Research, 3*, 269-287.

Hickey, M.G. (1993). Computer use in elementary classrooms: An ethnographic study. *Journal of Computing in Childhood Education, 4*, 219-228.

Hine, M.S., Goldman, S.R., & Cosden, M.A. (1990). Error monitoring by learning handicapped students engaged in collaborative microcomputer-based writing. *The Journal of Special Education, 23*(4), 407-422.

Hlawati, B. (1985). *Effects of Logo and problem-solving CAI on the cognitive processes of gifted children*. Unpublished doctoral dissertation, Kent State University.

Hohmann, C. (1994). Staff development practices for integrating technology in early childhood education programs. In J. L. Wright & D. D. Shade (Eds.), *Young children: Active learners in a technological age* (pp. 104). Washington, DC: National Association for the Education of Young Children.

Holmes, D.J., & Godlewski, J.B. (1995). *The attitude toward writing of first grade students using computers with the help of peer coaches*. Paper presented at the The Twelfth International Conference on Technology and Education, Orlando, FL.

Hoover, J.M., & Austin, A.M. (1986, April). *A comparison of traditional preschool and computer play from a social/cognitive perspective*. Paper presented at the meeting of the American Educational Research Association, San Francisco.

Horton, J., & Ryba, K. (1986). Assessing learning with Logo: A pilot study. *The Computing Teacher, 14*(1), 24-28.

Howard, J.R., Watson, J.A., & Allen, J. (1993). Cognitive style and the selection of Logo problem-solving strategies by young black children. *Journal of Educational Computing Research, 9*, 339-354.

Howland, J., Laffey, J., & Espinosa, L.M. (1997). A computing experience to motivate children to complex performances. *Journal of Computing in Childhood Education, 8*, 291-311.

Hungate, H. (1982, January). Computers in the kindergarten. *The Computing Teacher, 9*, 15-18.

Hutinger, P.L. (1987). Computer-based learning applications for young children with special needs. In J.L. Roopnarine & J.E. Johnson (Eds.), *Approaches to early childhood education* (pp. 213-236). Columbus, OH: Merrill.

Hutinger, P.L., Bell, C., Beard, M., Bond, J., Johanson, J., & Terry, C. (1998). *The early childhood emergent literacy technology research study. Final report*. Macomb, IL: Western Illinois University. (ERIC Document Reproduction Service No. ED ED 418 545)

Hutinger, P.L., & Johanson, J. (2000). Implementing and maintaining an effective early childhood comprehensive technology system. *Topics in Early Childhood Special Education, 20*(3), 159-173.

Ishigaki, E.H., Chiba, T., & Matsuda, S. (1996). Young children's communication and self expression in the technological era. *Early Childhood Development and Care, 119*, 101-117.

Israel, B.L. (1968). *Responsive environment program: Brooklyn, N.Y.: Report of the first full year of operation. The Talking Typewriter.* Brooklyn, NY: Office of Economic Opportunity. (ERIC Document Reproduction Service No. ED 027 742)

Johnson, J.E. (1985). Characteristics of preschoolers interested in microcomputers. *Journal of Educational Research, 78*, 299-305.

Jones, I. (1998). The effect of computer-generated spoken feedback on kindergarten students' written narratives. *Journal of Computing in Childhood Education, 9*(1), 43-56.

Jones, I., & Pellegrini, A.D. (1996). The effect of social relationships, writing media, and microgenetic development on first-grade students' written narratives. *American Educational Research Journal, 33*, 691-718.

Jones, M., & Liu, M. (1997). Introducing interactive multimedia to young children: A case study of how two-year-olds interact with the technology. *Journal of Computing in Childhood Education, 8*, 313-343.

Kajs, L.T., Alaniz, R., Willman, E., & Sifuentes, E. (1998). Color-coding keyboard functions to develop kindergartners' computer literacy. *Journal of Computing in Childhood Education, 9*, 107-111.

Kelman, P. (1990, June). *Alternatives to integrated instructional systems.* Paper presented at the meeting of the National Educational Computing Conference, Nashville, TN.

Kent, J.F., & Rakestraw, J. (1994). The role of computers in functional language: A tale of two writers. *Journal of Computing in Childhood Education, 5*(3/4), 329-337.

King, J.A., & Alloway, N. (1992). Preschooler's use of microcomputers and input devices. *Journal of Educational Computing Research, 8*, 451-468.

King, M., & Perrin, M. (n.d.). *An investigation of children's use of microcomputers in an early childhood program.* Athens: Ohio University.

Kinsley, T.C., & Langone, J. (1995). Applications of technology for infants, toddlers, and preschoolers with disabilities. *Journal of Special Education Technology, 12*, 312-324.

Klein, P., & Gal, O.N. (1992). Effects of computer mediation of analogical thinking in kindergartens. *Journal of Computer Assisted Learning, 8*, 244-254.

Klinzing, D.G., & Hall, A. (1985, April). *A study of the behavior of children in a preschool equipped with computers.* Paper presented at the meeting of the American Educational Research Association, Chicago, IL.

Kokish, R. (1994). Experiences using a PC in play therapy with children. *Computers in Human Services, 11*(1-2), 141-150.

Kraus, W.H. (1981). Using a computer game to reinforce skills in addition basic facts in second grade. *Journal for Research in Mathematics Education, 12*, 152-155.

Kromhout, O.M., & Butzin, S.M. (1993). Integrating computers into the elementary school curriculum: An evaluation of nine Project CHILD model schools. *Journal of Research on Computing in Education, 26*(1), 55-69.

Kurth, R.J. (1988, April). *Process variables in writing instruction using word processing, word processing with voice synthesis, and no word processing.* Paper presented at the meeting of the American Educational Research Association, New Orleans.

Kurth, R.J., & Kurth, L.M. (1987, April). *A comparison of writing instruction using and word processing, word processing with voice synthesis, and no word processing in kindergarten and first grade.* Paper presented at the meeting of the American Educational Research Association, Washington, DC. (ERIC Document Reproduction Service No. ED 283 196)

Labbo, L.D., & Kuhn, M. (1998). Electronic symbol making: Young children's computer-related emerging concepts about literacy. In D. Reinking & M.C. McKenna & L. D. Labbo & R. D. Kieffer (Eds.), *Handbook of literacy and technology* (pp. 79-91). Mahwah, NJ: Lawrence Erlbaum Associates.

Lahm, E.A. (1996). Software that engaged young children with disabilities: A study of design features. *Focus on Autism and Other Developmental Disabilities, 11*(2), 115-124.

Lane, A., & Ziviani, J. (1997). The suitability of the mouse for children's use: A review of the literature. *Journal of Computing in Childhood Education, 8*(2/3), 227-245.

Lavin, R., & Sanders, J. (1983). *Longitudinal evaluation of the C/A/I Computer Assisted Instruction Title 1 Project: 1979-82.* Chelmsford, MA: Merrimack Education Center.

Lehrer, R., & deBernard, A. (1987). Language of learning and language of computing: The perceptual-language model. *Journal of Educational Psychology, 79,* 41-48.

Lehrer, R., Harckham, L.D., Archer, P., & Pruzek, R.M. (1986). Microcomputer–based instruction in special education. *Journal of Educational Computing Research, 2,* 337–355.

Lehrer, R., Levin, B.B., DeHart, P., & Comeaux, M. (1987). Voice-feedback as a scaffold for writing: A comparative study. *Journal of Educational Computing Research, 3,* 335-353.

Lehrer, R., & Randle, L. (1986). Problem solving, metacognition and composition: The effects of interactive software for first–grade children. *Journal of Educational Computing Research, 3,* 409-427.

Lemerise, T. (1993). Piaget, Vygotsky, & Logo. *The Computing Teacher,* 24-28.

Lewin, C. (1997). "Test driving" CARS: Addressing the issues in the evaluation of computer-assisted reading software. *Journal of Computing in Childhood Education, 8*(2/3), 111-132.

Lewis, C. (1981). A study of preschool children's use of computer programs. In D. Harris & L. Nelson-Heern (Eds.), *Proceedings of the National Educational Computing Conference* (pp. 272-274). Iowa City, IA: National Educational Computing Conference.

Lieberman, D. (1985). Research on children and microcomputers: A review of utilization and effects studies. In M. Chen & W. Paisley (Eds.), *Children and microcomputers: Research on the newest medium* (pp. 59-83). Beverly Hills, CA: Sage.

Lin, S., Vallone, R.P., & Lepper, M.R. (1985, April). *Teaching early reading skills: Can computers help?* Paper presented at the meeting of the Western Psychological Association, San Jose, CA.

Lipinski, J.M., Nida, R.E., Shade, D.D., & Watson, J.A. (1986). The effects of microcomputers on young children: An examination of free–play choices, sex differences, and social interactions. *Journal of Educational Computing Research, 2,* 147-168.

Liu, M. (1996). An exploratory study of how pre-kindergarten children use the interactive multimedia technology: Implications for multimedia software design. *Journal of Computing in Childhood Education, 7,* 71-92.

Mayfield-Stewart, C., Moore, P., Sharp, D., Brophy, S., Hasselbring, T.S., Goldman, S.R., & Bransford, J. (1994, April). *Evaluation of multimedia instruction on learning and transfer.* Paper presented at the meeting of the American Education Research Association, New Orleans, LA. (ERIC Document Reproduction Service No. ED ED 375 166)

McCollister, T.S., Burts, D.C., Wright, V.L., & Hildreth, G.J. (1986). Effects of computer–assisted instruction and teacher–assisted Instruction on arithmetic task achievement scores of kindergarten children. *Journal of Educational Research, 80,* 121-125.

McCormick, L. (1987). Comparison of the effects of a microcomputer activity and toy play on social and communication behaviors of young children. *Journal of the Division for Early Childhood, 11,* 195-205.

McKenna, M.C. (1998). Electronic texts and the transformation of beginning reading. In D. Reinking, M.C. McKenna, L.D. Labbo, & R.D. Kieffer (Eds.), *Handbook of literacy and technology* (pp. 45-59). Mahwah, NJ: Lawrence Erlbaum Associates.

Mikropoulos, T.A., Kossivaki, P., Katsikis, A., & Savranides, C. (1994). Computers in preschool education: An interactive environment. *Journal of Computing in Childhood Education, 5,* 339-351.

Miller, G.E., & Emihovich, C. (1986). The effects of mediated programming instruction on preschool children's self–monitoring. *Journal of Educational Computing Research, 2*(3), 283-297.

Mitterer, J., & Rose-Drasnor, L. (1986). LOGO and the transfer of problem solving: An empirical test. *The Alberta Journal of Educational Research, 32,* 176-194.

Moxley, R.A., Warash, B., Coffman, G., Brinton, K., & Concannon, K.R. (1997). Writing development using computers in a class of three-year-olds. *Journal of Computing in Childhood Education, 8*(2/3), 133-164.

Muhlstein, E.A., & Croft, D.J. (1986). *Using the microcomputer to enhance language experiences and the development of cooperative play among preschool children.* Cupertino, CA: De Anza College. (ERIC Document Reproduction Service No. ED 269 004)

Muller, A.A., & Perlmutter, M. (1985). Preschool children's problem–solving interactions at computers and jigsaw puzzles. *Journal of Applied Developmental Psychology, 6,* 173-186.

Murphy, R.T., & Appel, L.R. (1984). *Evaluation of Writing to Read.* Princeton, NJ: Educational Testing Service.

Nastasi, B.K., Clements, D.H., & Battista, M.T. (1990). Social-cognitive interactions, motivation, and cognitive growth in Logo programming and CAI problem-solving environments. *Journal of Educational Psychology, 82,* 150-158.

National Association for the Education of Young Children and the International Reading Association. (1998, July). Learning to read and write: Developmentally appropriate practices for young children. *Young Children,* 30-46.

National Council of Teachers of Mathematics. (2000). *Principles and standards for school mathematics.* Reston, VA: Author.

Neufeld, K. (1989). When children use word processors for writing: Some problems and suggestions. *Reading Improvement, 26*(1), 64-70.

Niemiec, R., & Walberg, H.J. (1987). Comparative effects of computer-assisted instruction: A synthesis of reviews. *Journal of Educational Computing Research, 3*, 19-37.

Niemiec, R.P., & Walberg, H.J. (1984). Computers and achievement in the elementary schools. *Journal of Educational Computing Research, 1*, 435-440.

Olson, J.K. (1988, August). *Microcomputers make manipulatives meaningful.* Paper presented at the meeting of the International Congress of Mathematics Education, Budapest, Hungary.

Orabuchi, I.I. (1993). *Effects of using interactive CAI on primary grade students' high order thinking skills: Inferences, generalizations, and math problem-solving* [doctoral dissertation].

Owston, R.D., & Wideman, H.H. (1997). Word processors and children's writing in a high-computer-access setting. *Journal of Research on Computing in Education, 30*, 202-220.

Paris, C.L., & Morris, S.K. (1985, March). *The computer in the early childhood classroom: Peer helping and peer teaching.* Paper presented at the meeting of the Microworld for Young Children Conference, College Park, MD.

Parker, J. (1984, *Some disturbing data: Sex differences in computer use.* Paper presented at the meeting of the National Educational Computing Conference, Dayton, OH.

Perlmutter, M., Behrend, S., Kuo, F., & Muller, A. (1986). *Social influence on children's problem solving at a computer.* Unpublished manuscript, University of Michigan, Ann Arbor.

Phenix, J., & Hannan, E. (1984). Word processing in the grade one classroom. *Language Arts, 61*, 804-812.

Picard, A.J., & Giuli, C. (1985). *Computers as a free–time activity in grades K-4: A two year study of attitudes and usage.* Unpublished manuscript, University of Hawaii, Honolulu.

Plourde, R.R. (1987, December). The insignificance of Logo—Stop "mucking around" with computers. *Micro-Scope*, 30-31.

Poulin-Dubois, D., McGilly, C.A., & Shultz, T.R. (1989). Psychology of computer use. The effect of learning Logo on children's problem-solving skills. *Psychological Reports, 64*, 1327-1337.

Prinz, P.M., Nelson, K., & Stedt, J. (1982). Early reading in young deaf children using microcomputer technology. *American Annals of the Deaf, 127*, 529-535.

Ragosta, M., Holland, P., & Jamison, D.T. (1981). *Computer-assisted instruction and compensatory education: The ETS/LAUSD study.* Princeton, NJ: Educational Testing Service.

Reed, W.M. (1996). Assessing the importance of computer-based writing instruction. *Journal of Research on Computing in Education, 28*, 418-437.

Reimer, G. (1985). Effects of a Logo computer programming experience on readiness for first grade, creativity, and self concept. "A pilot study in kindergarten." *AEDS Monitor, 23*(7-8), 8-12.

Rhee, M.C., & Chavnagri, N. (1991). *Four year old children's peer interactions when playing with a computer.* Wayne, NJ: Wayne State University. (ERIC Document Reproduction Service No. ED 342466)

Riding, R.J., & Powell, S.D. (1987). The effect on reasoning, reading and number performance of computer-presented critical thinking activities in five-year-old children. *Educational Psychology, 7*, 55-65.

Riding, R.J., & Tite, H.C. (1985). The use of computer graphics to facilitate story telling in young children. *Educational Studies, 11*, 203-210.

Riel, M. (1985). The Computer Chronicles Newswire: A functional learning enviornment for acquiring literacy skills. *Journal of Educational Computing Research, 1*, 317-337.

Riel, M. (1994). Educational change in a technology-rich environment. *Journal of Research on Computing in Education, 26*(4), 452-474.

Robinson, M.A., Gilley, W.F., & Uhlig, G.E. (1988). The effects of guided discovery Logo on SAT performance of first grade students. *Education, 109*, 226-230.

Robinson, M.A., & Uhlig, G.E. (1988). The effects of guided discovery Logo instruction on mathematical readiness and visual motor development in first grade students. *Journal of Human Behavior and Learning, 5*, 1-13.

Roblyer, M.D., Castine, W.H., & King, F.J. (1988). *Assessing the impact of computer-based instruction: A review of recent research.* New York: Haworth Press.

Rosegrant, T.J. (1985, April). *Using a microcomputer to assist children in their efforts to acquire beginning literacy.* Paper presented at the meeting of the American Educational Research Association, Chicago.

Rosegrant, T.J. (1988). Talking word processors for the early grades. In J.L. Hoot & S.B. Silvern (Eds.), *Writing with computers in the early grades* (pp. 143-159). New York: Teachers College Press.

Rosengren, K.S., Gross, D., Abrams, A.F., & Perlmutter, M. (1985, September). *An observational study of preschool children's computing activity.* Paper presented at the meeting of the "Perspectives on the Young Child and the Computer" conference, University of Texas at Austin.

Ross, J.A., Hogaboam-Gray, A., & Hannay, L. (2001). Collateral benefits of an interactive literacy program for grade 1 and 2 students. *Journal of Research on Computing in Education, 33.*

Ryan, A.W. (1993). The impact of teacher training on achievement effects of microcomputer use in elementary schools: A meta-analysis. In N. Estes & M. Thomas (Eds.), *Rethinking the roles of technology in education* (Vol. 2, pp. 770-772). Cambridge, MA: Massachusetts Institute of Technology.

Samaras, A. (1991). Transitions to competence: An investigation of adult mediation in preschoolers' self-regulation with a microcomputer-based problem-solving task. *Early Education and Development, 2*, 181-196.

Saracho, O.N. (1982). The effects of a computer-assisted program on basic skills achievement and attitudes toward instruction of spanish-speaking migrant children. *American Educational Research Association Journal, 19*, 201-219.

Sarama, J., Clements, D.H., & Vukelic, E.B. (1996). The role of a computer manipulative in fostering specific psychological/mathematical processes. In E. Jakubowski, D. Watkins, & H. Biske (Eds.), *Proceedings of the eighteenth annual meeting of the North America Chapter of the International Group for the Psychology of Mathematics Education* (Vol. 2, pp. 567-572). Columbus, OH: ERIC Clearinghouse for Science, Mathematics, and Environmental Education.

Schery, T.K., & O'Connor, L.C. (1992). The effectiveness of school-based computer language intervention with severely handicapped children. *Language, Speech, and Hearing Services in Schools, 23*, 43-47.

Schery, T.K., & O'Connor, L.C. (1997). Language intervention: Computer training for young children with special needs. *British Journal of Educational Technology, 28*, 271-279.

Schrader, C.T. (1990). *The word processor as a tool for developing young writers.* (ERIC Document Reproduction Service No. ED ED321276 CS212431)

Sexton, D., King, N., Aldridge, J., & Goodstat-Killoran, I. (1999). Measuring and evaluating early childhood porspective practitioners' attitudes toward computers. *Family Relations, 48*(3), 277-285.

Shade, D.D. (1994). Computers and young children: Software types, social contexts, gender, age, and emotional responses. *Journal of Computing in Childhood Education, 5*(2), 177-209.

Shade, D.D., Nida, R.E., Lipinski, J.M., & Watson, J.A. (1986). Microcomputers and preschoolers: Working together in a classroom setting. *Computers in the Schools, 3*, 53-61.

Shade, D.D., & Watson, J.A. (1987). Microworlds, mother teaching behavior, and concept formation in the very young child. *Early Child Development and Care, 28*, 97-113.

Shapira, D. (1995). *Learning to read with joy by using computer-based graphics.* Paper presented at the The Twelfth International Conference on Technology and Education, Orlando, FL.

Shaw, E.L., Jr., Nauman, A. K., & Burson, D. (1994). Comparisons of spontaneous and word processed compositions in elementary classrooms: A three-year study. *Journal of Computing in Childhood Education, 5*(3/4), 319-327.

Sheingold, K. (1986). The microcomputer as a symbolic medium. In P.F. Campbell & G.G. Fein (Eds.), *Young children and microcomputers* (pp. 25-34). Reston, VA: Reston Publishing.

Sherman, J., Divine, K.P., & Johnson, B. (1985, May). An analysis of computer software preferences of preschool children. *Educational Technology, 39-41.

Shields, M.K., & Behrmann, R.E. (2000). Children and computer technology: Analysis and recommendations. *The Future of Children, 10*(2), 4-30.

Shilling, W.A. (1997). Young children using computer to make discoveries about written language. *Early Childhood Education Journal, 24*, 253-259.

Shrock, S.A., Matthias, M., Anastasoff, J., Vensel, C., & Shaw, S. (1985, January). *Examining the effects of the microcomputer on a real world class: A naturalistic study.* Paper presented at the meeting of the Association for Educational Communications and Technology, Anaheim, CA.

Shute, R., & Miksad, J. (1997). Computer assisted instruction and cognitive development in preschoolers. *Child Study Journal, 27*, 237-253.

Silfen, R., & Howes, A.C. (1984). A summer reading program with CAI: An evaluation. *Computers, Reading and Language Arts, 1*(4), 20-22.

Silvern, S.B., Countermine, T.A., & Williamson, P.A. (1988). Young children's interaction with a microcomputer. *Early Child Development and Care, 32*, 23-35.

Sivin, J.P., Lee, P.C., & Vollmer, A.M. (1985, April). *Introductory computer experiences with commercially-available software: Differences between three-year-olds and five-year-olds.* Paper presented at the meeting of the American Educational Research Association, Chicago, IL.

Smithy-Willis, D., Riley, M., & Smith, D. (1982, November/December). Visual discrimination and preschoolers. *Educational Computer Magazine, 19-20.

Spiegel-McGill, P., Zippiroli, S., & Mistrett, S. (1989). Microcomputers as social facilitotors in integrated preschools. *Journal of Early Intervention, 13*(3), 249-260.

Sprigle, J.E., & Schaefer, L. (1984). Age, gender, and spatial knowledge influences on preschoolers' computer programming ability. *Early Child Development and Care, 14,* 243-250.

Steg, D.R., Lazar, I., & Boyce, C. (1994). A cybernetic approach to early education. *Journal of Educational Computing Research, 10,* 1-27.

Stone, (1996). The academic impact of classroom computer usage upon middle-class primary grade level elmentary school children. *Dissertation Abstracts International, 57-06,* 2450. (University Microfilms No.)

Strommen, E. (1993). *Joystick, mouse, or trackball? Preschoolers' competence with three common input devices.* Atlanta, GA: American Educational Research Association.

Swan, K., & Black, J.B. (1989). *Logo programming and the teaching and learning of problem solving* (CCT Report 89-1). Teachers College, Columbia University.

Swigger, K., & Campbell, J. (1981). Computers and the nursery school. In D. Harris & L. Nelson-Heern (Eds.), *Proceedings of the National Educational Computing Conference* (pp. 264-268). Iowa City, IA: National Educational Computing Conference.

Swigger, K.M., Campbell, J., & Swigger, B.K. (1983, January/February). Preschool children's preferences of different types of CAI programs. *Educational Computer Magazine, 3,* 38-40.

Swigger, K.M., & Swigger, B.K. (1984). Social patterns and computer use among preschool children. *AEDS Journal, 17,* 35-41.

Talley, S., Lancy, D.F., & Lee, T.R. (1997). Children, storybooks, and computers. *Reading Horizons, 38*(2), 116-128.

Teague, G.V., Wilson, R.M., & Teague, M.G. (1984). Use of computer assisted instruction to improve spelling proficiency of low achieving first graders. *AEDS Journal, 17,* 30-35.

Turkle, S. (1997). Seeing through computers: Education in a culture of simulation. *The American Prospect, 31,* 76-82.

Vaidya, S., & McKeeby, J. (1984, September). Computer turtle graphics: Do they affect children's thought processes? *Educational Technology, 24,* 46-47.

Villarruel, F. (1990). Talking and playing: An examination of the effects of computers on the social interactions of handicapped and nonhandicapped preschoolers. *Dissertation Abstracts International, 51-11,* 3630. (University Microfilms No. AAD91-08303)

Walker, S.-L., Elliott, A., & Lacey, d. P.R. (1994). Enhancing language development for young children at risk: the role of computer-based and direct-instruction teacher. *Australian Journal of Early Childhood, 19.*

Warash, B.G. (1984, April). *Computer language experience approach.* Paper presented at the meeting of the National Council of Teachers of English Spring Conference, Columbus, OH. (ERIC Document Reproduction Service No. ED 244 264)

Wartella, E., & Jennings, N. (2000). Children and computers: New technology—old concerns. *The Future of Children, 10*(2), 31-43.

Watson, J.A., & Brinkley, V.M. (1990/91). Space and premathematic strategies young children adopt in initial Logo problem solving. *Journal of Computing in Childhood Education, 2,* 17-29.

Watson, J.A., Chadwick, S.S., & Brinkley, V.M. (1986). Special education technologies for young children: Present and future learning scenarios with related research literature. *Journal of the Division for Early Childhood, 10,* 197-208.

Watson, J.A., Lange, G., & Brinkley, V.M. (1992). Logo mastery and spatial problem-solving by young children: Effects of Logo language training, route-strategy training, and learning styles on immediate learning and transfer. *Journal of Educational Computing Research, 8,* 521-540.

Watson, J.A., Nida, R.E., & Shade, D.D. (1986). Educational issues concerning young children and microcomputers: Lego with Logo? *Early Child Development and Care, 23,* 299-316.

Wiburg, K.M. (1987). *The effect of different computer-based learning environments on fourth grade students' cognitive abilities.* Unpublished doctoral dissertation, United States International University.

Wild, M., & Ing, J. (1994). An investigation into the use of a concept keyboard as a computer-related device to improve the structure of young children's writing. *Journal of Computing in Childhood Education, 5*(3/4), 299-309.

Wood, E., Willoughby, T., & Specht, J. (1998). What's happening with computers technology in early childhood education settings? *Journal of Educational Computing Research, 18,* 237-243.

Woodward, E.H.I., & Gridina, N. (2000). *Media in the home 2000: The fifth annual survey of parents and children.* Philadelphia: Annenberg Public Policy Center, University of Pennsylvania.

Wright, A., Read, P., & Anderson, M. (1992). Contrasting computer input devices for teaching children with severe learning difficulties to read. *British Journal of Educational Technology, 23,* 106-112.

Wright, J.L. (1994). Listen to the children: Observing young children's discoveries with the microcomputer. In J.L. Wright & D.D. Shade (Eds.), *Young children: Active learners in a technological age* (pp. 3-17). Washington, DC: National Association for the Education of Young Children.

Wright, J.L., & Samaras, A.S. (1986). Play worlds and microworlds. In P.F. Campbell & G.G. Fein (Eds.), *Young children and microcomputers* (pp. 73-86). Reston, VA: Reston Publishing.

Wright, J., Seppy, J., & Yenkin, L. (1992). The use of digitized images in developing software for young children. *Journal of Computing in Childhood Education, 3*(3/4), 259-284.

Xin, J.F. (1999). Computer-assisted cooperative learning in integrated classrooms for students with and without disabilities. *Information Technology in Childhood Education Annual,* 61-78.

Yelland, N. (1994). A case study of six children learning with Logo. *Gender and Education, 6,* 19-33.

Yelland, N. (1995). Young children's attitudes to computers and computing. *Australian Journal of Early Childhood, 20*(2), 20-25.

Yelland, N.J. (1998). Making sense of gender issues in mathematics and technology. In N.J. Yelland (Ed.), *Gender in early childhood* (pp. 249-273). London: Routledge.

Yost, N.J.M. (1998). Computers, kids, and crayons: a comparative study of one kindergarten's emergent literacy behaviors. *Dissertation Abstracts International, 59-08,* 2847. (University Microfilms No.)

CHAPTER 10

STRENGTHENING THE ROLE OF CURRICULUM IN CHILD CARE

Douglas R. Powell and Gary E. Bingham

INTRODUCTION

Education is increasingly viewed as a necessary part of children's out-of-home child care experiences. Our society's concern about the quality and outcomes of schooling has extended to the care of young children, with growing numbers of policymakers, professionals, and parents seeking ways to maximize the learning potential of the early years. Child care is a logical target of this interest because a sizeable number of young children now spend a significant amount of time in child care arrangements, and because research repeatedly points to the mediocre quality of most out-of-home child care settings.

Curriculum is an obvious focus of efforts to improve learning opportunities and outcomes in child care. A curriculum provides a coherent framework for delineating program content, process, and desired outcomes, and for guiding staff development and program evaluation efforts (Evans, 1982; Goffin, 1994; Spodek, 1973). There is a rich history of curriculum development work in early childhood education (Spodek & Brown, 1993), and currently a renewed interest in curriculum as a vehicle for providing good educational experiences in the preschool years that positively influence subsequent school learning (Bowman, Donovan, & Burns, 2001).

Efforts to strengthen the role of curriculum in child care face three major challenges: (1) curriculum, a term central to the field of education, is not a core concept in the child care field; (2) education is not consistently a primary goal across child care programs; and (3) existing early childhood curriculum models do not easily transfer to the typical full-day child care program context. At the same time, the expansion of child care and growing interest in curriculum provide an opportunity to design and implement programs that integrate early education and care in the context of research on young children's learning capacities.

This chapter identifies challenges and opportunities in strengthening the role of curriculum in child care. The chapter is divided into two major sections. The first section describes historical and contemporary contexts of the three major challenges noted above. The second section sets forth three strategies for improving learning opportunities in child care settings. The strategies pertain to refining the definition of child care quality, integrating early education and care in curriculum approaches, and personnel preparation. For this chapter, child care entails full-day nonparental care of children outside the child's home in a child care center or a family child care home.

CONTEXT OF CHALLENGES

Interest in early childhood curriculum has escalated in the past decade. Most educational reform initiatives view learning experiences in the early childhood period as a foundation of school success. The first goal of the National Education Goals adopted in 1989 by President William Clinton and the 50 governors focuses on the early years, for example, and a Carnegie Corporation blueprint for reform of elementary education devotes an entire chapter to "getting serious about early learning" (Carnegie Task Force on Learning in the Primary Grades, 1996). No doubt, the inclusion of the early years in school reform plans is partly the result of well-publicized longitudinal research on the positive effects of early childhood programs. While some observers correctly note that research findings from programs serving low-income populations have been inappropriately generalized to middle-class populations (e.g., Olsen & Zigler, 1989), there appears to be widespread belief that early childhood education is generally beneficial (Shonkoff & Phillips, 2000). At the same time, there are nagging concerns about whether prevailing early childhood program practices are sufficiently supportive of young children's learning. Parents have long asked about the educational benefits of children's play in early childhood classrooms, for example, and it is common for parents to press for or prefer programs that employ educational flashcards and other didactic approaches to learning (Powell, 1997). Recently a prestigious National Research Council panel of early childhood experts concluded that a convincing body of research indicates children are more capable learners than current practices reflect (Bowman et al., 2001).

Nomenclature and Purpose

Most child care programs are not well positioned to readily embrace the growing interest in improved learning opportunities for young children. At a surface level, there is a challenge of nomenclature. Child care has developed in this country largely outside of the nation's educational systems, and child care terminology generally has come from the field's professional roots in child and social welfare. Accordingly, the field's semantic traditions do not include educational concepts and terms. For example, the topic of "curriculum" receives scant or no attention in recent scholarly treatments of child care research and issues (e.g., Howes & Ponciano, 2000; Lamb, 1998; Spodek & Saracho, 1992).

At a deeper level, there is a challenge regarding the purpose of child care. The creation and expansion of child care have occurred mostly to accommodate adult needs. Child care has been supported by governments and philanthropies as a way to enable parents, especially mothers, to enter the work force and to participate in education and training programs, including welfare-to-work initiatives; as an aid to increased productivity in the workplace; as a win-the-war support during World War II; and, during the Great Depression of the 1930s, as a job program for unemployed teachers, nurses, and social workers. Full-day child care programs, called day nurseries in their earlier form, also have been enlisted in societal reform movements wherein training in religion, morality, cleanliness, nutrition, and character building for young children was deemed a central step toward an improved social order. The targets of these efforts typically were neglected and abandoned children associated with "troubled" families as well as children of poor or immigrant families (Fein & Clarke-Stewart, 1973). In general, supporting children's learning and school-related competence has not been the primary aim of child care programs; the tendency has been to focus on custodial care that keeps children safe and protected. Data collected in 1990 indicate that the majority of a nationally representative sample of centers and family child care programs indicated their goal was to provide a warm, loving environment for children (56% of centers, 78% of home-based programs). School preparation was the main goal of 13% of centers and 6% of family child care providers, while 20% of centers and 7% of family child care providers identified child development as the main goal. Programs based in public schools were about twice as likely as other types of centers to indicate that child development and school preparation were their main goals (Kisker, Hofferth, Phillips, & Farquhar, 1991).

The history of child care is in contrast with the evolution of nursery school programs, which typically were organized for the purpose of studying or enhancing child growth and development and, prior to Head Start and other early intervention programs, tended to serve preschool children from intact middle-class and privileged families who viewed the experience as an opportunity to enrich their child's social development (Fein & Clarke-Stewart, 1973). Importantly, half-day preschool programs traditionally have been the venue for the development and evaluation of early childhood curriculum models, which received significant attention and resources in the 1960s and 1970s as part of the dramatic growth of preschool programs such as Head Start for economically disadvantaged populations (Goffin, 1994; Powell, 1987).

Historically, then, child care has a stronger alignment with the child welfare field than with education. A structural implication of this legacy today is that usually the state and local agencies responsible for licensing and supporting child care programs are the social service, not education, divisions of government. A functional implication of this history is that the "care" tradition is linked to child welfare and social services professions while the "education" function of early childhood programs is linked to the education profession.

Caldwell (1989) has argued that the "education" and "child care" labels comprise two distinct turfs that "once established, have to be guarded by both semantic and programmatic manipulations" (Caldwell, 1989, p. 407). She illustrates this point with a 1960 definition of day care in the Child Welfare League of America's Standards for Day Care Service, which notes that the primary purpose of a day care service is the care and protection of children while the primary purpose of a nursery school is the education of young children (Child Welfare League of America, 1960).

The debate over institutional sponsorship of child care also offers an example of the maintenance of "education" and "care" turfs. Among the main sponsorship contenders (churches, for-profit enterprises, public non-profit agencies, schools, and employers), the most intense debate has been generated over the prospect of public schools serving as the dominant sponsor of child care. The remarkably strong appeals of public school sponsorship of child care include a universal delivery system for families of all social classes, the focus on a service expressly for children, and the improved status of child care staff affiliated with the teaching profession (Klein, 1992). However, opponents of public school sponsorship of child care often argue that the care/nurturance function of child care would be diminished or lost in favor of an academic approach to child care operated by public schools (for an analysis of the arguments, see Klein, 1992), perhaps through downward extension of an elementary school curriculum (e.g., Elkind, 1987). For example, in response to an American Federation of Teachers plan for public school sponsorship of child care, Greenman (1978) submitted that nurturance is missing in the school paradigm, which emphasizes knowledge and skill attainment in the context of state and community mandates. In contrast, child care centers are institutions and extensions of the home and family; "parent control of schools may be controversial, but parent control of child-rearing is an American tradition" (Greenman, 1978, p. 10). Many observers contend that the intensity of the debate over public school child care stems from adversarial relations between the social service and education communities (e.g., Caldwell, 1986).

In practice, the care and education functions of early childhood programs are not mutually exclusive. The inseparable nature of care and education is commonly acknowledged in proposals for quality improvements in early childhood programs (e.g., Bowman et al., 2001). Further, the institutional domains of child care and early education have been far from completely separate. While staff in the earliest forms of day nurseries ensured that children were cared for, cleaned, and fed, day nurseries started offering educational programs on a regular basis by the 1920s (Spodek, Saracho, & Davis, 1991). Nursery school methods continued to be assimilated into some full-day child care programs through the 1940s (Fein & Clarke-Stewart, 1973), and by 1950 a prominent book in early childhood education treated the full-day child care center as one kind of nursery school identical to other early childhood programs in curriculum and general approach to working with children (Read, 1950).

In recent years recommendations to combine the traditions of early education and child care have increased while the historically sharp distinctions between child care and preschool education have decreased. The term "early care and education" is used with greater frequency in references to the broad, patchwork field of early childhood programs (e.g., Bowman et al., 2001; Kagan & Cohen, 1997), although there continues to be a lack of a clear, widely accepted definition of this label (Kagan & Neuman, 2000, p. 345).

Realities of Child Care

What are beneficial ways to combine the traditions of early education and care in full-day arrangements for children? One option is to coordinate children's participation in separate early education and child care programs. An example here is for child care to "wrap around" a part-day Head Start program, with child care services provided before and after the Head Start day and on days when Head Start is not in session (Poersch & Blank, 1996). A variant of this model applied to a full-day setting is for the morning to be viewed as "educational" and the afternoon as "care." This approach to providing education and care falls short of achieving the true integration of education and care advocated by leaders in the field who view the two functions as inseparable.

Length of day is not the only challenge in efforts to strengthen children's learning opportunities through curriculum in child care. Staffing patterns and generally weak infrastructures for high-quality child care programs also diminish the supports for thoughtful curriculum work. Consider, for example, efforts to incorporate into child care centers the dialogic reading program developed by Whitehurst and his colleagues (Whitehurst, Epstein, Angell, Payne, Crone, & Fischel, 1994). The program involves small groups of no more than four children engaged in shared reading with a staff member in the classroom. During a six-week period the program was being closely evaluated, child care teachers adhered to the design of small groups of no more than four children but they did not continue the four-child group limit during a subsequent six-month follow-up period. Arnold and Whitehurst (1994) suggest several ways the current organization of child care classrooms was unable to support the design of the reading program long term. First, although there were two or more adults in each classroom, rarely did they engage in teaching at the same time. One adult was responsible for the group while the other staff member engaged in other activities (e.g., preparing or putting away materials). Second, Arnold and Whitehurst (1994) speculate that the developmental (vs. instructional) philosophy of child care centers leads to a "supportive environment for a child's naturally unfolding interests and needs . . . (and) makes it difficult to motivate staff to utilize a technique based on teaching children specific skills" (p. 121). The researchers also emphasize that the dialogic reading program requires careful attention to individual children for extended periods but teachers seldom devote individual attention to children. This pattern does not appear to be unique to full-day child care programs. A study of one half-day university preschool program found that teacher interaction with individual children was limited in frequency even when a teacher was within close proximity to a child (Wilcox-Herzog & Kontos, 1998), and another study of both full-day and half-day programs found that, at least during researchers' observation periods, some children received no individual attention from a teacher (Layzer, Goodson, Moss, & Farquhar, 1993).

The weak infrastructure supports for child care—including low salaries, minimal staff qualifications and staff development opportunities, and often inappropriate standards for staff-child ratio and group size—are well documented in the literature (e.g., Lamb, 1998). Limited or nonexistent time for teacher planning of children's experiences is among the numerous consequences of this general situation. Cryer and Phillipsen (1997) concluded from an analysis of strengths and weaknesses of 390 child care center classrooms serving preschool-aged children that curriculum-related areas needing improvements require teacher thought and preparation (e.g., art activities, dramatic play, meals/snacks, cultural awareness). For example, meaningful art or dramatic play activities require teacher time devoted to planning, including careful attention to children's interests. Similarly, time and preparation are needed for serving nutritious snacks and meals in a way that enables adults to sit with children, engage them in pleasant interactions, and teach them self-help skills during mealtimes.

STRATEGIES FOR IMPROVING THE ROLE OF CURRICULUM

Today full-day child care programs are the fastest growing segment of the early childhood field and are steadily evolving into a mainstream service as growing numbers of middle-class mothers enter the labor force. There is an emerging consensus in the country, especially among parents, that young children should be afforded educational experiences, and an increasingly widespread belief that many existing early childhood practices fall short of fully supporting young children's learning capacities (Bowman, et al. 2001).

This context provides an opportunity to add programmatic details to repeated calls for an integration of early education and child care traditions. More than a decade ago Caldwell (1989) proposed use of the term "educare" for representing the inextricably combined functions of education and care. Zigler (1989) endorsed the idea in his proposal for incorporating child care into a School of the 21st Century model. More recently, Kagan and Cohen (1996) have called for early care and education to function as a single seamless system, not as a set of disparate programs. Three broad strategies are necessary for realizing this general goal.

Refine the Definition of Child Care Quality

Efforts to improve the role of curriculum in child care would likely benefit from definitions of child care quality that emphasize children's actual experiences in child care. Currently the nature of children's experiences in child care is overshadowed by attention to structural features of child care (e.g., staff-child ratio, group size, education and training of staff) in policy and professional considerations of child care quality. The strong interest in structural features is understandable because they are cost-sensitive characteristics of child care settings that are readily amenable to regulation. They are predictors or correlates of child care quality, however, and should not be confused with children's daily experiences in child care or what researchers call "process quality" (e.g., interactions with staff).

Structural attributes of child care settings also cannot be treated as proxies for child care quality because the presence of good structural factors does not guarantee quality interactions between teacher and child (Scarr, Eisenberg, & Deater-Deckard, 1994). For example, an observational study of life in 119 early childhood classrooms with approximately even institutional sponsorship by Head Start, public schools, or private child care agencies in five sites found that the classrooms resembled one another in many ways and provided little variation in structural features such as staff-to-child ratios. The programs generally provided adequate levels of quality experiences, but none was rated as excellent. Teachers and aides spent most of their time actively involved with the children, but the largest proportion of their time was spent with the group as a whole and little time was spent with individual children. For example, in 12% of all classrooms, more than half of the children received no individual attention during two observation periods. The investigators suggest that "while regulating program characteristics can ensure adequate care, it does not necessarily produce the high quality experience that we would want for all children" (Layzer et al., 1993, p. 67).

Curriculum is well represented in measures used to quantify the "process quality" or actual experiences of children in child care. Consider the focus of a widely-used measure of process quality in child care, the Early Childhood Environment Rating Scale (ECERS) (Harms & Clifford, 1980; Harms, Clifford, & Cryer, 1998) and a related measure of infant-toddler classrooms, the Infant/Toddler Environment Rating Scale (ITERS) (Harms, Cryer, & Clifford, 1990). Curriculum-related items are part of six of the measure's seven subscales (activities, language and reasoning, interaction, program structure, space and furnishings, personal care routines). Overall, this measure gives attention to such mainstream curriculum content as literacy, fine motor experiences, art, music and movement, blocks, sand and water, dramatic play, nature and science, math and number experiences, and use of television, video and/or computers.

Curriculum also is well represented in the six areas of the 150-item Assessment Profile for Early Childhood Programs (Abbott-Shim & Sibley, 1987), another prominent measure of process quality. The curriculum area is divided into subsections focused on use of varied materials, materials encouraging cultural awareness, alternative teaching techniques to facilitate learning, and individualization of the curriculum. Further, curriculum issues are addressed in the profile's other five areas: safety and health, learning environment, caregiver-child interactions, scheduling of time, indoor and outdoor play spaces, and individualizing the program to meet students' needs. For example, the learning environment area includes items pertaining to the use of manipulative materials, creative activities, and motor activities.

While dimensions of curriculum are central to measures of child care quality, the term "curriculum" is not prominent in descriptions of these measures or in the usual benchmarks of child care quality. Most commonly the recognition of children's child care experiences in definitions of quality comes in the form of a general reference to the developmentally appropriate practice (DAP) guidelines set forth by NAEYC (Bredekamp & Copple, 1997). The widespread acceptance of DAP guidelines is a milestone development in the early childhood field, but NAEYC is quick to acknowledge that DAP represents a framework for practice and not a curriculum (Bredekamp & Rosegrant, 1992).

The task of moving children's actual child care experiences to a more central position in definitions of child care quality may be aided by asking some basic questions about how we want children to spend their time in out-of-home settings. For example, what knowledge, skills, and values do we want children to learn and how should they learn them? Presumably a large number of child care programs already are explicitly or implicitly answering this question in their decisions about curriculum. Although the stereotype is that most child care settings are void of curriculum, a 1994 survey of a random sample of members of the NAEYC found that a relatively high percentage of early childhood personnel indicated that their child care setting used a curriculum model. Specifically, the following percentages of respondents in various settings reported using a curriculum model: 82% of public school early childhood programs, 76% of nonprofit child care centers, 72% of for-profit child care centers, 67% of group child care homes, 63% of family child care homes, 74% of for-profit child care centers. These patterns compare to 82% of public school early childhood programs. Interestingly, nearly all respondents reported being aware of at least one early childhood curriculum model (Epstein, Schweinhart, & McAdoo, 1996).

It would be unreasonable to claim that curriculum is alive and prevalent in child care. But it also would be unreasonable to assume it is a huge stretch for child care programs to consider curriculum as a core part of program quality. Definitions of child care quality are still in development (Larner, 1996; Phillips, 1996), and a clear vision of goals and experiences for children that encompasses both the caring and learning functions of an early childhood program should be integral to delineations of quality.

Curriculum Approaches That Integrate Education and Care

A true integration of early education and care traditions in child care settings requires careful adaptation of existing curriculum approaches, most of which were generated in half-day programs. The early childhood field has a number of curriculum models, including some with longitudinal research evidence regarding effectiveness (Epstein et al., 1996; Goffin, 1994). Available evidence indicates that no single curriculum approach is best, and that children tend to learn more and do better in mastering the demands of formal schooling when they participate in well-planned, high-quality early childhood programs in which curriculum goals are specified and integrated across content domains (e.g., science) (Bowman et al., 2001).

Early childhood curricula that intentionally integrate education and care functions require thoughtful consideration of the educational dimensions of care and the caring dimensions of education. Key elements of a framework for this task are available in a recent report of the Committee on Early Childhood Pedagogy organized by the National Research Council for the purpose of exploring implications of recent behavioral and social science research on early learning for the education and care of young children ages 2 through 5 years (Bowman et al., 2001). A central premise of the report is that care and education cannot be treated as separate entities in dealing with young children. Specifically, the Committee submits that "adequate care involves cognitive and perceptual stimulation and growth, just as adequate education for young children must occur in a safe and emotionally rich environment" (Bowman et al., 2001, p. 32). Moreover, the Committee argues that "neither loving children nor teaching them is, in and of itself, sufficient for optimal development; thinking and feeling work in tandem" (Bowman et al., 2001, p. 2).

A well-planned curriculum that enables "thinking and feeling" to work in tandem for young children requires a theoretical point of view that transcends a narrow focus on content knowledge and skill development. Potentially helpful in this regard is a relationship perspective on early childhood programs that emphasizes the quality of teacher-child, child-child, and adult-adult relationships, particularly adult responsiveness to children's interests and needs. A growing body of research demonstrates that the quality of children's early relationships is strongly related to social and cognitive development outcomes and to children's exploration of learning opportunities (Elicker, 1997).

Conventional terminology and thinking about learning and caring are formidable obstacles to overcome in developing curriculum approaches that integrate early education and care. Leaders of one effort aimed at providing "educare" consistently referred to the program as an extended-day school and attempted to eliminate distinctions between education and child care services. However, staff, parents, and children continued to view the day as divided into school and child care. For instance, at the end of the "regular" school day, most children would say "I'm going to day care now" as they reported to the check-in point for extended-day activities (Caldwell, 1989).

Staffing arrangements for early childhood programs also are a serious obstacle. Spodek and Saracho (1990) have predicted that there will continue to be a distinction between the care and education of young children and between the practitioners who provide those services due to the economics of child care costs and the difference in standards for teachers in education programs and child care programs. Indeed, Olsen and Zigler's (1989) proposal for organizing a full-day program for kindergarten-age children entails a half-day of school complemented by a half-day of high-quality child care provided at the school by staff with a Child Development

Associate credential. The school portion would include "more structured activities and a greater focus on academics" while the child care component would offer "opportunities for outdoor and exploratory play and for social interaction" (Olsen & Zigler, 1989, p. 181). Olsen and Zigler note that, under this plan, "teachers are not asked to assume a care-taking function outside their traditional role" and "costs are kept to a minimum" because child care staff will be paid less than teachers (Olsen & Zigler, 1989, p. 182).

This strategy is in contrast with an arrangement that incorporates a kindergarten curriculum into an extended-day or full-day arrangement. An observational study of children's use of time in full-day and half-day kindergarten classrooms found that children in full-day programs spent more time engaged in self-initiated learning activities (e.g., at learning centers), direct one-to-one teaching situations, small group activities, and individual teacher-specified work (e.g., writing in a journal) than children in half-day programs, who spent a majority of their time in large group teacher-directed activities. In general, there was a greater balance between child-initiated and teacher-directed learning in the full-day programs (Elicker & Mathur, 1997).

We cite kindergarten as an example of issues faced in the integration of early education and care. We also highlight kindergarten because the way in which public schools accommodate the growing public interest in extended-day kindergarten—by dividing the day into "education" and "care" components *or* reworking a half-day kindergarten curriculum to spread across a longer day—may provide a salient model in local communities for how parents, policymakers, and teachers think about and support children's education and care in the early years.

The integration of early education and care takes on special importance in the context of profound demographic changes in the United States. The growth of child care in this country is indicative of rapidly changing circumstances for families and communities. Early childhood curriculum advances need to be cognizant of the contemporary needs of children and families, especially regarding the daily schedules of families, the availability of informal and formal family support systems, opportunities for extended parent-child interaction, and the impact of family structure and adult work demands on children's experiences at home. Moreover, growing numbers of children and families represent cultures and languages that require full accommodation and support in early childhood programs (Tabors, 1997). Children's approaches to learning (e.g., value placed on working quietly), social rules of conversation (e.g., appropriateness of child initiating conversation with teacher), and the contribution of cultural background to children's social and emotional capacities are among the factors that research suggests are important for teachers to understand in working with young children (Bowman et al., 2001).

Personnel Preparation

We propose a focus on personnel preparation as the third major strategy for strengthening the role of curriculum in child care programs for three research-based reasons: teacher training and education levels are significant predictors of the quality of children's experiences in child care programs; early childhood teachers with bachelors' degrees are far more likely than those without a bachelor's degree to use an early childhood curriculum model; and child care staff often lack two- or four-year degrees in early childhood education or a related field.

A growing body of research indicates that personnel preparation is a major pathway to an improved quality of children's experiences in child care. Howes (1997) found that child care teachers with specialized training or education in early childhood education provided better quality care for children than teachers without this training. Specifically, teachers with a bachelor's degree or higher in early childhood education were rated as more sensitive than teachers with either an associate's degree in early childhood education or Child Development Associate (CDA) training, who in turn were rated as more sensitive than teachers with high school or vocational training only. The frequency of children's language play was higher in classrooms where teachers had a bachelor's degree in early childhood education or CDA training than in classrooms where teachers had high school backgrounds only. Also, children in centers where teachers had at least a bachelor's degree in early childhood education engaged in more complex play with objects and in more creative activities than children in other classrooms. Children in classrooms with teachers who had either CDA training or a bachelor's degree or higher in early childhood education engaged in the most complex play with peers and engaged in the most language activity. Howes (1997) also found that child outcomes were associated with levels of teacher preparation in early childhood. Children in classrooms with teachers who had at least an associate's degree in early childhood education scored higher on a standardized test of receptive language than did children in classrooms with teachers who had high school backgrounds only. In another study, results of a survey of a random sample of NAEYC members found that 81% of respondents with a bachelor's degree or more used one or more early childhood curriculum models while 65% of respondents with less than a bachelor's degree used a curriculum model (Epstein et al., 1996).

A limitation of most research on the relation between teacher education levels and classroom quality or child outcomes is that usually data are collected at one time only. A more rigorous test of the efficacy of professional preparation in early childhood would examine teachers' classroom performance before and after participation in a post-baccalaureate education program. To this end, Cassidy and colleagues investigated the effects of the first year of an associate degree program in early childhood on a sample of child care classroom teachers who had no college level coursework at the time of acceptance into the early childhood degree program. The associate degree program was a component of the TEACH (Teacher Education and Compensation Helps) Early Childhood Project in North Carolina, an initiative aimed at improving the educational qualifications and compensation levels of early childhood personnel. The associate degree program was targeted at individuals employed in the child care field who had no college coursework. Persons selected for the program received a scholarship plus support for release time from work. Thirty-four teachers participated in the study; 19 were teachers who had received scholarships to pursue an associate degree program in early childhood education and in child development at community colleges, and 15 were comparison teachers. All participants had high school diplomas and some in-service training. At posttest, the degree program participants had completed at least 12-20 academic credit hours of community college coursework, primarily in methods of early childhood education. Results indicated that the classrooms of the program participants had made significant gains on measures of classroom quality and provided more developmentally appropriate practices in their classrooms than comparison teachers at time of posttest (Cassidy, Buell, Pugh-Hoese, & Russell, 1995).

For the vast majority of child care personnel, associate and baccalaureate degree programs in early childhood education are out of reach and certainly not a requirement of employment. Short-term training programs for staff are often viewed as a stopgap measure for improving program quality, but available evidence suggests that short-term training programs may not be a viable way to contribute to significant improvements in child care quality. One illustrative effort is the Family-to-Family training program offered to family child care providers in three states. The training entailed between 15 and 25 hours of actual class time and some trainer visits to providers' homes, and focused on a range of content, including child development and age-appropriate activities for children, environments to promote learning, guidance and discipline, and diversity issues. Training was based on well-known training curricula and was provided by experienced trainers through community colleges in two states and through a child care resource and referral agency in a third state. A study of the training found that ratings of global quality of care provided by those who participated in the training program were higher after the training than the ratings of global quality of care provided by those in a comparison group that did not participate in training. However, there were no differences in process quality as assessed by measures of provider sensitivity to children and intensity of adult-child involvement. Also, almost one-half of the providers who participated in training made no change in the frequency of planning activities for children after the training. Of the 55% who did make changes in planning, some actually planned less (26%) while others planned more

(29%). These modest findings from a relatively rigorous training program prompted the investigators to suggest that it may be easier to modify global aspects of a child care environment through changes in equipment, planning, daily schedule, menus and the like than to change the nature of teacher-child interactions (Kontos, Howes, & Galinsky, 1996).

Sustained changes in child care staff behaviors probably are more likely to be achieved when feedback on performance is provided through coaching and other forms of one-on-one mentoring work that takes the trainer or mentor into the trainee's classroom or family child care home. Research suggests that training delivered through workshop and adult classrooms can increase participants' knowledge and awareness, but usually does not lead to behavioral change (Kontos, 1992; Kontos & File, 1993). Individualized, site-based coaching and other forms of mentoring are valuable tools to this end (e.g., Gallacher, 1997) and, as Kontos and colleagues (1996) note, these are infrequent occurrences in in-service training programs such as the Family-to-Family intervention.

The length of training and inclusion of in-service training supports also may strengthen the efficacy of training. For example, consider the training and other supports to family child care providers provided through the national Head Start program. Eighteen Head Start family child care demonstration projects began in 1992 to determine whether Head Start Performance Standards could be met in family child care homes through additional training and support services. The providers received a median of 96 hours of pre-service training and an average of 63 hours of in-service training over an approximate one-year period. Training was provided through workshops, courses, and occasionally a home visit. Training content pertaining to education focused on a range of subjects, including developmentally appropriate practices, literacy development, social development, and classroom management. An experimental study compared the impact on children and families in family child care with those participating in center-based classroom programs. Results indicated no significant differences between Head Start family child care homes and centers on quality indicators, except the centers surpassed the family child care homes in Head Start indicators of parent involvement. The children assigned to family child care performed at least as well as children in centers on measures of cognitive, socioemotional, and physical development (Faddis, Ryer, & Gabriel, 1997).

At first blush these results may seem insignificant in substance, but in fact they hold value in the context of important differences between Head Start classroom and family child care provider backgrounds. Specifically, the classroom teachers had attained higher levels of education (60% of classroom teachers versus 27% of family child care providers had college degrees), and center staff were far more likely (48%) to have a degree in early childhood education than family child care providers involved in the program (9%). Overall the classroom teachers had five more years of child care experience and six more years of Head Start experience than the family child care providers. The training provided through the Head Start demonstration program appears to have compensated for these educational and background disadvantages in the family child care provider sample. In the fall the family child care homes were less developmentally appropriate than center classrooms, but by spring the two settings did not differ in this regard. Family child care providers were rated as significantly higher than classroom teachers in attentive and encouraging behaviors, and were more likely to maintain a balance of staff-directed and child-initiated activities (Faddis et al., 1997).

Personnel training programs also may be more effective when in-service training content focuses squarely on a particular early childhood curriculum. A study of in-service training on teachers' use of the High/Scope curriculum found that training, provided through workshops and classroom visits by trainers, was positively associated with program quality. Teachers' experience and in-service training also were significant predictors of children's developmental outcomes. Teachers involved in this study represented the top 20% of the early childhood profession in terms of background (an average of 10 years of experience in the field) and qualifications (more than 70% had early childhood degrees or credentials) (Epstein, 1993).

A major problem in the use of personnel preparation as a means of strengthening curriculum in child care is the minimal set of standards regarding staff qualifications. States typically require almost no formal education in early childhood education or child development, and incentives and supports for staff participation in training or degree programs often do not exist. Individuals who participate voluntarily in personnel preparation offerings are likely to have a strong interest in or commitment to work with young children. In the Family-to-Family training program, for example, the family child care providers who participated in the training were similar to the typical regulated providers in each respective state, but there were some differences between those who sought training and those who did not in terms of their intentionality in the family child care provider role. For example, the training group providers were more likely to have chosen family child care work as a way to work with children and to see it as a stepping stone to other work. They also were less likely to do housework while providing care and to never plan activities for children (Kontos et al., 1996). These patterns have potentially important implications for the widespread impact of voluntary training programs, and also raise the question of whether training is more beneficial when participants see it as a step toward larger professional goals.

CONCLUDING COMMENT

Curriculum is not a panacea for the many problems facing child care in the United States. Yet a focus on curriculum offers significant opportunities to improve the quality of child care. Chief among these is the opportunity to alter the definition of child care quality, and to plan and implement environments where education and care are intentionally integrated as core experiences for children. Fortunately, there is much to support these efforts: a growing press (especially from parents and policymakers) for improved learning opportunities for young children; heightened concern about the condition of child care in this country; useful knowledge from a growing body of research on children's intellectual and social development; well-developed early childhood curriculum models that are conducive to adaptation; and, importantly, a tradition of professional creativity among early childhood teachers.

REFERENCES

Abbott-Shim, M., & Sibley, A. (1987). *Assessment profile for early childhood programs.* Atlanta, GA: Quality Assist.

Arnold, D.S., & Whitehurst, G.J. (1994). Accelerating language development through picture book reading: A summary of dialogic reading and its effects. In D.K. Dickinson (Ed.), *Bridges to literacy: Children, families, and schools* (pp. 103-128). Cambridge, MA: Blackwell.

Bowman, B., Donovan, M.S., & Burns, M.S. (Eds.). (2001).*Eager to learn: Educating our preschoolers.* Washington, DC: National Academy Press.

Bredekamp, S., & Copple, C. (1997).*Developmentally appropriate practice in early childhood programs, revised edition.* Washington, DC: National Association for the Education of Young Children.

Bredekamp, S., & Rosegrant, T. (1992). Reaching potentials: Introduction. In S. Bredekamp & T. Rosegrant (Eds.), *Reaching potentials: Appropriate curriculum and assessment for young children* (pp. 2-8). Washington DC: National Association of Young Children .

Caldwell, B.M. (1986). Day care and the public schools—Natural allies, natural enemies. *Educational Leadership, 5,* 34-39.

Caldwell, B.M. (1989). A comprehensive model for integrating child care and early childhood education. *Teachers College Record, 90,* 404-414.

Cassidy, D.J., Buell, M.J., Pugh-Hoese, S., & Russell, S. (1995). The effect of education in child care teachers' beliefs and classroom quality: Year one evaluation of the TEACH early childhood associate degree scholarship program.*Early Childhood Research Quarterly, 10,* 171-183.

Child Welfare League of America. (1960). *Standards for day care service.* New York: Child Welfare League of America.

Cryer, D., & Phillipsen, L. (1997). Quality details: A close-up look at child care program strengths and weaknesses. *Young Children, 52,* 51-61.

Elicker, J. (1997). Developing a relationship perspective in early childhood program research. *Early Education and Development, 8,* 5-10.

Elicker, J., & Mathur, S. (1997). What do they do all day? Comprehensive evaluation of a full-day kindergarten. *Early Childhood Research Quarterly, 12,* 459-480.

Elkind, D. (1987). Early childhood education on its own terms. In S.L. Kagan & E.F. Zigler (Eds.), *Early schooling: The national debate* (pp. 98-115). New Haven, CT: Yale University Press.

Evans, E.D. (1982). Curriculum models. In B. Spodek (Ed.), *Handbook of research in early childhood education* (pp. 107-134). New York: The Free Press.

Epstein, A.S. (1993). Training for quality: Improving early childhood programs through systematic inservice training. *Monographs of the High/Scope Educational Research Foundation, 9.* Ypsilanti, MI: High/Scope Press.

Epstein, A.S., Schweinhart, L.J., & McAdoo, L. (1996). *Models of early childhood education.* Ypsilanti, MI: High/Scope Press.

Faddis, B., Ryer, P., & Gabriel, R. (1997). *Cohort 2 report: Evaluation of Head Start family child care homes.* Portland, OR: RMC Research Corp.

Fein, G.G., & Clarke-Stewart, K.A. (1973). *Day care in context.* New York: Wiley.

Gallacher, K.K. (1997). Supervision, mentoring, and coaching: Methods for supporting personnel development. In P.J. Winton, J.A. McCollum, & C. Catlett (Eds.), *Reforming personnel preparation in early intervention: Issues, models, and practical strategies* (pp. 191-214). Baltimore, MD: Paul Brookes Publishing.

Goffin, S.G. (1994). *Curriculum models and early childhood education: Appraising the relationship.* New York: Merrill.

Greenman, J. (1978). Day care in the schools? A response to the position of the AFT. *Young Children, 33,* 4-13.

Harms, T., & Clifford, R. (1980). *Early childhood environment rating scale.* New York: Teachers College Press.

Harms, T., Clifford, R., & Cryer, D. (1998). *Early childhood environment rating scale: Revised edition.* New York: Teachers College Press.

Harms, T., Cryer, D., & Clifford, R. (1990). *Infant/toddler environment rating scale.* New York: Teachers College Press.

Hayes, C.D., Palmer, J.L., & Zaslow, M.J. (1990). *Who cares for America's children? Child care policy for the 1990s* (Report of the Panel of Child Care Policy, Committee on Child Development Research and Public Policy, Commission on Behavioral and Social Sciences and Education, National Research Council). Washington, DC: National Academy Press.

Howes, C. (1997). Children's experiences in center-based child care as a function of teacher background and adult : child ratio. *Merrill-Palmer Quarterly, 43,* 404-425.

Howes, C., & Ponciano, L. (2000). Child care. In J.L. Roopnarine & J.E. Johnson (Eds.), *Approaches to early childhood education* (3rd ed., pp. 39-53). Columbus, OH: Merrill.

Howes, C., Phillips, D.A., Whitebook, M. (1992). Thresholds of quality in child care centers and children's social and emotional development. *Child Development, 62,* 449-460.

Kagan, S.L., & Cohen, N.E. (1996). A vision for a quality early care and education system. In S.L. Kagan & N.E. Cohen (Eds.), *Reinventing early care and education* (pp. 309-332). San Francisco: Jossey-Bass.

Kagan, S.L., & Neuman, M.J. (2000). Early care and education: Current issues and future strategies. In J.P. Shonkoff & S.J. Meisels (Eds.), *Handbook of early childhood intervention* (2nd ed., pp. 339-360). New York: Cambridge University Press.

Klein, A.G. (1992). *The debate over child care 1969-1990: A sociohistorical analysis.* Albany: State University of New York Press.

Kisker, E.E., Hofferth, S.L., Phillips, D.A., & Farquhar, E. (1991). *A profile of child care settings: Early education and care in 1990* (Vol. 1). Princeton, NJ: Mathematica Policy Research.

Kontos, S. (1992). The role of continuity and context in children's relationships with nonparental adults. In R.C. Pianta (Ed.), *Beyond the parent: The role of other adults in children's lives. New directions for child development, 57* (pp. 109-199). San Francisco: Jossey-Bass.

Kontos, S., & File, N. (1993). Staff development in support of integration. In C.A. Peck & S.L. Odom (Eds.), *Integrating young children with disabilities into community programs: Ecological perspectives on research and implementation* (pp. 169-186). Baltimore, MD: Paul H. Brookes Publishing.

Kontos, S., Howes, C., & Galinsky, E. (1996). Does training make a difference to quality in family child care? *Early Childhood Research Quarterly, 11,* 427-445.

Lamb, M. (1998). Nonparental child care: Context, quality, correlates, and consequences. In W. Damon, I.E. Sigel, & K.A. Renninger (Eds.), *Handbook of child psychology: Child psychology in practice* (5th ed., pp. 73-133). New York: John Wiley & Sons, Inc.

Larner, M. (1996). Parents' perspectives on quality in early care and education. In S.L. Kagan & N.E. Cohen (Eds.), *Reinventing early care and education* (pp. 21-42). San Francisco: Jossey-Bass.

Layzer, J.I., Goodson, B.C., Moss, M., & Farquhar, E. (1993). *Life in preschool. Volume 1 of an observational study of early childhood programs for disadvantaged four-year-olds.* Final report to the Office of Policy and Planning, U.S. Department of Education. Cambridge, MA: Abt Associates.

Olsen, D., & Zigler, E. (1989). An assessment of the all-day kindergarten movement. *Early Childhood Research Quarterly, 4,* 167-186.

Phillips, D. (1996). Reframing the quality issue. In S.L. Kagan & N.E. Cohen (Eds.), *Reinventing early care and education* (pp. 43-64). San Francisco: Jossey-Bass.

Poersch, N.O., & Blank, H. (1996). *Working together for children: Head Start and child care partnerships.* Washington, DC: Children's Defense Fund.

Powell, D.R. (1997). Parents' contributions to the quality of child care arrangements. In S. Reifel (Series Ed.), C.J. Dunst & M. Wolery (Vol. Eds.), *Advances in early education and day care, Vol. 9: Family policy and practice in early child care* (pp. 133-155). Greenwich, CT: JAI Press.

Powell, D.R. (1987). Comparing preschool curricula and practices: The state of research. In S.L. Kagan & E.F. Zigler (Eds.), *Early schooling: The national debate* (pp. 190-211). New Haven, CT: Yale University Press.

Read, K.H. (1950). *The nursery school: A human relationships laboratory.* Philadelphia: Saunders.

Scarr, S., Eisenberg, M., & Deater-Deckard, K. (1994). Measurement of quality in child care centers. *Early Childhood Research Quarterly, 9,* 131-151.

Shonkoff, J.P., & Phillips, D.A. (Eds.). (2000). *From neurons to neighborhoods: The science of early childhood development.* Washington, DC: National Academy Press.

Spodek, B. (1973). *Early childhood education.* Englewood Cliffs, NJ: Prentice-Hall.

Spodek, B., & Brown, P.C. (1993). Curriculum alternatives in early childhood education: A historical perspective. In B. Spodek (Ed.), *Handbook of research on the education of young children* (pp. 91-104). New York: Macmillan.

Spodek, B., & Saracho, O.N. (1990). Preparing early childhood teachers for the twenty-first century: A look to the future. In B. Spodek & O.N. Saracho (Eds.), *Early childhood teacher preparation* (pp. 209-221). New York: Teachers College Press.

Spodek, B., Saracho, O.N., & Davis, M.D. (1991). *Foundations of early childhood education, second edition.* Englewood Cliffs, NJ: Prentice-Hall.

Tabors, P.O. (1997). *One child, two languages.* Baltimore, MD: Paul H. Brookes Publishing.

Whitehurst, G.J., Epstein, J.N., Angell, A.L., Payne, D.A., Crone, D.A., & Fischel, J.E. (1994). Outcomes of an emergent literacy intervention in Head Start. *Journal of Educational Psychology, 86,* 542-555.

Wilcox-Herzog, A., & Kontos, S. (1998). The nature of teacher talk in early childhood classrooms and its relationships to children's competence with objects and peers. *Journal of Genetic Psychology, 159,* 30-44.

Zigler, E.F. (1989). Addressing the nation's child care crisis: The school of the twenty-first century. *American Journal of Orthopsychiatry, 59,* 484-491.

CHAPTER 11

WHAT COUNTS IN EARLY LEARNING?

Tony Bertram and Christine Pascal

INTRODUCTION

We are currently living through a revolution in our understanding of early learning and its importance in determining a child's life chances. We now know that it is at this time deep-seated attitudes and approaches to life are established that will endure and shape the future progress of an individual. In this way, the early childhood educators who build the foundations of life long learning are not politically neutral, they are politically active, paving the way for progress or retrenchment in children's lives. It is also evident from this new knowledge that certain kinds of early learning, particularly social, attitudinal and affective learning, are powerful indicators of long term achievement in children. Yet many of the early years curriculum frameworks which dominate in many developed countries, including England, with an emphasis on subject knowledge, particularly language and mathematical competency, appear to ignore this important new knowledge and are requiring practitioners to conform to other curriculum requirements, even at this early stage of children's lives. Laying the foundations on which a child's life is to be built is increasingly acknowledged to be a complex, skillful and very responsible task. It requires practitioners who understand the importance of establishing robust footings in those areas that will stand the test of time, withhold the stresses of a lifetime and provide stability for further construction. How and what we should build to ensure a strong and enduring structure are key questions for the early childhood educator as they construct their curriculum for young children because their work has a long term and formative time scale. The foundations that are laid down early will fundamentally shape a child's future, eventually allowing the child to thrive or fail. Those involved in early childhood education and care should never forget that their role is both as co-constructor and advocate of the empowered and effective learner.

The new knowledge which has emerged recently on cognition is welcomed but it generates an urgent need for a robust and critical debate about the aims and purposes of early education, what an early childhood curriculum should contain, what kind of learners we want to create for the future and whether education should develop critical, active citizens who can promote democracy and equity in their communities. These questions also highlight the need for more work on identifying and describing the key elements of effective early learning within an early years curriculum, how these might be assessed and how these might be nurtured in our youngest children. It is these big questions that are being addressed in the Accounting Early for Life Long learning (AcE) Project (Pascal & Bertram, 2000), the early findings of which are reported in this chapter. The essential starting point for our work has been that promoting certain curricula and assessment regimes is not politically neutral, it is politically manipulative and, ultimately, coercive because it determines a child's long term ability to make and shape the world in which they live. Curricula and assessments have the capability to generate for some an exclusive and, for others, an excluding experience which will be carried for life. As Freire (1985) argued, education that pretends to be neutral and does not encourage critical, competent and questioning learners, supports the dominant ideology in society. It also ultimately suppresses achievement and attainment for many groups of children, the very goals it professes to promote. The point we are making is that the content and pedagogy of early childhood carry political and professional choices which should be open to challenge and critical debate. The AcE Project is an attempt to stimulate and provide a forum for this debate to begin, drawing on the best professional knowledge we have about young children's learning.

Research from a variety of disciplines is providing us with rich and powerful evidence about how children learn; the nature of such learning; and the ways in which early experiences shape the pattern of progress, achievement and fulfilment, throughout an individual's life. The research highlights the importance of, for example, dispositions to learning (Katz, 1995); mastery orientation (Heyman, Dweck & Cain, 1992); pro-social development (Rogoff, Mistry, Goncu & Mosier, 1993); conflict resolution (Lantieri, 1990); multiple intelligences (Gardner, 1983); involvement, linkedness, emotional well being and emotional literacy (Goleman, 1996; Laevers, 1995, 1996). As Sir Christopher Ball pointed out in the influential Start Right Report,

Modern educational research is on the threshold of a revolution. The findings of brain science, for example, or the theory of multiple intelligence, or the idea of different styles of learning, or the recognition that people can learn to learn faster, are all pointing the way towards a new and powerful theory of learning which will be able to satisfy the three tests of explanation, prediction and aspiration. Central to the new theory will be a clearer understanding of learning development, and the sequence whereby people progress from infancy to become mature learners. In the (recent) past the professionalism of teachers has often been thought to reside in mastering the subject or discipline. But these are merely the tokens of learning. The art of learning (learning how to learn) is also concerned with the types, or "super skills" and attitudes, of learning - of which motivation, socialisation and confidence are the most important. These are the fruits of successful early learning. (Ball, 1994, para. 2.17)

In short, there is much recent evidence that has identified the important learning characteristics associated with later achievement, such as aspiration, pro-socialisation, self-esteem, motivation and confidence, and demonstrates that these attributes are established in the early years. These enabling attitudes have been called the "super skills" of learning (Ball, 1994). These ideas about what is fundamental in developing lasting, positive attitudes to learning are the focus of the AcE Project. While we recognize the importance of skills and knowledge in early learning, we believe that such a simplistic focus should not be the sole view of the early years curricula. We need to widen our perspective on "outcomes" in early childhood and strengthen the practitioners' ability to support and assess those other areas of children's development that may be equally crucial to long-term success.

In our work with practitioners, we acknowledge the recent neuropsychological research on brain growth in infants (Phillips, 1995; Trevarthan, 1992) that supports the view that environments for young children that are staffed by caring, responsive and dependable adults are critical in the development of these attributes and dispositions in children. We believe there is a need to develop the ability of practitioners to support "the child's learning in sensitive, stimulating and empowering ways (Bertram, 1996). To sustain development in young minds, practitioners must be prepared to look at wider outcomes than academic knowledge and skills, and include dispositions to learn, social competence and emotional well being, in their aspirations and intentions for young children. Developing practitioners' awareness of these important aspects of children's learning, and providing them with the means to assess and enhance them, will be a major challenge in developing a nation of life long learners.

A report by the influential U.S. National Center for Clinical Infant Programs (Brazelton, 1992) suggests that academic success rests predominantly on children's early knowledge of how to learn, as well as what is learned. Goleman (1996) claims,

> that school success is not predicted by a child's fund of facts or a precocious ability to read so much as by emotional and social measures; being self-assured and interested; knowing what kind of behaviour is expected and how to rein in impulse to misbehave; being able to wait, to follow directions, and to turn to adults and peers for help; expressing needs whilst getting along with other children. (p. 193)

Our interest is targeted at birth to six year olds because there is evidence to show that this is the critically important phase for establishing learning attitudes. Gender and race studies (Siraj-Blatchford, 1996) show that life long attitudes are set early. Attitudes to "self as a learner" follow the same pattern. Goleman (1996) talks of a "window of opportunity" analogous to Lorenz's (1946) notion of "imprinting." These studies show that there is a biologically determined period when it is crucial to establish certain semi-permanent attitudes about learning. The stronger these are embedded, the greater their resilience to inevitable, climatic periods of poor stimulation, and the more likely that they will persist. The importance of this early period of social consciousness to life long achievement is recognized by Donaldson, Grieve, and Pratt (1983),

> Early childhood is ". . . a period of momentous significance for all people growing up in our culture. . . . By the time this period is over, children will have formed conceptions of themselves as social beings, as thinkers, and as language users, and they will have reached certain important decisions about their own abilities and their own worth." (Donaldson et al., 1983, p. 1)

We live in an audited society where that which is measurable is seen as significant. We need to ensure that what we are measuring is significant and that we are not simply focusing on those things that are easily measured. We need to be aware that a focus on simplistic outputs may mean that more subtle outcomes are neglected. A focus on measured targets for literacy and numeracy may impact on deeper and more important attitudes to learning. Hospital administrators, for example as an analogy, faced with targets to reduce waiting lists, increased the throughput of minor surgery cases rather than the more needy, long term chronic and difficult cases. Similarly, administrators faced with numerical indicators of measuring success, found ways of preventing people from getting on the waiting list in the first place in order to meet their targets. Parallels in education in the narrowing of the curriculum and in the exclusion by some SAT conscious schools of children with special needs, make the point that target setting needs to be treated cautiously and to incorporate the specialist knowledge of the experienced practitioner. Our view would be that accountability rests in three domains incorporated in the different meanings of accounting. The first, and unfortunately sometimes the only, meaning of "accounting" is the "numerical audit." As far as we can and it is accurate and helpful practitioners should use agreed measurements for achievement but in itself it is not sufficient. A second meaning of "accounting" is "to give an account," a multi-voiced narrative of what a child is achieving which allows the child, her parents and the early years worker to contribute to her story of achievement. The third meaning of "accounting" is "giving an explanation of events" and here we touch on the reflective practitioner, evidence-based practice and professional development. If we know what the explanations are for achievement we can make adjustments in our pedagogy. It would seem to us that this sort of approach to accountability would be much more helpful than the current centralized concern with dubious target setting.

Using this approach to accountability, the identification, development and measurement of young children's aptitudes, dispositions and inclinations are the subject of the AcE Project. This work is based on a clear exposition of what we believe to be an effective learner.

THE EFFECTIVE LEARNER

Effective learners are children who can sustain their ability to explore the world in an open, critical, creative and joyful way in order to extend their knowledge and understanding. Central to this ability is a sense of "agency." Agency is fundamentally about empowerment. The learner with agency is able to function effectively within a social community but is capable of acting upon and within that community with sensitivity and a sense of belonging. This sense of agency and empowerment frees the child's exploratory drive and allows their natural curiosity to emerge. They will also have a sense of participation and influence upon their world, which motivates them to engage in a socially constructive, inclusive and equitable way. They will have the social and emotional skills and competencies to engage with others, access opportunities and express their needs as they take their learning forward. In short, the Effective Learner:

- is empowered and operates as a subject not an object;
- has a sense of instrumentality and causality;
- is able to assert and articulate her sense of self and self-direction in relation to others;
- acts on her own behalf and her actions come from her sense of self and self-will;
- takes her own decisions in relation to her life;

- is able to, and enjoys, taking responsibility for herself, her decisions and her actions;
- has a sense of belonging and interconnectedness;
- is able to negotiate authority;
- has empathy and operates in reciprocity with others;
- has autonomy within the boundaries of accountability. (Pascal & Bertram, 2000)

Through our work with practitioners and our understanding of the current professional and research literature on effective learning we have been able to identify three core constituent elements of the Effective Learner:

- dispositions to learn;
- social competence and self-concept;
- emotional well being.

We shall define each of these core elements, outline the supporting evidence for its place within our framework of the Effective Learner, and describe how these characteristics may be identified in young children.

Dispositions to Learn

Definition

Dispositions are the first key element to be identified in an effective learner and may be defined as behavioral characteristics and attitudes, exhibited frequently in young children and in the absence of external coercion, threat or reward, which indicate internalized habits of mind under conscious and voluntary control. Dispositions can be positive or negative. Educative dispositions are seen as positive when these behavioral characteristics are intentionally oriented to achieving broader goals than specific curriculum knowledge. Positive educative dispositions, which have long term effects on life long learning, include independence, creativity, self-motivation and resilience. Dispositions are environmentally sensitive. They are acquired from and affected by interactive experiences with the environment, significant adults and peers. Unlike genetic predispositions, dispositions are not fixed at birth but are dynamic. Positive dispositions are learnt but they are rarely acquired didactically. These dispositions are central not only to educational achievement but to personal fulfilment.

Supporting Evidence

Dispositions are different from predispositions, which are the genetic biological determinants. Resnick (1987) suggests dispositions can be cultivated and acquired through habit and through learning. They are part of intrinsic motivation and relatively lasting but they are not didactically acquired. They are not skill or knowledge acquisition but something else. Dispositions require another level of involvement and, we believe, are very strongly linked to life long learning.

Research in this area is developing fast and there is increasing evidence from U.S. and cross-national empirical studies that these learning orientations and abilities, or dispositions, are evident in very young learners (aged three and four years) and continue to shape a child's progress and attitudes toward learning throughout their schooling and beyond. For example, Resnick (1987) shows that dispositions to learn are acquired early by children and are an important part of a child's motivation to explore the world. She also found that they were relatively long lasting. Stevenson and Lee (1990), in a study of cross national achievement in mathematics compared large samples of children (aged 7 and 8) from the United States, China and Japan and found significant differences in levels of achievement between U.S. children and children in the two Asian countries. They argue that the difference in achievement was due, not to IQ, but rather to differences in motivation and attitudes to learning. Heyman et al.'s work (1986, 1988, 1992) supports this view. For the past fifteen years this group of American psychologists have been exploring academic motivation, learning characteristics and attitudes in children from the age of three and four. They have carried out scores of experiments which have demonstrated that most children fall somewhere on a continuum of "helplessness" or "mastery" in their approach to learning, and that these behavioral patterns go hand in hand with differing goal structures. They found that children with a "mastery" orientation to learning manage to coordinate their performance and learning goals successfully and set in motion cognitive and social processes which facilitate educational and social progress in the long term. Their most recent work has focused on young children aged three and four (Heyman et al., 1992) and has shown that such characteristics are already well established and affecting the child's approach to learning and exploration of the world. Another major U.S. report on infant development (Brazelton, 1992), worryingly, finds such characteristics already established in very young babies, whose, demeanour is "hang dog," a look that says, "I'm no good. See, I've failed." Such children are likely to go through life with a defeatist outlook, expecting no encouragement or interest from teachers and finding school joyless, perhaps eventually dropping out. (Brazelton, 1993, p. 58)

Major longitudinal studies of achievement further support this evidence. The High/Scope Program (Schweinhart & Weikart, 1993) has followed children through from the age of five to adulthood and found that children with high aspirations, independence and who experience an early education curriculum (at the age of five to seven) that encourages a mastery orientation are significantly more effective learners and achievers in the long term. The authors of this major empirical study point out,

> It was the development of specific personal and social traits that enabled a high quality early education programme to significantly influence participants performance . . . while no single factor ensures success in life, the sense of personal control is certainly a major force. (Schweinhart & Weikart, 1993)

Description

We have identified four educative dispositions which characterize "The Effective Learner."

Independence. A disposition toward independence is revealed by a child's ability to be self-sufficient, to self-organize, and self-manage. The independent child is as equally comfortable in exercising choice as she is in taking responsibility for her decisions and actions and their consequences. Independently disposed children enjoy opportunities for autonomy and choice making. They are strong enough to ask for support when required from adults or their peers, to ask questions and to negotiate opportunities for choice. They can be assertive when needed but without resort to threat or dominance. Independently oriented children are capable of making selections and of locating and using resources appropriately. They develop competencies in organizing their environment, including the human environment, which allow them to have agency and affect change.

Creativity. A disposition toward creativity is characterized by those children who show curiosity and interest in their world, reveling in especially in serendipity and originality. Such children enjoy exploring their environment, looking for patterns of meaning and comparing similarity and difference. The creative child is imaginative, spontaneous and innovative. They instigate and expand play ideas. They are secure enough in their immediate world to venture forth to explore new boundaries especially within the exciting zone of proximal development. They enjoy developing and extending their knowledge and thinking. They are rarely timid or fearful but have a confidence, which allows them to embrace the undiscovered with enthusiasm, boldness and wonder. They can think laterally, innovatively and reflectively. Their confidence, originality and creativity is often expressed through humor. Satisfaction and reward from their exploration, allows them to feel comfortable with the original and the different. Internally strongly located with an established self-identity based on secure notions of belonging, they can take risks and have satisfying adventures and face their world openly.

Self-Motivation: A disposition toward self-motivation allows children, independently, to become deeply involved and engrossed in activities and challenges. Characteristically, they have plenty of self-initiated purposes, plans and objectives. They often will declare aims and goals and the intention to achieve them. Highly self-motivated children appreciate effort as a strategy and they show determination, persistence and precision. These well-motivated children are self-driven toward achieving their goals and the energy of their exploratory drive will be apparent. They also understand that mastery is a continual process of trial, error and adjustment. They see "failure" as a temporary state, simply an intermediate part of the learning process and certainly not an indication of any fundamental and continuing personal inadequacy. They develop positive mindsets, such as: "let's try," "have a go" and "can do." They are smilingly keen to display newly acquired knowledge and skills, "watch me," "look at this" and "did you know?". These children will self-manage, develop self-efficacy, and make choices to achieve their goals.

Resilience: A resilient child has the disposition to bounce back after setback, hindrance or frustration and retain temperament, personality and spirit. Such children develop a varied range of strategies for coping with change, recovering quickly and rebounding from disappointments. They are usually confident with an internal locus of control. Their resilience makes them happy with new challenges and often keen to try to tackle problems themselves. Although they appreciate the need for boundaries and structures, when routines are altered they are flexible and remain secure. They will sometimes develop self-survival mechanisms which allow them to vary their dependence on significant others without losing the bond. When reprimanded, they can separate errant behavior from personal identity. They appreciate their right and that of others to have a different opinion. They understand the rewards to be gained from the processes of engagement, negotiation, assertion and persuasion. They understand that usually authority is logical but they are strong enough to know that sometimes adults get things wrong and, temporarily, that is something with which you may have to live. They understand that, in endeavor, setbacks are inevitable but they also know that there are limits to the extent one should strive without reward. They appreciate that sometimes it is reasonable to persist and sometimes it is reasonable to quit, sometimes you need to stand up and shout out and sometimes you need to be quiet and give way. They have strategies for conflict resolution.

Social Competence and Self-Concept

Definition

Social competence is the second core element of the effective learner and may be defined as the ability of the child to reach out to others and to make connections and relationships that help them to survive and thrive. These competencies provide the child with the mechanisms to interact and interrelate with their community, a precondition for successful social living. The need for interdependency, a moral conscience and inner discipline are central to participation within a social network. A further precondition for developing effective relationships is that of self-concept, which provides the child with a strong sense of their own identity or worth. Self-esteem provides the child with the inner confidence to reach out and explore the unknown and forms a base from which they will form respectful relationships with others. These competencies are critical for learning which is essentially a social process.

Supporting Evidence

It is now a well-established tenet in the field of cultural, social and neural psychology that, from birth, learning is a process which occurs in a social context. Even as helpless neonates, young humans have the ability to reach out to others to help them make sense of their world (Bruner, 1996; Caxton, 1997; Trevarthan, 1992; Vygotsky, 1962). The burgeoning of work in the field of brain science and social cognition is underlining the importance of the social and affective domain in learning, and revealing the extent to which educational progress is affected by a child's view of herself in her world and her ability to reach out and connect to others within her world. As Ball has pointed out in his review of the importance of early learning,

> The most important learning in pre-school education has to do with aspiration, socialisation and self esteem . . . no-one learns effectively without motivation, social skills and confidence. (Ball, 1993, para 2.16)

The experiences and interactions of a child with others create internalized perceptions of self which then become predictors of their future behavior. The child's main care giver has a particularly strong influence in establishing respect for self and in "empowering" children to be strong (Whalley 1996). With the increasing institutionalization of young children's upbringing, early childhood practitioners need to be more aware of the dangers of undermining and distilling parents by offering one "best" model of practice. At the same time, they need to be able to offer guidance and support which, while acknowledging parents' capabilities, needs and cultural differences allows parents to fully support their child's social psychological development (Dahlberg & Asen, 1994; Moss & Pence, 1994). Practitioners need to work with parents to create the development of children's self-respect and a strong self-esteem (Roberts, 1996). The "Advancement Attributes" that cluster around a strong sense of worth and a feeling of self-esteem need to be explored. Children with high levels of respect for self have the courage to stand up for themselves, to express their needs self-confidently, and know how to handle life. There is a need for child, parents and practitioners to recognize these attributes and to develop the "emotionally literacy" to discuss them (Goleman, 1996).

As with respect for self, young children also need to develop a respect for others. Again, there is a growing body of empirical evidence which demonstrates the influence such personal and social "attributes" have on a child's educational progress. For example, Lipman's pioneering work (1989) in the United States on the importance of respect for self and respect for others in young children aged 6 has demonstrated how programs which develop these "attributes" directly benefit a child's cognitive and social development and educational progress. Lipman shows that young children can be encouraged to express preferences and opinions, to articulate their viewpoint and to have it acknowledged and given credence by peers and by their educators and significant carers. Such children are more likely to be able to acknowledge that there are other alternative views held by others which are equally valid and should be given respect. This understanding of multiple perspectives has been shown to reduce classroom tensions and advance learning achievements. Gardner's (1983) ground breaking work on multiple intelligence has shown that children with the same IQ can differ significantly in terms of school performance and he attributes this to differences in the children's inter- and intrapersonal intelligence, which he sees as critical factors in educational achievement and long term progress. This work has been followed up by Salovey and Mayer (1990) who have developed the concept of "emotional intelligence" suggesting that it is more significant than IQ in determining an individual's life chances.

Laevers (1996) recent work on the notion of "linkedness" and the dangers inherent in feeling unconnected to the world is relevant here. Those who are, or become, delinquents lose their ability to connect to their inner self or to others. They become "de-linked" delinquents. But this issue is wider than self-connection. It is about societal cohesiveness. We live in an increasingly plural society and if we are to do this harmoniously then we need to be able to respect each other and to acknowledge and celebrate difference. This celebration of difference makes us have a great sense of belonging and community. The origins of these attitudes and their development are in early childhood (Siraj-Blatchford, 1996). We need to sensitize children, parents and practitioners to these issues and define and measure the attributes which create them.

Finally, support for outcome measures to include "respect for self and others" comes from Goleman. In Goleman's (1996) influential review of the evidence on the importance of the affective domain in children's development he argues,

> school success is not predicted by a child's fund of facts or a precocious ability to read so much as by emotional and social measures; being self-assured and interested; knowing what kind of behaviour is expected and how to rein in impulse to misbehave; being able to wait, to follow directions, and to turn to adults and peers for help; expressing needs whilst getting along with other children. (Goleman, 1996, p. 193)

Description

We have identified five social competences which characterize "The Effective Learner."

Establishing Effective Relationships: A key social competence is the ability of the child to establish effective relationships with other children and adults. These relationships are crucial to the child's survival and healthy development. It requires the child to have the ability to initiate interactions, to cooperate with others, to accept others ideas and suggestions and to share experiences. The ability to make strong and close friendships with more than one person signals a child's connectedness and interdependency, and will support their place within a learning community.

Empathy: The ability to empathize is a social competence by which the child can understand the world from another's perspective. This is required for developing social relationships and cooperating within collaborative group learning situations. The empathetic child behaves considerately toward others and shows respect for other people, their feelings and intentions. A sensitivity to the social context in which they are operating and the effect this context has on themselves and others is reflected in the child's actions and responses.

Taking Responsibility: The ability of the child to take responsibility for their own thoughts, intentions and actions is a core social competence for successful learning. This competence is an essential determinant of effective social functioning. This indicates the child's developing sense of right and wrong and awareness of appropriate behavioral expectations; the child will have a moral self and an inner discipline. The child's actions show a strong internal locus of control along with an ability to treat others with respect, care and concern.

Assertiveness: The ability of the child to be assertive is a social competence that provides the child with the capacity to influence and shape their learning and their lives. This gives the child the capacity to make and carry through decisions and to have a sense of themselves as an active and valued member of a community of learners. The assertive child will communicate and voice their opinions and ideas, offer suggestions and negotiate. They will question and be inquisitive but listen to others opinions and suggestions. This will be reflected in their interactions which will be without aggression or undue deference or evasiveness.

Awareness of Self: A key precondition for effective social interaction is the child's developing sense of self and self-worth in relation to their personality, their family, their home and their culture. This competence is reflected in the child's understanding of their own personal identity and sense of belonging. The child with self-worth will have a positive self-image and demonstrate self-esteem. They will show a sense of control over their decisions and rights and have pride in their achievements. They will also have a developing capacity to reflect upon their sense of self in relation to the world.

Emotional Well Being

Definition

Emotional well being is the third core element of the Effective Learner and focuses on the child's ability to feel comfortable with themselves. This is demonstrated in the child displaying an open, receptive attitude to the environment. This enables the child to be assertive and to show and manage their emotions. They will also reflect peace, vitality and zeal for life and will enjoy participating without too much anxiety. Such qualities are seen to be critical in sustaining learning in the long term and to sustain the child through difficulties and learning challenges.

Supporting Evidence

The importance of the emotional aspect of learning has been well documented (Goleman, 1996), and most educationalists work hard at kindling in young children an enthusiasm and passion for learning, which will provide a foundation for life. In contrast, studies of children with behavioral and learning difficulties have shown that such children do not possess these qualities of "well being." The growing number of children with psychological and emotional difficulties in many developed countries has been shown to be a major factor in increasing underachievement and school dropout (Achenbach & Howell 1989; Goleman, 1996; Thomas, 1989). Examples of studies which demonstrate the link between "well being" and educational performance include Salovey and Mayer (1990) who found that children with "ego resilience" or emotional well being are more able to be self-regulating, adaptive, to control impulses, to have a sense of self-efficacy and to operate in a social environment. In a longitudinal study of about 100 children they found these factors were significant to long term achievement and educational success. Nowicki and Duke (1989) in their study of children who had the ability to be sensitive to others feelings and in touch with their own feelings, found they were more popular, more emotionally stable, and achieved more in school than children with an equivalent IQ. Evaluations of a number of preschool and school programs which aimed to enhance children's social and emotional abilities, reported in Goleman (1996), demonstrate enhanced adjustment and progress in school, providing further evidence of a link between "well being" and academic performance. Rutter's (1997) overview of the link between "resilience" attributes and achievement further underlines the importance of "well being" to educational achievement.

Laevers (1996) describes young children as readily displaying the level of their "well being" in eight observable signals. Children with high levels of well being are, he says, "like fish in water" in their educational environments and maximize their learning potential. Laevers has developed a five-point scale to be used by practitioners to assess children's "well being." The New Zealand Early Childhood Curriculum, Te Whiriki, (New Zealand Ministry of Education, 1996) uses the strand of "well being" as a permeation issue which interweaves with their curriculum principles. Health, safety and nurture and sensitively handled transitions develop consistency, trust and security. "Well being" leads to the establishment of the confidence to explore, and the foundation of remembered and anticipated places and experiences. It encourages the positive development of that innate exploratory drive that characterizes humans. Above all, children who display the quality of "well being" have learnt the joy of empowering contact with responsive people. The identification of the "Advancement Attributes" associated with "well being" is the final element in the creation of a comprehensive typology of the outcomes of young children's learning which we are developing as part of the AcE Project.

Description

We have identified four elements of emotional well being that characterize the Effective Learner.

Emotional Literacy: A key element of emotional well being is the ability of the child to be emotionally literate. This reflects the child's fluency in both feeling and expressing their emotions and being able to pass through a range of feelings toward a sense of equilibrium. The emotionally literate child is aware of their emotions and is able to articulate and express them.

The child shows self-control and is able to manage a range of emotions. They are able to be self-motivated and persist in the face of adversity. The child shows the ability to empathize with others and has a growing understanding of the effect of their actions on others. The fundamental influence of emotions on learning and on the child's ability to free their exploratory drive is often under estimated.

Empowerment: The empowered child has an inner strength and robust self-will which encourages self-direction and self-management of new learning. The child has a strong sense of self-worth, identity and confidence. The child feels able to trust and is able to determine her own actions, appreciate the consequences of these actions and to make choices. An empowered child can cope with changes in their life and has a sense of self-value, knowing that their emotional needs will be met, being unafraid to ask for support when required.

Connectedness: A further precondition for emotional well being is that of connectedness. To learn effectively the child requires an ability to relate to others, to interlink events and situations in their life and to feel a part of the whole. They also need to have a sense of attachment and belonging to the people with whom they come into close and regular contact, both adults and children. The community in which the child operates provides the context in which a child feels their sense of value and within which they are able to participate. The connected child will have a working knowledge of the pattern of their day to day life, how things function and will feel able to contribute to and shape this.

Positive Self-Esteem: A major contributing factor to emotional well being is positive self-esteem. This indicates the child's sense of self-worth and personal identity and the way in which this is perceived by the community of adults and children within which they operate. Self-esteem is shaped first by the experiences of the child in relation to others, but reflects the child's own perception of self and the value that they believe this self is given in relation to others. The child with positive self-esteem feels capable, significant and worthy but not necessarily perfect, and does not feel the need to strive for perfection. Positive self-esteem allows the child to have a realistic appraisal of self and to deal with her feelings, both positive and negative, in relation to risk, success and failure. These are key skills for the effective learner.

CONCLUSION

As Ball (1993, para 2.17) points out, "major educational research is on the threshold of a revolution," a view echoed by Bruner (1996), who talks of a "cognitive revolution" which is changing the way we think about learning. The knowledge base which supports our understanding of early learning is developing fast, and clearly showing that a focus on curriculum frameworks which view education as the injection of facts, subjects and disciplines of knowledge alone, particularly in the early years, provides only a partial explanation of what makes for effective and life long learning. Our focus on defining and describing the "Effective Learner" has two main thrusts. Firstly, we are attempting to encourage those who work with young children to apply this new knowledge to their practice and their curricula to ensure their work is at the forefront of professional knowledge. Secondly, we are aiming to communicate this newly acquired professional knowledge to those who create policy so that they also may act from an informed base when developing curricula requirements for the field. The need to review and evaluate both curriculum practice and policy in relation to current educational research is a priority. We should aim for the knowledge revolution in early learning to come off the shelves and feed directly into the actions of those who shape young children's early educational lives. We believe the early years curricula needs a radical rethink to catch up with our twenty-first century knowledge.

REFERENCES

Abbott, J. (1994). *Learning makes sense: Recreating education for a changing future.* Hertfordshire: Education 2000.

Achenbach, T., & Howell, C. (1989, November). Are America's children's problems getting worse? A 13 year comparison. *Journal of the American Academy of Child and Adolescent Psychiatry.*

Ball, C. (1994). *Start right: The importance of early learning.* London: RSA.

Bertram, A. D. (1996). *Effective early educators: A methodology for assessment and development.* Ph.D. Thesis, Coventry University.

Brazelton, T.B. (1992). *Heart Start: The emotional foundations of school readiness.* Arlington, VA: National Center for Clinical Infant Programmes.

Britton, J. (1992). *Language and learning: The importance of speech in children's development.* Harmondsworth: Penguin.

Bruner, J. (1996). *The culture of education.* London: Harvard University Press.

Caxton, G. (1997). *Hare brain, tortoise mind.* London: Fourth Estate.

Dahlberg, G., & Asen, G. (1994). Evaluation and regulation: A question of empowerment. In P. Moss & A. Pence (Eds.), *Valuing quality in early childhood services: new approaches to defining quality.* London: Paul Chapman Publishing.

Department for Education and Science. (1990). *Starting with quality.* (The Rumbold Report of the Committee of Inquiry into the Quality of the Educational Experience offered to 3 and 4 year olds.) London: HMSO.

Department for Education and Employment. (1996). *OFSTED Inspection framework for nursery education.* London: Department for Education and Employment.

Department for Education and Employment. (1997). *Baseline assessment schemes: Submission guidelines.* London: Department for Education and Employment.

Donaldson, M., Grieve, R., & Pratt, C. (1983). *Early childhood development and education: Readings in psychology.* Oxford: Basil Blackwell.

Dweck, C.S., & Leggett, E. (1988). A socio-cognitive approach to motivation and achievement. *Psychological Review, 95*(2), 256-273.

Elliott, E., & Dweck, C.S. (1988). Goals: An approach to motivation and achievement. *Journal of Personality and Social Psychology, 54*(1), 5-12.

Freire, P. (1985). *The politics of education: Culture, power and liberation.* Westport, CT: Greenwood, Bergin-Garvey.

Gardner, H. (1983). *Frames of mind: The theory of multiple intelligences.* London: Fontana Press.

Goleman, D. (1996). *Emotional intelligence: Why it can matter more than IQ.* London: Bloomsbury.

Goswami, U., & Bryant, P.E. (1990). *Phonological skills and learning to read.* Hove: Lawrence Erlbaum.

Handy C. (1994). *The empty raincoat: Making sense of the future.* London: Hutchinson.

Heyman, G., Dweck, C.S., & Cain, K. (1992). Young children's vulnerability to self blame and helplessness: Relationship to beliefs about goodness. *Child Development, 63,* 401- 415.

Katz, L.J. (1995). *Talks with teachers of young children: A collection.* Norwood, NJ: Ablex.

Kryiacou, C. (1994). *Effective teaching in schools.* Hemel Hampstead: Simon and Schuster Education.

Laevers, F. (1989). *Ervoringsgericht werken in der basisschool.* Leuven: Leuven Projectgroep EGO.

Laevers, F. (1994). *The Leuven Involvement Scale for Young Children LIS-YC, Manual and video tape.* Experiential Education Series No. 1. Leuven: Centre for Experiential Education.

Laevers, F. (1996, September). *Social competence, self organisation and exploratory drive, and creativity: Definition and assessment.* Paper presented at the 6th European Early Childhood Education Research Association Conference on the Quality of Early Childhood Education, Lisbon, Portugal.

Laevers, F., & Van Sanden, (1995). *Basic book for an Experiential Pre-Primary Education.* Leuven: Centre for Experiential Education.

Lantieri, L. (1990). *The resolving conflict creativity problem 1989: Summary of significant findings of RCCP.* NJ: Metis Associates.

Leggett, E.L., & Dweck, C.S. (1986). Goals and inference rules: Sources of causal judgments. *Psychological Review, 95*(2), 256-273.

Lipman, M. (1989). *Philosophy goes to school.* Philadelphia: Temple University Press.

Lorenz, C. (1946). *Studies in animal and human behaviour* (Vol. 1). Cambridge, MA: Harvard University Press.

Moss, P., & Pence, A. (Eds.). (1994). *Valuing quality in early childhood services.* London: Paul Chapman.

National Commission on Education. (1993). *Learning to succeed: A radical look at education today and a strategy for the future.* Report of the Paul Hamlyn Foundation National Commission on Education. London: Heinemann.

New Zealand Ministry of Education. (1996). *Te Whariki, early childhood curriculum.* Wellington: Learning Media.

Nowicki, S., & Duke, M. (1989). *Helping the child who doesn't fit in.* Atlanta: Peachtree Publishers.

Organisation for Economic Cooperation and Development. (2001) *Thematic review of early childhood education and care thematic review: UK country note.* Paris: OECD.

Olsen, P., & Zigler, E. (1989). An assessment of the all day kindergarten movement. *Early Childhood Research Quarterly, 4,* 67-187.

Pascal, C., & Bertram, A.D. (1997). *Effective early learning: Case studies in improvement.* London: Hodder and Stoughton.

Pascal, C., & Bertram, A.D. (2000). *Accounting early for life long learning: Phase 2 report.* Worcester: University College, Amber Publications.

Pascal, C., Bertram, A.D., Ramsden, F. (1997) *Effective early learning: Phase 3 final report.* Worcester: Amber Publications.

Pascal, C., Bertram, A.D., Ramsden, F., Georgson, J., Saunders, M., & Mould, C. (1996). *Evaluating and developing quality in early childhood settings.* Worcester: Amber Publications.

Phillips, D. (1995). Giving voice to young children. *European Early Childhood Education Research Journal, 3*(2).

Qualifications and Curriculum Authority. (1998). *Desirable outcomes for children's learning on entering compulsory education.* London: HMSO.

Qualifications and Curriculum Authority. (2000). *The foundation stage curriculum guidance.* London: HMSO.

Resnick, L.B. (1987). *Education and learning to think.* Washington, DC: National Academy Press.

Roberts, R. (1996). *Self-esteem and sccessful early learning.* London: Hodder and Stoughton.

Rogoff, B. , Mistry, J., Goncu, A., & Mosier, C. (1993). Guided participation in cultural activity by toddlers and care givers. *Monographs of the Society for Research in Child Development, 58*(8), (Serial No. 236.

Rutter, M. (1997, September). *Resilience and recovery in young children.* Paper delivered at the Seventh Conference on the Quality of Early Childhood Education, European Early Childhood Education Research Association, Munich.

Salovey, P., & Mayer, J. (1990). Emotional intelligence. *Imagination, Cognition and Personality, 9,* 85-211.

Schweinhart, L.J., & Weikart, D. (1993). *A summary of significant benefits: The High/Scope Perry Pre-school Study through age 27.* Ypsilanti, MI: High/Scope Educational Foundation.

Shorrocks, D., Daniels, S., Frobisher, L., Nelson, N., Waterson, A., & Bell, J. (1992) *Enca 1 project: The evaluation of National Curriculum assessment at key stage 1.* University of Leeds.

Siraj-Blatchford, I. (1996). *The early years: Laying the foundation for racial equity.* Stoke on Trent: Trentham Books.

Stevenson, S., & Lee, T. (1990). *Asian-American achievement beyond IQ.* Hillsdale, NJ: Lawrence Erlbaum.

Thomas, A. (1989). Longitudinal study of negative emotional states and adjustments from early childhood through adolescence. *Child Development, 54,* 52-71.

Tizard, B., Blatchford, P., Burke, J., Farquhar, C., & Plewis, I. (1988). *Young children at school in the inner city.* Hove: Lawrence Erlbaum.

Trevarthan, C. (1992). An infants motives for thinking and speaking. In A.H. Wold (Ed.), *The dialogical alternative.* Oxford: Oxford University Press.

Tymms, P. (1996). *Baseline assessment and value added.* Middlesex: School Curriculum and Assessment Authority.

Walkerdine, V. (1985). Child development and gender: The making of teachers and learners in nursery classrooms. In C. Adelman et al. (Eds.), *Early childhood education: History, policy and practice.* Reading: Bulmershe.

Whalley, M. (1996). *Learning to be strong.* London: Hodder and Stoughton.

Wiltshire, J., & Sylva, K. (1993). The impact of early learning on children's later development. *European Early Childhood Education Research Journal, 1*(1), 17-40.

Wolfendale, S. (1993). *Baseline assessment: A review of current practice, issues and strategies for effective implementation.* Paris: OMEP.

Vygotsky, L.S. (1962). *Thought and language.* Cambridge, MA: MIT Press.

CHAPTER 12

NEW DIRECTIONS IN
CURRICULUM DEVELOPMENT

Bernard Spodek and Olivia N. Saracho

The chapters in this volume examine the foundation for selecting appropriate practices and integrating knowledge from different disciplines to create a "balanced curriculum." Olivia N. Saracho and Bernard Spodek provide a framework for developing an appropriate early childhood curriculum. They probe the theories and history of early childhood curriculum and identify the conflicting concepts of knowledge in human growth and development similar to those identified by Seifert in his chapter. These are represented in the historical curriculum models of the 1960s and 1970s. They continue to impact today as we use this knowledge and our knowledge of social and cultural forces as well as knowledge of the different disciplines, blending them all in the creation of an early childhood curriculum and teaching methods designed to educate young children.

The volume considers the nature and knowledge of young children in planning and designing the early childhood curriculum. Kelvin Seifert discusses the various conceptions of children's cognitive development. Olivia N. Saracho presents developmental theories in children's social pretend play. Children's diversity and both individual and cultural differences are discussed by Barbara Wasik and her colleagues and by Eugene E. Garcia's. The issues they have identified and the research they present are helpful as we plan an early childhood curriculum for all children.

Our knowledge of how young children approach the different content areas of school is essential to developing an integrated curriculum that is both effective and consistent with the concepts we want children to acquire. These different content areas are approached by Joseph Becker and Daniel Miltner who discuss young children's reasoning in mathematics, by Thomas Weible and Ann J. Dromsky who discuss the social studies curriculum, and by Olivia N. Saracho who discusses young children's literacy development. Douglas H. Clements and Julie Sarama focus on our knowledge relating to the use of computers in the early childhood classroom. This current technological innovation is impacting on young children both at home and in school. The more we know about the appropriate uses of computers, the more effective our programs can be. Child care setting requires special attention in any discussion of early childhood curriculum because they are generally not considered as educational institutions. Douglas Powell and Gary E. Bingham discuss the research we have on curriculum in child care settings and suggest approaches to improving child care services by strengthening their curriculum content. Tony Bertram and Christine Pascal alert us to the fact that issues relating to early childhood curriculum are not limited to concerns in the United States. They suggest ways to determine what is important for young children to learn that transcend our borders.

CURRENT TRENDS IN THE EARLY CHILDHOOD CURRICULUM

In examining the practices observed in the early childhood education curriculum, a number of trends have been appearing, some of which may be adopted and adapted to other cultures. Some that are particularly pertinent today include the following:

1. Educating all children in inclusive classes.
2. Dealing with both vertical and horizontal transitions.
3. Providing programs serving the need both for the education and for care of young children.
4. Building school-family-community relations.
5. Focusing on language learning, not as a form of reading readiness, but as a reflection of emergent literary.
6. Organizing integrated learning in the classroom.
7. Using technology in the early childhood classroom.

These trends are discussed in the following sections.

Educating All Children in Inclusive Classes

Over the last 30 years there has been an increased emphasis in our country on educating children with disabilities. Recently, the focus has been on providing this education in inclusive settings, that is, in classes where children with and without disabilities are educated together. The research shows that this trend is more effective for the children with disabilities. They perform more like their peers who have no disabilities. At the same time the children without disabilities do not lose out academically and they gain by learning to live with other children who are different from themselves in a variety of ways.

This approach demands a great deal of teachers. Often additional personnel are needed to work with the teacher to meet the particular needs of some of the children. It also requires that teachers be trained to work with a broader range of children than has been the case in the past. For this reason increasing numbers of teacher training programs in the United States are redesigning their programs to prepare teachers to teach both children with and without disabilities in inclusive classrooms. To do this requires the cooperation of teacher training faculties from both regular early childhood education programs and early childhood special education programs.

Having children with disabilities in a classroom has several curriculum implications. It increases the range of individual differences in a classroom and requires that teachers individualize their instruction. It also requires that teachers plan differently. The Individualized Educational Programs (IEP's) requires that a specific instructional plan be developed for a child with a disability. This might be useful to do for all children. In doing so, individual assessment of children becomes increasingly important to determine each child's capabilities and goals for each child should be set accordingly. It also suggests that a careful assessment of classroom resources be made of the use time, space, equipment, materials, and personnel in terms of what is needed to support the curriculum.

The creation of inclusive classrooms and the preparation of teachers to work in them is a trend that we believe will continue. Teachers prepared to teach in these classrooms are better at teaching all children.

Dealing with Both Vertical and Horizontal Transitions

We have different kinds of early childhood programs in the United States, both half-time and full-time. We have half-day preschools and all-day (or extended-day) child care programs for 3-and 4-year-olds. Most of these are sponsored by non-public school agencies. We also have some special programs for children this age within the public schools. These are primarily designed for children with disabilities and for those who are assessed as at risk of future educational failure. In addition, the Head Start programs, which usually function outside of the public schools, serves the same populations as those just noted. Usually these are half-day programs. We also have public school kindergarten programs for 5-year-olds, some of which are half-day and some of which are full-day (full-day here means full school day). Many of the children in half day or full school day programs are in need of child care during the rest of the day. They may be put in child care centers, or provided care in their home or the home of a care giver (child care homes).

Children may have very different experiences as they move from program to program or from center to center during the day. For example, a child may be in a Head Start program in the morning and in a public school at-risk program in the afternoon, or in a public school kindergarten in the morning and a child care center in the afternoon.

The need arises to deal with these horizontal transitions. On the one hand children may need to be prepared to respond to many different adults each day as well as to different expectations and even different rules for behavior. If possible, programs may be coordinated with one another. Representatives of the various program may meet together to coordinate activities so that children have the best of each program. They may also work to make the daily transition easier.

As children grow up, they go to different early childhood programs and must make the transition from one to another. There may be different expectations in different programs and children must learn the behavior appropriate for each program. The programs may also vary from less academic to more academic and the style of teaching may differ as well. Parent, too, will experience different expectations as their children move from one program to another. Both children and parents must learn to adjust to each situation. Often they need help.

Many Head Start and preschool programs design specific activities at the end of the school year to support the transition. Teachers may rearrange the classroom or the schedule to reflect the anticipated change. They may take children to visit the new school, if possible.

The transition may be complicated by the lack of coordination and by the absence of information about the child's previous school experience. Too often, teachers in the public schools pay little attention to the information they receive from the child's prior teachers. Public school teachers may not take the reports of preschool or child care teachers seriously or they may refuse to meet with them. They feel that the information they receive may be inadequate and invalid. They will look down upon the preschool teachers because they have lower teacher qualifications.

Many public schools and Head Start programs are taking the initiative in creating formal transition programs. They are holding joint conferences on the children. Public school teachers are invited to visit preschool or prekindergarten programs. Preschool programs and child care centers are being made aware of the expectations of the public school kindergartens and primary classes. The sharing of information and the interaction of teachers from different programs is lowering the amount of misinformation that both sets of teachers have.

Considering the transitions that children make is important in curriculum building. One needs to anticipate the expectations of classes into which the children will move, just as one must be aware of the learning and experiences the children have had before they enter the classroom. In addition, teachers may need to pay more attention to the experiences children have outside the classroom on a day-to-day basis. Cooperation and coordination of plans and activities will make for a better educational experience for all children.

Programs Serving Both the Need for Education and for Care of Young Children

Because of the needs of children, neither custodial child care nor early education programs that are school-based adequately serve all the needs of young children. Increasingly, as the number of single parents increase along with the number of working mothers of young children, there is a need for coordinated programs that provide both education and care. These programs have been characterized as *educare*.

There are few such programs that exist in the United States, though they are increasing. We also see programs of child care and programs of education cooperating with one another, sometimes to the point of public schools placing certified teachers in designated child care centers. However, programs of *educare* are expanding in other places. In Iceland, for example, the preschools which are called "play schools" in Icelandic are operated by the public schools. They offer programs for an extended day. However, parents may choose to enroll their children for only a part day.

In Japan, the curriculum of the kindergarten and the child care center is now the same. There is also a move to prepare kindergarten teachers and child care teachers in the same university programs. As a result, programs for children in both types of centers will have similar curriculums taught by teachers with similar backgrounds and qualifications.

In planning for *educare* teachers must develop a new sense of curriculum. The curriculum needs to expand. Activities we generally view as routines can be designed as a source of learning. This is no different from how the curriculum of the pioneer nursery school in England was conceived. Margaret Macmillan used the term nurturance to characterize her curriculum. In a sense it means that the admonition that teachers deal with, the whole child is taken seriously in curriculum planning.

Building School-Family-Community Relations

Since the 1960s, educators in the United States, especially in the area of early childhood education, have focused on building relations with the parents of children in their programs. The early childhood models of the 1960s were especially effective when work with parents was related to work with children. Thus, when Head Start was established, parent involvement was a required component of all Head Start programs.

Today, some form of parent program is required in prekindergarten programs offered to children who are considered to be at risk of future school failure. In addition, programs for children with disabilities have some parent component to them and parents of these children are required to approve the individualized educational programs that educators created for these children.

Some educators believe that all early childhood programs should be an extension of the family itself. Schools should coordinate support services for families and the culture of the family should be reflected in the educational programs provided to children. Parents should also be involved in making decisions concerning the programs provided for their children and teachers should see that the school culture is not in conflict with the home culture.

This concern for family-school cooperation is not limited to kindergarten and elementary school programs alone, but extends even into child care programs. Ellen Galinsky and Bernice Weissbourd (1992) advocate the creation of family centered child care programs in which coordinated services are provided to families through the center. In America there is increasing support for improved home-school-community relations. Goals 2000 for Education, an educational initiative supported by former President Clinton, establishes such partnerships as one of its goals.

Joyce Epstein (1995) developed a framework which characterizes six types if family/ community involvement. These types are:

1. *Parenting.* This type helps families build home environments to support children's learning and development. Parents are helped to learn parenting skills or are given information on health, nutrition and other services in the community.
2. *Communicating.* This type provides forms of home-school communication. Communications may be about school programs and about children's progress in school. Teachers hold regular parent conferences in most schools. They also send home notes, memos, and newsletters letting parents know what is happening in school. They may also use newer technology, creating school or class web pages that parents can access.
3. *Volunteering.* This type leads to increasing parent involvement in the school by recruiting and organizing parents to help and support school activities. Parents may read to children in class, or work with groups of children in a particular skill area, such as sewing or painting. They may also help with administrative tasks, or even cleaning and acting as a teacher aide as they do in parent cooperatives.
4. *Learning at home.* This type helps parents to help their children at home by providing information and ideas in regard to curricu-

lum-related activities that parents can do. They may be helped to work with their own children in literacy related activities. Schools may provide parents with packets of materials they can use with their children at home.

5. *Decision making.* This type consists of ways to include parents in school decisions, through advisory councils and parent teacher organizations. Head Start programs, for example, have parent advisory committees. Parents in such committees may be involved in preparing budgets and hiring personnel.

6. *Collaboration with the community.* This type is concerned with identifying and integrating services and resources from the community to strengthen school programs, family practices, and children's learning and development. Schools can help parents work with schools, civic, health recreation and other agencies in the community.

While almost all early childhood programs include some sort of parent program, few include many of those noted above.

In designing a program to serve families as well as children, the teacher expands the range of her clientele. Families become the unit of service not just individual children. Parents become the clients as well as children. Activities must be organized beyond the classroom. A new relationship must be established between parents and teachers with parent becoming partners as well as clients.

Focusing on Language Learning Not as a Form of Reading Readiness, but as a Reflection of Emergent Literary

Conventional approaches to beginning reading instruction have used a concept of reading readiness to determine when reading instruction should begin. Once the teacher determined that the child was ready to learn to read, she could begin to teach him. Depending on the theory, readiness could be determined either by intellectual maturation or by the child's acquisition of skills that were seen as needed to become a successful reader.

Based on a number of studies that were done more than 60 years ago, the suggestion was that reading instruction not begin until a child had reached a mental age of six years and six months. This conclusion was arrived at by an analysis of the mental ages of children who were introduced to reading instruction. Those with a mental age of six years, six months were more successful in learning to read. Thus, teachers could give children intelligence tests to determine when to begin teaching children to read.

More recently reading readiness has been determined by the degree to which a child had acquired those skills that were considered to be the necessary requirements for reading. These requirements included such skills as being able to associate letters with sounds (English is a phonetic language where symbols represent sounds, not ideas). Also important

was the ability of the children to discriminate among the shapes of letters, to move one's eyes from left to right on the page, and to listen to and recall a story. They should also show an interest in learning to read. As many as 28 child attributes might be assessed in order to determine if children have achieved their prerequisites for reading, what was referred to as reading readiness. Then formal reading instruction would begin, often without reference to the child's former experiences with the written word.

Even more recently, the notion of emergent literacy has replaced the idea of reading readiness in early childhood education. This is a process that is supported by the developmental theory of L.S. Vygotsky. Emergent literacy suggests that the process of learning to read does not begin suddenly after a child is considered ready. Rather, the process of learning to read is one that emerges slowly over a long period of time as children gain knowledge of and experience with their language. All of the language activities that children engage in, at least from toddlerhood, can be used to support the process that leads to formal reading. Preschool teachers and parents can help literacy emerge in the following ways:

- They can read regularly and often to children;
- They can help children learn the symbols of their language;
- They can model reading and writing activities so children can see what adults do when they read and write;
- They can help children seek meaning in the reading that they do;
- They can make the children aware of the signs and symbols in their environment; and
- They can link learning to read to learning to write.

Preschool teachers, even if they do not provide formal reading instruction are teachers of reading.

Integrated Learning in the Classroom

In traditional classes each subject is taught separate from all other subjects. The purpose of this approach is to increase the probability that key ideas will be taught systematically. Recently, proposals have been made to provide an integrated curriculum in the early childhood classroom. One of these proposals suggests that schools for young children emulate the program offered in Reggio Emilia centers in Italy. The other calls for using projects as a way of organizing classroom learning.

In both of these approaches teachers are expected to create situations in which children inquire into specific topics. Often the topics allow the children to explore their immediate environment. The children collect information that they later use in designing simulations through arts and crafts activities as well as through play. This enables the children to reconstruct the knowledge gained from their inquiries. In these activities the children act as scientists and social scientists. They observe situations in the immediate surrounding area of the school and collect data to be used in their study. The Reggio Emilia approach also suggests that children work with artists to create representations of what they have observed in an artistic fashion.

The rationale for these approaches is that children learn best when ideas are presented in a context with which they are familiar. It also suggests that children construct their own knowledge as a result of personal inquiry. In time they decontextualize what they have learned, abstracting their knowledge as they transfer the key ideas to other situations.

The key to providing intellectualized learning in this method is to use the topics' studies as vehicles for accessing organized knowledge. As John Dewey wrote in 1902,

> It is just to get rid of the prejudicial notion that there is some gap in kind (as distinct from degree) between the child's experience and the various forms of subject-matter that make up the course of study. From the side of the child, it is a question of seeking how his experience already contains within itself elements—facts and truths—of the same sort as those entering into the formulated study; and, what is of more importance, of how it contains with in itself the attitudes, the motives and the interests which have operated in developing and organizing the subject matter to the plane which it now occupies. From the side of the studies it is a question of interpreting them as outgrowths of forces operating in the child's life and discovering the steps that intervene between the child's present experience and their richer maturity. (pp. 15-16)

Integrated learning made sense for young children in 1902 when John Dewey wrote *The Child and The Curriculum*. It made sense when William Kilpatrick wrote *The Project Method* fifteen years later. It made sense during the era of Progressive Education. It made sense when the British infant schools organized their programs into the Integrated Day and when American educators created Open Education. And it makes sense today.

This is an approach that attracts educators periodically . . . but it never has attracted a majority of educators at any one time. Essentially, these programs have reflected a Progressive ideology regarding children and learning. This is one of three ideological positions that continue to compete with one another. A second ideology has been characterized as romantic.

From this point of view young children are given maximum freedom with little imposition from the school. Children are expected to use this freedom to select activities that match their developmental levels. This ideology is reflected in the idea of Developmentally Appropriate Practices (DAP) in the United States. The third ideology, the cultural transmission ideology, suggests that the role of the school is to pass on the accumulated knowledge of the culture to the next generation. This, too, is an approach that has its advocates in America, including E.D. Hirsch who published a book on cultural literacy and those who have raised issues of standards in American schools and universities.

Using Technology in the Early Childhood Classroom

The one recent trend that can truly be considered new is the use of electronic technology in early childhood classes . . . especially the use of computers. Computers were introduced some years ago in our society; they are now found everywhere. When they first entered the classroom, educators were worried about the appropriateness of providing computers for young children. Some worried that computers would isolate children from one another. Some were concerned that computers were too sophisticated for young children. Some worried that using computers would take time away from children learning activities based on play and experience with concrete materials.

While there are possible problems with using computers in the classroom, they can be used very successfully to enhance early childhood programs. Used properly, computers can enhance young children's learning. They should be one option among many exciting learning options in the classroom. The programs should meet the criteria for all good quality programs and the computers themselves should be powerful enough to run available programs. Additionally, if they are going to be used well, teachers must know about how best to use them and what high quality programs are available.

Concerns need to be raised about software that is available for young children. There are good software programs and there are poor ones. The better ones help children learn higher order thought processes. The poorer ones focus primarily on drill and practice, emphasizing memorization and giving the one right answer.

Computers are also a good place for children to learn collaborative learning with one another. Rather than isolating individual children from their peers, computers are often places for children to come together and work together in pairs or in small groups.

Most important is the selection of good software and good websites for children. In the United States there are a number of sources for evaluating computer software and websites for young children and a number of educational clubs that support the purchase of good software. Articles in recent journals, such as *Young Children* also provide advice regarding the use of computers with young children. Most important, young children are living in an age of computers. They must not only learn from computers, they need to learn about computers.

Conclusion

We have tried to focus on what we consider to be some of then most significant trends in early childhood education today. Some of these trends are truly new. Others are expressions of issues that have arisen time and again in the field of early childhood education. Our final caution is to suggest that as early childhood educators, we do not quickly and mindlessly adopt anything that is current. Nor should we reject an idea or approach simply because it is new.

We need to assess each idea, each program, each innovation to determine whether it is worthwhile in and of itself, and also whether it is applicable to the culture and community in which we teach.

THE FUTURE

In the final decade of the twentieth century, American society is presenting us with the possibilities of an unknown future. Even as this book was written, we saw the hopes for universal peace, generated by the opening of Eastern Europe, dashed in the turmoil of a Middle East crisis. A year before that, political conflict in Tiananmen Square changed our relations with the People's Republic of China. Such situations seriously influence early childhood education programs. Societies can become less open when threatened. Governments must rechannel resources from domestic to international programs during periods of crises. In addition, people's willingness to accept certain programs may change as they see their security threatened.

In spite of the pitfalls of predicting the future, one still must prepare for it. While we cannot be sure of what the future holds in store, we can make some best guesses. We can also be flexible so that our plan the future can be modified as the future unfolds.

Planning for the future cannot be linear; it must be open-ended and flexible. Educational futurists acknowledged the problems of linear reformation. Shane (1970) suggests that the future be construed as a fan-shaped array of possibilities of alternative futures, rather than a linear one.

Curriculum developers in early childhood education must identify educational goals in relation to a transforming society. Education in the United States, and in other nations, has always delayed in responding to changing social, cultural, technological, and economic conditions. Some delays are due to the process of cultural diffusion. But schools must learn to respond more rapidly to change.

A consequence of the rapid social change in our society has been the condition called *transience*, a mood or sense of impermanence in the relationships among people, things, places, organizations, and information. Extreme transience jeopardizes social stability by diminishing the cultural preservation and transmission framework. The historic role of early childhood programs and society's conforming stratagem is challenged in a culture where impermanence is a periodic state. Yet we must learn to accommodate to this change.

SUMMARY

American society is continuing to encounter colossal ameliorations in the twenty-first century. Transience in our society, cultural delay in educational institutions, and the deficiency of conventional direct expectations of the future question the future of curriculum development.

Researchers, scholars, and educators offer numerous explanations to depict young children's educational future. Dispersed programs advocate for individual or definite audiences in American society. Unified programs satisfying the state have also been considered.

The philosophies and composition of curriculum specialists will resolve the nature of the future educational programs in the United States. This is an ordeal to early childhood curriculum specialists who have to compose more divergent and attainable learning alternatives for young children.

REFERENCES

Dewey, J. (1902). *The child and the curriculum.* Chicago: University of Chicago Press.
Kilpatrick, W. (1917). *The project method.* New York: Macmillan.
Shane, H.G. (1971). Future-planning as a means of shaping educational change. In R.M. McClure (Ed.), *The curriculum: Retrospect and prospect,* 70th Yearbook, Part I, National Society for the Study of Education (pp. 185-215). Chicago: University of Chicago Press.

ABOUT THE AUTHORS

Joe Becker is an Associate Professor at the University of Illinois at Chicago. His research interests are theories of intellectual development, semiotic aspects of cognition, and children's understanding in mathematics and science. He is also interested in the relation of research in domain-specific knowledge, expert-novice, and everyday cognition traditions to constructivist theory.

Tony Bertram is Senior Research Fellow at University College Worcester, England, where he is Director of the Centre for Research in Early Childhood, (which has two sites, one in Worcester and one in Birmingham). He is Co-Director of the Effective Early Learning (EEL) Project and The Accounting Early for Life Long Learning (AcE) Project and is National Evaluator of the Government's Early Excellence Centre Programme. He is President of the European Early Childhood Education Research Association and has recently worked as an Early Childhood Review Expert for the Organisation for Economic Cooperation and Development (OECD) on an International Thematic Review of Early Childhood Education and Care. He has published widely in the field of quality evaluation and development in early childhood, and the development of integrated services.

Gary E. Bingham is a Ph.D. candidate in the Department of Child Development and Family Studies at Purdue University. He has served as head teacher in a university preschool program and as supervisor of student teachers in early childhood programs. His research interests include quality and curriculum issues in early childhood programs, children's emergent literacy development, and family socialization practices. He received his master's degree from the Department of Family and Human Development at Utah State University.

Mary Alice Bond earned her master's degree in early childhood education from Towson University. She is a Senior Curriculum Specialist and Program Facilitator for the Early Learning Program at the Johns Hopkins University Center for Social Organization of Schools. She has been developing and training language and literacy pre-school programs for the last ten years.

Douglas H. Clements, Professor of Mathematics, Early Childhood, and Computer Education at University at Buffalo (SUNY), was a kindergarten teacher for five years. He has conducted research and published widely in the areas of the learning and teaching of geometry, computer applications in mathematics education, the early development of mathematical ideas, and the effects of social interactions on learning. He has co-directed several NSF projects, producing Logo Geometry, Investigations in Number, Data, and Space and over 70 referred research articles. Active in the NCTM, he is editor and author of the NCTM Addenda materials and was an author of NCTM's Principles and Standards for School Mathematics (2000). He was chair of the Editorial Panel of NCTM's research journal, the *Journal for Research in Mathematics Education*. In his current NSF-funded project, Building Blocks-Foundations for Mathematical Thinking, Pre-Kindergarten to Grade 2: Research-based Materials Development, he and Julie Sarama are developing mathematics software and activities for young children.

Ann Dromsky is a doctoral student and graduate teaching assistant at the University of Maryland at College Park where she also earned her Masters in Reading Education. She obtained her B. A. in Elementary Education at Saint Marys College, Notre Dame, IN. She has held both elementary and middle school teaching positions. Her research interests center around the use of content area texts in the primary grades and early literacy comprehension. She has published several chapters; articles in state and national literacy journals; and designed literacy curriculums for area schools. In addition to her academic work, she consults with Reading Is Fundamental in Washington D. C. and the Walters Gallery in Baltimore, MD.

Eugene García is Professor of Education at the University of California, Berkeley. He received his B.A. from the University of Utah in Psychology and his Ph.D. in Human Development from the University of Kansas. He has served previously as a national research center director and an academic department chair and dean. He has published extensively in the area of language teaching and bilingual development authoring and/or co-authoring over 150 articles and book chapters along with 8 book length volumes. He served as a Senior Officer and Director of the Office of Bilingual Education and Minority Languages Affairs in the U.S. Department of Education from 1993-1995 and he is conducting research in the areas of effective schooling for linguistically and culturally diverse student populations.

Annemarie Hindman is a Research Assistant with the Early Learning Program at the Center for Social Organization of Schools. Her past work includes experience with Head Start and other programs targeting disadvantaged young children, and she is currently working on a language and literacy training program for early childhood educators. She holds a bachelor's degree in history from Yale University.

Dan Miltner is a Program Associate at the University of Illinois at Chicago working on the Big City Teacher Initiative Project. He is working towards his PhD in mathematics education. His interests are in teacher preparation in mathematics, constructivist theory, and children's understanding in mathematics.

Christine Pascal is Professor of Early Childhood Education at University College Worcester, England, where she is Director of the Centre for Research in Early Childhood, (which has two sites, one in Worcester and one in Birmingham). She is Co-Director of the Effective Early Learning (EEL) Project and The Accounting Early for Life Long Learning (AcE) Project and is National Evaluator of the Government's Early Excellence Centre Programme. She is also currently a Specialist Adviser to the UK House of Commons Select Committee Inquiry on Early Years and is a member of the UK DfEE Foundation Stage Working Group. She co-founded the European Early Childhood Education Research Association and works extensively across Europe in her early childhood research and development work. She has written widely on the subject of quality early childhood education and is committed to developing integrated services for all children and their families.

Douglas R. Powell is Professor and Head, Department of Child Development and Family Studies, Purdue University, West Lafayette, Indiana. His areas of interest include relations between families and early childhood programs, family contributions to children's learning, and early childhood personnel preparation. He is former Editor of the *Early Childhood Research Quarterly* and author of numerous scholarly publications, including *Enabling Young Children to Succeed in School* (American Educational Research Association).

Julie Sarama is an assistant professor of mathematics education at the University at Buffalo (SUNY). She is currently Principal or Co-Principal Investigator on four projects funded by the National Science Foundation, including Building Blocks-Foundations for Mathematical Thinking, Pre-Kindergarten to Grade 2: Research-based Materials Development and Planning for Professional Development in Pre-School Mathematics: Meeting the Challenge of Standards 2000. She has taught secondary mathematics and computer science, gifted math, and mathematics methods and content courses for elementary to secondary teachers. She designed and programmed microworlds for the National Science Foundation-funded Investigations in Number, Data, and Space project and is co-author of several of the geometry units for that curriculum. She is co-author of the award-winning Turtle Math, as well of 19 refereed articles, 13 chapters, 7 units of the Investigations in Number, Data, and Space project, and more than 50 additional publications.

Kelvin Seifert is professor of educational psychology and coordinator of early years education at the University of Manitoba. He is author of several university textbooks, including *Child and Adolescent Development* (with Robert Hoffnung), now in its fifth edition. His current research concerns early childhood teachers' beliefs and interpretations of science and science teaching. He is co-editor of the newly founded journal Teaching Educational Psychology, and author of other articles about the relationship of teachers' informal beliefs to formal academic theory.

Olivia N. Saracho is Professor of Education in the Department of Curriculum and Instruction at the University of Maryland. Her areas of scholarship include cognitive style, teaching, and teacher education in early childhood education. Dr. Saracho's most recent books are *Right From The Start: Teaching Children ages Three through Eight* (Allyn & Bacon), *Dealing with Individual Differences in the Early Childhood Classroom* (Longman) (both with Bernard Spodek), and *Foundations of Early Childhood Education* (Allyn & Bacon) with Bernard Spodek and Michael J. Davis. She is also editor, with Roy Evans of *Early Childhood Teacher Education: An International Perspective* (Gordon & Breach). Dr. Saracho was also co-editor of the *Yearbook in Early Childhood Education* Series (Teachers College Press).

Bernard Spodek is Professor Emeritus of Early Childhood Education at the University of Illinois. He received his doctorate from Teachers College, Columbia University. His research and scholarly interests are in the areas of curriculum, teaching, and teacher education in early childhood education. He has written and edited 31 books, 48 chapters in books, and 67 scholarly articles. Dr. Spodek's most recent books are *Multiple Perspectives on Play in Early Childhood Education*, with Olivia Saracho (SUNY Press), *Issues in early Childhood Educational Research* (Teachers College Press), with Olivia

Saracho and Anthony Pellegrini and the *Handbook of Research on the Education of Young Children* (Macmillan). Dr. Spodek has been president of the National Association for the Education of Young Children (1976-78) and is currently president of the Pacific Early Childhood Education Research Association.

Barbara A. Wasik, Ph.D. is a Principal Research Scientist and the Director of the Early Learning Program at the Johns Hopkins University Center for Social Organization of Schools. Her area of research is emergent literacy and early intervention in beginning reading with a specific focus on disadvantaged children. She has extensive experience in program and curriculum development and was the original developer of the tutoring and early childhood program in Success for All, a school-wide restructuring program. Dr. Wasik has written extensively about tutoring as an early intervention strategy for children at risk of reading failure. Currently, she is developing a language and literacy training program for early childhood educators. Dr. Wasik has co-edited a book on *Early Prevention of School Failure* and is co-authoring a forthcoming book, *Kindergarten: Four-and Five-Year-Olds Go to School.* She received her Ph. D in developmental psychology.

Thomas Weible is Professor of Social Studies and Acting Chair of the Department of Curriculum and Instruction at the University of Maryland. He received his doctorate in social studies education at the University of Iowa. His research and scholarly interests are state certification standards for social studies teachers and teacher education. In addition to his responsibilities at the department level, Dr. Weible currently serves as Associate Dean and has served as Acting Dean of the College of Education. He is also an appointed member of the Maryland State Professional Standards and Teacher Education Board.